Crucibles
Selected Readings in U.S. Marine Corps History

Second Edition

Edited by
Robert S. Burrell

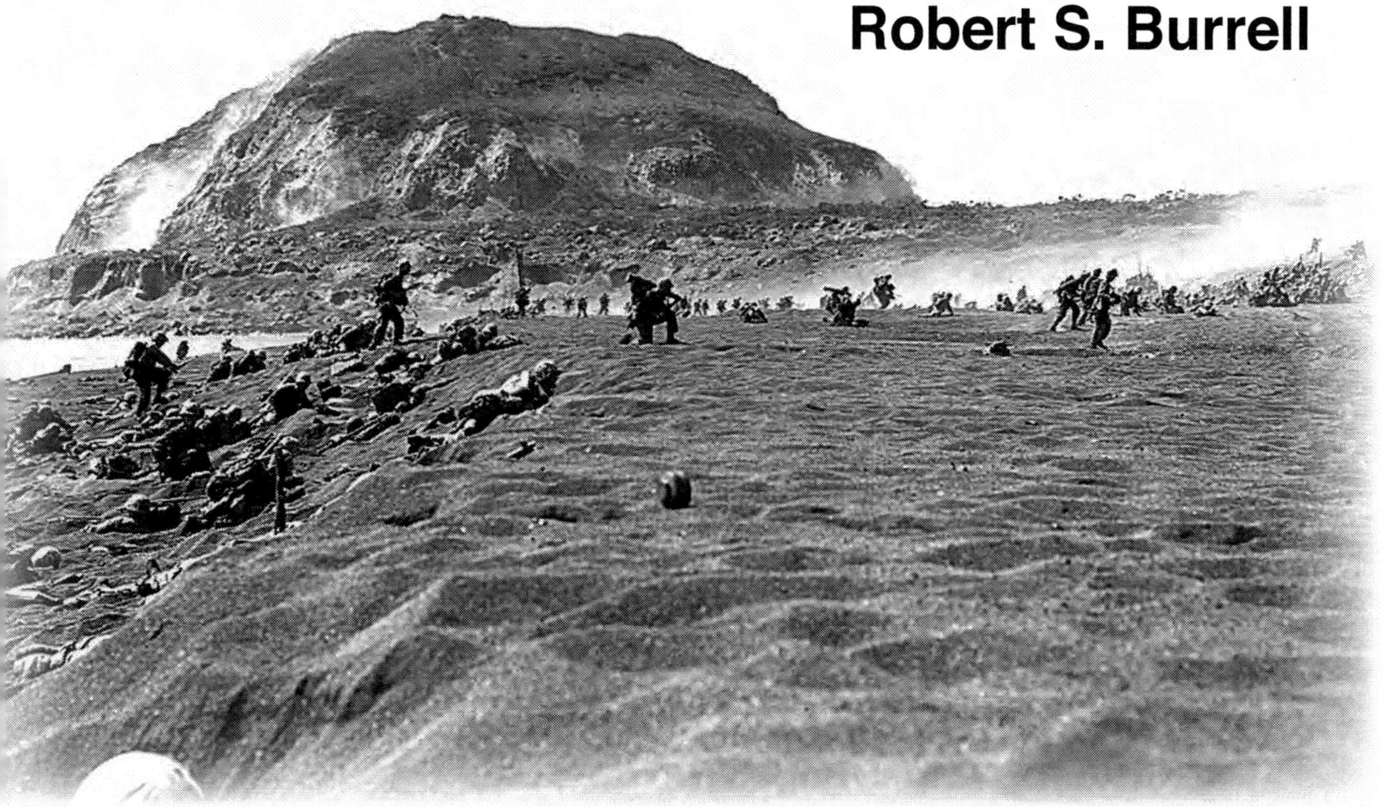

Editor: Joann Manos
Cover Designer: Doris Bruey
Cover Image: The cover photo of two Marines attacking a Japanese pillbox on Iwo Jima in 1945 is provided courtesy of the Marine Corps University Research Archives.

CRUCIBLES: Selected Readings in U.S. Marine Corps History, 2E
Copyright © 2004 by Robert S. Burrell

The author declines any royalties derived from the use of this book in history courses at the U.S. Naval Academy.

All rights reserved. No part of this publication may be reproduced or transmitted in any form or by any means, electronic or mechanical, including photocopying, recording, or any information storage and retrieval system, without the written permission of the publisher.

Requests for permission to make copies of any part of the work should be mailed to:

Permissions Department
Academx Publishing Services, Inc.
547 Country Ridge Circle
Bel Air, Maryland 21015

Copyright acknowledgments appear on page 311-312, and constitute a continuation of the copyright page.

Printed in the United States of America

ISBN-13: 978-1-932768-08-4
ISBN-10: 1-932768-08-4

This book is dedicated to the History Department faculty of U.S. Naval Academy. Professors and military officers who have worked at the Academy at one time or another composed a significant portion of the essays included in this work. The institution continues to serve as the premier source for naval history. For the positive impact the terrific faculty of academic years 2002, 2003, and 2004 has made on my historical scholarship and personal growth over the past three years, I am eternally grateful. Thank You.

Marines raise the American flag atop Mount Suribachi on the Japanese island of Iwo Jima, 23 February 1945.

TABLE OF CONTENTS

Introduction
    Robert S. Burrell   1

Evolution of the U.S. Marine Corps as a Military Elite
    Dennis E. Showalter   3

The Cat With More Than Nine Lives
    Robert D. Heinl, Jr.   21

With Fidelity and Effectiveness:
Archibald Henderson's Lasting Legacy to the U.S. Marine Corps
    Joseph G. Dawson   43

We Will Go Heavily Armed:
The Marines Small War on Samar, 1901-1902
    Brian McAllister Linn   67

The China Marines and the Crucible of the Warrior Mythos, 1900-1941
    Heather P. Marshall   83

Teddy Roosevelt and the Corps' Seagoing Mission
    Jack Shulimson and Graham A. Cosmas   97

The Culebra Maneuver and the Formation of the U.S. Marine Corps Advance Base Force, 1913-14
    Graham A. Cosmas and Jack Shulimson   109

Sea Soldiers Ashore: U.S. Marines in World War I
    Joseph Alexander   125

Cacos and *Caudillos*: Marines and Counterinsurgency in Hispaniola
    Graham A. Cosmas   135

U.S. Marines and Miskito Indians: The Rio Coco Patrol of 1928
David C. Brooks — 147

Sandino Against the Marines: The Development of Air Power for Conducting Counterinsurgency Operations in Central America
Kenneth A. Jennings — 161

Pete Ellis: Amphibious Warfare Prophet
John J. Reber — 175

The Prototype U.S. Marine: Evolution of the Amphibious Assault Warrior, 1942-1945
Robert S. Burrell — 191

The Truth About Peleliu
Jon T. Hoffman — 207

The Vital Role of the U.S. Marine Corps Reserve, 1893-1951
Chris Morton — 215

'Issue in Doubt': The Unification Crisis, 1945-1952
Robert S. Burrell — 235

Inchon
Robert D. Heinl Jr. — 255

A Feather in Their Cap? The Marines' Combined Action Program in Vietnam
Lawrence A. Yates — 277

Why the Army and Marine Corps Should Be Friends
Allan R. Millett — 291

Biographical Digest — 301
Suggested Readings and Film — 307
Commandants at a Glance — 309
Battle History — 310
Bibliography — 311
Index — 313

INTRODUCTION

Of all the American services, the history of the Marine Corps presents the most dynamic evolution of an organization. In both preparatory and career schools, Marines are taught a fluid and unchanging narrative of Marine Corps heritage. However, the vibrant history of the Corps offers a wealth of information for investigative study and argumentative interpretation. Consequently, this book was compiled to present some of most exciting new research on this subject in a single volume.

Concerning the time periods covered herein, the focus of this text is thematic rather than chronological. In his definitive work, historian Allan R. Millett divides Marine Corps history into four phases: Soldiers at Sea, 1775-1909; Colonial Infantry, 1899-1941; Amphibious Assault, 1900-1945; and Force in Readiness, 1945-1990s.[*] Of those stages, little of the readings here discuss the "Soldiers at Sea" period. This fact is mainly due to the straightforward mission of the institution that differed little from similar organizations around the world. That is not to say that the period was uneventful, but it certainly mirrors that of other marines.

Conversely, from its "Colonial Infantry" phase onward (in stark contrast from its sea service phase), the U.S. Marine Corps began an entirely distinctive divergence from other nation's marines. Essentially, it greatly expanded its roles until it no longer resembled its previous "Age of Sail" structure. In theory, Marines obtained a mission to defend advance naval bases. However, during the Philippine War (1899), the Corps made a revolutionary change from protection of vessels and naval stations to an occupational land force that resembled the Army. At the same time, the Corps kept a strong naval tie. In fact, this link to the Navy remained the most significant organizational aspect of the "Colonial Infantry" that differed from that of the U.S. Army. Additionally, we also see the unique development of close air support during this period, especially in the Nicaraguan insurrection of the 1920s and 1930s; it could certainly be argued that battling Sandino, a noteworthy opponent, made one of the largest impacts on the culture of the Marine Corps. Often overlooked in Marine Corps heritage, the "Colonial Infantry" phase requires the greatest degree of scholarly scrutiny because it offers the most important lessons on the Corps' exceptional fruition.

The United States' retraction from its imperialist phase endangered the mission of the Marines as "Colonial Infantry." Rather than returning to sea service roles, the Corps developed "Amphibious Assault." The foresight of Marine leadership during this period

---

[*] Allan R. Millett, *Semper Fidelis: The History of the United States Marine Corps* (1980, New York: Free Press, 1991). A highly respected scholar, Millett currently serves as the primary authority on Marine Corps history and, consequently, is either mentioned or cited in nearly every article in this book.

cannot be overstated, especially the profound influence and impact of Naval Academy graduate, John. A. Lejeune. The principle place of amphibious assault's employment would eventually become the Pacific Theater in World War II against the Japanese Empire. The Marine Corps made such a momentous impact in the Central Pacific, both militarily and culturally at home, that amphibious assault remains the mission that most Americans, if not the world, associate with Marines.

Despite Americans' love affair with Marines in regard to amphibious assault, "force-in-readiness" proved the Marine Corps' greatest departure from its traditional role. After World War II, the need for future amphibious assaults appeared unlikely. By this time, developing a new mission had become culturally engrained into the fabric of the Corps. The Marines instinctively sought a mission that would keep the organization a viable fighting force, which resembled the Army but remained naval. The transition to force-in-readiness was difficult and fraught with controversy, yet, once completed, solidified the Corps' new role in America's Armed Forces. From Korea (1950) to the second war in the Persian Gulf (2002), the Marine Corps has remained the nation's foremost weapon at the tip of the spear.

The articles selected herein, provide insight into how all these changes took place. *Crucibles* seeks to help the reader understand the dynamic aspects of the Corps' unique history, an institution constantly in a state of flux. Through such study, we can better appreciate the gifted leadership and rare opportunities that made such extraordinary transitions possible.

Semper Fidelis,

Robert S. Burrell
Captain, U.S. Marine Corps
History Department, U.S. Naval Academy

EVOLUTION OF THE U.S. MARINE CORPS AS A MILITARY ELITE

Dennis E. Showalter

Perhaps one of the best ways to begin study on the Marine Corps is through an examination of its perceived elite status. Is the Marine Corps a privileged few, a specialized unit, or simply one of many conventional forces? Dr. Showalter, former Chair of Military Affairs at Marine Corps University, investigates how the perception of the Marine Corps as elite developed over time – determining if the charge is imagined, real, or a combination of the two.

The United States Marine Corps occupies an ambiguous position in American history and American mythology. The Corps is so commonly accepted as an "elite" that it is often awarded the adjective by the media even when being sharply criticized. It has risen triumphantly above training-camp scandals, attacks on its tactics as murderously unimaginative commitments to frontal assault and descriptions of its staff work as inefficiency tempered by anarchy. Its boast of "looking for a few good men" is likely to remain unmodified by revelations of questionable recruiting practices. The fighting Marine symbolized by John Wayne's Sgt Stryker in *Sands of Iwo lima* is part of American folklore.(1) Yet these images exist alongside Michael Herr's portrait – in his bestseller, *Dispatches* – of a Corps which in Vietnam "came to be called by many the finest instrument ever devised for the killing of young Americans" and Harry Jeffers' invitation to *See Parris and Die*. Similarly the self-revelations of Philip Caputo's *A Rumor of War* seem at once more shocking and more believable because Caputo was a Marine officer.

This ambivalent attitude toward the Marines is fostered by the fact that most accounts of the Corps, popular or scholarly, expose or glorification, have been written from the inside. The authors are Marines or retired Marines, Marine reservists, or civilians with a case to argue. It is also encouraged by the academic military historian's tendency to ignore elite military forces as such. When he discusses military elites, he usually refers to the position of armies and their components within the societies to which they belong. Discussion of elite fighting formations is generally left to popularizers or to historians working within official or semi-official frameworks. The result too often is a composite image of war stories and institutional infighting which contributes little more than surface impressions to an understanding of the subject. One notable exception to this generalization is Roger Beaumont's, *Military Elites*. This work, however, is restricted in scope to the period beginning with World War II and is so vague in its definition of what constitutes an elite that it cannot be called definitive. Finally, military men themselves, particularly in the United States, seem uncomfortable when attempting to define an elite force. Usually their definition involves an ability to perform assigned missions regardless of constraining circumstances with the "constraining circumstances" frequently being a euphemism for heavy casualties. This definition, while possessing some merit, is so broad as to be almost valueless for purposes of analysis, as opposed to description. It confers, by implication at least, elite status on any organization or formation able to fight well for any reason over an unspecified period of time longer than a single campaign, or a battle or two.

In this essay, I offer a definition of elite forces as characterized by a combination of recruitment and function: their personnel are specially selected or self-selected for combat purposes. I admit that this definition is narrow. It excludes intellectual elites such as the 19th-century U.S. Army's Corps of Engineers, whose officers included a disproportionate number of West Point's top-ranking graduates. It excludes social elites such as the bodyguards of the later Hapsburg emperors, which never took the field as organized formations. Its specificity, however, enables a clear focus on units deliberately created to be better in battle than the ordinary cross-section of an army: true fighting elites.(2)

While such elite forces have deep roots in military history, their flowering came only with the Napoleonic Wars. Romanticism, with its cult of the heroic individual, contributed something to their development. More concretely, an era combining mass armies and universal conscription with long years of field service generated an internal demand for distinctions and honors. Probably more significant than these factors combined, however, was the heroic aura surrounding the Imperial Guard of France. In practice, the Guard frequently only functioned as the Emperor's bodyguard and an army reserve which "put on full dress to stand with folded arms." Yet its mystique, culminating in the glorification at Waterloo, inspired imitators and emulators for more than a century and made the Guard a model for all subsequent elite combat forces.(3)

In the course of the 19th century, three categories of elites emerged. Each incorporated both recruitment and function, but to different degrees and for different purposes. The first category, the guardsmen, stressed recruiting. The rank and file of the British, Russian and Prussian household troops were selected almost exclusively on physical grounds. Their training and battlefield missions were not essentially different from those of the armies to which they belonged, though their training might be more rigorous. The character of their officer corps was determined largely by social factors. These might seem flimsy reasons for describing the guards formations of 19th century Europe as elites. Their sense of being set apart, however, generated a spirit contributing so frequently to results out of proportion to numbers and training that the guardsman must be allowed his place in any general model of modern elite force.

The second form of modern elite force is built around technicians. It is composed of men whose skills or experience seem to qualify them for combat missions deemed too complex or exacting for the ordinary soldier. From the grenadiers of the 17th century to the paratroopers of the 20th, the constantly changing conditions of warfare have generated demands for corps of specialists distinguished from their fellow soldiers primarily, though not exclusively, by the task they do – a task seen as requiring some kind of special training or preparation. It usually requires little time for the functional or technical elite to put itself out of business. Its skill may become unnecessary or be proved impractical. More likely, the skill will become common property among the ordinary rank and file. Skirmishing, which in Prussia during the Wars of Liberation had become by default the task of the best of the active soldiers, was during peacetime an official mission of half of every infantry regiment in the army. An elite of 50 percent is a contradiction in terms.

As functional elites grow larger, they tend to supply part of their heritage to the third type of modern elite, the warriors. Such elites often resemble functional elites in their possession of a special combat mission. Like guardsmen, warrior elites also stress recruiting. Their personnel, however, are chosen on a basis of proved or potential superiority as fighters. Frequently their selection process involves a rite of passage different in essence or degree from that required of the ordinary soldier. Thus for the airborne warrior, parachute training is part of an initiation into a brotherhood. The technical skills involved in jumping from an aircraft are means to a moral end. And because of the quality of their personnel, warrior elites frequently tend to lose their specific mission orientation and become general-purpose shock troops like the French paras in Indochina and Algeria.(4)

The criteria of recruitment and function can be used to establish three kinds of elite: guardsmen, technicians, and warriors. They can also be used to eliminate from consideration two types of pseudo-elite relevant to the U.S. Marine Corps. The media elite is simply a military force whose tasks provide an opportunity for publicity credits giving it an image of special selection or special missions without the reality. Examples include the U.S. Navy's PT crews and the Royal Navy's coastal forces of World War II. The performance elite, on the other hand, gains its stature by its effectiveness. The Iron Brigade of the Army of the Potomac in our Civil War, the British 29th Division of World War I, the U.S. Army's 1st Division from 1942 to 1944 – all have been legitimately recognized as first-rate fighting formations by contemporaries and historians. None was distinguished by either recruitment or function. To qualify as elites for the purpose of this analysis, they would have had to incorporate the pattern made familiar by the Soviet Union during World War II: giving units with distinguished operational records a new title as guards or shock troops, favoring them in allocating replacements and equipment and assigning them the most exacting combat missions.

II

Any application of this model to the place of the Marine Corps in United States military history must take into account a historic national lack of hospitality to elite forces. Before 1900, peacetime defense establishments were too small to support these specialized fighting formations. The experiences of two world wars seemed to support the concept that mass armies whose units were roughly equal in quality were the true keys to victory. Army Ground Forces Chief Lesley McNair's hostility during World War II to specialized divisions is a case in point. Finally, after 1945 patterns of career advancement could put significant obstacles in the way of mavericks who wore special insignia or special items of clothing and also excluded outsiders. Ranger training, for example, has periodically been required of all regular Army line officers. Airborne training, accompanied at times by a tour of duty with the Special Forces, has tended to become part of the professional life cycle of every ambitious Army officer. Elite status, therefore, becomes associated with the individual rather than the organization to which he belongs.

In this general context, recruiting literature and Marine myths to the contrary, there is no evidence that the Corps was regarded, or regarded itself, as anything militarily special before the turn of the 20th century. During the American Revolution, Marine roles were functional. But manning some ships' guns, acting as sharpshooters in close action and forming parts of landing forces did not automatically confer elite status. In the course of the next century, since ship-to-ship actions were relatively few, Marines tended to develop a primary combat mission almost by default. They served as elements of landing parties. The scale of operations ranged from battalion-sized assaults to 20-man platoons landed to intimidate Pacific island chieftains. The degree of success ranged from the triumphs before Mexico City to the fiasco of the second attack on Fort Fisher.(5)

In the process the Marines established a certain internal mystique and morale, but these attitudes tended to be defensive, negative rather than positive. In what Peter Karsten aptly describes as an emerging naval aristocracy, Marine officers were at the bottom of an increasingly stratified pecking order. The function of the Corps, moreover, was increasingly called into question by junior officers of the new Navy of the 1890s. The role of the Marines as policemen, a reliable force to suppress mutiny or disorder among polyglot ships' crews, was described as an un-American insult to the new-model bluejacket. Technological changes had rendered unnecessary the use of Marines in fighting tops or as gun crews. As for the Marines' place in landing parties, naval enthusiasts argued that a well-trained ship's crew could provide an efficient striking force for shore operations from its own resources. The Marines, in short, were presented as an anachronism, surviving more because of influence in Congress than because of either merit or mission.(6)

The change in the Marine Corps' status is inseparable from the emergence of the modern war correspondent. It began with the exploits of the battalion which landed at Guantanamo Bay in 1898. The Marines may have fought more mosquitos than Spaniards, but by the time Stephen Crane finished filing his dispatches and writing his short stories, no American reader would have known it. The Marine detachment which participated in the defense of the foreign legations in Peking during the Boxer Rising of 1900 similarly covered itself with glory in the newspapers if not always in the opinions of eyewitnesses. During the first two decades of the 20th century, numerous occupations and landings in the Caribbean – mostly again, well-reported – contributed further to the image of the U.S. Marine as a hard-bitten warrior, able for the honor of the flag to turn his hand to anything from ruining a municipal water system to founding a disciplined police force.(7) The scale of these operations also helped silence the Navy's argument that sailors could perform equally well on land and sea. The modern warship was unable to spare a large proportion of its crew for a long time without a significant loss of operational efficiency. And a commander or captain whose expertise had been developed at sea was likely to find himself disastrously out of his element commanding a battalion-sized landing party. George Dewey's complaint about the lack of Marines at Manila in 1898 was bloodily reinforced at Vera Cruz in 1914, when an experienced Navy captain led a regiment of white-uniformed sailors, in proper parade formation, into a costly and embarrassing ambush.

World War I carried the Marines over any remaining media gap. There were no significant differences between the initial combat performances of Marine and Army units. However, Army regulations forbidding or restricting precise identification of individual units led correspondents and newspapers alike to publicize the activities of the Marines, an organization they were at least allowed to identify. The process might also have been fostered by the fact that only a single Marine brigade saw combat service with the AEF. In a war of corps and armies a formation only 7,000 strong could generate a sense of community among reporters as well as its own members.(8) Some of the best-known descriptive accounts of America's participation in the war have Marine Corps settings: Laurence Stallings' and Maxwell Anderson's *What Price Glory*, John W. Thomason's *Fix Bayonets,* Thomas Boyd's *Through the Wheat*. The images they conveyed were mixed: horror and hi-jinks, heroics and metaphysics. But each in its own way, these works and others stimulated continuing public interest in the Marine Corps.

By 11 November 1918, the U.S. Marine Corps had become a performance elite as well as a media elite. The 4th Marine Brigade's parent command, the 2nd Division, gained more ground and captured more prisoners and guns than any division in the AEF. Their German adversaries regarded the Marines as shock troops, the best America had to offer and equal to any fighting men on the Western Front in ferocity, if not always in operational skill. Yet neither press clippings nor battle records by themselves could make the Marine Corps anything but a pseudo-elite. The Corps took its first step towards true elite status by maintaining its status as a volunteer force until September 1918.

The relative military merits of volunteers and conscripts is an abstract question. On the other hand, the preparedness campaign of 1914-1917 combined with long-standing American myths to link volunteering with both patriotism and servicemen. Marine recruiting appeals stressing the Corps' role as "first to fight" brought in thousands of men who accepted the premises behind that slogan. Marine officers and NCOs as a whole regarded these enlistees as excellent raw material, even going so far as to boast of the high percentage of college men in the ranks of the wartime Corps.(10)

It is also certain that by 11 November 1918, the volunteer principle had come to be one of the most important ways of distinguishing Marines from soldiers. A Marine was there because he wanted to be rather than at the behest of his draft board. And the Marine brigade's achievements and image combined to support the Corps' emerging status as America's version of the Old World's guards formations, a force of men who had placed themselves above the ordinary soldier not by simple physical measurements, but democratically, by the free moral act of volunteering. As with their European counterparts, moreover, the American guardsmen solidified their position by performing ordinary combat missions extraordinarily. Marines were not specialists like the German storm battalions or the Italian *arditi*. They did everything that accompanied warfare on the Western Front. And they did it all superbly well.

III

Although the United States abandoned conscription after 1918, the Marine Corps did not sacrifice entirely its position as a force of guardsmen. Volunteering for military service involved making choices. The Army was largely stationed in the United States or in relatively comfortable colonial garrisons. The Navy offered regular hours, opportunities for travel and a chance to learn a trade. The Marine Corps, on the other hand, was involved in frequent action in China and the Caribbean. Unlike their counterparts in the other services, Marines had to expect a reasonable possibility of seeing combat or field duty during their term of service. This fact was likely to discourage at least some men seeking three meals and a bunk. And as the Great Depression grew more severe, a Corps less than 20,000 strong could afford to be increasingly selective in the recruits it accepted.

During the interwar years the Marine Corps also began establishing itself as a functional elite by developing a special mission, amphibious warfare. The process began at the turn of the century, according to Marine historians Graham Cosmas and Jack Shulimson, with practice exercises in occupying and defending advanced bases for the Navy. Nineteenth-century fiction was replete with accounts of hypothetical invasions: Great Britain by France or Germany, Germany by Great Britain, the United States by European and Asian powers. Most of these works tended to simplify the problems of the initial landing. Usually they described naval landing parties seizing an undefended beachhead or forcing their way ashore against ineffectual opposition.

Fact and fiction, however, proved two different things between 1914 and 1918. Wartime experience seemed to provide overwhelming evidence of the insuperable difficulties and unacceptable risks in landing on a hostile shore against even reasonably alert, efficient opposition. Gallipoli is only the most familiar example. For all the heroism displayed in the British raid on Gallipoli in 1918, losses in men and ships were abortively high for anything but a one-time operation against a target of supreme importance. Sir John Fisher's project for an amphibious invasion of Germany's Baltic coastline produced nothing more significant than an assortment of poorly designed warships. The most effective amphibious operation of the war, the German attack on the Baltic islands of Oesel, Moon and Rugen, was conducted against a Russian garrison demoralized by the winds of revolution and without any hope of relief from the mainland. It was supported by a large proportion of the High Seas Fleet. Yet in spite of these favorable conditions, enough ships were damaged or sunk, especially by mines, that the Imperial German Navy could hardly draw optimistic conclusions about the prospects for a repeat performance against an enemy who wanted to fight.

The U.S. Marine Corps defied accepted military wisdom for both internal and external reasons. For two decades Marines had performed every variety of military task, whose common denominator had frequently been nothing more than Army and Navy disinterest. Certainly they did not add up to a mission, a task for which the Corps could prepare in peacetime.

During the 1920s, however, a debate developed between the career officers who had spent 1917 and 1918 fighting in France and those who had remained involved in small-scale counterinsurgency operations in the Caribbean. Should the Marines orient themselves towards participation in a major war, most probably to be waged in Europe, or should they concentrate on developing a coherent doctrine supporting a role as Imperial America's fire brigade? The actual and projected strength of the Corps suggested that it was hardly likely to be able to support more than a division or two under any conceivable circumstances, an insignificant numerical contribution to a general war and one which experience with Pershing and his staff suggested would not be welcomed with open arms. No Marine could forget that one of the two brigades sent to France during World War I had been split into detachments for duties on the lines of communication instead of being formed with the veterans of Belleau Wood into a separate Marine division. Concentration on small wars, however, implied acceptance of a secondary role, one, which risked disappearing entirely as the United States became increasingly reluctant to use military intervention as a primary tool of diplomacy.(12)

At the same time that the Corps was trying to solve its internal dilemma, the U.S. Navy faced another set of challenges. For two decades naval planners had been preoccupied with resolving the strategic problem created by the Spanish-American War, which had left a thin line of American possessions strung like beads across the Western Pacific. The emergence of Japan as a great power and, the only potential enemy in the Pacific further complicated the situation. How would it be possible to defend or reconquer colonies and at the same time defeat the world's third-largest navy? Bases on the China coast, bases in the Philippines and massive fortifications of Guam were all considered. Before 1918, interservice rivalry, diplomatic considerations and budget constraints combined to defeat any proposals to maintain a significant United States military presence west of Hawaii. Then the Versailles Treaty gave Japan control of former German territory astride the most likely route of advance. The Washington Naval Treaty guaranteed Japan de facto superiority in the Western Pacific and prohibited significant improvement of existing American facilities in Guam and the Philippines. These international agreements, however, merely set final seals on the argument hardliners had been advancing for years. The Navy should abandon illusions and prepare itself to do what it was likely to have to do in any case, fight its way across the Pacific with its own resources.

This involved major changes in doctrine and practice. Developing a fleet train became a priority consideration. The aircraft carrier gained importance because of a growing belief even among gun-oriented admirals that the Navy would have to carry at least its own spotter planes and fighter support along with it during its advance in the face of a highly competent enemy. The Japanese could be expected to make few significant mistakes. The U.S. Navy, steaming ever farther from its major bases, could afford none. Warships by themselves, moreover, were not going to be enough. At the least, Japanese air and submarine bases would have to be cleared from the line of advance. And all but the most incurable optimists accepted the need for establishing American supply bases and elementary repair facilities as the fleet pushed deeper into Japanese controlled waters. A ship forced to return to the United States, or even to Pearl Harbor, for maintenance might just as well be out of the war altogether. This in turn meant landing operations, almost certainly on a scale far beyond the capacities of naval landing parties, ships' Marine detachments or the improvised battalions and regiments which had proved effective enough in the West Indies. And even discounting traditional service rivalries, the diluted Army of the Harding-Coolidge era was too concerned with digesting the lessons of war in Europe and too stretched by existing colonial defense commitments, static and mobile, to have either energy or personnel to spare for planning amphibious operations in the Pacific.(13)

Suddenly the Marine Corps was something more than a stepchild looking for a role. The Navy's needs had given the Marines a primary mission. From the early 1920s Marine planners immersed themselves in the studies of equipment and techniques required to land on a hostile shore and stay there.

In the process the Corps also began defining, albeit indirectly, the kind of fighting man who could best perform such a mission. Both the lessons of Gallipoli and the demands of the Navy indicated that time was the most important factor in the kinds of landings the Marines would be expected to perform. Enemy positions must be overrun promptly and enemy facilities must be occupied before they could be destroyed. This emphasized aggressiveness, dash and readiness to accept high casualties in a short time span in order to accomplish a mission. Experience in Haiti, Nicaragua, Mexico and the Dominican Republic further reinforced the hypothesis that quick, decisive action could establish the kind of moral superiority over an enemy that helped reduce one's own losses in the long run. This heroic vitalism was relatively untempered by the casualty lists of the Marine brigade in France. The Marines, like the AEF in general, never experienced attrition on the grand scale of Verdun or the Somme. And after 15 years, "What cold statistics could compete with images of Belleau Wood: the profane exhortation of GySgt Dan Daly to his wavering platoon; Capt Lloyd Williams' informing a discouraged French major, "Retreat, hell. We just got here"; and Capt Donald Duncan leading his company forward pipe in mouth and swagger stick in hand? The Marine Corps of the 1930s, in short, had an ample supply of the precise kind of traditions it considered valuable in its new mission as amphibious warfare specialist. All that was required were men to fit the mold and equipment to get them ashore. In World War II the Corps would have both.

IV

World War II marked the evolution of the Marine Corps into the third type of elite, the warriors. The process began with Guadalcanal where the 1st Marine Division's successes against the Japanese, the climate and the Navy could be and were sharply contrasted with the Army's initial debacle on the other side of the world at the Kasserine Pass. From Tarawa and Bougainville to Iwo Jima and Okinawa the legends continued to grow.

The emergence of the Marine as warrior, however, also reflected two significant modifications of his role as a technician. First, the Corps never had a monopoly of amphibious warfare. Army divisions also executed landing operations, exclusively in Europe and increasingly in the Pacific, without manifesting general and conspicuous incompetence. Particularly as the scale and complexity of amphibious operations increased, the Marine Corps had to justify its expansion against charges that it was simply duplicating the U.S. Army. The Marines answered on two levels. Officially the Corps asserted not that soldiers could not carry out amphibious missions, but that Marines were inevitably better at a mission in which they specialized. Unofficially this argument was accompanied by a strong implication that Marines were simply better fighters, man for man and unit for unit, than their Army counterparts.

This was not necessarily simply interservice boasting. As part of the naval service, the Corps did not have to accept draftees officially until December 1942. Particularly when allowances are made for bureaucratic delays, this meant that for well over a year of war, Marine recruiters were able to choose from among volunteers. Throughout the conflict, moreover, men below the legal draft age were able to volunteer for service with the Marines. As in World War I, the Corps could count on a substantial cadre of men who wanted to fight, expected to fight or could be motivated to fight.

And the developing "Marine machine" in turn generated a snowball effect. The adolescent who thought he was tough or who dreamed of martial glory could find an immediate outlet for his fantasies by joining the Marines. Volunteering for airborne or ranger training with the Army did not guarantee acceptance. The prospective paratrooper might just as easily find himself counting cans of beans in a supply dump. The Marines' boast that every Marine was a rifleman first and a specialist second offered far superior possibilities for civilian wish-fulfillment. The "Leatherneck" who ended as a truck driver or an orderly at least had had his chance and might well eventually find himself in a rifle company in any case.

The concept of an essential equality of quality within the Corps contributed significantly to the eventual disbanding of Marine airborne and raider battalions and the elimination of distinctive division, wing and other shoulder patches. Simply being a Marine was considered distinction enough for anyone in the Corps.(14)

The role of the Marine Corps as a technical elite was modified by a second factor as well. Marine divisions were never used purely as amphibious shock troops. They did not capture and consolidate beachheads, then await immediate relief by the Army in the same way that, for example, airborne formations depended on establishing prompt contact with supporting forces driving overland. Even in the Solomons, Army and Marine formations increasingly performed similar tasks in a similar environment, often fighting side by side. This made comparisons of methods and performances inevitable. And the best illustration of the nature of these comparisons came in the famous – or notorious – Smith versus Smith controversy. When Marine LGen Holland Smith relieved Army MGen Ralph Smith because of the alleged failure of the latter's troops to advance during the battle of Saipan, he touched off a debate which three decades later has left nerves exposed.

The military merits of the case remain open to debate.(15) Holland Smith was not considered a tactful man even by his fellow Marines. The 27th Division was not considered a particularly first-class unit even by the Army. The Army's Board of Officers appointed to investigate the circumstances of Ralph Smith's relief probably came closest to the truth when it declared in its report that a major problem was the "considerable amount of loose talk" existing at all levels of command on Saipan. The nature of that talk, however, is significant. Army officers like LGen Robert Richardson, commanding general, U.S. Army Forces, Pacific Ocean Areas, regarded the Marine emphasis on unity of command in amphibious operations as involving unnecessary duplication of effort at all levels. They questioned the Corps' ability to train staff officers and form efficient units of specialist troops: heavy artillery, supply and engineer units. They argued that Marines tended to define a good fighting division in terms of the casualties it sustained and that the Marine Corps had become so contemptuous of the Army's fighting ability that no Army unit could expect fair treatment when operating under Marine command. Nor could it expect recognition from correspondents bamboozled by the Marine public relations steamroller or honestly impressed by the Marine mystique.

The Marines for their part claimed that the derogatory comments only began when the 27th Division repeatedly failed to perform missions Marine units were expected to handle as routine. They cited their own examples of Army prejudice. Holland Smith, for example, accused Richardson of calling the Marines a bunch of "beach runners" unqualified to conduct operations out of sight of a shoreline and of declaring Marine officers less qualified than their Army counterparts to control large bodies of troops.

Richardson, who was the kind of officer who spoke to service clubs on his lunch hour and always remembered his superiors' birthdays, admitted that he did discuss differences in tactical doctrine, but only in general terms. In no manner could his attitude be interpreted as criticism of the Marines "unless one were seeking to attribute criticism where none existed." His denial has never achieved wide credibility among either Marines or Marine historians.(16)

In the final analysis, the U.S. Marine Corps had excellent mute witnesses, lines on a map. There was no way to deny that the Marines on Saipan had advanced while the Army had not. As for comparative casualty lists, the Marines were able by V-J Day to cite other statistics. If certain Army officers continued to regard operations like Iwo Jima as nothing but "Marine slaughter houses," conducted from beginning to end without regard for losses, Army divisions committed to the kind of battles the Marines had been fighting in the Central Pacific also suffered proportionately heavy casualties. On Guam, Peleliu and Okinawa, differences in losses between Marine and Army divisions were marginal and explainable by operational circumstances as opposed to tactical doctrines.

Significant general discrepancies in performance between Marines and soldiers are equally difficult to discern. Nevertheless, the Army in the Central Pacific always seemed to be playing catch-up, to be justifying or defending its performance *vis-à-vis* the Marines. This attitude may have reflected the reality that the Army was for the first time in its history fighting side by side with Marines on what amounted to Marine Corps terms, landing on and capturing the kind of island fortresses against which Marine planning had been directed for two decades. Whatever its roots, Army defensiveness set a final seal on the characterization of the U.S. Marines as warriors elite, the men who set the standards of performance on the battlefield.

V

After 1945, however, the Marine Corps was reluctant to describe or defend itself in these terms, at least officially. Instead, it emphasized its role as a functional elite. To some extent this was influenced by the Corps' concern for its position in the reorganized American defense establishment. Dwight Eisenhower's argument that Marine combined-arms units were "assuming and duplicating" Army functions was accompanied by a recommendation that the Cops be limited to a strength of 50,000 to 60,000. Its functions would resemble those of the British Royal Marines: furnishing battalion-sized formations for security or raiding missions and providing landing craft crews, beach parties and personnel for similar waterborne aspects of larger-scale amphibious operations – assuming these were still possible in the atomic age. The Marine Corps responded directly by emphasizing the enduring necessity of amphibious operations to a maritime power like the United States. If they were necessary, they were possible. The challenge lay in developing techniques appropriate to a nuclear environment. Indeed, the more difficult amphibious warfare was likely to be, the more necessary it was to maintain a force specializing in that form of warfare.

A line of argument presenting the Marine as a technician almost certainly carried more weight in defense planning than would a defense of the Corps as a warrior elite. The National Security Act of 1947 gave the Marine Corps legal responsibility for developing amphibious capability and doctrine. For three decades the Corps has continued to regard this mission as important, if not essential, to its institutional survival in its post-1945 configuration.

The Marines, however, have also continued to emphasize, especially for external consumption, their nature as a force of elite volunteers. America's real "old guard." This required little intellectual or emotional innovation. While the United States maintained an active selective service system, the Marines' position that a volunteer force was superior to its conscript equivalent, developed in World War I and continued through World War II, remained unchallenged. The Corps accepted draftees and directed accessions only with reluctance during part of the Vietnam era. And while the Navy and the Air Force might also consist of volunteers, their recruits, in Marine terms, were men who did not wish to serve in ground forces under any conditions. Marines, on the other hand, enlisted to close with the enemy, whether in 1918 or 1968. Even since the introduction of a volunteer military, the Marine Corps has continued to imply that the fact of joining the Marines involves a moral statement, a deliberate opting for membership in an elite. It is the element of choice that has been important, not available alternatives or even the recruit's intellect and character – assuming that he lives up to his new status once he enlists. Not until 1975 did Marines begin admitting for public consumption that there were limits to what even the Corps could achieve with some of its volunteers. And this admission has been made with extreme reluctance.

Yet for all the importance the Corps continues to place on its specialized function and its unique recruiting policies, its dominant emphasis over the past three decades has been on the Marine as warrior. The Corps has retained and in many ways enhanced its World War II image as a force of super soldiers – not necessarily death-worshipping fanatics, but men who accept death as an inevitable part of war and who are at home with violence under any circumstances. With the major exception of the television series "Gomer Pyle, USMC," the image of the enlisted Marine in America's media is that of a fighter, a man who even in dress blues always seems to be looking for a sharp rock with which to cut throats. Can one readily imagine, for example, a credible comic-strip series featuring "Beetle Bailey, USMC"? The stereotype of the completely ignorant junior officer whose sergeant leads him by the hand through his initiation to battle is also absent for all practical purposes from popular culture dealing with the Marine Corps. Whether second lieutenant or two-star general, a Marine officer is presented as a combat leader in the mold of John Wayne in *Flying Leathernecks* and Robert Conrad in TV's "Baa, Baa Black Sheep" or the prose characterizations in Pat Frank's *Hold Back the Night* and James Webb's *Fields of Fire*, one set in Korea, the other in Vietnam.

The extent to which myth and reality overlap is questionable. What is certain is that the Corps accepts and reinforces its own mythic images. A Marine intellectual is certainly not a contradiction in terms. Nevertheless, the Marine stereotype emphasizes jawlines instead of foreheads. Nicknames like "Chesty" (Puller) or "Brute" (Krulak) are borne with pride. The contrast demonstrated between Smith and Richardson on Saipan has been replicated many times since 1944, most recently in Vietnam where the life styles and command approaches of Gens Walt and Westmoreland offered a contrast that in other contexts might have been an amusing example of two men trying to live up to respective stereotypes of hardnosed Marine and inevitable general.(17)

A Marine of any rank is in a sense expected by his counterparts in other services to be somewhat unimaginative, able enough to storm a beach or demolish a pillbox but lacking in operational subtlety. To his professional critics, at least, the Marine is excessively prone to trade lives for time at unfavorable rates, prone to turn a defensive position like Khe Sanh into a potential death trap because he is too proud to entrench and then expect the Air Force or the Army to make good history. The respective service studies of Khe Sanh prepared by the Air Force and the Marine Corps are studiously polite, but seem to describe entirely different battles.

Once again, images and realities conflict sharply. It can be argued legitimately that many significant operational innovations developed by the Marine Corps, from the tactical use of helicopters in Korea to the combined-action platoon in Vietnam, have been overlooked or de-emphasized because the other Services cannot quite believe Marines are that clever. And this innovative capacity has been fostered by a concrete factor which has in turn contributed significantly to the development of the Marine as warrior. The U.S. Marine Corps has since 1945 essentially functioned as a force in readiness, able and willing to go anywhere and do anything, in any strength from a battalion landing team to a corps-level amphibious force. This emphasis on flexibility has not involved ad hoc improvisations. It is institutional, antedating by years the 1976 Brookings Institution study by Martin Binkin and Jeffrey Record criticizing the Marine Corps for its excessive commitment to an obsolescent form of warfare. The Corps has been too much of a military anomaly, and regards itself as too much of a military outsider, to link its destiny willingly to one specific mission, even if that mission is defined by law. This does not imply complete internal harmony. Particularly in the aftermath of Vietnam, the Corps has been racked by conflicts regarding prospective future missions and policies. The debates, outlined for public consumption in such journals as the *U.S. Naval Institute Proceedings*, the *Marine Corps Gazette* and the *Naval War College Review* are significant proof that the Marines are not, in fact, committed blindly to an endless refighting of the Battle of Iwo Jima.

In practice, moreover, current emphasis on Marine flexibility tends to emphasize the Marine's status as a warrior rather than a technician. The Corps has executed only one major opposed amphibious landing in three decades, at Inchon in 1950. In Vietnam the Army conducted riverine operations in the Mekong Delta, while the Marines remained locked in land combat in the north. Marines in Korea functioned as MacArthur's fire brigade in the Pusan Perimeter and participated in the trench warfare along the 38th Parallel. Marines in Vietnam did almost everything but land on a beach against serious resistance. Operations in Lebanon (1958) and the Dominican Republic (1965) provided further tests of Marine flexibility.

As American military planning increasingly focuses on Western Europe, the long-standing Marine commitment as a strategic reserve for NATO is being given new life. While the Corps' current primary concept is to support NATO's northern flank, deploying in Scandinavia as an emergency reinforcement, operations elsewhere in Europe are not excluded. Mechanized Marine formations are even being considered for deployment in Central Europe in a manner reminiscent of 1917. This scenario is generally regarded as an unlikely response to an extreme emergency, but its very existence reinforces the Corps' increasing self-identification as the most general of the nation's general purpose forces, ready to fight any time in any environment regardless of how its units enter the operational zone.

This self-identification in turn reflects increasing comfort with the thesis that as long as armed forces and societies seek counterpoises to mass, as long as they respond consciously or unconsciously to models of the extraordinary, the United States Marine Corps will maintain its de facto role as America's warrior elite. In this sense at least, the Corps has come far from Belleau Wood and Guadalcanal.

It would, however, be highly inappropriate to end here with a simple paraphrase of the "Marines' Hymn." The Marine Corps' concern for its place in the defense establishment may focus on missions and budgets. Yet Marines might do well to remember that elite forces can decay as well as be destroyed by jealous rivals. Historically, fighting elites have faced two major risks. The first is loss of perspective, with the corresponding tendency to degenerate into a parody of past deeds and present images. Self-confidence bordering on cockiness and pride of service bordering on arrogance are major ingredients of military morale. By themselves, however, they are at best winning tickets for membership in the "Order of the Plastic Bag." At worst they can intensify the shock of defeat to the point of disaster. The cry of "the Guard is retreating" did not by itself touch off the panic of the French at Waterloo, but it certainly helped discourage mere soldiers from making any attempts to rally. More serious than the perils of arrogance are the risks of stagnation. The exclusive nature of any elite can be seductive. To be part of an elite which has combined selective recruitment, a unique mission and the status of super-soldiers can readily generate a chorus of "this is right because it is the way we do it," with a corresponding reluctance to entertain new ideas. Its history of flexibility and its self-image as a military stepchild, however, combine to suggest that the Corps will not merely play the role of an elite. It will fulfill elite functions as well.

And perhaps "if the Army and the Navy ever look on heaven's scenes," they may indeed "find the streets are guarded by United States Marines"!

NOTES

The U.S. Marine Corps has inspired an immense bibliography. Of the general histories, three stand out. Clyde H. Metcalf, *A History of the United States Marine Corps* (New York, 1939) has the advantage of being able to concentrate on the early and middle years. Robert Debs Heinl Jr., *Soldiers of the Sea: The United States Marine Corps, 1775-1962* (Annapolis, 1962) is substantial and reasonably well-balanced. J. Robert Moskin, *The U.S. Marine Corps Story* (New York, 1977) carries its account through Vietnam. Edwin H. Simmons, *The United States Marines* (New York, 1976) is a recent and readable short account, despite a certain tendency to slide into Corps pieties. All can expect to be superseded by Allan Millett's forthcoming study in the Macmillan series. On the other hand, hundreds of articles on operations and doctrine have been published in dozens of journals, while even the guides to primary printed and oral sources form a substantial bibliography by themselves. To avoid submerging my argument beneath the weight of its scholarly apparatus, footnote citations have been kept to a minimum. They are presented largely as suggestions for additional general reading illustrating my theme.

1. Lawrence Suid, "Hollywood and the Marines," *Marine Corps Gazette* (April 1978).
2. For a slightly different approach, see Eliot A. Cohen, *Commandos and Politicians: Elite Military Units in Modern Democracies* (Cambridge, Mass., 1978).
3. See particularly David Chandler, *The Campaigns of Napoleon* (New York, 1966) and the somewhat idealized Henry Lachoque, *The Anatomy of Glory*, adapted by Anne S. K. Brown (Providence, R.I., 1961). The quotation is from Lachoque.
4. Among the best of many analyses of the paratroop mystique are two essays by
Ramon Lopez-Reyes, "Airborne Training and Group Dynamics," and "Airborne Rituals, Symbols and Behavior," in *Power and Immortality* (New York, 1971). See also James K. McCollum, "The Airborne Mystique," *Military Review* (November 1976) and John E. Talbot, "The Myth and Reality of the Paratrooper in the Algerian War," *Armed Forces and Society* (1976).
5. H. A. Ellsworth, *One Hundred Eighty Landings of United States Marines, 1800-1934* (Washington, D.C., 1974) is a useful compendium.
6. A brief treatment of these issues can be found in Peter Karsten, *The Naval Aristocracy* (New York, 1972), the more detailed discussion in Frederick S. Harrod, *Manning the New Navy: The Development of a Modern Naval Enlisted Force, 1899-1940* (Westport, Conn., 1978).
7. Among the more familiar pieces to emerge from the Spanish-American War is Stephen Crane's, "Marines Signaling Under Fire at Guantanamo," *McClure's Magazine*, (February 1899), reprinted in Fredson Bowers, ed., Stephen Crane, *Tales of War, Vol. VI of The University of Virginia Edition of the Works of Stephen Crane* (Charlottesville, Va., 1970); also "The Red Badge of Courage Was His Wig-Wag Flag," *New York World*, 1 July 1898, reprinted in *The War Dispatches of Stephen Crane*, ed. by R. W. Stallman and E. R. Hagemann (New York, 1964). For Marine versions of Peking, see Oliver P. Smith, "We Will Do our Best," *U.S. Naval Institute Proceedings* (1928) and Capt John T. Myers, "Military Operations and Defenses of the Siege of Peking," *Proceedings*, (1902), which tells the detachment commander's story. Peter Fleming, *The Siege at Peking* (New York, 1959) and Richard O'Connor, *The Spirit Soldiers* (New York, 1973) offer accounts more critical of Marine morale and performance. For the Corps in the Caribbean, J. H. McCrocklin, *Garde d'Haiti: Twenty Years of organization and Training by the U.S. Marine Corps* (Annapolis, 1959) and Capt Stephen M. Fuller and Graham A. Cosmas, *Marines in the Dominican Republic 1916-1924* (Washington, 1974) are excellent.
8. For the evolution of the censorship policies of the AEF see the "Historical Statement" in Reports of Commander in *Chief A.E.F., Staff Sections and Services Vol. XIII of United States Army in the World War, 1917-1919* (Washington, 1948). Its impact on the behavior and attitude of correspondents is discussed in Emmet Crozier, *American Reporters on the Western Front, 1914-1918* (New York, 1959).
9. Edward M. Coffman, *The War to End All Wars* (New York, 1968) puts the Marine experience in the general context of American intervention. John A. Lejeune, *Reminiscences of a Marine* (Philadelphia, 1930, reprinted Quantico, Va., 1979), and A. W. Catlin, *With the Help of God and a Few Marines* (Garden City, N. Y., 1919) are important memoirs. U.S. Army, Records of the Second Division (Regular), Vols. 1-9

(Washington, D.C., 1927) is a valuable collection of undigested documentary material. For those with less patience or more common sense, O. L. Spaulding and J. W. Wright, *The Second Division American Expeditionary Force in France 1917-1919* (New York, 1937) is solid and makes a successful effort to be fair to the Army and the Marine halves of the division. Robert Asprey, *At Belleau Wood* (New York, 1965) is a well-written modern account of the Marines' most familiar battle.

10. This conclusion involves a minor paradox. A major theme of the preparedness movement was its advocacy of universal military training. As a first step towards such a program, the movement stressed volunteering for peacetime training. See John G. Clifford, *The Citizen Soldiers: The Plattsburg Training Camp Movement, 1913-1920* (Lexington, Ky., 1972) and John Patrick Finnegan, *Against the Specter of a Dragon* (Greenwood, Conn., 1974). See also the general account in Russell F. Weigley, *History of the United States Army* (New York, 1967) and the discussion of Marine recruiting during World War I in R. G. Lindsay, *This High Name: Public Relations and the U.S. Marine Corps* (Madison, Wis., 1956).

11. The standard general account is I. F. Clarke, *Voices Prophesying War* (London, 1966). Familiar treatments of the specific problem of landing operations include [G. T. Chesney], "The Battle of Dorking: Reminiscences of a Volunteer," *Blackwood's Magazine*, (May 1871); William Le Quex, *The Great War in England in 1897* (London, 1894) and *The Invasion of 1910* (London, 1906); and Hudson Maxim, *Defenseless America* (New York, 1915).

12. See the surveys in Ronald Schaffer, "The 1940 Small Wars Manual and the 'Lessons of History,'" *Military Affairs* (April 1972); Raymond G. O'Connor, "The U.S. Marines in the Twentieth Century: Amphibious Warfare and Doctrinal Debates," ibid., (October 1974); and K. J. Clifford, *Progress and Purpose: A Developmental History of the United States Marine Corps 1900-1970* (Washington, 1973). Valuable longer discussions include J. A. Isely and Philip A. Crowl, *U.S. Marines and Amphibious War* (Princeton, 1951); G. C. Dyer, *The Amphibians Came to Conquer, Vol. I* (Washington, 1969); and Frank O. Hough, et al., *Pearl Harbor to Guadalcanal, Vol. I, History of U.S. Marine Corps Operations in World War II* (Washington, 1958).

13. The best general analyses of American naval policy during this period include William R. Braisted, *The United States Navy in the Pacific, 1919-1922* (Austin, 1971); Gerald E. Wheeler, *Prelude to Pearl Harbor: The United States Navy and the Far East, 1921-1931* (Columbia, Mo., 1963); and Stephen E. Pelz, *Race to Pearl Harbor: The Failure of the Second London Naval Conference and the Onset of World War II* (Harvard, 1974). William R. Braisted, "On the American Red and Red-Orange Plans," in Gerald Jordan, ed., *Naval Warfare in the Twentieth Century, 1900-1945* (London, 1977) shows the Army's continued focus on RED (Great Britain) as a more useful hypothetical enemy than ORANGE (Japan). Hector Bywater, *The Great Pacific War* (Boston and New York, 1925), in its original edition, is an excellent fictional analysis of America's strategic problem by a British civilian expert. C. M. Melhorn, *Two-Block Fox: The Rise of the Aircraft Carrier, 1911-1929* (Annapolis, 1974) interprets the evolution of this vessel principally in terms of increased recognition of the need for air support in the proposed reconquest of the Pacific.

14. For a summary of Marine recruitment and training procedures see H. I. Shaw and Maj Douglas Kane, *Isolation of Rabaul, Vol. II of History of U.S. Marine Corps Operations in World War II* (Washington, 1963). C. L. Updegraph Jr., *Special Marine Corps Units of World War II* (Washington, 1972), presents an official critique of the concept of elite units for special missions. Among the proliferation of personal narratives stressing Corps pride and an accompanying sense of membership in an elite, Robert Leckie, *Helmet for My Pillow* (New York, 1957) and S. E. Smith, ed., *The United States Marine Corps in World War II* (New York, 1969) are worthwhile introductions. Leon Uris, *Battle Cry* (New York, 1948) remains the archetypal "Marine Corps novel" with a World War II setting.

15. The case is best presented from the Marines' perspective in H. I. Shaw Jr., et al., *Central Pacific Drive, Vol. III of History of U.S. Marine Corps Operations in World War II* (Washington, 1966). Philip A. Crowl, *Campaign in the Marianas, Vol IX of United States Army in World War II* (Washington, 1960) tells the Army's side. Holland M. Smith, *Coral and Brass* (New York, 1949) and E. Q. Love, *The 7th Infantry Division in World War II* (Washington, 1949) are mutually vitriolic. Perhaps the best-balanced summary, written from the perspective of the overall commander, is Thomas B. Buell, *The Quiet Warrior: A Biography of Admiral Raymond A. Spruance* (Boston, 1974).

16. Statements from Army officers are contained in notes, letters, memos and official statements found in R. C. Richardson Papers, Saipan Incident, Hoover Institution on War, Revolution and Peace, Stanford, Calif.

17. This point has been stressed over and over in informal or off-the-record comments to me by serving officers, Army and Marine alike. For corroboration compare pieces such as "The Two Wars of General Walt," *Life*, 26 May 1967 or "Leader for all Reasons," *Time*, 9 June 1967 and L. W. Walt, *Strange War, Strange Strategy* (New York, 1970), with E. B. Ferguson, *Westmoreland: The Inevitable General* (Boston, 1968) or Westmoreland's own memoirs, *A Soldier Reports* (New York, 1976).

THE CAT WITH MORE THAN NINE LIVES

Robert D. Heinl, Jr.

> *The following essay presents a prevalent view held by many Marines that the most significant threat to the Corps derives from the jealousy of its opponents within the U.S. Government. This historical perspective is important to keep in mind when considering nearly every event in which the Marine Corps has participated – especially those that Marines themselves have written about. Heinl, a retired Marine Colonel and prolific writer, provides this institutional perspective on the frequent assaults by the War and Navy Departments to dismember the Marine Corps since its establishment. Undeniably, the Marines have tenaciously responded to such adversity by seeking out an expanded role in the Armed Forces. Although the U.S. Congress has always come to its aid, perhaps a strain of paranoia regarding the "sinister" motives of its sister services has left its mark on Marine Corps' culture?*

On a rough average of once every eleven years since 1829, the U.S. Marine Corps has found itself compelled to fight for existence – not against enemies of the United States, but against enemies of the Marine Corps.

These attacks have come equally from all quarters, from War Department, Navy Department, White House; from efficiency experts, budgeteers, brass-hats, and Presidents. Habitually, every attack has been justified as a move to get rid of "needless duplication." No attempt has ever succeeded, and several have touched off legislative action which further strengthened the Marine Corps. The rock on which all but one of these proposals foundered has been Congress – in other words, the will of the people.

If ever an organization has thrived on attempts to abolish it, it is this small Corps with one foot in the sea, one foot on land, and its head perpetually under the sword of Damocles. The battlefield and beachhead victories of the Marine Corps need no advertisement. Not so well known, on the other hand, is the Corps' durability in the face of ten successive attempts (all launched from within the U.S. Government) to legislate, administer, or remodel the U.S. Marine Corps out of existence.

Like a cat with more than nine lives, however, the Marine Corps has emerged safe and sound from each ordeal, and, if anything, it has prospered on opposition.

Andrew Jackson's Waterloo

On December 8, 1829, President Andrew Jackson, himself a fighting general of no mean standing, struck consternation throughout the Marine Corps by a passage in his first annual message to Congress:

> I would also recommend that the Marine Corps be merged in the artillery or infantry, as the best mode of curing the many defects in its organization. But little exceeding in number any of the regiments of infantry, that corps has, besides its Lieutenant-Colonel Commandant, five brevet lieutenant colonels, who receive the full pay and emoluments of their brevet rank, without rendering proportionate service. Details for Marine service could well be made from the artillery or infantry, there being no peculiar training requisite for it.

The Marine Corps had been in existence 54 years. Its Commandant, Lieutenant Colonel Archibald Henderson (who was destined, before retirement, to outlast ten Presidential administrations), had already had his worries in keeping the tiny Corps (1,800 strong) a going concern. In 1821, less than a year after he had taken office on the heels of a ne'er-do-well predecessor deposed by general court martial, the Secretary of the Navy had tried to abolish the offices of Commandant and Quartermaster of the Corps and to replace the two key Marine officers by civil servants. In 1824, things were still far from rosy, as witness Henderson's prophetic plaint to the Secretary of the Navy:

> Our isolated Corps, with the Army on one side and the Navy on the other (neither friendly), has been struggling ever since its establishment for its very existence. We have deserved hostility from neither, especially the Navy.

To make matters worse, real doubt existed as to the legal and administrative status of the Corps. Some believed the Marines to be part of the Army; others, part of the Naval Establishment; and still a third faction held the Corps to be autonomous. These administrative headaches had begun to throb in the late 1820s, and it is hardly a surprise to find the incumbent Secretary of the Navy, John Branch, firmly aligned with the President on the Marine Corps problem. Said Branch, in effect, to Congress, "Either settle the status of the Corps or get rid of it."

So, in early 1830, the survival of the Marine Corps was squarely up to Congress. "On this point," to quote Secretary Branch,

> the opinions of many of the superior officers of the Navy were called for, and presented to the honorable Chairman of the Committee on Naval Affairs by the Senate, during the last session of Congress. These, it appeared, were by no means in accordance with each other; and this diversity of sentiment amongst persons best qualified to determine the question has induced the Department to withhold any recommendation on the subject.

Andrew Jackson, Army man by long experience and predilection with his conviction that the Marines needlessly duplicated the Infantry and Artillery of the Army, had also, however, steered his recommendation into the House Committee on Military Affairs. That committee, turgidly reported the Honorable William Drayton, its chairman, "took cognizance of the Marine Corps, in consequence of the expediency of merging it in the Army," (whatever that meant), and finally did not "think proper to interfere with" the status of the Marine Corps, but rather to pass the buck back to the Committee on Naval Affairs, where the President's proposals were put to sleep and died.

Meanwhile, Colonel Henderson, quick and prompt in legislative matters as he was in combat, had laid down an aggressive defense with both the Naval and Military Affairs Committees, whom he bombarded with statistics and arguments regarding continuation of the Marine Corps. Equally to the point, when a new Secretary of the Navy, Levi Woodbury, succeeded Branch, Henderson undertook his education as well, in a characteristic letter:

> Sir –
> The Corps of Marines is one of the oldest in the service. As the exigencies of the Country required, it has served in time of War both the Navy and Army. No want of military efficiency nor of honorable performance of duty was then heard of. In peace no dereliction of duty has ever been more than once charged upon it, at least as far as I have heard. The propriety of any change in the organization of such a Corps is at the least questionable. As the Commandant of the Corps, if I thought such change necessary for the public interests, I should be among the first to recommend it. It is my fixed opinion that no such change will eventuate in the promotion of either economy or utility.

Further Congressional action was definitely aborted, confessed Congressman Drayton to Henderson – President Jackson or no Jackson. The public, setting a pattern which still holds, had jumped into the foray with both feet, and the press (notably in New England) rallied to support the Marines.

The time now seemed ripe for counter-offensive, and Colonel Henderson pressed for Congressional action to protect the Corps and to remedy the organizational weaknesses which the controversy had uncovered. The result was that, on June 30, 1834, Congress passed "An Act for the better Organization of the Marine Corps." This statute (spurred by Henderson and even by petitions from all the Marine officers on duty at Headquarters) firmly constituted the Marine Corps as a part of the Naval Establishment (although not a part of the U.S. Navy), directly under the Secretary of the Navy, and gave Archibald Henderson a substantially increased Corps to lead toward new laurels.

Andrew Jackson, having been afforded a good look at the back of Archibald Henderson's hand, let go of the Marines in favor of more digestible game and signed the bill. The

Marines, able at length to abandon the foxholes of Capitol Hill, returned with a single mind to normality – which then consisted of swamp and jungle fighting against insurgent Indians in the Creek and Seminole Wars.

Because the Jackson foray was the first of many to come and because it foreshadowed, crudely perhaps and in miniature, basic elements to be found in subsequent anti-Marine proposals, it might be well to examine it on the postmortem slab.

Woven through the 1829 controversy ran threads of thinking which were destined to become deadly familiar to Marines during the next 120 years. Those propositions ran as follows:

a. The Marine Corps must be eliminated as a unit because it duplicated someone else (the Army, said General Jackson), and because it was administratively troublesome.
b. On the other hand, there never arose any question but that the functions or duties being performed by Marines had to be done by someone (the Army again, said General Jackson).
c. The proponents of the measure could never show that, even if someone else took over essential Marine functions, the latter would be any better performed.
d. Perceiving the closed-circle character of the foregoing propositions and realizing that this was manifestly an attack on the entity of the Marine Corps and not on its functions, Congress acted with logic and soundness on the side of the Marines.

This was a pattern destined to appear and reappear whenever opponents of the Marine Corps plotted its downfall.

Saved by the Admirals

It never took a house to fall on Archibald Henderson where matters concerning the security or improvement of the Marine Corps were concerned, and, by 1852 (six Presidents after Andrew Jackson), the venerable but vigorous Colonel-Commandant had amassed a special file of testimonials from the flag officers of the Navy regarding the usefulness and need of Marines in any well run Naval Establishment: "All urge in the strongest terms," it was stated,

> an increase in the Marine Corps, basing their view on the specific-necessity of Marines for duty on board ship, owing to their usefulness and efficiency,

In 1859 (as if this were not enough) in his Annual Report of December 2, the current Secretary of the Navy brought a reminiscent smile to brave old Colonel Henderson, by his comment:

> The Marine Corps is an indispensable branch of the naval service....It is a gallant little band upon which rests the most widely extended duties at home and in every sea and clime, without sufficient numbers to perform them.

Only six years later, incredibly, after Archibald Henderson had finally sheathed his sword, the Marine Corps found itself at low ebb.

Most Marine fighting in the Civil War had taken place on shore, under the Army, and only one successful amphibious assault – that by Major Reynolds' battalion against the Hilton Head forts – marked the Leathernecks' record. True, Marines had fought and died on Henry House Hill at the first Bull Run (where, as a later Commandant, Major General Ben H. Fuller, observed, "Surely they were among the last to run"); they had soldiered at Island No.10 and with Grant at Vicksburg. It was not surprising, therefore, in 1864, to see a Congressional resolution introduced with the aim of transferring the Corps intact to the Army.

Colonel Commandant Jacob Zeilin, newly appointed, heavily bearded, much shot-at since entering the Corps in 1831, and already famous as the first Marine officer to land on Japanese soil, moved aggressively in this crisis. Having learned his techniques as Henderson's aide and protégé, Zeilin without hesitation canvassed the senior flag officers of the Navy for their ideas on the status of Marines. The Admirals' response was unanimous. With David G. Farragut, David D. Porter, and Samuel DuPont heading the list, the naval hierarchy opposed any such change, and Congress, wisely respectful of such authority, tabled the resolution.

Encore for the Admirals

On February 21, 1867, Colonel Zeilin – now, it might be said, a veteran of such affairs – was notified that a resolution had just been introduced in the House of Representatives, not merely to transfer the Marine Corps to the Army, but to abolish it entirely, after detaching its members to the latter service. The resolution, he noted, was being referred to the House Naval Affairs Committee, then headed by the Hon. Alexander Rice, a salty and conservative member from Massachusetts. In the course of hearings on the proposal, Zeilin again produced the sheaf of testimonials which he had employed with such success in 1864, together with new ones as well, and the Committee elected to concur with the views of Farragut, Porter, DuPont, Wilkes, Stribling & Co. The resolution was reported out adversely and died stillborn, on the floor of the House of Representatives.

The Sailors Object

The early 1890s marked the end of the doldrums in which the Naval Establishment had drifted since the Civil War. The Marine Corps, under efficient command of its 8th Commandant, Charles Grymes McCawley, seemed never safer. In 1890, the Admiral of the Navy, David D. Porter, had written:

> I have had the Marines under my observation since the year 1824, since I first joined an American man-of-war, a period of 66 years, and during that time I have never known a case where the Marines could not be depended on for any service. Without that well drilled force on shipboard, an American man-of-war could not be depended on to maintain discipline and perform the arduous duties assigned her. There is not an intelligent officer of the Navy who can speak anything but praise of the Marine Corps, or, if there are any, I cannot conceive upon what they can ground their opposition.

If Admiral Porter had only known it, his closing sentence, quoted above, had a prophetic ring. Within four years, in 1894, a determined minority group of younger Navy officers, spark-plugged by Lieutenant William F. Fullam, U.S. Navy, had launched a full-fledged attempt to force Marines off the ships of the Navy and, ultimately, into the Army.

Fullam's initial test case (there were destined to be several during the succeeding fifteen years) had to do with U.S.S. *Raleigh*, whose Marine detachment, it was proposed, should be radically pared in strength and duties. This the Navy Department, after weighing pro's and con's, disapproved in favor of the Marines. What followed can be described in a subsequent letter from Major General George F. Elliott, 10th Commandant, to the Secretary of the Navy:

> The wishes of the movers of this proposition being thus frustrated by the Department, petitions were circulated for signature among the crews of the vessels of the Navy addressed to the Congress of the United States, asking for withdrawal of Marines on board ship. The attention of the Department being called to said petitions, the Secretary deemed it his duty to issue a Special Order reprobating this procedure on the part of the enlisted men, which was nurtured by the few officers previously referred to.[1]

Although the sailors' complaint undoubtedly had sub-structure in the occasional bad feeling which arose in those days between bluejackets and Marines (who were unaffectionately termed "policemen"), such an agitation could not have lasted five minutes without countenance by ships' commanding officers.

Be that as it may, on July 31, 1894, Vice President Adlai E. Stevenson, presiding over the Senate, read into the Record the sailors' petition, and, less than a month later on August 24, Senator Charles F. Manderson of Nebraska (a land-locked state in which almost half the counties are named for Army generals) introduced on behalf of Senator John Sherman (brother of Army General William T. Sherman) Senate Bill 2324, designed to consolidate five artillery regiments of the Army with the Marine Corps; to redesignate this body as a Corps of Marine Artillery; and then to transfer the whole Corps to the Army. This approach, novel to American ideas on the subject of Marines, followed closely the prevailing European fad which considered Marines primarily as coast-defense and fortress-artillery troops.

At this juncture, the sailors' petition went to the Senate Naval Affairs Committee, which pigeonholed it promptly, on the very same day that Secretary of the Navy Hilary A. Herbert issued official reprimands to certain officers whom he believed responsible for instigating the petition and went further by promulgating Navy Department Special Order 16 (previously mentioned by General Elliott), in which the Department stated:

> Advantage is taken of this opportunity to state that the Department, after maturely considering the subject, and particularly in view of the honorable record made by the Marine Corps . . . is convinced of the usefulness of the Corps, both ashore and afloat, and of the propriety of continuing it in service on shipboard.

Senator Manderson's bill was referred to the Senate Military Affairs Committee, where it collided head-on, as in 1864 and 1867, with the disapproval not only of the Secretary of the Navy just expressed, but that of senior admirals of the Service. Following precedent, the Senators concurred in expert opinion and decided in favor of the Marine Corps as it was.

Fighting Bob Fights the Leathernecks

Captain Robley D. Evans, U.S. Navy, carried throughout his Service career the well-deserved nickname of "Fighting Bob." He had begun earning it on the fire-swept beaches short of Fort Fisher, North Carolina, on January 15, 1864, by holding a pistol to the head of a surgeon who had announced intention of amputating his wounded leg. On this occasion – "about as bloody a place as a lot of men ever got into," Admiral Evans later mused – he had observed the relative inefficiency of ships' landing forces (including Marines) in the assault of a defended beach.

Almost thirty years later, still fighting and quite evidently undaunted by the Secretary of the Navy's expressed views on Marines afloat, Captain Evans, now prospective commanding officer of the new huge (10,288-ton) battleship *Indiana*, asked that the customary Marine detachment be left off the complement of the ship, inasmuch as her demands in the way of a working crew left neither accommodations for Marines, nor billets, he felt, in which they could economically be employed.

On November 1, 1895, Secretary Herbert replied to "Fighting Bob." First, to make matters clear, the basic request was disapproved. Second, for the record, it was prescribed that *Indiana*'s Marine detachment would be composed of "One Captain, one subaltern and 60 noncommissioned officers, privates and musics." These Marines were to be considered part of the working force of the ship; they would man certain guns of her battery, wherever possible under command of their own officers; and they would assist in all-hands evolutions such as provisioning, coaling, ammunitioning, and the like. To the present day, in fact, this letter sets a pattern of duties and responsibilities for Marines on board ship.

As if to set the seal on the matter and to follow up his repeated expressions during the past two years, the Secretary embodied in his Annual Report for 1895 a rationale of his views on Marines afloat. The modern ships of the "New Navy," he pointed out, were complicated pieces of machinery, in which the crews had of necessity to be much more concerned with precise evaluations, drills, and weapons than in the days of sail. Following this generalization on the modern warship came his clinching particularization about Marines:

> It is precisely in infantry and gun drills that the Marine is, or may be, an expert. It would therefore seem that there is far more propriety in having the ship's crew composed in part of Marines now than could have been in the days of the sailing ship. The having on board of two organizations, if a proper spirit of rivalry between the two is encouraged, ought to be considered another advantage.

As far as Secretary Herbert was concerned, therefore, Marines were here to stay.

"The Marine Has No Place . . ."

Stubborn and combative as Marines themselves, the Navy opponents of the Corps were still bound to have their way. Evidence of their determination, and of the headway which their views had gained, may be found in the first 1896 issue of the *U.S. Naval Institute Proceedings*. This issue contained the Institute's annual Prize Essays; the Honorable Mention paper, submitted by Lieutenant Fullam, was entitled, "Organization, Training, and Discipline of Navy Personnel as viewed from the Ship." Under this full-rigged title, Fullam moved swiftly to his ancient quarry, the Marine Corps. His essay contains such gems as "The Marine officer has no *raison d'etre* . . ." It is followed by a printed "Discussion" which is extraordinary revealing, not only because of the intense anti-Marine feeling made manifest, but because it identifies many officers, destined for naval renown, who overtly espoused Fullam's views. Extracts from this discussion follow:

> *Captain Robley D. Evans*: That I am opposed to Marines on board ship is pretty well known. . . . The more Marines we have, the lower the intelligence of the crew.
> *Lieutenant H. S. Kapp*: As regards the Marines, every day's experience strengthens my conviction that they detract from rather than add to the discipline of ship life, and that they are room-takers and 'idlers.'
> *Lieutenant Harry P. Huse*: The Marine has no place . . .
> *Lieutenant Bradley A. Fiske*: I am strongly in favor of withdrawal of Marines from our modern ships. My reasons are exactly those stated by Lieutenant Fullam.

Lieutenant A. P. Niblack: It would seem the part of real wisdom to draw on the artillery of the Army for marine duty on board ship, if we are to have the present system.
Lieutenant C. E. Colahatt: They have no place on board ship.
Commander I. N. Heinphill: Regarding the Marines, I think they should be turned over bodily to the Army.

The foregoing statements have little significance unless we realize that those who made them (together with many others not quoted here) were largely destined to hold flag rank in subsequent years and would represent a definite hurdle for the Marine Corps to cross in the future. It must have heartened the Marine of 1896, however, to find such Navy men as Luce, Wainwright, and Ellicott supporting him and to read the spirited, closely reasoned papers submitted for the defense by Lieutenants Lauchheimer and Doyen, two young Marine officers destined to go far.

The spatter of this bitter eruption was not long in coming to earth. A new presidential administration was in office, and with it a new Assistant Secretary of the Navy; the impetuous New York gentleman-politician and naval historian, Mr. Theodore Roosevelt, a "mover and shaker." Under his chairmanship, in the all-powerful Bureau of Navigation, a Departmental board was soon convened in 1897 with the mission of studying and recommending measures for reorganization of the personnel of the Navy (Fullam's project). Before the board had been long underway, one of its members arose with the resolution, "It is desirable that Marines be not embarked as a part of the complement of sea-going ships." After heated discussion, a majority of the board disapproved, and the motion, like the sailors' petitions, died on the table.

For the time being, the status of Marines afloat was safe if shaky. The Fullam wing was still a minority, though an increasingly influential one. Their cause, originally baldly aimed at getting rid of the Marine Corps, was now much strengthened by a refinement in tactics; the Marines made available by disbandment and withdrawal of ships' detachments, urged Fullam, should be formed into shore-based battalions for employment with the Fleet. Had this proposal been wholly candid, rather than a stalking-horse to get the Marines ashore, and thence out of the Naval Establishment, it might have anticipated by a third of a century the formation of the Fleet Marine Force.

Nor should the involvement of Assistant Secretary Theodore Roosevelt be overlooked. A radical reorganizer by temperament and intellectual bias, Roosevelt had, at the outset of his naval association, fallen in with a keenly ambitious, articulate group of "radicals," so pro-Navy (as they would have described themselves) that they were apparently eager to maim the Naval Service by amputation of a trusted member.

The Marines Should Be Incorporated in the Army

On November 10, 1906 (the 131st Birthday of the Marine Corps), Rear Admiral G. A. Converse, Chief of the Bureau of Navigation, testified before the House Naval Affairs Committee that Marines should be taken off sea duty and should be grouped ashore for expeditionary service and to safeguard Navy property. Less than four months later, Fullam, now a commander, was back in the ring, breaking his (official) silence of ten years by a letter to the Secretary of the Navy, Victor H. Metcalf, in which he reiterated his own and Admiral Converse's proposals, now emphasizing the expeditionary battalions which might result. As endorsed by the Major General Commandant, Elliott, the Marine Corps views indicate a sense of weariness after more than a decade of nagging by Fullam & Co.:

> In view of the fact that this is simply a suggestion of Commander Fullam, and as it is not believed that the Department will consider such suggestion seriously, it is not deemed necessary on the part of the undersigned to enter into a lengthy argument to show that neither the Navy nor the Marine Corps will be benefited by said suggestion, but that on the contrary the efficiency of both services would be impaired. The continued desultory agitation of this subject simply tends to injure the efficiency of both the Navy and Marine Corps, and causes dissension amongst its various officers, which cannot but be injurious to the service as a whole.[2]

If General Elliott really believed that Fullam's proposal was unworthy of comment or concern, he was whistling in the dark, for he had already received intimations in early 1907 from Secretary Metcalf and from the Attorney General that trouble was brewing for the Marines.

Although Metcalf inclined toward the Corps as an essential part of the Naval Establishment, he in turn was well aware of the President's feeling, which has been summed up by an eminent Roosevelt scholar in these words:

> Roosevelt considered that the Marine Corps' major function was to act as an overseas garrison and police force. He believed that it could carry out this function more effectively as part of the Army . . . [3]

While Metcalf remained in office, however, the line held, despite a proposal advanced in 1908 by the Army Chief of Staff that the Marine Corps be absorbed into the Coast Artillery. Fullam's letter was consigned to the wastebasket, and his idea was shelved for the time being.

On October 16, 1908, Rear Admiral I. E. Pillsbury, still another Chief of the Bureau of Navigation, as a final act prior to retirement from the Navy, addressed to a new Secretary of the Navy, Truman H. Newberry, an old suggestion:

> SIR: The Bureau is of the opinion that the time has arrived when all Marine detachments should be removed from United States naval vessels, substituting bluejackets instead . . .

The Bureau of Navigation, long a center of anti-Marine feeling (and perhaps somewhat nettled by the Corps' traditional autonomy directly under the Secretary), was now in the position of urging a proposal very near to President Theodore Roosevelt's heart. He too, it seemed, wished not only to get the Marines on shore, but, moreover, to transfer the Corps, as he possessed Executive authority to do, to service under the Army.

> They have augmented to themselves. [wrote Roosevelt] . . . such importance, and their influence has given them such an abnormal position for the size of their Corps that they have simply invited their own destruction. . . . They cannot get along with the Navy.[4]

On October 23, 1908, therefore, over the vehement protest of General Elliott, the Secretary, acting on Presidential mandate, approved Admiral Pillsbury's suggestion, and directed progressive withdrawal of the Marine detachments serving afloat.

In reply to Elliott's agonized reclama, Secretary Newberry merely quoted President Roosevelt: "I know all about it – *take them off*."

On November 9, 1908, eve of a Corps birthday which many Marines feared might be its last, General Elliott made his final plea, in person, to the President. "TR" was obdurate in his reply: "I believe in their removal."

As Elliott subsequently testified before the Senate Naval Affairs Committee, this interview coincided closely with a proposal in the Washington Post (never a friend of the Marine Corps) that a force of infantry, artillery and cavalry forthwith replace the Marines stationed at Pearl Harbor Navy Yard. In Elliott's subsequent words.

> Indeed, the Marines had reached the vanishing point. There was not a duty left. About three days after the President's order, a general officer of the Army expressed a strong desire to embrace the Corps into the Army as infantry. While we had been quietly following our duties, elimination and absorption were casting, unknown to us, their shadows at our heels.[5]

"The vanishing point" seemed at hand indeed when, on November 12, 1908, President Roosevelt signed Executive Order 969. This order restated the roles and missions of the Marine Corps, omitting conspicuously the time-honored function of service at sea.

To intimates, the President added that this was the first step toward transferring the Corps to the Army. In this inner circle, which included TR's great and good friend, General Leonard Wood, Chief of Staff of the Army, Roosevelt's views were not exactly secret, but Wood, nonetheless, sought a green light before openly proceeding for all-out annexation of the Marines. On November 28, 1908, the President wrote Wood:

> Dear Leonard:
> I have your letter of the 26th: You are quite welcome to quote me publicly in the matter. I think the marines should be incorporated in the Army. It is an excellent corps and it would be of great benefit to both services that the incorporation should take place.[6]

During the winter of 1908-09, Marines were removed, by orders of Secretary Newberry, from thirteen major combatant ships, namely, the USS *California, Idaho, Montana, South Dakota, Washington, Tennessee, New Hampshire, Mississippi, Connecticut, Maine, North Carolina, Vermont,* and *Charleston.*

Congress, traditional preserver of the Marine Corps, was not so ready to swallow all this. On January 7, 1909, the House Naval Affairs Committee summoned before it Newberry, the Secretary of the Navy; Pillsbury, the offending Chief of the Bureau of Navigation; the Major General Commandant, Elliott; and a full panel of lesser advocates on both sides, including Fullam and Evans. For the next week, the fur flew. All the testimony unfolded, it became clear that Congress, in its own fashion, was conducting not merely an inquiry into a matter of ships' detachments, but into the justification for the Marine Corps; and that Congress was using the hearings as a means of driving home to the Executive Branch (just as it would on many future occasions) the legislature's conception of what the Marine Corps should be and do.

Foremost among those who testified in support of the Executive Order were: Fullam, Pillsbury, Helm, Winslow, Sims, Rodgers, Ingersoll, Evans, and Taussig. On the other hand, the Marines, outside their own ranks, could claim generous support from such naval officers as Schley, Goodrich, Brownson, and Badger. Within the Corps, the witnesses in support of General Elliott read like a Marine Corps roll of fame: Littleton Waller Tazewell Waller; Lauchheimer, father of Marine Corps marksmanship; Feland and Dunlap, already marked as leaders and thinkers; "Whispering Buck" Neville, destined to serve as Commandant; Mahoney, Doyen, Denny, and Murphy.

The Naval Appropriations Act of 1910 returned the verdict. Passed by Congress on March 3, 1909, hours before the sands of TR's administration ran out, that act included the following unequivocal proviso:

> Provided that no part of the appropriations herein made for the Marine Corps shall be expended for the purposes for which said appropriations are made unless officers and enlisted men shall serve as heretofore on board all battleships and armored cruisers and also upon such other vessels of the Navy as the President may direct, in detachments of not less than eight per centum of the strength of the enlisted men of the Navy on said vessels.

And with that Congressional thunderclap, the issue of the ships' detachments closed forevermore.

The affair of 1909 brought to a rousing finish the fifteen-year cycle of opposition to the Marine Corps within the Navy. To students of these matters, these attempts to do away with the Marine Corps brought in real innovations in technique. Item one was the device not of attacking the entity of the Corps by all-out demand for its abolition, but of urging curtailment of the roles and missions which gave it vitality and *raison d'etre*. By depriving the Marine Corps of its then primary shipboard role, its ill-wishers reasoned that they would soon see the Corps withering on the vine, just as, under similar enforced constriction of roles and missions, the Royal Marines of Britain were shortly destined to fade into desuetude. The device was subtle and destined to reappear less than half a century later.

Item two in the innovations of 1909 was the bold use of Presidential executive powers to constrict the Marine Corps. Prior to the day of Theodore Roosevelt, executive steamroller par excellence, none had questioned the prerogative of Congress to arrive at all major decisions regarding the status of the Marine Corps. From that time on, however, the possibility of unexpected executive action, without recourse to Congress, remained a threat to the Corps.

Then as later, however, Congress possessed the insight to protect its Marines, and neither the attempted surgical removal of Marine Corps missions nor the danger of conference-table knifing by executive fiat met with any more success than the frontal attacks of years gone by.

Quiet Interlude, 1909-1932

The Corps was now destined for an interlude of quiet – one of the longest in the history of the Corps, at least as far as its domestic tranquility was concerned.

Even during this period, however, two attempted incursions deserve mention, although neither could be fairly described as endangering the existence of the Marine Corps as a whole.

The first of these forays was a seemingly obscure piece of legislation (drafted and proposed by the still new War Department General Staff) which essayed to regularize inter-Service command relationships. When mixed forces of the Army and Navy (including Marines) served together ashore, read this War Department bill, the senior Army officer present was to exercise command, regardless of the relative seniority of Marine or Navy officers with the force. This bill was actually passed by the Senate in 1912, but was stopped dead in the House of Representatives as its implications became clear. Colonel John A. Lejeune, subsequently to become 13th Commandant of the Marine

Corps, had an active part in exposing the fallacy of this proposal insofar as the capability of Marine officers to command joint forces (which was at the heart of the matter) was concerned.

The second foray against the Corps marked the valedictory effort of the tenacious Fullam, now a Captain.

By 1912, the Marine Corps Advanced Base Force (precursor of the Fleet Marine Force) had become a reality. It was to be tested in the Atlantic Fleet Maneuvers of January, 1913 by an exercise involving the seizure and defense of the island of Culebra, P.R., a spot destined to hear the tread of many a Marine field-shoe in years to come.

Without the knowledge of Marines, Captain Fullam secured audience with the Secretary of the Navy's "Aide for Operations" (as CNO was then known) and demanded that he – Fullam, a Navy officer – be detailed by the Secretary to command the new Marine Advanced Base Force. Fullam's argument at that crucial conference speaks volumes for the mentality of those who had worked so unceasingly against the Corps: " . . . the Marine Corps would never successfully accomplish the very difficult task assigned to it, of its own volition, *but would have to be driven to do it*." (Italics supplied.)

Fortunately for the future of the FMF, Admiral Badger was then Commander-in-Chief of the Atlantic Fleet, and was present at Fullam's conference. Badger had been one of the few Navy witnesses to take the part of the Marines in the Naval Affairs Committee hearings of 1909. If Fullam epitomized the Navy officer in opposition to the Marine, then surely Badger spoke for the long tradition, past and future, of admirals who have resolutely defended the Corps against intrigue and vendetta. Replied Badger to Fullam, ". . . he had never known the Corps to fail in any duty which it undertook, and that it would be an uncalled for humiliation of its officers and men to accede to Captain Fullam . . . and that he would not stand for it."[7]

It was to be almost twenty years before the Marine Corps again found itself in jeopardy.

Trouble in the Thirties

In the two decades between 1909 and 1932, both the Nation and the Marine Corps had changed perceptibly. The Corps had come through World War I with a sterling combat record, and fully as important, it had gotten well launched in its systematic rationalization of the tremendous problem of amphibious warfare. Ships' detachments were no longer the principal characteristic organization of the Corps, and, in the lean years of the pacifist, anti-military 1920s, the appropriations and troop strength of the Corps, frugal though they were, attracted wishful attention from without.

At the turn of the 1930s, the President of the United States was Herbert Hoover and the Army Chief of Staff was Douglas MacArthur. Neither had particular reason to be counted among the many friends of the Marine Corps. From where General MacArthur then sat, the Marines represented competition and diversion of funds and manpower which the attenuated Army wanted badly.

The 1931 strength of the Corps was 18,000. In 1932, the Bureau of the Budget recommended appropriations for 15,343 Marines. And for 1933, President Hoover, whose controversy with Major General Smedley Butler had made headlines in 1931, recommended a further cut in Marine Corps strength to 13,600. As a yardstick for comparison, the total proposed reductions in the armed forces strength, 1931-33, were: Army, none; Navy, 5.6% reductions; and the Marines, urged the President, were to receive a 24.4% cut.

Shortly after Mr. Hoover's economy message hit Congress, it was widely rumored that the President had on his desk an executive order which would transfer the Marine Corps (as the President legally could) to service under the War Department. This order, it was said, had been drafted in the War Department for or by General MacArthur.

At the same time, the War Department set on foot a project to convert the 29th Infantry, then stationed at Fort Benning, Georgia, into a sort of expeditionary regiment which might attempt to carry out the type of expeditionary-force, readiness missions traditional to the Marine Corps.

Between the known fact of the ruthless budgetary mauling and the less known information as to the projected Executive Order, a public-opinion shock wave developed. Press and public rallied to defend the Corps. Major General Harbord, U.S. Army, (now retired and Chairman of the Board, Radio Corporation of America), went on the air over a national hook-up to defend the Corps whose 4th Brigade he had so dauntlessly led at Belleau Wood. Congress, ever quick to champion the Marine Corps, was johnny-on-the-spot in the persons of two outspoken members, Representatives Fiorello H. LaGuardia and Melvin J. Maas. Very little behind were the Naval Affairs Chairmen of the two Houses of Congress, Representative Vinson (long a Marine friend) and Senator Hale.

After a heated conference at the White House, the draft Executive Order disappeared from sight. A steady fire of statements and testimony from the Navy supported the hardpressed Marines, as elder statesmen of seapower, like Admirals Hugh Rodman and Pratt and Secretary Adams, rallied to the cause. In January, 1933, the House Naval Affairs Committee, piloted by Vinson, voted down the proposed cut, restored the 18,000 strength, and, once again, Congress had proved to be the Marines' champion. It would be fourteen years, with nothing intervening more eventful than a world war, before the Marine Corps would again fight for existence.

Merged, But Not Submerged

The conclusion of World War II, like the end of every other major war in American history, brought to the United States a mood of profound self-examination in military matters, True, we had just won victory in a Herculean contest, unequalled in the world's history, But was this enough? Couldn't we have done it better? Would not "a proper organization" have achieved miracles – and achieve them sooner and more miraculously than the undoubted miracles of 1941-45?

In such a mood as this, in the spring of 1946, the Joint Chiefs of Staff began a searching enquiry and debate into the proper future roles and missions for the U.S. Armed Forces. In the course of this great debate (whose proceedings, because of their national interest and implications, were ultimately made public by Congress), it became clear that the War Department (more particularly, its General Staff), abetted by the all-but-autonomous Army Air Forces, favored reduction of the Marine Corps to military non-entity. The missions of the Marine Corps, proposed the War Department, should in future be as follows:

1. Security forces at Navy Yards and aboard ship.
2. Maintenance of "lightly armed forces no larger than the regiment" for minor police actions.
3. The "waterborne aspects of amphibious operations" (e.g., shore party, landing craft crews, amphibious communications personnel, and such – like miscellaneous jobs).

To effectuate such roles for a Corps which had lately fielded six elite divisions and spearheaded the greatest amphibious campaign in history, the Army and Air Force Chiefs proposed:

1. That the Marine Corps be limited permanently to a ceiling of 50,000, with no expansion in wartime or on mobilization.
2. That the Corps not be permitted to conduct combined-arms operations (with the unspoken but evident corollary that the Marine Corps should not be permitted use of the combined arms). Also that any amphibious operation requiring the combining of arms be commanded by the Army.
3. That Marine Corps aviation be ceded to the Air Force.

Despite the candid and direct manner in which these recommendations were urged, they were anything but palatable to the 18th Commandant, General A. A. Vandegrift, victor of Guadalcanal. On May 6, 1946, General Vandegrift appeared before the Senate Naval Affairs Committee and presented the facts in a public statement which awakened Congress to the peril in which the Marine Corps stood. The following passage indicates the tenor of Vandegrift's forthright testimony:

> In its capacity as a balance wheel, the Congress has on five (sic) occasions since 1829 reflected the voice of the people in examining and casting aside a motion which would damage or destroy the United States Marine Corps. In each instance, on the basis of its demonstrated value and usefulness alone, Congress has perpetuated the Marine Corps as a purely American investment in continued security. Now I believe that the cycle has again repeated itself, and that the fate of the Marine Corps lies solely and entirely with the Congress.

How accurately and forcefully General Vandegrift had estimated the situation can be demonstrated by the ultimate Congressional reaction to his testimony, when, more than a year later, in passing the National Security Act of 1947, the Congress laid down in Section 206(c) what is now the charter of the modern Marine Corps:

> (c) The United States Marine Corps, within the Department of the Navy, shall include land combat and service forces and such aviation as may be organic therein. The Marine Corps shall be organized, trained, and equipped to provide fleet marine forces of combined arms, together with supporting air components, for service with the fleet in the seizure or defense of advanced naval bases and for the conduct of such land operations as may be essential to the prosecution of a naval campaign. It shall be the duty of the Marine Corps to develop, in coordination with the Army and the Air Force, those phases of amphibious operations which pertain to the tactics, technique, and equipment employed by landing forces. In addition, the Marine Corps shall provide detachments and organizations for service on armed vessels of the Navy, shall provide security detachments for the protection of naval property at naval stations and bases, and shall perform such other duties as the president may direct: Provided, that such additional duties shall not detract from or interfere with the operations for which the Marine Corps is primarily organized. The Marine Corps shall be responsible, in accordance with integrated joint mobilization plans, for the expansion of peacetime components of the Marine Corps to meet the needs of war.

Crisis in 1949

The feeling of surcease and security which descended on the Marine Corps after passage of the National Security Act of 1947 was relatively short-lived. By 1948 it was apparent that forces hostile to the Corps still enjoyed audience. The operation of these forces was made manifest by such gestures as the point-blank refusal of Secretary of Defense Louis Johnson to allow the Marine Commandant to attend Joint Chiefs of Staff meetings, even on an informal basis, when Marine Corps matters were under discussion, and by evidence that, in lieu of the proven Marine division, some personnel planners of the Pentagon favored the Marine battalion landing team as the largest organized tactical unit which the Corps should have – a direct echo of 1946's proposals.

Still more alarming was the Senate testimony in April, 1949, of Army Secretary Kenneth C. Royall that the President should, in the former's picturesque verbal counterpoint, "make the Marines part of the Army, or the Army part of the Marines." When asked by Senator Leverett Saltonstall if he were advocating that the Secretary of Defense "abolish the Marine Corps and make it part of the Army," Royall shot back, "That is exactly what I am proposing."

The Marine Corps had cause for further apprehension, as General C. B. Cates, 19th Commandant, testified before the House Armed Services Committee in 1949, when it was learned in the nick of time that unpublicized Defense Department plans were all but signed to transfer Marine Corps aviation to the Air Force. This transaction was aborted by Chairman Carl Vinson of the House Armed Forces Committee, who presented the entire question directly to the then Secretary of Defense, Mr. Louis Johnson, and secured the latter's assurance that any such policy actions would be referred to the Congressional committee involved.

And here again the Congress had thrown decisive weight toward preservation of the anomalous but effective entity in which the Corps of Marines had won its great victories.

Korea would demonstrate soon enough that the Marine Corps was still fit, ready, and worthy of preservation to fight another day.

Epilogue, 1951-52

In 1951 and 1952, the 82d Congress, its members seemingly hoped, brought the 120-year Marine Corps cycle of unrest to full stop by passage of the Douglas-Mansfield Bill, sometimes called "The Marine Corps Bill." This bill affords the Commandant place among The Joint Chiefs of Staff on Marine matters and provides the Corps with a legally stable division and air wing organization.

This notable legislation passed in final form only after lengthy hearings before the Armed Services Committees of both the Senate and the House, unanimously by the Senate and after a floor debate in the House of Representatives in which the 8-to-1 pro-Marines majority swept away the few arguments which the bitter-end opposition attempted to raise.

In the Douglas-Mansfield Bill, students of Marine Corps history could see strong similarities to the 1834 legislation with which this article opened. As in 1834, Congress had acted once again to clear up misunderstanding as to the status and organization of the Corps and to guarantee it an effective strength. The Congressional method of approaching the question was definitely reminiscent of 1909, and much of the quality and reasoning of the opposition was similar – strikingly so. Students of Marine Corps history could say truthfully that not since 1909 had the Corps been the subject of so-single-minded, detailed Congressional examination – an examination which, like that in 1909, found the Corps no whit wanting.

Thus it may be, if history is any guide, that, just as after the 1834 and 1909 Congressional debates, the Marine Corps may look forward to a long period of tranquility, at least as far as its domestic opponents are concerned.

After 1834, it was thirty years before trouble brewed again; after 1909, it was more than twenty. Today's Marines hope that history may, at least on this score, repeat itself.

Down through the twelve decades from 1829 to 1949, a historical pattern stands clear. Most striking in that pattern is the fact that the proposals to eliminate or hamstring the Marine Corps originated, very nearly fifty-fifty, from both sides of the State, War, and Navy Building.

Six of these jihads (1829, 1864, 1867, 1932, 1946, and 1949) took form, in greater or less degree, as attempts to amalgamate the Marine Corps with the Army (or latterly, the Air Force). Four, however (1894, 1895, 1896-97, and 1907-09), had their origin within the Navy. Thus it is a fair conclusion that the Marine Corps, in its day, has withstood storms from every quarter. Conversely, no one (except Congress) has been the Marines' consistent protector.

A second rather striking observation is that, regardless of origin, every proposal to modify or abolish the Marine Corps has been justified at some point by its proponents as a move to eliminate duplications of one kind or another within the armed forces. In 1829, 1864, 1867, 1932, 1946, and 1949, the Corps was stated to be in duplication of the Army. In 1894, 1895, 1897 and 1909, it was maintained that Marine detachments aboard ship needlessly duplicated the functions of seamen. Curiously enough, however, it appeared that, whatever these duplicating functions were, they had to be performed by someone. For example, in 1908, when Secretary Newberry finally acceded to removing the Marines from on board ship, he was forced to direct a *gradual* withdrawal – for the simple reason that the departing Marines would have to train equivalent bodies of sailors to perform distinctive duties hitherto assigned to Marines. Conversely, as early as 1829, Andrew Jackson's proposal stipulated that "details for the Marine service" would, upon abolition of the Corps, be made from the Army. Ninety-eight years later, in 1932, a necessary preliminary to disbandment of the Marine Corps was the projected conversion of the 29th Infantry into a sort of miniature Fleet Marine Force.

In other words, it may well be observed that all these proposals, each directed toward getting rid of a supposed (or claimed) duplication, have been aimed, not as might appear, at the functions of the Corps, but rather at the existence of the Corps as a separate entity. Superficial similarities between the Marine Corps and the Navy (in some respects), or between the Marine Corps and the Army (in other respects), or between the Marine Corps and the Air Force (in still other respects), have thus repeatedly bemused outsiders into accepting as real, rather than apparent, "duplications" which functionally do not exist.

What perpetually laid the Marine Corps open to attack, at least prior to the 1920s, was its anomalous character, not a body of seamen, and yet by no means conventional shoregoing soldiers. In theology this indefinable status would be called a "mystery," and, in the case of the Marine Corps, it was disastrously easy to oversimplify.

Commencing in the twentieth century, the Marine Corps mounted a fulldress attack upon the reputedly insoluble problems of amphibious warfare, particularly that of the opposed landing. History records how well the Corps succeeded, and how, prior to 1941, it had not only evolved the doctrines for, but had actually organized the only amphibious striking force of, the United States. This development demolished the factual groundwork of any claimed duplications of function leveled against the Marine Corps, which had, in effect, invented and then executed in the best style a new military function of crucial importance. And this unique role of the Corps has now been recognized in law.

With all said and done, why – we may still ask – have the American people (through Congress) sided unanimously with the Marines?

There are a multitude of well-reasoned, logical answers, and it is on these that Congress has so often reached conclusions in favor of the Corps. But it is not enough to say that Marines have pioneered where military orthodoxy has lagged; that the readiness of the Marine Corps is a national insurance policy; that dollar for dollar, man for man, the Marine Corps represents economy and efficiency unsurpassed.

Perhaps, on the whole, it is not too much to conclude that the Corps is just a little more than a mere "component" in our Armed Forces. The U.S. Marines have become, a unique, vital, and colorful part of the American scene. Perhaps, indeed, the Corps has matured into a national institution.

NOTES

[1] As to the admitted identity of the ringleaders, the following quotation from hearings before the Senate Naval Affairs Committee on 9 January 1909, is illuminating:
Gen. ELLIOTT: Were you not aboard the Chicago when the crew of that ship circulated petitions to come to Congress to have the Marines withdrawn from ships?
Cdr. FULLAM: Yes, sir.
Gen. ELLIOTT: And did not the Secretary of the Navy, Mr. Herbert, get out a general order that really referred to you?
Cdr. FULLAM: I do not know whether it referred to me or not; but I will say that if it did, I am willing to take the responsibility.

[2] Endorsement by MGC to SecNav on Fullam letter, February 26, 1907.

[3] Letter from Alfred D. Chandler, Jr., Assistant Editor, *The Letters of Theodore Roosevelt*, December 5, 1951.

[4] Letter quoted in "The Marines' First Spy," by John L. Zimmerman, *Saturday Evening Post*, November 23, 1946.

[5] "Hearings Before the Committee on Naval Affairs, House of Representatives, on 'The Status of the U.S. Marine Corps'," Government Printing Office, 1909, pp. 216-220.

[6] Letter made available through the kindness of Mr. A. D. Chandler, Jr., Theodore Roosevelt Research Project, Massachusetts Institute of Technology.

[7] *The Reminiscences of a Marine*, by Maj. Gen. John A. Lejeune, Philadelphia, 1930, p. 202.

WITH FIDELITY AND EFFECTIVENESS: ARCHIBALD HENDERSON'S LASTING LEGACY TO THE U.S. MARINE CORPS

Joseph G. Dawson

Review of the Marines' early history requires assessing the substantial impact of this legendary figure who served from 1806-1859. During the Age of Sail period, the Marine Corps' structure – divided into numerous ships detachments and Navy yards – was in dire need of centralized organization. Through both personal ambition and devotion to duty, Archibald Henderson provided the necessary leadership to establish a fundamental identity to this small service. Traditionally, Archibald Henderson has been endeared as the "Grand Old Man" of the Marine Corps. Professor Dawson explains why that title is justly deserved.

Archibald Henderson wore the uniform of the United States Marines for nearly fifty-three years, and for almost thirty-nine years he served as Commandant of the Corps. He guided the marines through shoals of criticism and set a personal example for leadership. Supervising new officers' initial training that began their transition from civilian to military life, Henderson made himself the exemplar of duty for nineteenth-century marines. Henderson's personal supervision partially compensated for the lack of formal training courses during the early decades of the Corps. From the 1820s through the 1850s he advocated increasing the number of enlisted marines and officers in order better to fulfill the variety of tasks assigned to the Corps by the Navy Department.

This essay highlights significant aspects of Henderson's career, emphasizing that he not only preserved and built up the Corps but also moved it beyond such traditional duties as manning fighting tops and guarding naval yards. Alertly taking advantage of opportunities presented by crises, Henderson organized select marine battalions to serve in field campaigns with the U.S. Army and led one of them himself. These battalions marked a significant departure in the way marines had been employed. This essay also contends that during the course of his service, especially during his last years as Commandant, Henderson proposed other reforms that would add to the basic capabilities of the Marine Corps. Most importantly, by advocating that the marines should acquire their own artillery units, in order to strengthen forces landing on hostile shores, Henderson foreshadowed things to come in the future of amphibious warfare. Henderson's actions and accomplishments confirm that he was an exemplary American military leader deserving wider recognition for his success in shaping as well as preserving the Marine Corps.

Naturally, historians of the Marine Corps have devoted attention to this officer who held the position of Commandant for so many years. These historians unanimously credit Henderson with being an excellent officer whose importance to the Corps was unmatched by any other marine of his day. In evaluating Henderson's career, however, some of the writers either neglect or only hint at how Henderson's personal leadership, in the battalion deployed during the Indian Wars, for instance, linked with his detailed management of the Corps to set the stage for his reforms. Most have not examined in detail the Commandant's personal role in suppressing civil disturbance in Washington, D.C., in 1857, and none recognized that, among Henderson's several reform proposals, he won approval for his most innovative concept: adding artillery units to marine landing forces.

The best overviews of Henderson's life are chapters in general histories of the Marine Corps, and in each case they shift from Henderson's point of view in order to present a survey of the service. In his comprehensive work *Semper Fidelis*, Allan R. Millett entitles his substantial chapter "Archibald Henderson Preserves the Corps, 1815-1859." Describing the growth of the Marine Corps from the 1820s through the 1850s, Millett covers Henderson's many duties, challenges, and accomplishments, stressing that the Commandant's signal contribution was to prevent the Corps from being incorporated into the U.S. Army. No other treatment of Henderson matches Millett's depth of research or breadth of coverage. In another substantive history of the marines, *Soldiers of the Sea*, Robert Heinl reached similar conclusions about the importance of Henderson's commandancy to the Marine Corps, maintaining that "The debt which the Marine Corps owes its fifth Commandant [Henderson] is incalculable." Heinl ranked among Henderson's achievements improving the "status," building the "strength," and increasing the "efficiency" of the Corps. J. Robert Moskin's well-written narrative in *The Marine Corps Story* jumps from topic to topic and adds little to the accounts of Millett and Heinl. Other one-volume histories offer briefer treatments of Henderson's commandancy than Millett's and Heinl's, and sometimes lack analysis and documentary support. Among several journal articles and essays, only a few stand out as exceptional. Studies by Ralph W. Donnelly, recognized as an expert on the early Marine Corps, summarize Henderson's command abilities and administrative success.(1)

Born near the village of Dumfries, Virginia, in 1783, Archibald Henderson was the son of Alexander Henderson, an upper middle-class businessman who had emigrated to America from Scotland in 1756. Well connected politically, Alexander Henderson served in the Virginia House of Burgesses and was a justice of the peace. Young Archibald gained his education at local schools as well as from tutors hired by his father. After trying his hand as an employee in his father's iron works, Archibald accepted a commission as a marine second lieutenant in 1806.(2)

In 1806 Marine Corps registers showed a paid strength of only eleven officers and 307 noncommissioned officers and enlisted men. Henderson's Corps was naturally patterned after the British Royal Marines. Its main duties at sea focused on guarding against mutinies in U.S. Navy ships. In combat, marines fired their muskets at enemy ships' officers and crew during battle, formed contingents to board enemy ships or attack enemy shore installations, and repelled enemy boarders. On shore, marines guarded U.S. Navy yards in several American cities.(3)

During his first years in uniform, Henderson served mostly in routine assignments typical for new lieutenants. He was promoted to first lieutenant on 6 March 1807, in keeping with the Marine Corps system of promotions coming when vacancies occurred. Henderson's postings included command of the marine detachment in the sloop *Wasp* in 1807, service at the Brooklyn Navy Yard in 1808, command of the detachment at Charleston, South Carolina, from 1809 to 1811, leading the marines in the frigate *President* from 1811 to 1812, and duty at the Charlestown (Boston) Navy Yard, 1812-13. His only extraordinary assignment was holding the temporary position of acting adjutant of the Corps in Washington, D.C., for three months in 1809. Until war erupted with Great Britain in 1812, Henderson contemplated seeking a commission in the U.S. Army or resigning from military life altogether because he was dissatisfied with the slow rate of promotions in the Corps, though he attained the rank of captain on 1 April 1811.(4)

His next posting at sea helped to make his reputation as a marine officer. In June 1814 he took command of the marine detachment in the frigate *Constitution* (forty-four guns) under Captain Charles Stewart, USN. Avoiding blockading British ships, *Constitution* slipped out of Boston in December 1814. A few weeks later Captain Stewart spoke to a merchantman, who revealed the news of the Treaty of Ghent, intended to end the war. Although the treaty had been negotiated, Stewart knew that several more days might pass before both sides approved it; Congress ratified it on 17 February 1815. Meanwhile, on February 20, not having learned of the treaty's approval, *Constitution* chanced upon two English warships, the frigate *Cyane* (thirty-two guns) and the sloop *Levant* (twenty guns). Using remarkable ship-handling, Stewart overhauled and engaged the British ships, inflicting great damage and forcing both to strike their colors. Henderson commanded his marines during the battle, maintaining what Stewart called a "lively and well directed fire." After the war, Congress awarded Henderson its thanks and a medal for his role in the action. In April 1816 Secretary of the Navy Benjamin Crowninshield notified him of his promotion to brevet major, to date from August 1814.(5)

No doubt appreciative of the brevet, Henderson still seemed unsure of his place in the Corps. In August 1815, for example, one of his sisters recalled that he again considered resigning his commission. The next spring one of his brothers complained that Henderson called for help in paying a $2,000 debt and thought of leaving the military to go into private business. Once more, Henderson reevaluated his situation and remained in the service.(6)

In 1817, every marine officer took sides during a remarkable courtmartial. Commanding the detachment at Portsmouth, New Hampshire, Brevet Major Henderson brought charges against Lieutenant Colonel Franklin Wharton, Commandant of the Corps.

Henderson acted out of concern for the reputation of the Marine Corps, but he may also have had a personal motive – the chance to maneuver into Wharton's job. The specifications grew out of Wharton's conduct during the British attack on the District of Columbia in 1814. Evidently, Wharton had fled the city as the British approached, and most marine officers were disgusted by the Commandant's behavior. Speaking for many of his fellow officers, Henderson asserted that Wharton had failed "to take any effectual measures to put a stop to reports so highly injurious to his own character, and of great disadvantage to the Corps under his command." The court had to decide if Wharton was guilty of neglect of duty and conduct unbecoming an officer. It rendered its remarkable verdict of not guilty on all counts on 22 September 1817. The Wharton imbroglio indicated how egotism and professional rivalry could flare into the open in a small military organization. Wharton died a year after the court-martial and Secretary Crowninshield summoned Henderson to Washington.(7)

Crowninshield appointed Henderson acting Commandant on 16 September 1818. During five months in that role, Henderson took care of routine duties and anticipated that, according to seniority, Major Anthony Gale would be made Commandant. Having his personal interests and those of the Corps in mind, Henderson undercut Gale, who was known to be a heavy drinker. Henderson informed the Secretary of the Navy that marine officers had "frequently seen Major Gale intoxicated at New Orleans and that his associates were of such a description and his habits of such a nature as to prevent the respectable officers on that station from having any social or friendly intercourse with him." Hoping to spare the Corps the embarrassment of having such a man as its leader, Henderson plunged into political waters. In a letter to Acting Secretary of the Navy John C. Calhoun, Henderson asserted that Gale was incompetent and put his own name forward as the right choice for Commandant. Calhoun endorsed Henderson. When Smith Thompson became the new naval secretary, Henderson supplied him with several documents relating to Gale's public intoxication and indicated that Captain Francis B. DeBellvue, an officer who had served in New Orleans, held a low opinion of the "moral and military character of Major Gale."(8)

New to his job, Smith Thompson decided to call a court of inquiry in Washington to examine Henderson's allegations. Taking testimony from several officers, the court found in favor of Gale, who became Commandant on 3 March 1819. Thompson soon regretted not heeding Henderson's advice. Gale was arrested in August 1820 and faced charges of public intoxication and conduct unbecoming an officer and a gentleman, specifically, that he had visited a known house of prostitution. Gale was court-martialed, found guilty, and cashiered on 18 October 1820. His ignominious behavior and disgraceful departure from office cast a pall over the marines and brought them into disrepute.(9)

To refurbish the image and reputation of the Corps, Secretary Thompson announced that Henderson would become Commandant. Notified of his promotion to the rank of lieutenant colonel as of 17 October 1820, Henderson officially assumed his new duties in Washington on 2 January 1821. According to procedure, Henderson replaced Gale on the basis of seniority, but no better choice could have been made, as far as personality, experience, and dedication to the Corps were concerned. Not only did Henderson possess the experience to serve as Commandant, he was the beau ideal of a nineteenth-century military officer. Receding hair gave his head a high-domed intellectual appearance. He carefully combed bushy side-whiskers above the high collar of his uniform. A prominent nose divided penetrating eyes. Prim lips added a touch of grace to his face. His overall appearance gave the impression of a refined, determined gentleman and capable officer. As for Henderson's willingness for the job, Secretary Thompson already knew that the colonel was alert to innovative deployment of marines, over and above their standard tasks in ships and at naval yards. In April 1820 while in New Orleans, Henderson advised Thompson that he had "volunteered my services [to Major General Andrew Jackson] should there be a forcible occupation of the Floridas." Under Jackson, U.S. Army soldiers had crossed into Spanish Florida at Pensacola in 1818 and created an international incident by hanging two English citizens suspected of selling weapons to Indians in the southeast. Prompted by Jackson's belligerent move, U.S. diplomats set out to acquire Florida, and closed the deal through the Adams-Onis Treaty, ratified by Congress in 1821.(10)

In the months to come, Henderson took steps to operate his entire command efficiently, reaffirm the marines' duties, and restore the reputation of the Corps. During his years as Commandant, Henderson acquired a personal knowledge of each marine officer – there were only thirty-five of them in 1821 and would never be more than seventy-five in any one year during Henderson's service. Each new lieutenant usually opened his career with about six weeks of training at Headquarters, which might be considered, unofficially, as an officer's basic course of instruction. Henderson told the secretary of the navy that "nothing is so well calculated to give character to a Corps, as a uniformity of system, and the initiation of your officers into the duties of their profession . . . under the immediate notice and auspices of its Commanding Officer." Therefore, Henderson concluded that "a young officer should never be permitted to leave Head Quarters before he is perfectly competent to [conduct] the drill of a Battalion – so that should he succeed by accident, or other causes, to command, he might be able to do justice to his situation." Henderson never wavered from that view during the next thirty-five years. The Commandant's training regimen set the examples not only for Corps officer training during the rest of the nineteenth century but also for the modern Basic School at Quantico, indicating the longevity of Henderson's influence. Moreover, he gave scrupulous daily attention to everything involved in running a military organization totaling around fifteen hundred personnel, including recruiting, assignments, furloughs, promotions, courts-martial, discharges, rations, uniform design, weapons selection, and construction of quarters. No detail missed Henderson's sharp eye. Intending to forestall criticism of marine fiscal operations from any source, he insisted that every penny should be accounted for and that no weapon or piece of equipment should be declared surplus if someone in the Corps could use it. Frugality and a Spartan attitude pervaded the Marine Corps from that time forward.(11)

In addition to casting the hallmarks of efficiency, strengthening practical training, and rebuilding the marines' reputation, Henderson also forged his personal authority and the design of Headquarters' staff. He ordered marine officers in charge of ships' detachments and barracks to report to him, not to the Secretary of the Navy, as had been the case before. Furthermore, he reassigned the officers serving at Headquarters as paymaster, quartermaster, and adjutant, replacing them with his own choices. While these jobs had rotated previously on an ad hoc basis, the new Commandant took the step of appointing three new staff members at once, thus indicating that their appointments were his prerogative and putting his imprint on the Headquarters composition. The Corps continued to use Henderson's staff system of depending upon these three officers and their departments through the Great War of 1914-18.(12)

During the 1820s, Henderson vigilantly blocked threats that would have undermined the Corps and responded with a counteroffensive calling for more marines. Threatening moves from politicians included proposals to replace marines with landsmen aboard ships and substituting civilian guards for marines at navy yards. Time and again, Henderson argued to secretaries of the navy and leading members of Congress that any reduction in the marines would be "injurious to the [naval] Service." For instance, substituting landsmen would be inefficient because marines, who received training as soldiers, formed the nucleus of naval landing parties. Marines often began their enlistments as guards at navy yards, where they took training in infantry drill and musketry before being assigned to ships. Rather than accede to any reduction in the Corps, Henderson consistently advocated increasing the numbers of enlisted men, noncommissioned officers, and officers, relying on the appropriate analogy of the British Royal Marines: if Great Britain's excellent Royal Navy continued to require marines, in proportion to the number of ships in service, then the U.S. Navy must have marines too.(13)

Calling for more marines was one of Henderson's most consistent themes as Commandant, but he sought other ways to improve the Corps. For example, in November 1823 he made his first pitch to the Secretary of the Navy to add artillery training and an integral artillery capability to the corps, thus increasing the strength of its landing forces. This is a subject Henderson would return to more emphatically later in his career. On another matter, Henderson knew from personal experience that marine officers often endured lengthy separations from shore and family due to extended cruises. Some officers became discouraged or lackadaisical, or concluded that they would try other pursuits. It disturbed Henderson to note that about half of the lieutenants entering the service since 1815 had been asked to resign because they were deficient in skills and leadership. These facts led him to advocate that vacancies or new appointments of officers should be made either from graduates of the U.S. Military Academy at West Point or from its former cadets, some of whom would leave without graduating with their class. The Secretary declined to approve Henderson's proposals in 1823, but that did not discourage him from reiterating such recommendations from time to time in letters or annual reports over the next four decades.(14)

Disappointed that reluctant secretaries of the navy and a penny-pinching Congress would not authorize an increase in the size of the Marine Corps, Henderson devised his own subterfuge – a sort of shell game – to tailor the marines' strength as he wanted. In annual reports, or in answer to inquiries from the secretary or other politicians, Henderson noted that the adjutant carried supernumerary sergeants or corporals above the authorized limit, but other categories, especially privates, were under enlisted. At any one time, the total rank and file of the corps might be slightly above authorized levels by twenty or thirty or forty men, and by this means Henderson often had the Corps technically over its legal limit. His reliance on this minor deception, particularly in assignments to ships' detachments, demonstrated that the Corps did need more men, especially noncommissioned officers for shipboard duty. At the same time as he admitted that the levels were slightly more than authorized, Henderson explained that two or three navy ships carrying marine detachments were scheduled to return to port, and several enlisted men were due to be mustered out. Henderson asserted that if a small number of extra men had not been enlisted in anticipation of the mustering out of an equal number of others, then the Corps would fall under strength, a circumstance he never wanted. Moreover, the Commandant contended that he was careful never to spend more than his appropriated budget and therefore his tinkering with the numbers of marines never meant spending beyond his legal limits.(15)

Secretary of the Navy Samuel Southard asked Henderson to consider another procedural matter. Recruiters routinely enlisted men who were in satisfactory health regardless of age or nationality. Southard directed Henderson to enlist only "native American citizens" who were at least twenty-one years of age, in order to meet legal requirements. Those underage needed parental consent to become a leatherneck, but most officers accepted the word of recruits that they were twenty-one. The Secretary made some limited concessions: noncitizens could be signed up for the Marine Band, and its members and other "musics," as drummers and fifers were called, could be under twenty-one. Henderson issued these guidelines to his recruiting officers, located in major eastern cities, such as New York, Boston, Philadelphia, and Baltimore. Accepting underage recruits who were not citizens continued to be facts of life for the Corps, however. Years later, the Commandant admitted to Lieutenant Frederick McNeill that the marines gladly accepted German immigrants because they usually made good soldiers and "they very soon learn our language." Henderson also had to acknowledge to Captain John Reynolds that "the order to enlist none but natives had never been fully carried out," and that recruiters were only guided by the preference for citizen recruits. Thus, the issues of citizenship and age of enlistees were ones never completely resolved while Henderson was Commandant.(16)

Meanwhile, Henderson turned his attention to the weapons his marines carried. Officers had traditionally carried a sword of the Mameluke pattern, worn by marines since 1805. Opting for uniformity, in 1826 the Commandant made it official and ordered that the Mameluke sword be the standard; it has been worn by marine officers ever since Henderson authorized it, with only a brief interruption during the Civil War era. Next, the

Commandant authorized the testing of a new shoulder weapon, the Hall's rifle, Model 1819, which passed its trials in 1827. Henderson recommended the innovative breech-loading rifle to the Secretary of the Navy in September, and the weapons began arriving at marine units the next year. A .52 caliber flintlock, the Hall's rifle weighed ten pounds, carried a sixteen-inch bayonet, and was accurate to 250 yards. The breech mechanism was durable and reliable, but it did allow some seepage of gas from the chamber. Despite that deficiency, as a breech-loader the Hall was much easier to load than the muzzle-loading muskets issued to most U.S. Army units at the time, and its range was more than four times that of the standard smoothbore musket. Henderson's choice of the Hall's rifle over smoothbore muskets and adoption of the sword in the Mameluke pattern were examples of his involvement in the operation of the Corps.(17)

Henderson delighted in the details of administering the marines, but at the end of the 1820s he faced one of his most critical challenges – a formidable threat to Corps' very existence. In his annual message to Congress on 8 December 1829, President Andrew Jackson denigrated the duties of marines, noting that, since in his opinion "no peculiar training [was] required" for marines, their "service could well be made from the [U.S. Army] artillery or infantry." Accordingly, Jackson recommended "that the Marine Corps be merged in the [army's] artillery or infantry, as the best mode of curing the many defects of its organization." Jackson considered that several public professional disagreements between naval officers and marines marked one defect in how the organization operated. Moreover, the President also asserted that the Marine Corps had, "besides its Lieutenant-Colonel Commandant [Henderson], five brevet lieutenant-colonels, who receive[d] the full pay and emoluments [including expensive extra rations] of their brevet rank." By raising this issue, Jackson used a political ploy. Officers with brevets usually were not paid at their honorary rank, but Jackson's contention made it appear that the marines, whose total strength equaled about one army regiment, carried a top-heavy echelon of ranking officers, many more than would be found in a typical army unit of similar size. Therefore, Jackson struck personally at Henderson's claim to operate the most financially efficient branch of the military. Eventually, in a case before the U.S. Supreme Court, the justices ruled that officers were not to be paid at their brevet rank, but in the meantime, those interested turned their focus to the heart of the matter: would the Marine Corps survive as a special service within the U.S. Navy?(18)

Jackson's merger proposal prompted committee hearings in both houses of Congress and drew comments pro and con from numerous naval officers. Leading the anti-marine contingent were Isaac Hull and Alexander S. Mackenzie. Captain Mackenzie judged that marines on ships were a source of "perpetual discord." Mutiny had ceased to be a serious threat in the U.S. Navy, and, therefore, in Captain Hull's opinion, marines were not "necessary to the armed equipment of a vessel of war." In contrast, several other navy captains supported keeping marines in ships' companies. Supporters included distinguished officers such as John Rodgers, William Bainbridge, Thomas Catesby Jones, and Henderson's old captain of the *Constitution*, Charles Stewart. With their help, Henderson and the marines weathered Jackson's storm of criticism, but similar calls for merging the corps with the army or disbanding the marines were staples in American politics for over a century.(19)

Henderson successfully turned aside attacks against the Marine Corps. Sending persuasive letters to each secretary of the navy, he emphasized the fact that marines were versatile and performed their duties "with fidelity and effectiveness." Not only did they sail in navy ships around the world and guard navy yards in America, they could be called out to suppress a slave revolt in Virginia or turn back a riotous mob in Boston.(20)

Having defended the existence of the Marine Corps, Henderson made his constant drumbeat for increasing its size pay off handsomely in the summer of 1834. On 30 June Congress passed "An Act for the Better Organization of the Marine Corps" and President Jackson signed it. This act was significant in several ways. It confirmed, against the wishes of its critics, that the Corps would remain part of the navy. The marines would be administered by the Navy Department and the position of Commandant would be continued. Henderson was promoted to the rank of full colonel, the first marine to hold that distinction. The Corps would be increased by 360 officers and men, approximately a 40 percent addition in manpower, and would reach a total of over 1,400 when the new personnel were sworn into service. In order to make the marines more attractive to recruits, the minimum enlistment was reduced from five years to four. To clarify a point of contention within the navy, marine officers could not command any ship or naval installation; such responsibility always would devolve on the senior navy officer present. Marine officers would be in charge of their detachments in ships or on shore, but would be subject to the orders of the ship's captain and the naval officer in command of the shore installation. Settling a long-standing issue, marine officers were to be paid the same salary as officers of the same rank in the army. Going beyond procedural matters, and opening up significant new vistas for the marines, the 1834 law authorized the President to designate a portion of the Marine Corps to serve ashore with army expeditions; otherwise, the Corps would be governed by navy regulations. Henderson concluded that this law "finally settled that the Marine Corps is to continue [as] the Military Arm of the Navy."(21)

In 1836 Henderson welcomed the opportunity to lead marines with a U.S. Army expedition against the Creek and Seminole Indians in the southeast. Although inherently risky, creating a special marine battalion to campaign against the Indians provided an opportunity to gain recognition for the Corps and perhaps overcome some of the criticism that President Jackson had leveled at the marines in 1829. Henderson's prompt response to form a contingent of marines for field duty was one of his most important acts as Commandant and was a major step in taking the Corps in a new direction.(22)

Anticipating specific orders, Henderson had directed the Marine Corps adjutant, Captain Parke G. Howle, to tell several officers to assemble at Charleston, South Carolina. To collect the largest possible battalion, Henderson directed senior officers to leave behind no more than a sergeant's guard (about a dozen men) "who are unable to perform field duty." Furthermore, about 20 to 30 percent of some ships' detachments were sent to Charleston. Eventually, 38 officers and 424 noncommissioned officers and privates, about half of the Corps' strength at the time, took to the field under Henderson's leadership. Choosing Lieutenant Colonel R. D. Wainwright to handle administrative duties at headquarters temporarily, Henderson left Washington in the transport Columbia on 2 June 1836.(23)

The trip from Charleston to Augusta, Georgia, the interior assembly point for the marine battalion, took fourteen days. A railroad aided the movement, which was completed by overland march. No one could anticipate how long the war would last. Shortly after arriving at Augusta, Henderson wrote Secretary Dickerson that "it is . . . universally believed the campaign will be short. In which case the necessity of the Corps being detained from its legitimate duties will soon cease." Nearly a month later, the marines had traversed Georgia, marching 224 miles, and set up "Camp Henderson" 15 miles south of Columbus, Georgia, on the Alabama side of the Chattahoochee River. There the fifty-three-year old Commandant began nearly eleven months of service in the field, setting the example for his officers to be with their men. In addition to having them construct storage buildings at the camp, Henderson sent out combat patrols "to show that we are prepared for fighting as well as for working." One patrol located an abandoned Creek campsite. Henderson again raised the hope that the campaign would end soon, but the summer stretched into fall and in October the marine battalion was transferred to Florida to join army units conducting operations against the Seminoles.(24)

The marine contingent came under the command of Brigadier General Thomas Jesup, U.S. Army, at Fort Brooke, near Tampa. Florida. Jesup divided his forces into two brigades, giving Henderson the 2d Brigade and army Brevet Brigadier General Walker K. Armisted the 1st. Each brigade had a nucleus of regulars. Henderson contained his marines and the army's 4th Infantry Regiment; Armisted's had the 6th Infantry Regiment. U.S. Army artillery companies (without cannon) plus units of southern volunteers and Indian auxiliaries supplemented each brigade. The marines, deploying 321 officers and men in Florida as of 18 November, comprised about 19 percent of Jesup's 1,680-man "Army of the South." Its mission was to establish supply depots and conduct sweeps through the scrub pine and swamps searching for Seminole bands. In a classic statement pertaining to guerrilla warfare, Jesup reported to the army adjutant general in Washington that "the difficulty is not to fight the enemy, but to find him."(25)

During one such search operation, on 27 January 1837, Henderson's brigade made contact with some Seminoles near Lake Tohopekaliga and pursued them toward the Hatcheelustee Creek. Retreating into the swamp, the Indians abandoned horses, mules, supplies, and several noncombatants. Henderson's units struck out into the swamp, catching glimpses of the Seminoles and exchanging shots with them. At around 12:30 p.m. the federal forces came upon an Indian rear guard at Hatcheelustee Creek. Leading the way, several officers scrambled into the water. Colonel Henderson balanced himself on a tree trunk that nearly stretched across the creek. Musket shots from the Seminoles killed one marine and wounded two others as they attempted to reach the far bank. Henderson ordered more soldiers to cross the stream. Their pursuit continued through a pine-studded field and into a cypress swamp. Two other soldiers went down with bullet wounds. Henderson decided to end the pursuit around 4:00 p.m. Gathering up prisoners, abandoned supplies, and captured horses, the 2d Brigade marched back to Jesup's camp, arriving about 10:00 p.m. The brigade had killed three Seminoles during the day but had suffered two dead and three wounded. General Jesup commended the brigade's action of 27 January, one of the sharpest engagements while he commanded U.S. forces against the Seminoles, and endorsed the conduct of several officers, including that of the "gallant colonel [Henderson] himself." Such engagements, however, could not defeat the Seminoles. The Florida war dragged on for several more years, leaving an indefinite number of Indians roaming the swamps and the U.S. military dissatisfied with its campaigns.(26)

By mid-April 1837 Henderson determined that he and his marine battalion had made a worthwhile contribution to fighting the guerrilla war but, as he revealed to his journal, he was "anxious to leave Florida & our connection with the Army." Henderson and Jesup had favorably impressed each other; the Commandant told his wife that the army general "has been a zealous and able officer." As he made plans to depart, Henderson told Secretary of the Navy Dickerson he expected that the Marine Corps had "added to its military reputation on this [Alabama and Florida] Service." Henderson and about two hundred marines boarded a steamboat in late May, leaving Lieutenant Colonel Samuel Miller in charge of two companies of leathernecks at Fort Brooke, near Tampa. Some of them remained in Florida until 1842.(27)

The Seminole War produced mostly positive results for the marines. Playing upon the generally favorable publicity given to the marine battalion, Henderson praised his "Soldiers" in a flowery proclamation, declaring that the service in the South was a "tour of duty equally honorable to yourselves and the Corps to which you belong." Henderson proudly contended that the marines had "elevated their Ancient Corps in the estimation of the Country." For Henderson, commendable field service resulted in a promotion to the rank of brevet brigadier general; he was the first marine to hold that rank. Furthermore, the Commandant's leadership and cooperation with General Jesup had proven the practicality of deploying a large portion of marine infantry for service with the army, supporting the conclusion that marines could be called upon in the future for similar duty. On the other hand, the experiment seemed to give credence to President Jackson's proposed merger of the marines into the army because the marines appeared to be similar to the army's soldiers.(28)

While he appealed for the return of all marines still on campaign in Florida, Henderson tried to use their service there to obtain another significant increase in the size of the Corps. He based his requests to the secretaries of the navy and members of Congress on the logical argument that as the U.S. Navy grew, so too should the Marine Corps. Accordingly, looking at the total navy personnel, which increased from around 4,900 in

1830 to about 8,000 in 1840, Henderson recommended that the strength of the marines be nearly doubled by adding 1,000 privates, around 50 noncommissioned officers and a handful of lieutenants. In the Commandant's view, such an expansion was necessary to provide the number of marines assigned to each ship, as specified in Navy Department guidelines. Thus, Henderson tried to show the politicians that the marines were shorthanded based on the Navy Department's own regulations.(29)

There had been no official approval for an increase in the numbers of marines since 1834, but Henderson recognized that the escalating tensions between the United States and Mexico raised the prospect of war, and he restated his plea for a larger Corps. In a stream of correspondence to Secretary of the Navy George Bancroft, the Commandant cogently argued that "the extension of our national domain [annexing Texas], and the interesting situation of our affairs in the Gulf of Mexico and on the shores of the Pacific" should lead to the enlistment of more marines.

Specifically, Henderson recommended forty sergeants, fifty corporals, thirty musicians, five hundred privates and twelve lieutenants, adding that actually one thousand privates would be the best figure and allow for replacing all civilians temporarily employed as watchmen at U.S. Navy yards. Henderson pointed out that "the annexation of so important a Country as Texas gives additional interest" to the naval depot at Pensacola, Florida, the closest active naval base to the incoming state. After describing in detail how the marine battalion had been assembled for duty in the southeastern Indian wars in 1836, Henderson concluded that "exigencies of a like or kindred character may again occur [calling for] . . . the assembling of the Corps as a Regiment or Regiments" for campaigns against Indians or on the frontier. He had planted the seed with Bancroft that another marine battalion could serve in a major land campaign with the army.(30)

After months of antagonistic relations between the United States and Mexico, the U.S. Congress declared war on Mexico on 13 May 1846. In the first weeks of the conflict, most of Henderson's time was taken up by routine matters – discharges, transfers, assignments for ships' detachments, officers' furloughs, and courts-martial. It must have warmed his heart when Secretary of the Navy Bancroft sent him an official inquiry asking if the number of marines should be increased. Seizing the opportunity Bancroft offered, Henderson urged boosting the Corps' by 1,500 more privates, 160 noncommissioned officers, 80 musicians, and 21 officers. Showing cogent strategic thinking, the Commandant forecast that unless the war came to a sudden end, "an [American] attack may be expected in the harbour [sic] of Vera Cruz, or at some other point [on the Gulf coast], the successful issue of which may be greatly promoted by a strong force of Marines." Despite Henderson's sound reasoning and the wartime excitement in the capital, Congress declined to increase promptly the size of the Corps. When John Y. Mason picked up the naval portfolio for the second time in September 1846, Henderson reminded him that "If the country requires effective cooperation with the Navy on the coast of Mexico, this increase [in the Corps] is indispensable." Congress received attention, too; Henderson sent a letter to Isaac E. Holmes, chair of the House

Naval Affairs Committee, urging a larger number of marines. On 2 March 1847, in a wartime measure supported by Henderson, Congress approved augmenting the marines by as many as 1,112 men. Henderson had gained another success at increasing the size of the Corps and immediately ordered recruiters to step up their efforts.(31)

In May 1847 Henderson sought and obtained permission from President James K. Polk to send a battalion of marines to serve with an American expedition invading Mexico. The Commandant selected Colonel Samuel Watson to lead the battalion, assembling at the army's Fort Hamilton, in New York City. Following his procedures of 1836, Henderson ordered detachment commanders to assign all available men for the campaign, leaving only a minimum number of guards at navy yards. Due to the weakness of the Mexican navy, Henderson knew that ship-to-ship encounters were unlikely. Therefore, he decided to reduce all ships' detachments in order to build up the infantry battalion. The army's quartermaster accommodated the marines by providing tents and other field equipment; Henderson traveled to New York to inspect the supplies and the battalion.(32)

Despite rapid preparations and Henderson's cautioning Colonel Watson to avoid being detained in New York, the marine battalion did not reach Mexico until 1 July 1847, three months after Veracruz fell to U.S. forces. In the first large-scale amphibious operation in American military history, General Winfield Scott had avoided the strength of the Mexican defenses by going ashore below Veracruz on 9 March. More than 8,000 U.S. Army soldiers and 180 marines from the ships' detachments of the U.S. invasion squadron had landed in five hours, but the landings were uncontested. Following a siege, Scott's army forced Veracruz to surrender on 29 March. Scott soon initiated an offensive with the objective of capturing the capital, Mexico City.(33)

Containing a large number of new recruits, Colonel Watson's battalion of 346 officers and men debarked at Veracruz and reinforced Scott's army at the Mexican city of Puebla on 6 August. Scott attached the marines to the division of Brigadier General John A. Quitman, a volunteer officer from Mississippi. Assigned to guard supply wagons, the marines saw little action until Scott had to use them in his series of attacks against the stout defenses of Mexico City. On 13 September the marines gained accolades for their part in the assault on Chapultepec Castle, site of the Mexican military academy. The capital fell the next day.(34)

In addition to the marines' participation in the Mexico City campaign, officers and men of the Corps' detachments assigned to ships of U.S. Navy squadrons made several landings on enemy coasts in California and the Gulf of Mexico. In California, marines and navy blue jackets landed near San Francisco, Monterey, Los Angeles, and San Diego, helping to secure a long stretch of the Pacific slope for the United States, and thus contributed to fulfilling one of the major war aims of the Polk administration. In the Gulf, marines went ashore at a number of locations, including Tabasco and Tampico, contributing to the American domination of that coast.(35)

Allowing his pride to show through over the accomplishments of his marines, Henderson wrote Secretary Mason that their actions were "a matter of record and will pass down to future ages unsurpassed if not unequalled in glory by any former achievements" of the Corps. In Henderson's opinion, marines serving "among the Storming party at Chapultepec" crowned the Mexico City campaign. When the battalion returned to Washington in 1848, a citizens' greeting committee handed Henderson a banner with the logo, "From Tripoli to the Halls of the Montezumas." Small though the battalion was, Henderson's arrangement for a marine unit to serve as part of Scott's Mexico City campaign successfully reinforced the concept of deploying part of the Corps with the army in event of war.(36)

The high-profile battalion deployments in 1836-37 and 1847-48 were a kind of duty marines did not have when Henderson joined the Corps in 1806 or became its Commandant in 1821. Henderson demonstrated how the marines could cooperate with the army in wartime and in doing so moved the Corps beyond its routine duties, such as serving in ships' detachments, guarding navy yards, and storming ashore with small naval landing parties. Although the battalion deployments actually included a limited number of marines, they involved a high percentage of the strength of the Corps and significantly improved the standing of the marines in the eyes of the public. Day by day, year in and year out, the marines' standard duties were about the same by 1848 as fifty years before, but after Henderson created successful battalions, the potential for using the Corps was greater than it was before he became Commandant.(37) Those modest battalions could have been written off as insignificant, but Henderson's examples helped set the stage for later commitments of marines, such as the Panama expedition in 1885 and the Guantanamo advanced base in 1898, as well as more distant overseas service in the Philippine War of 1899-1902, the Boxer Rebellion in 1900, and World War I, when first a marine regiment and then a marine brigade were attached to the army in the American Expeditionary Forces.

During the 1850s, familiar peacetime duties occupied Henderson, but the Commandant now considered and pushed for reforms in the Marine Corps more than he had done earlier. For example, Henderson renewed his call to secretaries of the navy for assigning West Pointers to fill officer vacancies in the Corps. He proposed to Secretary William Graham that a certain number of Military Academy graduates should become marines, and conferred with General Winfield Scott, whom he had known for years, about the matter. If Scott had granted permission for a few West Pointers to put on marine uniforms, Henderson might have been able to establish a precedent. When Captain A. H. Gillespie resigned in 1854, Henderson used the occasion to tell Navy Secretary James Dobbin that Gillespie's replacement should be "a young man of integrity, education and correct habits, who will do credit to himself and the Corps, in its various duties at home and abroad." These traits could be expected from graduates of West Point, which, as Henderson reminded the Secretary, regularly produced more lieutenants than the army needed. Therefore he called on Dobbin to work with the secretary of war and President Franklin Pierce to divert Academy graduates into the marines. Although Henderson was disappointed not to receive any West Pointers through his plan, he had demonstrated again his grasp of the needs of the military services and had offered an innovative way to meet those needs.(38)

Henderson raised other administrative reforms, ones that seemed prescient and became the focus of American military reformers in the 1870s and 1880s. In 1852 the Commandant urged the authorization for a marine officers' retired list so that older or infirm officers could honorably leave the service and make way for the promotion of younger leaders. Without a retired list, officers remained on active duty in order to continue being paid. As Henderson explained to Secretary of the Navy John P. Kennedy, "Some of the captains, from age and physical inability, are unfit to perform duty at Sea, [therefore] the consequences of the duty falls heavily on those who are efficient," that is, young and healthy. Furthermore, in 1858 Henderson declared that he wanted marine policy to be changed, requiring a routine physical examination for all new officers. Such an examination was logical – all enlisted recruits had to be examined by a doctor. Henderson expected that physicians could detect problems that would prevent someone from being able to carry out duties as a marine officer. Conservative officers blocked the policy change, but such proposals became part of the basic package of reforms sought twenty-five years later by reformers in all of the services. Henderson, while in his sixties, had anticipated them.(39)

Henderson's next reform concepts were his most important and related directly to the Corps' ability to project power ashore. Although he had raised the concept of artillery training to other secretaries of the navy, Henderson began emphasizing it in 1852 to Secretary Kennedy. The next year he became more insistent to Secretary Dobbin, reminding him that "the present drill of the Corps on shore is exclusively that of the infantry." The Commandant continued: "The Artillery drill, especially that of Light Artillery, would be highly beneficial in case of landing a force in a Foreign Country." Finally, Henderson recommended that "a battalion at headquarters [in Washington, D.C.] and at New York would be sufficient for uniting the artillery with the infantry drill, and thus add greatly to the efficiency of the soldiers of the Corps." Bringing their own artillery ashore would greatly strengthen the firepower of American naval landing forces.(40)

In 1854 and again in 1856 Henderson expanded his request. He called on Dobbin to authorize instruction for marines in heavy as well as light artillery, emphasizing that "in the event of [marines] landing upon hostile shores they should be prepared with artillery training." Coincidentally, at about that time U.S. naval forces, spearheaded by fifty marines led by Brevet Captain John D. Simms, went ashore against a series of "Barrier Forts" on the Pearl River near Canton, China. This action may have helped Henderson's case, for in the summer of 1857 marine First Lieutenant Israel Greene began a course of instruction in both heavy and light artillery at the U.S. Military Academy, with the goal of acquiring "a knowledge of Artillery for the purpose of introducing it into the Marine Corps." The Commandant asserted that Greene's assignment and the prospect of having one battery each of heavy and light artillery "will be an important step forward . . . for the Corps."(41)

Henderson hit upon another potential improvement. He anticipated the need for marine engineer officers who could design and supervise construction of gun emplacements and temporary fortifications on captured shores. He highlighted his latest reform idea: "When bodies of men are landed from vessels of war, their numbers are rarely large, but they may be made very formidable by properly constructed field works, or by more permanent works." In his 1858 annual report, Henderson wrote, perhaps with a trace of self-congratulation, that marine Headquarters now served as a "School for Drill" for both infantry and artillery.(42)

In his last years in uniform, Henderson was more than a placeholder edging to retirement. His lively mind generated practical ideas for making the Corps more powerful. He also cordially pushed politicians to consider such notions as commissioning West Point graduates into the marines, setting up medical examinations for new officers, and establishing a retired list for older officers. Variations on those concepts would be implemented by others in the years to come. It was his proposals for artillery training and engineer officers that really indicated the mind of an active professional military officer. Sending a single marine lieutenant for artillery training at the Military Academy meant winning a small skirmish in a larger campaign. While he deserves credit for gaining approval for a marine artillery capability, Henderson did not emphasize the artillery training after he got authorization for it in 1857. It may have been too late in his career for him to pour his energies into a new artillery training program but a logical option open to Henderson was to groom one or two top subordinates and dedicate them to promoting his concept of an enhanced infantry-artillery marine landing force. He knew which officers were most likely, by seniority and leadership, to be chosen as Commandant when he left the scene, but he did not single out a likely successor and pledge him to continuing the artillery program.(43)

Future plans for the Corps had to be set aside in the summer of 1857 when the Commandant personally responded to a crisis during the District of Columbia's municipal elections. Supporters of the Know-Nothing party and other anti-immigrant groups opposed voting by naturalized citizens. Hooligans, termed "plug-uglies" at the time, took to the streets, assaulting immigrants and trying to prevent naturalized citizens from voting. Washington's mayor doubted the ability of the district's police to keep order at the polling places. On the morning of 1 June, plug-uglies attacked a naturalized citizen near a ballot box in the first precinct of the fourth ward. A melee resulted: gunshots and paving stones filled the air, and a voting commissioner was seriously injured. Another outbreak of violence occurred in the second ward, injuring several people. The mayor concluded that the police were unable to protect the polls and appealed to President James Buchanan to "order out the company of . . . Marines now in this city to maintain the peace."(44)

The president informed the Secretary of the Navy, who in turn directed Henderson to select marines who would aid the mayor. Around noon, the Commandant met with Captain H. B. Tyler, who then "collected the available Marines at Headquarters and the Navy Yard," about one hundred privates and a few noncommissioned officers. The Commandant spoke to his men: "Soldiers, you have always done your duty in the face of enemies of your country; [and] I expect you to do your duty in upholding the laws of the country." All of the privates were recent recruits receiving training; based on typical marine recruiting practices, several of the new leathernecks were probably immigrants themselves.(45)

Tyler divided his men into two companies led by experienced officers and, accompanied by General Henderson wearing civilian clothes, the marines marched from the Washington Navy Yard toward city hall. Groups of plug-uglies heckled and threatened them along the way. A bold one shouted, "not a Marine should return to the Navy Yard alive." As they approached city hall, Henderson and Tyler saw a large crowd of around one thousand people gathered in the street and the general was informed that some plug-uglies had a small cannon nearby.(46)

The crowd blocked access to the polls and taunted the marines. The mayor wanted to continue the election and asked members of the crowd to make way so that the voting could begin again. The demonstrators hooted down the mayor's request. Then a man appeared at Captain Tyler's side saying that the plug-uglies would fire their cannon at the marines if they did not leave the area. Tyler ordered the marines to fix bayonets as a display of resolve and Henderson marched with a platoon to the cannon's location.(47)

Henderson walked up to the cannon and leaned his chest against the muzzle. The Commandant urged the plug-uglies to go home and directed words of warning to the people nearest the cannon: "Men, you best think twice before you fire this piece at the Marines." One of the ruffians nearest the cannon responded by pulling out a pistol, but a marine private knocked it aside. Other plug-uglies fired their pistols ineffectively at the marines while Henderson ordered Tyler to secure the cannon. Several more gunshots found their marks, hitting one marine in the shoulder and another in the face. On order, marines raised their rifles and fired into the mob, killing and wounding several people. The marines reloaded and prepared to fire again, sending the crowd "in full flight in all directions." Tyler and his soldiers remained on guard near city hall until 8:30 p.m. Then they marched to a railroad depot to check on a report that more plug-uglies were arriving from Baltimore. Finding nothing out of the ordinary at the station, the marines returned to their barracks, as an army contingent came into Washington to take their place. The show of force had broken the plug-ugly demonstrations.(48) It pleased Henderson that his marines had restored order in the capital. The incident at the cannon may be seen as foolhardy or as evidence of Henderson's flair for the dramatic. It served to demonstrate his personal leadership of the Corps and endeared him to his officers.

After the unrest subsided in Washington, Henderson naturally kept up his requests for additional marines, but he also accentuated calls for more funds to build new barracks around the country. His concern about marine barracks was not new. He routinely had asked for modest sums for repairing barracks, but during the 1850s the circumstances at some of them had become desperate. For example, Henderson pointed out that the barracks in Brooklyn, "abandoned as unfit for paupers," was a former alms house in a condition of near-collapse. Other barracks were "dilapidated," according to the Commandant. In the late 1850s Congress authorized funds for construction of new barracks in some cities and repairs of others.(49)

Such minor administrative victories dotted Henderson's calendar until his death on 6 January 1859, following his usual walk near the Marine Barracks in Washington, D.C. He was seventy-six years old. The Corps had lost its "grand old man" and its leader of thirty-eight years.

Henderson's significance to the U.S. Marine Corps may be calculated in several ways. First, he successfully increased the size of the corps. When he became Commandant, marine strength stood at 19 officers and 552 noncommissioned officers and enlisted men (571 total). In 1858 there were 52 officers and 1,555 other ranks – a total of 1,607. Although the organization was still small compared to the U.S. Army (about 10,500 in 1820 and 17,700 in 1858).(50) So the growth of the Corps during Henderson's commandancy reflected his tireless efforts to link the numbers of marines to the numbers and types of U.S. Navy ships in service as well as ceaselessly reiterating that if the British Royal Navy needed marines then the U.S. Navy must have them too. Second, Henderson blunted the drive by President Jackson to abolish the marines and merge them into the army. The Corps faced other challenges to its existence in the decades to come, but by 1859 Henderson had made marines staple fixtures on navy ships and at navy yards, and the Marine Band regularly played at many social and ceremonial events in Washington. Third, Henderson put his stamp on future generations of marines. He supervised officer training at Headquarters and created special battalions of marines to deploy with the U.S. Army expeditionary forces to fight in the Indian campaigns of the 1830s and the Mexico City campaign of 1847. Personally leading a detachment to suppress the plug-ugly disturbance in 1857 helped Henderson maintain the image of a vibrant and successful Marine Corps in the mind of the public and the Congress. Proposing and gaining approval for the new artillery training program pointed the way for the possibility of more powerful marine landing forces in the future.

In December 1859 Secretary of the Navy Isaac Toucey endorsed the soldiers of the sea in his annual report: "The Marine Corps is an indispensable branch of the Naval Service. . . . It is a gallant little band upon which rests the most widely extended duties at home and in every sea and clime, without sufficient numbers to perform them." Archibald Henderson could not have said it better himself. Not only was the respect for the Marine Corps in 1859 far higher than when he became Commandant in 1821, Henderson had given the marines a lasting legacy of excellence.(51)

NOTES

1. Allan R. Millett, *Semper Fidelis: The History of the United States Marine Corps*, rev. ed. (New York: Free Press, 1991), 26-86; Robert D. Heinl, *Soldiers of the Sea: The United States Marine Corps, 1775-1962* (Annapolis, Md.: Naval Institute Press, 1962), 31-68, quotes on p. 68; about half of Heinl's chapter concerns broad activities within the Corps without keeping the focus on Henderson; J. Robert Moskin, *The Marine Corps Story*, rev. ed. (New York: Little, Brown, 1992), 97-100, 105-9, 113-14, 118-19, 124-28, 178, 191-93. Other studies include Clyde H. Metcalf, *A History of the United States Marine Corps* (New York: G. P. Putnam's Sons, 1939), 83, 96-101, 189-90; Charles Lewis, *Famous American Marines* (Boston: L. C. Page, 1950), 75-88; Philip N. Pierce and Frank O. Hough, *The Compact History of the United States Marine Corps*, rev. ed. (New York: Hawthorn, 1964), 59-74; Edwin H. Simmons, *The United States Marines: The First Two Hundred Years, 1775-1975* (New York: Viking, 1976), 20-40, 48; Ralph W. Donnelly, "Archibald Henderson – Marine," *Virginia Cavalcade* 20 (Winter 1971): 39-47; and Ralph W. Donnelly, "Archibald Henderson," in Roger J. Spiller et al., eds., *Dictionary of American Military Biography*, 3 vols. (Westport, Conn.: Greenwood Press, 1984), 2: 461-63. See also Lynn Montross, "War with the Seminoles," *Leatherneck* 54 (November 1971): 42-45; Karl Schuon and Tom Bartlett, "Giants of the Corps," *Leatherneck* 58 (January 1975): 50-55.
2. Archibald Henderson Personal Papers, Henderson-Lee Collection, Headquarters, Marine Corps, Historical Division, Washington, D.C. (hereafter HQMC Historical Division); Secretary of the Navy (hereafter SecNav) Robert Smith to Archibald Henderson, 4 June 1806, Letters Sent by the Secretary of the Navy to Officers and Commandants of the Marine Corps, General Records of the Department of the Navy (Record Group 80), National Archives and Records Administration, Washington, D.C. (hereafter RG 80, NA; all citations are to entry 1 unless otherwise indicated). Donnelly, "Archibald Henderson – Marine," 39. Dumfries is only few miles from the modern Marine Corps schools at Quantico.
3. Edwin H. Simmons, "The Marine Corps," in John E. Jessup, ed., *Encyclopedia of the American Military* (New York: Charles Scribner's Sons, 1994), 397; Charles Nordoff, *Man-of-War Life* (1855; reprint, Annapolis, Md.: Naval Institute Press, 1985), 56, 63, 105-6.
4. SecNav Robert Smith to Henderson, 6 March 1807, SecNav Paul Hamilton to Henderson, 12 April 1811, RG 80, NA; Henderson to brother J. G. Henderson, 4 January 1808, 3 February 1809, Henderson-Lee Collection, HQMC Historical Division.
5. Edward L. Beach, *The United States Navy: 200 Years* (New York: Henry Holt, 1986), 129-30; Stewart quoted in James C. Jenkins, "Brig. Gen. Archibald Henderson, USMC," *Marine Corps Gazette* 25 (June 1941): 50; SecNav B. W. Crowninshield to Henderson, 22 April 1816, RG 80, NA.
6. Janet Henderson to Alexander Henderson, Jr., 24 August 1815, and Richard Henderson to J. G. Henderson, 13 February 1816, Henderson-Lee Collection, HQMC Historical Division.
7. Franklin Wharton Biographical File, HQMC Historical Division; Benjamin Thomas to Henderson, 21 July 1817, and Crowninshield to Henderson, 7 September 1818, RG 80, NA; *American State Papers, Naval Affairs* (Washington: Gales and Seaton, 1853), 1: 503-7; Heinl, *Soldiers of the Sea*, 31; Millett, *Semper Fidelis*, 54.
8. Henderson to Crowninshield, 16 September 1818, and Henderson to Smith Thompson, 29 January, 1 February 1819, Letters Sent, Headquarters, USMC, 1818-1859, Records of the United States Marine Corps (Record Group 127), National Archives (hereafter RG 127, NA; all citations are to entry 4 unless otherwise indicated); Henderson to John C. Calhoun, 15 November 1818, and Calhoun to James Monroe, 19 November 1818, *Papers of John C. Calhoun*, ed. Clyde N. Wilson (Columbia: University of South Carolina Press, 1967), 3: 278, 282; Heinl, *Soldiers of the Sea*, 31-32; Moskin, *Marine Corps Story*, 99.
9. SecNav Thompson to Gale, 16 February 1819, and Thompson to Henderson, 19 February and 23 March 1819, RG 80, NA; Henderson to Gale, 8 November 1819, Henderson Biographical File, HQMC Historical Division; Moskin, *Marine Corps Story*, 102-4; Millett, *Semper Fidelis*, 55; Pierce and Hough, *Compact History of the Marine Corps*, 59-61.

10. SecNav Thompson to Henderson, 2 January 1821, RG 80, NA; Henderson to Thompson, 12 April 1820, Henderson Biographical File, HQMC Historical Division; illustration of Henderson, in Moskin, *Marine Corps Story*, following p. 94.

11. Henderson to SecNav Samuel Southard, 22 November 1824, RG 127, NA; numerous letters sent by Henderson throughout his commandancy, ibid.; Millett, *Semper Fidelis*, 56; Metcalf, *A History of the Corps*, 83; Victor Krulak, *First to Fight: An Inside View of the Marine Corps* (Annapolis, Md.: Naval Institute Press, 1984), 142; Simmons, *U.S. Marines*, 36.

12. Brevet Major Samuel Miller, the adjutant Henderson replaced, believed that he had been improperly removed. Miller held a grudge against the Commandant, creating an acrimonious rivalry that lasted for the rest of their lives. Henderson saw to it that Miller was brought before a court-martial in 1822 on a charge of public intoxication. Miller appealed his conviction through Secretary of the Navy Smith Thompson to President James Monroe, who remitted Miller's suspension and restored him to duty. Years later, in 1836, Miller preferred several charges against Henderson, including misapplication of funds and approving improper furloughs to officers. Some of the raft of correspondence on reassignments and rivalries includes: Henderson to SecNav Thompson, 7 February, 4 and 20 December 1821, 26 March 1822; Henderson to Samuel Miller, 22 February, 26 November, 17 December 1821, 29 March 1822, Henderson to President James Monroe, 13 January 1823, all in RG 127, NA; Miller to SecNav Mahlon Dickerson, 7 May 1836, RG 80, NA, entry 14. See also Millett, *Semper Fidelis*, 56, and Moskin, *Marine Corps Story*, 106.

13. SecNav Thompson to Henderson, 3 July 1822; Henderson to Thompson, 22 November 1822; Henderson to SecNav Samuel Southard, 17 July 1827; and Henderson to SecNav Levi Woodbury, 22 October 1831, RG 127, NA. 14. Henderson to SecNav Southard, 18 November 1823 and 16 February 1824; and Henderson to Senator Robert Y. Hayne (Democrat of South Carolina), Chair of the Senate Naval Affairs Committee, 11 March 1828, RG 127, NA; Henderson to Southard, 23 November 1823, *American State Papers, Naval Affairs*, 2: 91. See also Millett, *Semper Fidelis*, 57, 63.

15. For example, see Henderson to SecNav Southard, 14 February 1825, and Henderson to SecNav James Paulding, 18 December 1839 (in which Henderson explained that "The necessities of the service have required a greater number of Sgts and Corporals than the law allows"), Henderson Biographical File, HQMC Historical Division. See also Henderson's letters to: Southard, 16 February 1826, 17 January 1827, and 25 November 1828; Acting SecNav John Boyle, 27 July 1838; Representative Henry A. Wise (Democrat of Virginia), 11 May 1842; Senator William Archer (Whig of Virginia), 1 July 1842; SecNav George Bancroft, 5 July and 13 October 1845, 7 August 1846; SecNav John Y. Mason, 9 December 1848; SecNav William Preston, 5 July 1849; and SecNav William Graham, 22 January 1851, all in RG 127, NA.

16. SecNav Southard to Henderson, 23 August and 8 November 1826; and SecNav Dickerson to Henderson, 23 March 1835, RG 80, NA. Henderson to Southard, 7 November 1826; Henderson to recruiters Captains Richard Smith, R. D. Wainwright, Samuel Miller and John Gamble, all dated 11 November 1826; Henderson to Lieutenant George Walker, 19 September 1833; Henderson to recruiters Lieutenant Colonel Samuel Miller, Major Samuel Watson, Major W. H. Freeman, Major John Harris, Captain William Dulany, Captain J. G. Williams, and Captain A. N. Brevoort, 1 April 1842 (in which Henderson wrote "the frequency of discharge of Aliens by civil authority in New York renders it necessary that their enlistment be prohibited as far as practicable"); Henderson to Captain John Reynolds, 25 March 1847; Henderson to Lieutenant Frederick McNeill, 18 February 1848; Henderson to recruiters English, Harris, Linton, Marston, and Caldwell, 11 March 1850; and Henderson to Mrs. Catherine Ulerick, in regard to her son who was an underage recruit, 30 April 1851, RG 127, NA. See also Millett, *Semper Fidelis*, 64.

17. On the sword, see Heinl, *Soldiers of the Sea*, 65, 108. On the Hall's rifle, see Henderson to SecNav Southard, 26 September 1827, Henderson Biographical File, HQMC Historical Division; and Navy Department to Henderson, 3 July 1828, RG 80, NA; Heinl, *Soldiers of the Sea*, 36. For the characteristics of the Hall's rifle, see Carl P. Russell, *Guns on the Early Frontiers* (Berkeley: University of California Press, 1957), 183-87.

18. James D. Richardson, *Messages and Papers of the Presidents, 1789-1897*, 10 vols. (Washington: GPO, 1897), 2: 460; Heinl, *Soldiers of the Sea*, 37-39; Krulak, *First to Fight*, 7; Millett, *Semper Fidelis*, 66. Details concerning the matters of extra pay and rations for certain breveted officers is found in U.S. vs. William L. Freeman, 3 Howard 557 [1845]. Freeman was one of the marine officers whose compensation at brevet rank was at issue.

19. Naval officers' letters in *American State Papers, Naval Affairs*, 3: 560-69 (Isaac Hull to SecNav John Branch, 5 March 1830; Jones to Branch, 5 March 1830; Rodgers to Branch, 8 March 1830; Bainbridge to Branch, 4 March 1830; and Stewart to Branch, 8 March 1830); Alexander S. Mackenzie, "Report of the Secretary of the Navy to the President of the United States," *North American Review* 30 (April 1830): 360-89. See also Millett, *Semper Fidelis*, 61.
20. Henderson to SecNav Levi Woodbury, 22 October 1831 (quotation), RG 127, NA; Acting SecNav John Boyle to Henderson, 17 September 1831; and Woodbury to Henderson, 11 December 1833, RG 80, NA.
21. The act of 1834 is in *American State Papers, Naval Affairs*, 4: 395-427. Henderson to SecNav Woodbury, 13 February 1834, and Henderson to SecNav Dickerson, 7 October 1834 (quotation), RG 127, NA. See also Millett, *Semper Fidelis*, 61, 66-68; Heinl, *Soldiers of the Sea*, 40-41.
22. SecNav Dickerson to Henderson, 23 May 1836, RG 80, NA; Millett, *Semper Fidelis*, 70.
23. P. G. Howle to Lieutenant Colonel Samuel Miller, 21 May 1836, RG 80, NA; Henderson to Lieutenant Colonel Samuel Watson, 21 May 1836; Henderson to Lieutenant Colonel William Freeman, 23 May 1836 (quotation); Henderson to Captain Levi Twiggs, 23 May 1836; Henderson to Lieutenant Colonel John Gamble, 23 May 1836; and Henderson to SecNav Dickerson, 27 May 1836, RG 127, NA. Washington National Intelligencer, 2 June 1836. An apocryphal story developed that Henderson had posted a notice on his office door at Headquarters. It read: "Gone to fight the Indians. Will be back when the war is over." Of course, the Commandant did not close down Headquarters, but the story has been cherished by generations of marines since the 1830s because it appeared to exemplify Henderson's grit and combativeness, traits that marines have adopted as their own. For sources that appear to take the story at face value, see Pierce and Hough, *Compact History*, 68; Lewis, *Famous American Marines*, 83; Karl Schuon, *U.S. Marine Corps Biographical Dictionary* (New York: Franklin Watts, 1963), 102; Philip N. Pierce and Lewis Meyers, "The Seven Years War," *Marine Corps Gazette* 32 (September 1948): 32; and J. D. Thacker, "Highlights of U.S. Marine Corps Activities in the District of Columbia," *Records of the Columbia Historical Society* 52 (1952): 84. Other histories appropriately use the word "legend" when describing the sign. Refer to Moskin, *Marine Corps Story*, 113; Lynn Montross, "War with the Seminoles," *Leatherneck* 54 (November 1971): 42; and Heinl, *Soldiers of the Sea*, 41.
24. Henderson to SecNav Dickerson, 9 June 1836 (first quotation), and 1 July 1836 (second quotation), RG 80, entry 14, NA; Henderson to wife, 4 May 1837, Henderson-Lee Collection, HQMC Historical Division; M. A. Aldrich, *History of the United States Marine Corps* (Boston: Henry L. Shepard, 1875), 73.
25. Jesup to Adjutant General Roger Jones, 12 January 1837, quoted in John T. Sprague, *The Origin, Progress, and Conclusion of the Florida War* (1848; reprint, Gainesville: University of Florida Press, 1964), 167; Moskin, *Marine Corps Story*, 125-26.
26. Henderson to Jesup, 28 January 1837, and Jesup to Adjutant General Jones, 7 February 1837, in Sprague, *Florida War*, 174-77, 172-73 (quotation on p. 173). See also Aldrich, *Marine Corps*, 6; John K. Mahon, *History of the Second Seminole War*, rev. ed. (Gainesville: University Press of Florida, 1967), 198-99. 27. Henderson journal extract, dated 13 April 1837, Henderson Biographical File, HQMC Historical Division; Henderson to Ann Henderson, 4 May 1837, Henderson-Lee Collection, HQMC Historical Division; Henderson to SecNav Dickerson, 11 May 1837, RG 80, entry 14, NA. Henderson was back at his desk by 20 June. See Dickerson to Henderson, 20 June 1837, RG 80, NA; Aldrich, *Marine Corps*, 77; Metcalf, *History of the Corps*, 101. It took much longer than Henderson expected to withdraw all the marines from Florida and have them back under his authority. Even a personal plea to General Jesup for their return was ineffective. Henderson to Jesup, 24 June 1837, RG 127, NA. Moskin, *Marine Corps Story*, 131-34, gives a summary of the marines who remained with the "Mosquito Fleet."
28. Henderson proclamation to Soldiers, 24 July 1838, Henderson Biographical File, HQMC Historical Division, and personal letter expressing similar sentiments, Henderson to SecNav James Paulding, 20 July 1838, RG 127, NA. Moskin, *Marine Corps Story*, 134, gives a more favorable overall assessment of the marines' role in the Florida War than most secondary works.
29. See Henderson's letters to: SecNav Dickerson, 18 November 1837, 8 January, and 6 February 1838; Representative Samuel Ingham (Democrat of Connecticut), 15 January 1838; SecNav Paulding, 7 October 1839; Representative William P. Fessenden (Whig of Maine), 10 February 1842 and 9 January 1843; SecNav Abel P. Upshur, 23 February 1842; SecNav David Henshaw, 1 September and 7 November 1843; and SecNav George Bancroft, 13 October 1845, all in RG 127, NA.

30. Henderson to SecNav Bancroft, 13 October (first and second quotations), 10 December (third quotation), 20 and 31 December 1845, and 13 April 1846, RG 127, NA. On the eve of a major war, Henderson had to contend with a challenge to his status and reputation. For several years Henderson had been accorded the pay and emoluments (such as additional rations and subsistence) of a brevet brigadier general, coming as a result of the award of the brevet in 1837. Secretary of the Navy John Y. Mason concluded that, due to technicalities of various laws pertaining to the American military establishment, the Commandant should be paid at his regular rank of colonel and be required to return $12,000 in what would be considered overpayments made since his brevet. Henderson protested the Secretary's decision and requested a ruling from higher authority. Asking them to offer advice on the issue, President John Tyler convened a special board of U.S. Army officers, chaired by Major General Winfield Scott, commanding general of the army. The board issued a finding that Henderson deserved the pay and emoluments of a brigadier general, and the President concurred. Overjoyed and letting his pride get the best of his common sense, Henderson relished his victory by personally paying for and distributing copies of the board's decision. Consequently, a congressional amendment to the Naval Appropriations Act of 1846 negated brevet pay for any marine officer who held the rank of brevet brigadier general, but did not require such an officer (only Henderson fit the description) to return money already paid. Henderson was disappointed, but not much chastened, by the terms of the new law, which thus lowered his pay back to that of a colonel. Heinl, *Soldiers of the Sea*, 40.

31. Henderson to SecNav Bancroft, 12 August 1846, RG 80, NA; Henderson to Sec Nav Mason, 7 November 1846 and 20 February 1847, RG 127, NA; Henderson to Representative Isaac Holmes (Democrat of South Carolina) 29 January 1847, ibid. Millett, *Semper Fidelis*, 73.

32. Diary of James K Polk, ed. Milo M. Quaife, 4 vols. (Chicago: McClurg Co., 1910), 3: 23-24. SecNav Mason to Henderson, 14 May 1847, RG 80, NA; Henderson to Watson, 13, 20, and 21 May 1847, RG 127, NA; Henderson to Major John Harris (Norfolk), Major Levi Twiggs (Philadelphia), and Lieutenant Colonel Samuel Miller (New York), 18 May 1847, ibid.; Henderson to Army Quartermaster Thomas Jesup, 22 May 1847, ibid.

33. Millett, *Semper Fidelis*, 74; K. Jack Bauer, *Surfboats and Horse Marines: U.S. Naval Operations in the Mexican War, 1846-48* (Annapolis, Md.: U.S. Naval Institute Press, 1969), 81-82.

34. Millett, *Semper Fidelis*, 77-80; Heinl, *Soldiers of the Sea*, 50-52. Watson's battalion comprised only about 3 percent of Scott's army at the time Mexico City fell. 35. Bauer, *Surfboats and Horse Marines*, 49-51, 102-5, 116-20, 194-95; Metcalf, *History of the Corps*, 138-65; Millett, *Semper Fidelis*, 72-75.

36. Henderson to SecNav Mason, 22 November 1847, RG 127, NA; Millett, *Semper Fidelis*, 81; Heinl, *Soldiers of the Sea*, 52; Simmons, *U.S. Marines*, 51. After Watson's battalion departed, it appeared that a second battalion was needed. Henderson devoted considerable time to the task and, of course, he could not know when the campaigning would conclude. The second battalion assembled under Major John Harris and sailed for Mexico in early March 1848, arriving too late to make any significant contribution to the war. The battalion returned home in the summer. 37. Millett appears to downplay the potential consequences of the battalion deployments. See *Semper Fidelis*, 81.

38. Henderson to: SecNav Graham, 15 October 1851; SecNav Dobbin, 17 November 1853, 16 October (quotation), and 10 November 1854; SecNav Isaac Toucey, 12 November 1857 and 20 November 1858, RG 127, NA. Millett, *Semper Fidelis*, 84. Eventually, the Naval Academy, which was established in 1845, began allowing its graduates to be commissioned in the Marine Corps, but it did not take that step until 1882. Before that year, the navy needed every Annapolis graduate.

39. Henderson to: SecNav Kennedy, 11 November 1852; SecNav Dobbin, 17 November 1853 and 10 November 1854; and SecNav Toucey, 20 November 1858, RG 127, NA. See also Millett, *Semper Fidelis*, 84, 110.

40. Henderson had also reminded SecNav Mason about his artillery concept; Henderson to Mason, 31 January 1848, RG 127, NA. Henderson to Kennedy, 11 November 1852 (emphasis added), and Henderson to Dobbin, 17 November 1853, ibid.

41. Henderson to: Dobbin, 10 November 1854 and 13 November 1856; Captain J. D. Simms, 7 May 1857; SecNav Toucey, 12 November 1857 (quotations), RG 127, NA. On the Barrier Forts, see Millett, *Semper Fidelis*, 84-85, and Heinl, *Soldiers of the Sea*, 57-59.

42. Henderson to SecNav Toucey, 12 November 1857 and 20 November 1858, RG 127, NA.

43. Unfortunately for the marines, the leader who followed Henderson, Colonel John Harris, Commandant from 1859 to 1864, was stodgy and failed to understand Henderson's proposal for the role of marine artillery as a part of a landing force. Instead, Harris changed Henderson's approach to the marines' use of artillery, distorting it to become all-marine guncrews on board ships, a dead-end step derailing Henderson's farsighted proposal of strengthening landing forces. Colonel Harris floundered in the office of Commandant. For instance, he failed to devise ways to bring the Corps up to authorized strength during most of the Civil War, even though the Union navy grew from forty-two ships in 1861 to almost seven hundred ships and vessels by 1865. More determined leadership from Harris, along the lines clearly established by Henderson in 1836 and 1847, could have attached marine battalions to the Union's Butler-Farragut expedition that captured New Orleans in 1862 and to the Army of the Potomac under the command of Major General George B. McClellan in the Peninsula campaign of that year, keeping alive Henderson's precedents of having marine battalions serve in army campaigns. Millett cogently concludes that there "was simply a failure of imagination within the Navy Department and Headquarters [USMC]. John Harris and his successor, Jacob Zeilin, simply did not recognize the amphibious assault mission or else rejected it for being too much like the Army's tasks." Millett, *Semper Fidelis*, 91.
44. *Washington National Intelligencer*, 2 June 1857.
45. Captain H. B. Tyler to Henderson, 2 June 1857, RG 80, NA, entry 14 (first quotation); *National Intelligencer*, 2 June 1857 (second quotation).
46. *Washington Evening Star*, 2 June 1857; *National Intelligencer*, 2 June 1857; Heinl, *Soldiers of the Sea*, 61-2. The location was near present-day 5th and K streets.
47. Tyler to Henderson, 2 June 1857, RG 80, entry 14, NA; *National Intelligencer*, 2 June 1857.
48. *Washington Evening Star*, 2 June 1857 (first quotation); *National Intelligencer*, 2 June 1857 (second quotation); *Washington National Era*, 4 June 1857; "Statement of Occurrences on Monday, 1st June 1857," Henderson Biographical File, HQMC Historical Division.
49. Henderson to SecNav Dobbin, 17 November 1853 (second quotation), 17 January 1855 (first quotation), and 13 November 1856; Henderson to SecNav Toucey, 20 November 1858, RG 127, NA.
50. For numbers of personnel, see Simmons, "Marine Corps," in Jessup, ed., *Encyclopedia of the American Military*, 397; and Russell F. Weigley, *History of the United States Army*, enlarged ed. (Bloomington: Indiana University Press, 1984), 597.
51. Annual Report of the Secretary of the Navy, 1859, 36th Cong., 1st sess., vol. 3, pt. 3, p.1141.

WE WILL GO HEAVILY ARMED:
THE MARINES' SMALL WAR ON SAMAR, 1901-1902

Brian McAllister Linn

After the Marine Corps' unremarkable performance in the Civil War, a variety of internal and external forces pressured its officers to make educational reforms, setting in motion crucial transformation toward a more modern and professional fighting force. Spurred on by a national mood of expansionism, the Navy began to increase in both numbers and technology in the 1880s, eventually producing a world-class naval power by the early 1900s. Correspondingly, the Marine Corps of the same period stood at the precipice of a new mission-in-being – Colonial Infantry. The Philippine War provided a test case for this new role as an occupational land force designed to suppress insurrections and provide governmental stability. However, the subsequent actions of Major Littleton W. T. Waller on the Philippine island of Samar have provoked controversy for over a century. Waller's supporters have maintained that the U.S. Army wrongly had him court-martialed in order to satisfy Congressional inquiries into American brutality. Professor Linn, an award-winning expert on the Philippine War, provides a far different account and holds Waller directly responsible for many of the tragic incidents that occurred. Perhaps this essay most importantly illustrates the challenges inherent to counterinsurgency operations – a mission in which the Marine Corps was just getting its feet wet.

On 28 September 1901 villagers and guerrillas attacked the 74 officers and men of Company C, Ninth U.S. Infantry at the town of Balangiga, Samar Island, in the Philippines. Surprising the men at breakfast, the Filipinos killed 48 soldiers, "mutilating many of their victims with a ferocity unusual even for guerrilla warfare."(1) The "massacre," which occurred when many believed the fighting between U.S. military forces and Filipino nationalists was virtually over, shocked Americans. Amidst public cries for vengeance, U.S. patrols, under orders to "make a desert of Balangiga," soon did such a thorough job that "with the exception of the stone walls of the church and a few large upright poles of some of the houses, there is today not a vestage [sic] of the town of Balangiga left."(2) Determined to crush the resistance on Samar, the army poured in troops, the navy sent gunboats, and a battalion of 300 marines was dispatched under the command of Major Littleton W. T. Waller. Some of these marines had served with the victims of Balangiga in the Boxer Rebellion a year earlier. Their attitude may have been best summarized by Private Harold Kinman: "we will go heavily armed and longing to avenge our comrades who fought side by side with us in China."(3)

Although only a small part of the total U.S. manpower on the island, the marine battalion soon became the most famous, or notorious, military force in the campaign – which in turn became one of the most famous, or notorious, episodes of the Philippine War. Even college freshmen may have read of Brigadier General Jacob H. Smith's orders directing Waller to take no prisoners to treat every male over ten as an enemy, to make the interior of Samar a "howling wilderness," and to "kill and burn. The more you kill and burn, the better you will please me."(4) Equally controversial are the marines' own exploits. Campaigning on Samar was such a hellish experience that for years afterwards, veterans would be greeted in mess halls with the toast, "Stand Gentlemen: He served on Samar." Yet in an early blunder, the marines lost ten men in one expedition without encountering a single enemy guerrilla. In another incident. Waller had eleven Filipino guides summarily executed, an action that President Theodore Roosevelt believed "sullied the American name" and led to Waller's court-martial for murder. Thus, both because it proved so controversial and because it represented the marines' first encounter with twentieth-century guerrilla warfare, the Samar campaign serves as an excellent starting point for a discussion of the small wars heritage of the U.S. Marine Corps.

Charles E. Callwell, the contemporary British expert in irregular warfare, noted that in small wars climate and terrain were often greater obstacles than the enemy forces. His observation is particularly true of Samar, where, as one saturnine marine noted there was no need for the orders to turn the interior into a "howling wilderness," because "nature had done it for us."(6) In the local dialect the name "Samar" means "wounded" or "divided' – an apt description for an island whose 5,200 square miles are replete with rugged mountains, jungles, tortuous rivers, razor-sharp grasses, swamps, and parasites. Because the mountains confined most of its population to a narrow coastal region, for most of its colonial history Samar was "an island of dispersed settlements only loosely bound together by a common religion, a lightly felt administrative structure, and a few ties between pueblos."(7) In the towns and barrios, authority was wielded by a few priests, merchants, land owners, and municipal officials; and in the mountains scattered groups practiced primitive slash-and-burn agriculture. The Samarenos exported abaca (Manila hemp) and coconuts from Calbayog, Catbalogan, and other ports; but they were unable to grow sufficient rice to meet their needs and suffered periodic food shortages. Although contemporary American officers described the population of the island as "savages" with a long and violent history of resistance to any authority, the Spanish praised the natives' docile acceptance of foreign rule.

Samar was untouched by the fighting between the Filipino nationalists and the Spanish in 1896; but with the declaration of Philippine independence by Emilio Aguinaldo on 12 June 1898, the Filipino revolutionaries, based predominantly on the island of Luzon, moved to secure the rest of the archipelago. On 31 December 1898, a month before the outbreak of the Philippine War between Filipino forces and the Americans, Brigadier

General Vicente Lukban (or Lucban) arrived and with some 100 soldiers formally placed Samar under Aguinaldo's Philippine Republic. Although he demonstrated commendable energy, Lukban was greatly hampered in his efforts to mobilize the Samarenos by the fact that he was an outsider. Moreover, a U.S. naval blockade prevented him from obtaining reinforcements or sending the money and supplies he collected to Aguinaldo. The blockade compounded Samar's precarious food situation: "Famine appeared as early as 1899 and Lukban wrote in 1900 that his troops were close to mutiny because of it."(8)

The American infantrymen who landed on the island on 27 January 1900 had little idea of either the precariousness of the insurgents' situation or the trouble that Samar was later to give them. Their mission was to secure the islands hemp ports and prevent a cordage crisis in the United States, a task they accomplished by brushing aside Lukban's forces and garrisoning a few towns. The soldiers' rapid seizure of the ports and the apparent collapse of the revolutionaries convinced the army high command that Samar was secured. With more important islands to pacify, army leaders quickly decided Samar was of minimal value. For the next eighteen months after their arrival, the isolated companies stationed on the island would cling precariously to little more than a few ports and river towns.

The weak occupation force allowed the Filipino revolutionaries, termed *insurrectos* by the Americans, to recover and counterattack. From the beginning the *insurrectos* attempted to confine the soldiers to the Catbalogan-Calbayog area while mobilizing the inhabitants against the invaders. In some places the revolutionaries depopulated entire areas, setting fire to villages and barrios and driving civilians into the mountains. They informed the Samarenos that the U.S. Army came for the purpose of raping, pillaging, and "annihilating us later as they have the Indians of America."(9) To support their military forces, the guerrillas confiscated crops and engaged in extensive smuggling, seeking both to continue the hemp trade and to bring in rice. Filipinos who collaborated with the soldiers or lived in the towns risked kidnapping or assassination, often in the most grisly manner. One U.S. officer complained, "The Insurgents have been guilty of all kinds of cruelty to those persons friendly to us, such as burying them alive, cutting off parts of the body, killing them, etc."(10)

Although the guerrillas lacked modern weapons, they showed remarkable tactical ingenuity and ability. They made cannons out of bamboo wrapped with hemp, gunpowder from community niter pits, and cartridges from brass fittings soldered with silver taken from churches. Their primitive firearms made the guerrillas more than able both to harass the soldiers and to force compliance from civilians. Against American patrols, they relied on an ingenious variety of booby traps: covered holes filled with poisoned bamboo, spring-loaded spears set off by carefully hidden trip wires, and heavy timbers or baskets of rocks hung over trails and rivers. One soldier who painstakingly removed dozens of obstacles from a trail returned in two weeks to find dozens more in place, "and such traps one could not imagine could be made and set so cunningly."(11) The ubiquitous traps, supplemented by an extensive system of pickets and vigilantes who signaled the approach of an American patrol through bells, bamboo and carabao horns, or conch shells, effectively precluded surprise. Occasionally the *insurrectos* would go on the offensive. From carefully concealed trenches, bamboo cannon or rifles would fire on American patrols struggling along narrow trails or river beds. This sniping might be followed by a sudden "bolo rush" of machete-wielding guerrillas pouring out of the thick grass or jungle to overwhelm detachments.(12)

It was not until May 1901 that the army began to give Samar more than a cursory interest, and then only because the end of military rule on neighboring Leyte Island made the continued turmoil on Samar intolerable. With much of the Philippines pacified, the army was able to reinforce Brigadier General Robert P. Hughes on Samar and by September he had twenty-three companies of infantry stationed in some thirty-eight towns located throughout the northern and central parts of the island. Hughes established two bases deep in the interior to allow U.S. troops to operate inland and he ordered patrols to converge at Lukban's headquarters on the Gandara River, in the process crossing the island and sweeping the countryside. He expanded the army's area of operations, stationing garrisons in heretofore ignored southern towns such as Basey and Balangiga. Through the laborious process of constructing roads, building supply camps, securing boats and porters, and constant patrolling, the Americans brought the war to the interior of the island.

Frustrated because the guerrillas rarely stood and fought, Hughes became convinced that the resistance would continue as long as the enemy could secure sufficient food. He determined to cut off smuggling and to destroy the guerrilla logistical base in order to give his soldiers "a fair opportunity to kill off the bands of utter savages who have hibernated in the brush."(13) He ordered the navy to step up its blockade and closed all ports in Samar, authorizing army and naval officers to seize all boats not deemed necessary for fishing and to arrest anyone found carrying food without a pass. To increase the pressure further, he ordered U.S. expeditions in the interior and along the coast to destroy crops, houses, and fields. Although Hughes did not formally implement a policy of concentrating the population into protected zones or camps, it was common for his soldiers to deport all Filipino civilians found in the interior to the coast. The result was that the towns, often already burned by the *insurrectos*, soon filled up with destitute Filipinos with no access to food. Within two months after Hughes's policies took effect, hunger was widespread and by September the situation was so critical that he had to authorize post commanders to purchase rice for the refugees.(14)

At the town of Balangiga, the American policies provoked a violent response. Despite his alleged sympathy for the Filipinos, the post commander, Captain Thomas Connell, destroyed much of the town's livestock, fishing supplies, and crops. In addition, he confined seventy townspeople in two tents designed for sixteen men each, forcing them to work all day in the sun and refusing to pay them or give them adequate food. His men also behaved poorly, taking food without payment and probably committing at least one rape. Such abuses, coupled with weak security measures, provoked a retaliatory attack by townspeople and local guerrilla forces who slaughtered most of the garrison on 28 September.(15)

The Balangiga "massacre" provoked an equally enraged American response. In what was undoubtedly one of the worst decisions of the war, Major General Adna R. Chaffee, the commanding officer of the army in the Philippines, selected Brigadier General Jacob H. Smith to take tactical command of the pacification of Samar. A product of the army's seniority system, Smith owed his general's stars to his longevity, his physical bravery, and the mistaken belief that he planned to retire. Having spent most of his life commanding little more than a company, he was bewildered by the complexity of handling the four thousand soldiers, marines, and native scouts in his Sixth Separate Brigade. To compound his problems, Smith displayed symptoms of mental instability and was subject to outbursts in which he urged the most violent and irresponsible actions.(16)

Unfortunately, among Smith's subordinates was an officer who himself was prone to rash and violent action: Major Littleton W. T. Waller, commander of the marine battalion. At first glance Waller would seem to have made an ideal commander. He was a twenty-two-year veteran whose combat exploits in Egypt, Cuba, and China had shown that he possessed several characteristics vital to a counterinsurgency fighter: he had tremendous powers of endurance and was personally brave, aggressive, and charismatic. These qualities would later make him a legendary combat leader in the marines' small wars in Latin America. Nevertheless, Waller consistently relied on physical courage and endurance to make up for deficiencies in planning and judgment. In China, for example, he had engaged a vastly superior enemy force and had been driven back, losing an artillery piece and a machine gun, suffering eleven casualties, and leaving his dead behind. Prone to both braggadocio and self-pity, he was convinced that his services in the Boxer Rebellion had not been properly recognized. Moreover, he arrived in Samar under a personal cloud, having recently gone on an alcoholic binge that culminated in a ten-day suspension from duty. This disciplinary action does not appear to have cured him: one marine later remembered that on operations in the field Waller "had a bottle of liquor for his own use, and when it gave out he was in bad shape."(17) His drinking may explain his boastfulness and irritability, his willingness to blame his superiors, and his inability to accept the consequences of his actions.

It is not surprising that the marines' organizational status within the Sixth Separate Brigade is still the subject of much misunderstanding, given the confusion engendered by Smith's instability and Waller's penchant for acting rashly. Assigned to the two southern towns of Basey and Balangiga, the marines fell under both army and navy authority. Not until after the campaign did the U.S. Army's judge advocate general rule that the marines on Samar were not detached from the navy but only engaged in a "cooperative" venture with the army.(18) Equally confused was Waller's area of responsibility. From 27 October 1902 on, he apparently believed he was in charge of an independent command he referred to as "Subdistrict South Samar," consisting of all territory south of a line from Basey on the west coast to Hemani on the east coast, an area totaling some six-hundred square miles and including two army posts. A careful reading of the extensive U.S. Army operational correspondence concerning Waller makes it clear, however, that he commanded the marines at Basey and Balangiga alone and that his army superiors never considered him more than the "Commanding Officer, Basey." The actual extent of Waller's authority would later become a major issue, but at the time nearly every army garrison and navy gunboat suffered from equally tangled command relations.(19)

The organizational vagueness surrounding Waller's command was compounded by his operational orders. Upon the arrival of the marines at Balangiga and Basey, Smith ordered Waller to "kill and burn," take no prisoners, and regard every male over ten as a combatant. In spite of these grim directives, Waller's own orders to the marine battalion on 23 October conformed to army policies already current on Samar. In common with American military efforts since June 1901, Waller focused on denying food to the guerrillas and ordered his marines to confiscate all rice, allowing families only a small daily ration on which to survive. In an effort to break up the guerrillas' extensive smuggling organization in the south of the island, he ordered all hemp confiscated and all boats registered and painted red. Waller attempted to organize the population into similarly identifiable groups by allowing a short grace period for male civilians to come into the towns and register or be treated henceforth as hostile. His orders emphasized that the Samarenos were "treacherous, brave, and savage. No trust, no confidence can be placed in them." Therefore, civilians were required to perform all manual labor and Filipino guides were to walk at the head of military columns with long poles and probe for pits and traps. The area around Balangiga, garrisoned by some 159 marines under Captain David D. Porter, was to be "cleared of the treacherous enemy and the expeditions, in a way, are to be punitive." Finally, Waller stressed that the marines were to "avenge our late comrades in North China" and "must do our part of the work, and with the sure knowledge that we are not to expect quarter."(20) There were also disturbing indications that Smith's illegal orders were passed on unchanged to the men. One marine wrote home that he and his comrades were "hiking all the time killing all we come across" and another veteran remembered that "we were to shoot on sight anyone over 12 years old, armed or not, to burn everything and to make the Island of Samar a howling wilderness."(21) Captain Porter later explained that although Smith had meant that the marines were only to "kill and burn" *insurrectos*, it was "understood that everybody in Samar was an *insurrecto*, except those who had come in and taken the oath of allegiance.(22)

Under these guidelines Waller pursued the objectives of destroying insurrecto supplies, bringing the guerrillas to battle, and establishing a defensive cordon. His men completed the destruction of the area around Balangiga and extended the devastation—between 31 October and 10 November the marines burned 255 houses and destroyed one ton of hemp, one-half ton of rice, thirteen carabao, and thirty boats while killing thirty-nine men and capturing eighteen. Waller also learned from a Filipino who had escaped from the *insurrectos* that the insurgents had established a base about fifteen miles up the Sojoton River. The first attempt up the river on 6 November resulted in the death of two marines and the loss of fifteen rifles. A second expedition was more successful. After ten days of struggling through the jungles, the marines launched an assault on 17 November that killed thirty guerrillas and drove the rest from their entrenchments. As congratulations poured in, Waller boasted that the "operations in the Sojoton were the most important of the whole campaign as far as their effect on the insurgents were concerned."(23)

This apparent success on the Sojoton River may have led Waller to overlook some of the campaign's hard lessons. He underestimated the crucial role the navy had played in supplying and transporting his expedition. Once separated from their waterborne logistical lifeline, his marines could neither carry enough food nor live off the country. Despite their victory, they had to withdraw from the Sojoton immediately and within a month the area was again a guerrilla stronghold. Waller could take pride in the fact that his men "can and will go where mortal men can go," but he apparently disregarded the human cost inflicted on them.(24) He seems to have drawn no lesson from the fact that after its ten-day ordeal his battalion was immobilized for almost a week.

Convinced that the Sojoton Valley was cleared, Waller launched operations into the interior to destroy other reputed guerrilla strongholds. He resolved the persistent problem of supply by ignoring it; in one telegram he arbitrarily decided that six days' rations could sustain his men for nine days. Unfamiliar with all of the deleterious effects of service in the Philippines and ignoring the lessons of the Sojoton campaign, he drove both himself and his men unmercifully. The marines slogged through Samara swamps and muddy trails, climbed the razor-backed mountains, and cut their way through jungles and *congon* grass. Constant rains, inadequate maps, and poor communications dogged them and patrols often wandered lost. One marine complained that "sometimes we do not have anything to eat for 48 hours and never more than 2 meals per day. Our feet are sore, our shoes worn out and our clothes torn. It rains [and] half of the time we sleep on the ground with nothing but a rubber poncho to cover us."(25)

In December, asserting that Smith had requested him to find a route for a telegraph line. Waller decided to march from the east coast to Basey, "belting the southern end of Samar."(26) Although the planned march covered only some thirty miles in a direct line, an earlier army expedition had already determined that no route existed in the region that Waller intended to cross. Not only would the marines be marching at the height of the monsoon season, but most of their journey would be over narrow, jungle-covered valleys, necessitating the constant crossing of both mountains and rivers. Between climbing the steep hills, cutting a path through the vegetation, and fording the swollen and treacherous streams, the marines would have to display epic stamina simply to cover a few miles on the map. The local army officers, far more experienced with the treacherous interior, urged Waller not to undertake the operation without establishing a secure supply line. Another officer who recently had returned from the very area Waller planned to explore warned the marine commander immediately before he departed "of the hardships of mountain climbing, even when he had a supply camp and shelters for his men."(27)

The ensuing march of six officers, fifty marines, two Filipino scouts, and thirty-three native porters from Lanang to Basey between 28 December 1901 and 19 January 1902 has been described by Allan R. Millett as "a monument to human endurance and poor planning."(28) The trail quickly disappeared and the expedition slowed to a crawl as each foot of the way had to be cut through the sodden and steaming jungle. As Waller's men crossed and recrossed rivers and inched up hills so sheer they were almost perpendicular, their shoes and clothes became little more than torn and rotting rags. The constant immersion, parasites, razor-sharp tropical grasses, and piercing rocks literally peeled their skin off in layers.

Although the survivors' recollections of the march are vague and contradictory, it is clear that after only five days of marching, supplies ran dangerously low and the men were exhausted. On about 2 January Waller and his officers decided to abandon their objective and return to the east coast along the Suribao River. The marines cut down trees and made rafts, but the water-logged timbers sank immediately Making a controversial decision, Waller took two officers and thirteen of his strongest men and set out in an attempt to blaze a trail to the Sojoton Valley. By 6 January they managed to cut their way through to a marine base camp. In the meantime the rest of the expedition disintegrated. Captain Porter, receiving no word from Waller, hacked his way back to Lanang with seven marines and six Filipinos. The remaining marines and Filipino porters were left on the trail under the command of Lieutenant Alexander Williams. Starving and suffering from prolonged exposure, Williams and several of his men became convinced that the porters not only had access to a large supply of food but also that they were plotting against the marines. The lieutenant later claimed that he was attacked by three of the porters, though his account of the event was somewhat confused. An army relief force, battling heavy floods, reached Williams' men on 18 January, but by that time ten marines had either died or disappeared and an eleventh was to die shortly afterwards. Starving, barefoot, and their clothes in rags, the marines who survived were literally helpless, and their rifles and ammunition had to be carried by the Filipino porters. Some of the marines were even crazed by their exertions. Although the expedition cost him over 20 percent of his command. Waller admitted: "As a military movement it was of no other value than to show that the mountains are not impenetrable to us."(29)

One result of Waller's ill-considered march was the virtual collapse of his battalion as an effective combat force. After they returned to their familiar quarters at Basey and Balangiga, the marines were incapable of further sustained operations. Instead of the large and protracted expeditions they had launched in the fall, the marines now sent between twenty and forty men out on "hikes" that seldom moved more than a day from camp. Marine patrols continued to destroy food and shelter and occasionally skirmished with guerrillas, but the real fighting of the campaign occurred elsewhere. Southern Samar returned to the backwater status it had enjoyed before Balangiga, and Waller's battalion may have been content to let the war be won elsewhere. Certainly neither Waller nor his men made any protest when the shattered battalion was withdrawn from Samar and returned to Cavite on 29 February.(30)

A second, more serious result of the march was the execution of twelve Filipinos without benefit of trial or even the rudiments of an impartial investigation. The first killing occurred on 19 January; the victim was a Filipino whom the mayor, or *presidente*, of Basey denounced as a spy. Because Waller was running a temperature of as high as 105 degrees, the camp surgeon judged him incompetent to command. As a result, authority in Basey fell to Lieutenant John H. A. Day. Through the use of "a real third degree," or torture, Day secured a confession, the specifics of which he later had trouble remembering. Acting "on the spur of the moment," he decided that the Filipino's confession warranted his immediate execution. Although Waller denied authorizing a summary execution, in a few minutes Day organized a firing squad, personally shot the suspect, and left his body in the street as a warning. Court-martialed for murder, Day was acquitted on the grounds that he was obeying Waller's orders.(31)

The following day saw an even bloodier incident. Williams and many of the survivors were in the hospital on Leyte Island; and no one at Waller's headquarters at Basey appears to have been certain of the magnitude of the disaster that had befallen their comrades. Some believed that not ten but twenty marines had died, and nearly everyone accepted the rumor that the porters had acted treacherously. Although Basey was connected by telephone with brigade headquarters on Leyte, Waller neither requested an investigation nor brought charges against the suspects. Instead, hovering between delirium and lucidity, he ordered that the surviving porters be brought over from Leyte and executed. He then apparently collapsed. When these men arrived, it fell to Private George Davis to pick out those who had been guilty of specific crimes. Davis identified three porters whom he recalled had hidden potatoes, stolen salt, failed to gather wood, and disobeyed orders. He then selected another seven men on the grounds that, as he later claimed, "they were all thieves, sir, that I know of; and they were all worth hanging, if I had anything to do with it."(32) Solely on the basis of this reasoning, ten civilians were promptly shot by Day's firing squad. At Waller's insistence, a final victim was executed later that afternoon—providing through his grim arithmetic a total of eleven Filipino victims in exchange for the eleven men he had lost on the march.

In a report written three months after the incident, Waller gave a variety of reasons for the executions: the hostility of the townspeople of Basey, an inquiry with his officers, "reports of the attempted murder of the men and other treachery by the natives," his own weakened physical condition, as well as his power of life and death as a district commander. He concluded: "It seemed, to the best of my judgment, the thing to do at that time. I have not had reason to change my mind."(33) Even after conceding him an unusual measure of moral obtuseness, it is hard to follow his reasoning. Clearly, he engaged in no procedure that either a civil or military court would recognize as an inquiry or investigation. Neither then nor since has any evidence emerged to prove that his victims were guilty of "attempted treachery" or any other action that warranted the death penalty under the laws of war. General Chaffee, who believed that Waller's actions were those of a man suffering from "mental anguish," drew attention to the fact that "no overt acts were committed by the *cagadores* [porters]; on the contrary those sent to their death continued to the last to carry the arms and ammunition after they [the marines] were no longer able to bear them, and to render in their impassive way, such service as deepens the conviction that without their assistance many of the marines who now survive would also have perished." Noting that the laws of war only justified summary executions in "certain urgent cases," Chaffee pointedly commented that after the march was over "there was no overwhelming necessity, no impending danger, no imperative interest and, on the part of the executed natives, no overt acts to justify the summary course pursued."(34) Chaffee drew attention to the fact that in executing the porters, Waller had assumed powers that both the "military laws of the United States and the customs of the service, confer only upon a commanding general in time of war and on the field on military operations." What made Waller's crime even more heinous was that he "was in telephonic communication with his Brigade Commander, but deliberately chose not to consult him regarding his contemplated action."(35) Concluding that Waller's acquittal was "a miscarriage of justice," the general chastised the major's illegal actions and publicly condemned the killings as "one of the most regrettable incidents in the annals of the military service of the United States."(36)

The subsequent court-martial of Waller for murder is almost as controversial today as it was ninety years ago. Taking place against the background of the last death throes of the Philippine War, the trials seem to embody the brutality, ambiguity, and frustration of the marines' first Asian guerrilla conflict. Waller's revelation that he had been ordered by General Smith to make the interior of Samar a "howling wilderness" and to regard every male Samareno over ten as a combatant provoked national outrage. American opponents of Philippine annexation, who had suffered a crushing defeat in the presidential election of 1900, now rallied behind the issue of atrocities to attack U.S. military policy in the Philippines.(37) Waller's acquittal did little to resolve the controversy, for both the military authorities who examined the trial transcript and the commander in chief himself, condemned Waller's actions as illegal and immoral. For years afterwards Waller was known as the "Butcher of Samar" and many attributed his being passed over for commandant to the notoriety he gained on the island.

Waller's supporters have since claimed that he was a scapegoat, a victim of politics, a Marine forced to stand trial for crimes that the US. Army committed with impunity in the Philippines. Joseph Schott entitled one of the chapters in *The Ordeal of Samar* "The Scapegoat"; Paul Melshen cites Waller's "high moral courage"; Stuart Miller praises him as an "honorable warrior" and a "sacrificial victim"; and Stanley Karnow terms Waller "a scrupulous professional" and a "scapegoat."(38) The charge that Waller was a victim of interservice rivalry is difficult to sustain. His conduct cannot be defended on the grounds that he was only following orders. In the first place, Waller claimed that as a marine he did not fall under U.S. Army authority. Moreover, he clearly understood that Smith's instructions to take no prisoners and regard all males over ten as enemies were illegal, for by Waller's own testimony he immediately told Captain Porter that despite Smith's instructions the marines had not come to make war on women and children.(39) The excuse that Waller did nothing that the U.S. Army had not been doing for years is not only morally bankrupt but factually incorrect. Although the army's operational records give ample evidence that throughout the Philippine War far too many Filipinos were indiscriminately fired on or shot "attempting to escape," the premeditated execution of prisoners was neither a common nor an accepted practice among American soldiers in the archipelago. Even on Samar, where both a thirst for vengeance and a lack of supervision led to war crimes and unnecessary cruelty, soldiers were expected to follow the laws of war. Smith, who openly advocated illegal policies, was relieved, court-martialed, found guilty and immediately retired in disgrace. Army officers on Samar suspected of atrocities were investigated, court-martialed, and, as in the case of Waller, either acquitted or given mild reprimands. Given the nature of their offenses and the lightness of their punishments, it is hard to view any of these men, soldiers or marines, as scapegoats.(40)

A third result of the marines' march and the tragic events that followed was that Waller's court martial and the charges of American brutality overshadowed Lukban's capture in February and the surrender of the last prominent guerrilla leader on 28 April. Despite Smith's attempts to turn his men into mindless butchers, the victory was due to careful planning, detailed organization, and persistence. In order to combat the guerrillas in Samar's rugged interior, the army constructed a string of supply dumps from which long-ranging columns could sweep the countryside. Through a combination of large expeditions and hundreds of small patrols that operated from towns and field camps, the soldiers demonstrated to the population that the Americans intended to stay. By recruiting Filipino volunteers, promising local autonomy, and offering generous surrender terms, the army began providing attractive alternatives to resistance. These methods, along with the destruction of most of the island's foodstuffs, eventually convinced all but the most intransigent rebels to accept American authority.

The brutality and excesses that characterized the conduct of soldiers and marines on Samar represented a radical departure from the pacification methods employed elsewhere in the Philippines. Too often lessons that had been painfully learned in the previous three years of warfare were disregarded, and only the most primitive elements were retained. Barring the first few months of American occupation, there was little attempt to found schools, build roads, or win over the population – methods that proved effective in other areas where the topography was only a little less daunting and the guerrillas better organized. Nor did the Americans on Samar later take advantage of their vastly expanded intelligence capabilities or seek to exploit the deep and bitter divisions among various sections and classes in Samareno society. With some exceptions, pacification methods remained crude and undeveloped. In part this was the result of Samar's isolation and topography which cannot be overemphasized. Yet it should not be forgotten that Samar's topography was equally harsh to the guerrillas, who, despite having little more experience of the interior than the Americans and being led by a "foreigner" from another island and culture, learned to control an unruly populace and to fight effectively with small units and with limited supplies. The marines, of course, fresh from China, could hardly be aware of this mass of tested lore; and in following their army superiors down the path of directionless retaliation, they wrote one of the most painful chapters in the history of the corps.(41)

In assessing the marines' performance in their first modern small war, it is essential to recognize that in the early twentieth century before most marines had any experience with expeditionary warfare and interventions and before the emergence of a specific doctrine for fighting "small wars," the character of the commanding officer was all important. Certainly the physical stamina and rugged endurance that the marines displayed on their disastrous attempt to march across the island may be sufficient justification for the old U.S. Marine Corps toast, "Stand Gentlemen. He served on Samar." Yet this glorification of suffering and tenacity should not obscure the fact that they did not display much expertise in their first modern guerrilla war. Inexperienced and, in the case of Waller, unwilling to learn, the marines' tactics were as physically devastating to themselves as they were punishing to their opponents.

Whether this ambiguous performance led to institutional growth or lessons learned is beyond the scope of this work. The Marine Corps took no action against Waller, and there is no indication that he displayed any remorse for his actions. He went on to become the mentor of a generation of counterinsurgency experts who emerged within the corps to fight the small wars of the Caribbean. Perhaps much of Waller's physical courage and endurance, his charismatic leadership, and his love of combat found their way into the marines' expeditionary forces. Yet it is important to note that his junior officers rejected Waller's headlong individual aggressiveness, choosing instead to discuss, disseminate, and eventually codify their experiences in the *Small Wars Manual* of the Marine Corps.

NOTES

Research for this article was made possible through a U.S. Marine Corps Historical Center Research Fellowship and a research grant from Old Dominion University. The author wishes to thank V. Keith Fleming, Jack Shulimson, Patricia Morgan, and the rest of the staff of the U.S. Marine Corps Historical Center for their professionalism, their willingness to discuss Marine Corps history, and their many helpful suggestions of sources to consult. He would also like to thank Daniel P. Greene and James R. Linn for their comments on drafts. The views expressed in this paper are the author's own and should not be taken to represent those of the U.S. Marine Corps Historical Center.

1. Richard B. Welch, Jr., *Response to Imperialism: The United States and the Philippine-American War, 1899-1902* (Chapel Hill, 1979), 41. For the Balangiga "Massacre," see Eugenio Daza y Salazar "Some Documents on the Philippine-American War in Samar," *Leyte-Samar Studies* 17 (1983): 165-87; Fred R. Brown, *History of the Ninth U.S. Infantry, 1799-1909* (Chicago, 1909), 578-96; James O. Taylor, *The Massacre of Balangiga* (Joplin, Mo., 1931); Brig. Gen. Robert P. Hughes to Adjutant General, 30 November 1901, Records of U.S. Army Overseas Operations and Commands, 1898-1942, Record Group 395, 2483, Box 39, no. 7825, National Archives, Washington, D.C. (hereafter cited as RG 395, NA); Edward C. Bumpus, *In Memoriam* (Norwood, Mass., 1902); Joseph Schott, *The Ordeal of Samar* (Indianapolis, 1964), 35-55.

2. Quote "make a desert" from Hughes to Col. Isaac D. DeRussy, 29 September 1901, RG 395, 2551, NA. Quote "with the exception" from Capt R. M. Blackford to Adjutant General, 8 October 1901, RG 395, 2571, Box 1, no. 164, NA. Capt. Edwin V. Bookmiller to Adjutant General, 1 October 1901, Annual Reports of the War Department, 1902, 1:9:625-27; DeRussy to Adjutant General, 5 October 1901, RG 395, 2552, NA. For the reaction to Balangiga, see Maj. Gen. Adna R. Chaffee to Maj. Gen. Henry C. Corbin, 25 October 1901, Henry C. Corbin Papers, Box 1, Library of Congress, Washington, D.C.; Testimony of William H. Taft, Senate Committee on the Philippines, Affairs in the Philippine Islands, 57th Cong., 1st Sess., 1902, Sen. Doc. 331, 363-64; John Morgan Gates, *Schoolbooks and Krags: The United States Army in the Philippines, 1898-1902* (Westport, Ct., 1973), 248-51.

3. Harold Kinman to Sister, 18 October 1901, Harold Kinman Papers, U.S. Marine Corps Historical Center, Washington, D.C. (hereafter cited as USMCHC). Cf. Kinman's sentiment with Maj. Littleton W. T. Waller's 23 October 1901 orders to his command, located in typescript copies of much of the marines' official correspondence during the Samar campaign, Waller File, USMCHC (hereafter referred to as Waller Report).

4. Records of the Office of the Judge Advocate General, Record Group 153, General Courts-Martial [G.C.M.] 30739, Brig. Gen. Jacob H. Smith, National Records Center, Suitland, Md.; Richard N. Current, T. Harry Williams, Frank Friedel, Alan Brinkley, *American History – A Survey*, 7th ed.(New York, 1987), vol. 2, Since 1865, 592.

5. General Orders 80, Headquarters of the Army, 16 July 1902, Records of the Bureau of Insular Affairs, Record Group 350, File 3490-27, National Archives, Washington, D.C.

6. John H. Clifford, *History of the Pioneer Marine Battalion at Guam, L.I. and the Campaign in Samar, P.I. 1901* (Portsmouth, N.H., 1914), 36; Charles E. Callwell, *Small Wars: Their Principles and Practice*, 3d ed. (London, 1906), 44.

7. Bruce Cruikshank, *Samar 1768-1898* (Manila, 1985), 106. For Samar's topography see Anon. to Adjutant, 2d Battalion, April 1900, Records of the Adjutant General's Office, Record Group 94, 117, 43d Inf., U.S.V., Co. "G," no. 8, National Archives, Washington, D.C. (hereafter cited as RG 94, NA); Capt. Murray Baldwin to Adjutant General, Sixth Separate Brigade [6SB], 21 November 1901, RG 395, 3750, Book 1, no. 5, NA; Capt. E. R. Tilton to Commanding Officer, 1st District, February 1900, Henry T. Allen Papers, Box 32, Library of Congress, Washington. D.C.; John R. M. Taylor, *The Philippine Insurrection against the United States, 1899-1903,* galley proof (Washington, 1903), 81 HS.

8. Holt, "Resistance on Samar: General Vicente Lukban and the Revolutionary War, 1899-1902," *Kabar Seberang Sulating Maphilindo* 10 (December 1982): 1-14; Brig. Gen. Vicente Lukban to Antonio Luna, 8 July 1899, in Taylor, *Philippine Insurrection*, Exhibit 1321, 58-59 HK.

9. Lukban to Local Residents of the Province of Samar, 14 February 1900, Charles G. Clifton File, 43d Inf., U.S.V. Box, U.S. Army Military History Institute (USAMHI), Carlisle, Pa.; Testimony of Lt. G. A. Shields, RG 153, G.C.M. 30739, NA; Lukban to *presidente* of Catubig, 15 September 1900, Philippine Insurgent Records, Select Document 502.8, National Archives Microfilms, Microcopy 254 (hereafter cited as PIR SD); 'Copy of Lukban's Speech on his Birthday," 1 February 1901, PIR SD 824.1; Col. Arthur Murray to Adjutant General, 4 June 1900, RG 94, 117, 43d Inf., Report No. 6, NA.

10. Maj. John C. Gilmore to Adjutant General, 30 June 1900, RG 94, 117, 43d Inf., 2d Battalion, NA.

11. Charles G. Clifton Diary, 10 January 1902 entry, 43d Iaf., U.S.V., USAMHI; Maj. R. A. Brown, "Inspection of the Post and Troops at Laguan, Samar," 31 March 1901, RG 395, 2483, Box 31, NA; Capt. William M. Swaine to Adjutant, 5 August 1901, RG 395, 3450, Box 1, no. 478, NA; Clifford, Pioneer Marine Battalion, 28-29; Brown, *Ninth Infantry*, 563; Taylor, *Philippine Insurrection*, 82-83 HS; Lukban to Local Chief of Cabalian, 3 March 1899, PIR SD 928.8; Maj. Narisco Abuke to Anon., 7 October 1900, PIR SD 846.1; Lt. Col. Francisco Rafael to Lt. Jorge Langarra, 16 July 1901, PIR SD 808.3; Hughes to Chief of Staff and Adjutant General, 3 June 1901, RG 395, 2550, Box 1, NA.

12. "Statement of Private Luther Jessup," in Maj. John J. O'Connell to Department Commander, 30 June 1901, RG 395, 2483, Box 36, NA; Capt. John S. Fair to Gilmore, 29 March 1900, RG 94, 117, 43d Inf., Co. "B," no. 38, NA; Gilmore to Adjutant General, 18 May 1900, RG 94, 117, 43d Inf., 2d Battalion, NA; Brown, Ninth Infantry, 573, 594-95.

13. Hughes to Smith, 15 October 1901, RG 395, 2483, Box 49, NA; Hughes Testimony, Senate, Affairs, 553.

14. Hughes to Chief of Staff and Adjutant General, 14 May 1901, RG 395, 2483, Box 28, NA; Capt. A. B. Buffington to Capt. Leslie F. Cornish, 14 June 1901, RG 395, 3447, no. 90, NA; Hughes to Adjutant General, 10 September 1901, RG 395, 2550, Box 1, NA.

15. Hughes to Adjutant General, 30 November 1901, RG 395, 2483, Box 39, no. 7825, NA; Schott, *Ordeal of Samar*, 16-17; Holt, "Resistance on Samar," 9; Interrogation of Joaquin Cabafies, 1 January 1902, RG 395, 2571, Box 3, no. 360, NA; Salazar, "Philippine-American War," 165-87; Richard Arens, "The Early Pulahan Movement in Samar," *Leyte-Samar Studies* 11 (1977): 59-66; Testimony of William Gibbs, Senate, *Affairs*, 2284-2310.

16. Chaffee to Hughes, 30 September 1901, RG 94, AGO 406865, NA; Chaffee to Adjutant General, 8 October 1901, Senate, Affairs, 1599; Chaffee to Corbin, 28 November and 9 December 1901, Corbin Papers, Box 1; Manila American (7 January 1902); Lt. W. R. Shoemaker to Senior Squadron Commander, 5 November 1901, Naval Records Collection of the Office of Naval Records and Library, Record Group 45, Area File 10, National Archives, Washington, D.C. For Smith's mental instability, see Capt. William M. Swaine Testimony, RG 153, G.C.M. 30739, Brig. Gen. Jacob H. Smith, NA; Allen to Taft, 7 February 1902, Allen Papers, Box 7; Luke Wright to Taft, 13 January 1902, William H. Taft Papers, Ser. 3, Library of Congress, Washington, D.C.; Chaffee to Corbin, 5 May 1902, Cotbin Papers; David L. Fritz, "Before the 'Howling Wilderness': The Military Career of Jacob Hurd Smith, 1862-1902," *Military Affairs* 43 (1979): 186-90.

17. Harry C. Adriance, "Diary of the Life of a Soldier in the Philippine Islands During the Spanish-American War by a Sergeant in the U.S.M.C.," photocopy in the USMCHC. For other evidence of Waller's alcoholism, see entries of 15 November 1900 and 14-16 February 1901, Henry Clay Cochrane Diary, USMCHC; Ben H. Fuller Papers, Box 1, Folder 9, USMCHC; "Record of Waller, Littleton Waller Tazewell," USMCHC. For the incident in China, see Waller to Second in Command, U.S. Naval Force, China, 22 June 1900, and Waller to Brig. Gen. Commandant, 28 June 1900, *Annual Report of the Brigadier-General Commandant of the United States Marine Corps to the Secretary of the Navy*, 62-66. For the marines' deployment, see Brig. Gen. Robert Hall to Hughes, 19 October 1901, RG 153, G.C.M. 30313, Maj. Littleton W. T. Waller, NA; Hughes to Chaffee, 21 and 25 October 1901, Corbin Papers; *Manila American* (20 October 1901); Rear Adm. Frederick Rodgers to Commander in Chief, Asiatic Squadron, 5 November 1901, RG 45, Area File 10, NA.

18. Brig. Gen. George Davis to Secretary of War, 27 June 1902, RG 153, G.C.M. 30313, NA.

19. Waller Report, 8-10. Waller's defenders have perpetuated the confusion over his authority by claiming he was in charge of all of southern Samar or even the entire island. Paul Melshen, "He Served on Samar,"

Proceedings 105 (1979): 45; Stanley Karnow, *In Our Image: America's Empire in the Philippines* (New York, 1989), 191.

20. Headquarters, Marine Battalion, Samar, 23 October 1901, Waller Report, 6-7. Quote "hiking all the time" from Harold Kinman to Sister, 23 December 1901, Kinman Papers; quote "we were to shoot" from *Modesto Bee*, 31 May 1965.

22. Testimony of Capt. David D. Porter, RG 153, G.C.M. 30313, NA. Waller to Smith, 31 October 1901, Waller Report, 10-12; Porter to Waller, 2 November 1901, Waller Report, 15-16; Waller to Anon., 10 November 1900, Waller Report, 21.

23. Waller to Anon., 10 November 1900, Waller Report, 25. See also ibid., 23-31; Waller to Adjutant General, 6 November 1901, RG 395, 2571, Box 1, no. 129, NA; Kinman to Sister, 23 November 1901, Kinman Papers.

24. Waller to Adjutant General, 65B, 19 November 1901, Waller Report, 26. Clifford, *Pioneer Marine Battalion*, 34; RG 153, G.C.M. 10196, Lt. John H. A. Day, NA.

25. Kinman to Sister, 23 December 1901, Kinman Papers; Waller to Adjutant General, 6SB, 30 November 1901, RG 395, 3451, Box 1, NA; Waller to Adjutant General, 6SB, 6, 18, and 20 December 1901, Waller Report, 43-48; Waller to Rodgers, 17 December 1901, RG 45, Area File 10, NA.

26. Waller to Smith, 19 November 1901, RG 395, 3451, Box 1, NA. For the confusion over Waller's mission, see Waller to Smith, 31 October 1901, and Judge Advocate's Summary, RG 153, G.C.M. 30313, NA; Waller Report, 42; Schott, *Ordeal of Samar*, 104-106; Smith to Chief Signal Officer, 2 November 1901, RG 395, 3451, Box 1, NA; Adjutant General, 65B, to Adjutant General, Division of Philippines, 1 December 1901, RG 395, 2571. Box 1, no. 1188, NA; Smith to the adjutant general, 11 December 1901, RG 395, 2573, Box 1, no. 166, NA.

27. Waller to Adjutant General, 65B, 25 January 1901, Waller Report, 49. For the army's 1901 expedition, see War Department, 1902, 1:9:601; Brown, Ninth Infantry, 561. It should be noted that judged by the campaign conditions on Samar, Waller's march was neither over particularly difficult terrain nor of more than moderate distance.

28. Allan R. Millett, *Semper Fidelis: The History of the U.S. Marine Corps* (New York, 1980), 154.

29. Waller to Adjutant General, 65B, 25 January 1902, Waller Report, 58. See also Cmdr. William Swift to Smith, 20 December 1901, RG 395, 2574, Box 1, NA; Lt. Kenneth P. Williams to C.O., Lanang, 19 January 1902, *War Department*, 1902, 1:9:446; Porter to Waller, 8 February 1902, Waller Report, 60-64; Lt. A. S. Williams to Waller, 18 February 1902, Waller Report, 64-68; Schott, *Ordeal of Samar*, chap. 5.

30. Waller Report, 68-88; Lt. Cmdr. J. M. Helms to Swift, 6 January 1902, RG 395, 2571, Box 2, no. 43, NA; Waller to Adjutant General, 8, 9, 18, and 20 February 1902, RG 395, 2573, Box 1, NA; 1902 entry, 1902, Charles G. Clifton Diary; Clifford, *Pioneer Marine Battalion*.

31. Quotations from Testimony of Lt. John H. A. Day, RG 153, G.C.M. 10196, NA. The identity of the victim was unknown at the time of the killing, but it was later alleged that he was an *insurrecto* leader named Captain Victor.

32. Testimony of Pvt. George Davis, RG 153, G.C.M. 30313, NA. Despite voluminous correspondence and records, the events of 19-20 January 1902 are still unclear and the evidence is inconclusive as to how many Filipinos were executed on 20 January. The above is based on the correspondence in the Waller Reports; RG 153, G.C.M. 30313 and G.C.M. 10196, NA; and General Orders 93, Headquarters, Division of the Philippines, 7 May 1902, RG 395, 2070, NA. For the confusion over the number of U.S. Marine deaths, see RG 153, G.C.M. 10196, NA; and Schott, *Ordeal of Samar*, 139, 142.

33. Waller Report, 76-77.

34. General Orders 93, Headquarters, Division of the Philippines, 7 May 1902, RG 395, 2070, NA.

35. For Waller's incapacity for command, see Testimony of Dr. George A. Lin~, RG 153, G.C.M. 10196, NA. General Orders 93, Headquarters, Division of the Philippines, 7 May 1902, RG 395, 2070, NA. For the judge advocate's ruling that Waller's acts were illegal and contrary to the laws of war, see Brig. Gen. George Davis to Secretary of War, 27 June 1902, RG 153, G.C.M. 30313, NA.

37. Millett, *Semper Fidelis*, 154; Gates, Schoolbooks and Krags, 256; Welch, *Response to Imperialism*, 138-41.

38. Schott, *The Ordeal of Samar*, chap. 9; Melshen, "He Served on Samar," 45; Stuart C. Miller, "Benevolent Assimilation" *The American Conquest of the Philippines, 1899-1903* (New Haven, 1982), 227; Karnow, *In Our Image*, 193.
39. RG 153, G.C.M. 30313, NA.
40. Maj. Charles H. Watts to Adjutant General, 1 April 1902, RG 94, AGO 482616, NA; RG 153, G.C.M. 30756, Lt. Julien E. Gaujot, NA; RG 153, G.C.M. 34401, Maj. Edwin F. Glenn, NA; RG 153, G.C.M. 30757, Lt. Norman E. Cook, NA.
41. An excellent discussion that demonstrates that the Samar campaign was an anomaly in Army pacification in the Philippine War can be found in Gates, *Schoolbooks and Krags,* chap. 9. For a study of Army pacification on Luzon, see Brian McAllister Linn, *The US. Army and Counterinsurgency in the Philippine War, 1899-1902* (Chapel Hill, N.C., 1989).

THE CHINA MARINES AND THE CRUCIBLE OF THE WARRIOR MYTHOS, 1900-1941

Heather P. Marshall

From the Spanish-American War onward, the Marine Corps initiated a process of constructing an elite self image, which eventually became a dominant perception held by Marines and others. Decades of duty in exotic China – where Marines continually interacted with the militaries of many European nations – was a key site for this dynamic process. Heather Marshall's research into this facet of institutional culture provides great insight into the mystique of "China Marines" and how this embryonic experience contributed to the formulation of a "warrior brotherhood."

Successfully passing his first test under fire in the Philippines, Marine legend Smedley Butler forever identified himself as a Marine after he "selected an enormous Marine Corps emblem to be tattooed across [his] breast . . . . [and] blazed forth triumphantly, a Marine from throat to waist."[1] Butler and other twentieth-century Marines sought to varying extents to affiliate themselves actively with their institution, even taking steps to mark themselves physically. The career of Smedley Butler (1898-1931) provides an opportunity to trace changes in the Corps' institutional culture, particularly if one zooms in on his service in China during the Boxer Rebellion of 1900 and again as Commander of the 3d Brigade from 1927-1928, because his career mirrors the era in which the Marine Corps defined itself once and for all as an elite warrior brotherhood. Only two years into his career during the Boxer Rebellion, Butler had been brevetted to captain at the age of eighteen when he, Lieutenant A.E. Harding, and four enlisted Marines carried a wounded Marine accidentally left behind during an engagement for six miles under Chinese fire.[2] If this and other trials of the Boxer Rebellion were Butler's initiation into the Corps' warrior brotherhood, his tenure as Commander of the 3d Brigade demonstrated the successful articulation of an elite institutional culture that had solidified during the previous decades.

Butler played an integral role in the construction of the Corps' institutional culture, and his youthful enthusiasm never waned over the course of his career. Gaining a commission in the Marine Corps at the impressionable age of sixteen in 1898 due to the political pull of his father, U.S. Congressman Thomas Butler, he began his training in Washington D.C. without even having finished high school. There, he would come under the guidance of the Corps' highest-ranking enlisted Marine, Sergeant Major Thomas Hayes, who had spent twelve years in the British Army during which he had served in India and Africa.[3] Hayes made such an impression on Butler that he recalled how "[t]hose first six weeks of intensive training planted the seed of soldiering in me. And from that time on I never felt entirely happy away from Marines."[4] Having missed the chance to accomplish great martial feats during the Spanish-American War, Butler eagerly accepted the opportunity for service in the Philippines where his commanding officer praised him for his poise during his first test under fire.[5] Major Littleton Waller then selected him and others to accompany him to duty on the desolate island of Guam until they were diverted to China after anti-foreign Chinese forces, known as The Society of Harmonious Fists or "Boxers" to those that fought against them, began besieging the International Legation Quarter. Austria, France, Germany, Great Britain, Italy, Japan, Russia, and the United States responded by forming the International Legation Force, consisting of marines and sailors, to rescue those trapped within the International Legation Quarter.

The Marines' service in China followed a larger pattern of colonial service that characterized the years between 1898 and 1934. The Navy's transition from sailing to steam-powered vessels in the 1880s had left Marines bereft of a mission. Without even unruly soldiers to police—hardly the most glamorous job to begin with—Marines had difficulty identifying with their institution. The Spanish-American War of 1898 resolved the Corps' crisis by giving it a new mission as an expeditionary force for the Navy, a solution eagerly espoused by naval officers given the difficulties they had experienced in coordinating landing operations with the Army.[6] As a result, the Corps became increasingly involved in the support and defense of a fledgling empire. In the Caribbean and Central America, Marines became caught up in what were termed "small wars," unconventional, low-intensity conflicts to protect American economic interests.[7] Although service in Central America and the Caribbean ranged from grueling jungle patrols to less taxing garrison duty, it failed to measure up even at its best to the luxurious lifestyle enjoyed by the so-called "China Marines."

While the Spanish-American War led to important changes in the Corps' mission, participation in the Boxer Rebellion and incursions in a spate of Latin American countries propelled the Corps toward the development of an elite image during a period of transition that in effect served as the crucible for the formation of the Corps' institutional culture. Many Marines who served during these decades began to envision themselves as a brotherhood of elite warriors, and the ramifications of this identity formation continue to influence the mindset of many modern-day Marines. The etymology of crucible—a pot used for melting metals—aptly indicates how an individual's traits merged into a larger force, in this case an institution. Examining the Corps' colonial service as the formative "cauldron" that stirred Marines' identity helps trace the construction of one of the world's most distinctive institutional cultures, as epitomized by the concept of the warrior brotherhood. Even when colonial exploits lost their place as the central mission of the Marine Corps, these experiences continued to shape and drive institutional culture.

This essay addresses how the Marine Corps' participation in the Boxer Rebellion of 1900 and service as a legation guard in Beijing between 1905 and 1941 acted as a catalyst for developments in its institutional culture. More specifically, service in China sparked developments in the Corps' growing elite identity and solidified the changing role of the enlisted Marine within institutional culture, linked as it was to the conceptual development of a warrior brotherhood. While the Boxer Rebellion proved particularly important in helping to cement ideas of the ideal Marine warrior, service as Legation Guards spurred refinement of the Corps' sense of status as Marines devoted themselves to perfecting appearances and developing new traditions that reinforced their privileged position in China.

Smedley Butler was not the only hero to emerge during the Boxer Rebellion. Pugnacious New Yorker and former newsboy Private Dan Daly began a distinctive career during which he became celebrated for the extent to which he epitomized the crystallizing image of the ideal Marine. The U.S. Marines had been assigned to defend an important section of the Tartar Wall abutting the American legation quarter. There, Daly entered the burgeoning pantheon of Marine Corps heroes after he single-handedly held back an offensive while waiting for relief.

Reflecting their improved position in the Marine Corps, enlisted Marines began entering the annals of the Marine Corps' mythology at the beginning of the twentieth century. By comparing the heroes of the Spanish-American War and the Boxer Rebellion, one can trace the developing image of the idealized warrior. Sergeant John Quick received accolades for his courage in signaling naval fire while engaged in a battle with guerrillas during the Spanish-American War, an event chronicled by Stephen Crane in a prominent war dispatch. As John Lejeune described Quick, "Perhaps of all the Marines I ever knew, Quick approached more nearly the perfect type of noncommissioned officer. A calm, forceful, intelligent, loyal and courageous man he was."[8] On the other hand, some continue to remember Dan Daly for allegedly killing 37 Chinese with one hand grenade.[9] As Butler recalled, Daly was "the 'fightingest man' I ever knew in the Marine Corps . . . . Hard-boiled as the devil, but fine clear through."[10] Although Quick's name figures prominently in Corps history, he has not been celebrated to the extent that Chesty Puller, Dan Daly, and Smedley Butler have. One historian has argued that the best-known events in military history are those that engrain themselves visually in the public's consciousness. Such was not the case for Quick who demonstrated bravery under fire but unlike Daly did not epitomize the warrior spirit that animated the Corps' developing mythos.[11]

The Boxer Rebellion provided an opportunity for Marines, relative latecomers to the imperial "scramble" that exercised many European armies during the late nineteenth century, to evaluate themselves in comparison to other westerners as well as non-westerners who constituted the International Task Force. Marines had mixed opinions of those they encountered. Some Marines praised the bravery and determination of the Japanese. Captain William Harllee expressed his respect for the military bearing and courage of the British Indian troops but criticized the lack of attention the French and Russians gave to hygiene.[12] Beyond simply observing the actions of the multinational forces, Marines forged varying relationships with the different nationalities. Private Oscar Upham, for example, believed that:

> When it comes to hard work the Ruskies are OK but cannot be depended on in any emergency although they would go any place with our men and have as much faith in us as they have in their officers.[13]

In this instance, "our men" referred to American enlisted Marines; in his view, the Marines' enlisted leaders were at least the equivalent of Russian officers. Quite possibly Upham based his distinction between Russian officers and enlisted Americans on the notion of a racial hierarchy in which Anglo-Saxons, regardless of their rank, took precedence over Slavs.[14] Other Marines assessed how they compared to other military forces. One officer "studied these troops of all nations closely. I came to the conclusion we were as good as they were. Naturally the English appealed to me more strongly from our common language."[15] His attitude reflected the gradual transition to an elite identity that intensified in the early decades of the twentieth century. It also hints at the strong sense of Anglo-Saxon solidarity that prevailed among many at that time. As one American observer noted, "The British and American are almost one people here; although the expressions, 'D--- Yankees!' and 'D____ lime-juicers!' are interchanged, they are used in a spirit of affection."[16] Although the Corps sought to establish itself as an elite institution by identifying with the British during the Boxer Rebellion, later China service witnessed the Marines sometimes foreswearing identification with the British in favor of competition once they had become more confident of themselves.

Marines had long looked to non-American military institutions as models, especially British ones. Itself a replica of the Royal Marines, the Corps often borrowed from the identity of its "parent" institution, as had occurred when the Corps used the Royal Marines' motto, "*Per Mare Per Terrum*" during much of the nineteenth century. Commandant Charles McCawley (1876-1891) later changed the motto to "*Semper Fidelis*" around 1883.[17] The new motto stressed loyalty and emphasized one's emotional attachment to Corps over a more prosaic description of the varied roles of marines. It also demonstrated McCawley's goal of providing the Corps with greater independence from the Army and the Navy. As McCawley wrote in a private letter presaging the Corps' colonial service, "It is my especial desire to see the Corps placed in its proper position as the most soldierly arm of the service."[18] The Corps, despite changing its motto, retained its friendship with the Royal Marines, as evident during joint operations in Egypt (1882) and again in Nicaragua (1899) where British and American Marines alternated command and exchanged uniform buttons.[19] While serving together in the Boxer Rebellion, American Captain John Twiggs Myers led both American and Royal Marines in what was hailed as the "bravest and the most successful event of the whole siege."[20]

Despite their historical ties to the Royal Marines, U.S. Marines seemed most drawn to the Royal Welch Fusiliers, with whom they also served during the rebellion.[21] They subsequently maintained their friendship by exchanging official greetings on the national holiday of Wales.[22] As there is no mention of the Fusiliers contacting the Marines on Independence Day, one can surmise that it was the Marines who sought to associate themselves with the Fusiliers given their elite status. Marines may have identified with the Fusiliers because of one of their regimental traditions—the "flash"—consisting of black ribbons tied to a wig. This fashion had become dated during the Fusiliers' long absence from Britain due to colonial service; the Fusiliers, however, gained royal permission to continue wearing the flash, which provided them with a distinct regimental identity.[23] U.S. Marines no doubt admired the Fusiliers' appreciation for traditions and could relate to their colonial service and frequent extended absences from home.

Joint operations continued to facilitate opportunities for the diffusion of military culture at this critical juncture in the Corps' history as it sought to demonstrate its distinctiveness from other branches of the United States military. Even as British colonial military culture seeped into the Corps, Americans prided themselves on retaining their more democratic instincts conducive to nurturing a brotherhood. One correspondent noted how British officers dined on gourmet fare served by Indian servants while American officers helped themselves to the same food eaten by the troops. He wrote that the "American officer prides himself upon the fact that he lives exactly as do the men in the ranks."[24] Smedley Butler also noticed this contrast, describing how the aristocratic British officers were "seated in state" while he and his fellow officers were "crouching with a chicken which had walked entirely too far in its life."[25] Within the Marine Corps, the difficult conditions of the Boxer Rebellion, including scorching heat and limited supplies, diminished distinctions between officers and enlisted men.[26]

Officers drew on these experiences to cultivate the Corps' growing identity, in which they reserved a sphere for the experiences of enlisted Marines to strengthen their claim as warriors. Although many officers credited their non-commissioned officers with helping them learn their jobs, Smedley Butler went one step further in according enlisted Marines the role of father figures, not surprising considering he was only nineteen years old during the Boxer Rebellion.[27] Experienced enlisted Marines taught him "the tricks of the trade." They also caused him "endless trouble" given their proclivity to become intoxicated on pay day, but he was grateful that when he "was dead tired, they carried my pack, and they shared with me the food they managed to steal."[28] Virginian Major Littleton Waller played an even more crucial role in promoting the Corps' developing mythos. He had initially hoped to become a cavalryman in the Army but his diminutive height prevented him from doing so. Despite becoming a Marine by default, he would play a key role in the establishment of the Marine Corps Association in Cuba several years after the Boxer Rebellion. The warrior culture that would sustain Marines through battles like Belleau Wood, however, was not fully operational during the Boxer Rebellion. Butler, acting for once without his customary flair for dramatics, noted that even the "dare-devil" Waller acted reasonably during the Rebellion, deciding that a handful of Marines could not single-handedly defeat China: "Waller turned to me. 'I hate to give the order. But if we don't retire at once, we'll be cut off.'" Butler claimed to have responded that he suggested they "run," to which Waller replied, "Marines never run, my boy."[29] Although the Corps' mythos was not yet fully operational, it was certainly increasing as Marines like Waller repeatedly emphasized that the Corps stood unparalleled among military services. Butler remembered that "[I]t was two thirty in the morning.... But 'Tony' Waller shot some pep into us with one of his typical orations on the honor and glory of the Corps, the finest fighting force in the world."[30] More Marines began to echo similar opinions. Sergeant George Herbert wrote after one military engagement that, "We are Russians, French, Germans, Italians, Britishers and last but not least 10 American Marines and we have been into every-thing so far and lost but 5 men. I don't know how long I shall be here, but as long as I stay I'm going where these Yankee Marines go. They are daisies!"[31] As nascent experiences of brotherhood intensified in part because of the less-than-convivial circumstances of the Boxer Rebellion, enlisted Marines could no doubt identity more fully with the Corps, especially when officers like Waller expressed a concern for them. This was exemplified in an incident related by one officer, who recounted Waller's response to an invitation from an Army officer:

> Major Waller and his Marines camped on a filthy flat piled high with Chinese fertilizer.... A trim orderly came to the Major with the message, "The General's compliments, sir, and he invites the major to move his bedding roll up the hill and spend the night there...."
>
> "Present my compliments to the General and tell him that Major Waller will stay with his men."[32]

Ignoring the privileges of rank, Waller remained with his men and displayed his preference for enlisted Marines over Army officers, no matter how unpleasant the circumstances.

The presence of the United States Army in China helped spur the Corps' growing efforts to define itself, especially as Marines believed that they were intentionally assigned to "guard the rear," enabling the Army to monopolize all of the opportunities for "glory."[33] Despite such seeming setbacks, Marines ensured that they received credit for their contributions, capitalizing on various "firsts" that appeared to be especially gratifying for western imperial powers. As one American proudly noted:

> [w]hen this polyglot contingent landed at the station in Peking there was great excitement as to which nationality should lead. Captain McCalla, who had come up with our fifty marines, hurried his men at the double-quick to get it, and our troops were the first to march up Legation Street.[34]

Although they had hoped to be the first to enter the so-called Forbidden City, from which foreigners had been prohibited previously, they found their ambitions quelled by Sikh troops. Some, however, continued to maintain that Marines had been the first to open the gates of the Forbidden City.[35] Writing in a 1915 edition of the Marine Corps' *Recruiter's Bulletin*, Private Hundertmark reminded readers "that it was a Marine who first entered Peking, that it was a Marine who opened the portals of the 'forbidden' city to the world at large."[36] By then, Marines had earned the reputation among some of being "first to fight" because of their tradition of operational readiness and efficiency. In this case, the "first" was slightly different, but just as important nonetheless—despite being historically inaccurate. By touting the "firsts" earned by Marines during the Boxer Rebellion, Hundertmark reinforced the Corps' elite image and demonstrated the need for the institution's continued existence.

Despite their chagrin at not being first at everything, Marines must have been reassured by the accolades they received for their participation in the Boxer Rebellion. Private Upham, for example, recorded the following encounter with Chinese troops in his journal:

> They keep up their sniping all day but we have taught them to respect us (during the truce a Chinese Colonel in command on the wall was holding conversation with our officers; he eagerly asked who those men were that wore the big hats? On being told they were American Marines, he shook his head and said, "I don't understand them at all; they don't shoot very often, but when they do I lose a man; my men are afraid of them.)"[37]

On one level, Upham's words hinted at the defensiveness of Marines that compelled them to prove their worth to observers on a consistent basis, as revealed in Upham's need to teach others to respect the Corps' martial abilities. On another level, his words reflected an emphasis on quantifiable differences, such as marksmanship and appearance, that later would be elevated into a mystique that could not be defined. Although Marines had gained a better understanding of how their institution compared with other military services, they did not yet display the security in their elite status that would later come to permeate the Corps.

The "China Marines," on the other hand, had a distinct understanding of what it meant to be a Marine. They eagerly coveted duty in China, drawn by the country's mystique. One officer noted, "I didn't hear one of the officers say he wasn't pleased to go. To China! China! Why, that's the place everyone wants to go! The one mystic land which defies civilization."[38] Another commented in a letter to his parents that "this is an Old Country and I would not take a thousand Dollars for what I seen."[39] The recruiting bureau, recognizing the importance of travel in shaping a Marine's experience, released a "Marine Corps Travel Series" consisting of pamphlets such as "Magic China" that demonstrated the Corps' fascination with Chinese customs:

> The sea soldiers are accustomed to travel to the out-of-the-way places of the world, but the Orient has a spell that is all its own. Thoughts of

China conjure visions of towering pagodas . . . .of purse-proud mandarins and humble coolies . . . and the veiled mysteries that still remain unsolved "Somewheres [sic] East of Suez."[40]

The lure of China partly stemmed from its antiquity and its seeming cultural continuity and timelessness; the itinerant life of the Marine contrasted significantly:

> His tour of duty is only transient, but the ancient Chinese city has existed almost beyond the memory of man. The vagaries of the service shuttle a Marine from place to place so fast sometimes, he scarcely has time to learn his destination before he is on his way. . . . The very uncertainty of where a Marine will go, or what duty he will be called upon to perform, is one of the greatest attractions of the service.[41]

The seeming changelessness of China clearly contrasted with the active lives of Marines. For one Marine, travel not only enlarged his horizons but transformed him into a man. He described to his parents how "Your son that was once a boy . . . now sees the world—and it was not all through a PORT HOLE."[42] In his letter, this Marine equated travel as a process through which he became a man; he also proudly distinguished his service as a Marine to that of a sailor whose vision resulted more from observation than experience. Other Marines fulfilled childhood fantasies of adventure. Future Commandant David Shoup remarked while serving as a second lieutenant that service in China enabled him to have "many experiences which I had always longed for as a boy, and even right now, I am riding through the streets of Shanghai, China, with a human for a horse and representing the U.S. Government. Interesting? Inexplicable!"[43] The availability of laborers ready to cater to their desires reinforced the sense of privilege Marines felt. This, as well as an abundance of material goods, contributed to an inflated sense of self-importance. As one officer noted retrospectively:

> It was China as it will never be again, with the standing and prestige of the white races, which had been established with the victories of the Opium War and the Boxer Rebellion, giving them prerogatives and privileges and a lordly way of life that was looked upon by them, as well as by the Chinese, as a natural order of existence.[44]

Some Marines recognized that their position in China depended on their own empowerment in relation to the denigration of the Chinese. A few demonstrated their respect for the Chinese and immersed themselves in Chinese language and culture. Others, however, acted in a more patronizing manner. Some Marines did not feel constrained by anything if it would accomplish their goals, as one made clear in his diary:

> a sentry had to detain the train which brought the liberty party from Tientsin. The method of detaining was none other than gently but

> firmly pressing a .45 pistol against the back of the slant-eyed engineer. This was necessary in order that the train would remain a bit longer than the customary minute . . . .[45]

As this Marine also noted sarcastically in regard to the subversive actions of the Chinese train employees, they were very "successful" in stopping the train with "unerring exactitude" so that Marines had to walk a quarter mile to arrive at the station.[46] In another incident, a drunk officer began whipping his rickshaw driver while shouting "Gidapp [sic]."[47] Alcohol and power were just a few of the intoxicating substances that Marines imbibed while in China.

They also absorbed traits and traditions from other legation forces, many of which were colonial armies that had a tendency to emphasize the trappings of military service, including "epaulettes, personal heroism, polo, and an archaizing courtliness among its officers."[48] These relationships, characterized by an atmosphere of competition, helped foster the developing identity of Marines, especially in regard to the British Army's elite regiments.[49] Throughout the nineteenth century, the British Army had emphasized the importance of appearance even at the cost of military efficiency. Given their own heritage as ship guards and the requisite attention to appearances, Marines easily drew on this British characteristic and began shining their weapons so brightly that they could serve no real military purpose.[50] Smedley Butler demonstrated this obsession with appearances, although he explained that the desire to best the British purportedly came from below, with enlisted Marines devising new ways to improve their appearance, motivated as they were by the "ambitious desire to rival the smart and dazzling appearance of the Coldstream Guards, Great Britain's crack regiment."[51] For Butler, equaling the Coldstream Guards became almost a mania, as evident in a letter to Commandant Lejeune:

> Of course the British have sent their crack troops . . . . they have no better military pedigree than have we, and within a month, we will push these coldstreamers into the creek, even in appearances. Our men are more intelligent and of a higher order than theirs .. . . . Don't worry, General, no outfit of Marines were ever licked yet, and this one won't be.[52]

Butler, convinced that his Marines were just as elite as any British regiment, set out to beat the Coldstream Guards at their own game by "secretly" training 150 Marines to "drive these limiest [sic] out of business."[53] Individual Marines sometimes expressed their competitiveness with the British in more informal ways. Second Lieutenant Shoup, for example, was enjoying his discussion of Russian customs (regarding the reputed ability of Russian children to handle vodka better than some of his fellow Marines) with an "ex-Countess" when the dictates of "Semper Fidelis" interfered and he found himself escorting his intoxicated friend home. The next day his friend excused himself, blaming his "overboisterousness" on General Butler's lessons regarding the necessity of despising

Many China Marines collected similar cartoons expressing the unique nature of their service. Simpson Cartoons, Walter F. Kromp Papers, Marine Corps University Research Archives.

the "English and all their ways" after a "Limey" had rudely refused his offer of a drink.[54] The friend's actions demonstrated the extent to which some Marines internalized the nature of Anglo-American competition in China. Competition, however, did not always characterize the interaction between British soldiers and American Marines. Some Marines were so impressed by a dinner hosted by the Green Howards that they initiated their own tradition of a mess night.[55] The China Marines' 4th Regiment Band also acquired the Corps' only fife and drums corps, again the result of the Green Howards' influence.[56]

Enlisted Marines expressed their own understandings of what it meant to be a Marine through poems, letters, and other forms of expression. Ralph Greenlee, for example, carefully pasted a copy of a poem, "Here Lies a Good Marine," in his scrapbook, along with ticket stubs, illustrations, and other memorabilia he collected while serving in China. The poem, a mock memorial, described the Marines' peculiar relationship to society, implying that the more closely one connected with the Corps, the more one severed connections with society:

> Now when I die, just bury me,
> In San Diego Bay
> So the China-bound old timers,
> Will know I've passed that way.
> Don't worry about the Honors,
> No one will cry for me
> I'm just an extinct Devil-Dog-
> Called soldier of the sea.[57]

Primarily self-identified as a Marine, the poet's author—and perhaps Ralph Greenlee—seemed satisfied that only fellow Marines would remember him as they sailed by his "grave" on their way to and from duty in China. The reference to the "extinct" devil dog also referred not only to the end of the Marine's life but to the feelings of persecution that provided further impetus for strengthening the Corps' identity. In their 1933 *Legation Guard Annual*, Marines confidently announced that they were "no longer 'boots' in the military profession; behind us we have one hundred and fifty eight years of traditions and experience."[58] As they became secure in their elite identity, they rewrote their "history" to reflect it. They also celebrated images of fighters and the iconoclastic model of leadership demonstrated at times by officers like Butler since the Boxer Rebellion. A 1951 novel about the China Marines' mascot—Soochow the dog—reflected the enduring legacy of Butler's iconoclastic personality and leadership style, especially in regard to enlisted Marines. When Soochow is throw in the military jail for excessive drinking, his "fellow" Marines console him with a plan to overcome his misfortune:

> "Don't give a thought about it, pal Sooch. Why, you're not the only good man to get fouled up. . . . Why, remember the words of the famous general, Smedley D. Butler, Sooch. 'If I want good men I'll take 'em out of the brig and the mess hall.'"[59]

The legacy of Butler, then, was an ideal world in which men could be molded and shaped into Marines and in which even cooks could become warriors.

Service in China and the growing strength of the Corps' institutional culture contributed to feelings of disjunction for Marines once they returned to the United States. The following letter, published in *The Walla Walla*, the newspaper of the 4th Marines in Shanghai, gives some indication of the bewilderment felt by former China Marines:

> I reckoned as how I'd drop you a line. I just arrived in this foreign country two weeks ago and have not seen a pagoda yet. . . .
>
> We came in through the Golden Gate in a fog, so the Indians didn't fire on us. In fact they don't seem to be much fighting going on around here. I haven't heard a machine gun yet, so I guess the Confederates or else the Cantonese won.
>
> . . . . I think I'll come back to God's Country. If I stay here, I'm liable to go native. A nurse wanted to see the things I brought back from China. I picked one off and showed it to her, and she screamed. Ain't women funny? I never could understand them. Don't be surprised if you see me in Shanghai some time, as I think I'll flee from this land of the Pale.[60]

Entitled, "The Asiatic Marine," the editors prefaced the letter with the words "speaks for itself".[61] The author's opening lines inverted the usual experience of a Marine, whereby the United States became a "foreign" country in which he played the role of an expectant tourist. The displacement he presumably had experienced when first arriving in China reversed and replicated itself upon his reentry into the United States. He now feared going "native," evident in his misunderstandings with an American female when he showed her one of his souvenirs. Instead of depicting the "inscrutability" of the Chinese, as would have been typical for an American at the time, he emphasized the enigmatic nature of a female horrified by his presumably grisly Chinese item of remembrance and, by extension, revealed his own identification with the "inscrutable" Chinese.

U.S. Marines and Royal Marines in China. Picture likely taken in the 1920s. C.L Fairbairn Papers, Marine Corps University Research Archives.

Furthermore, the Marine's convoluted references to Confederates and the Cantonese as he merged the various factions fighting for power in China's civil wars with the United States' Civil War showed his feeling of homelessness unless among other China Marines.

Relative newcomers compared to some of the more experienced participants of the International Legation Force, the Marines used the Boxer Rebellion to reflect on how they compared to other military services and to create some legends of their own which helped to strengthen the idea of a warrior brotherhood. By the 1920s, the China Marines had become polished warriors who retained their reputation as fighters even as they added to their budding mystique by borrowing traditions and creating some of their own, continuing to refine what exactly it meant to be a Marine. Although many of the China Marines' legacies have become distant memories, they still help to sustain the Marine Corps' distinctive institutional culture built as it is on the twin pillars of an elite identity and a warrior brotherhood.

NOTES

[1] Lowell Thomas, *Old Gimlet Eye: The Adventures of Smedley D. Butler as told to Lowell Thomas* (New York: Farrar & Rinehart, 1933), 40.

[2] Robert Heinl, *Soldiers of the Sea: The U.S. Marine Corps, 1775-1962* (Annapolis: Naval Institute Press, 1962), 132.

[3] Robert E. Barde, *The History of Marine Corps Competitive Marksmanship* (D.C.: Marksmanship Branch, G-3 Division, HQUSMC, 1961), 8-9.

[4] Thomas, 10.

[5] Hans Schmidt, *Maverick Marine: General Smedley D. Butler and the Contradictions of American Military History* (Lexington: The University Press of Kentucky, 1987), 11-12.

[6] Jack Shulimson, "The Influence of the Spanish-American War on the U.S. Marine Corps," in *Crucible of Empire* (Annapolis: Naval Institute Press, 1993), 88.

[7] For the operational component of "small wars," see Keith B. Bickel, *Mars Learning: The Marine Corps' Development of Small Wars Doctrine, 1915-1940* (Boulder: Westview Press, 2001).

[8] John A. Lejeune, *The Reminiscences of a Marine* (Philadelphia: Dorrance and Company, 1930. Reprinted by MCA, 1990), 99.

[9] Anthony Swofford, *Jarhead: A Marine's Chronicle of the Gulf War and Other Battles* (New York: Scribner, 2003), 14.

[10] Thomas, 190.

[11] Michael C.C. Adams, *Echoes of War: A Thousand Years of Military History in Popular Culture* (Lexington: The University Press of Kentucky, 2002).

[12] Diana Preston, *Besieged in Peking: The Story of the 1900 Boxer Rising* (London: Constable, 1999),144; William Harllee, *The Marine from Manatee: A Tradition of Rifle Marksmanship* (Washington D.C.: National Rifle Association, 1984), 73.

[13] Frederic A Sharf and Peter Harrington, eds., "Account of Private Oscar Upham, American Marine" in *China 1900: The Eyewitnesses Speak* (Mechanicsburg, Pennsylvania: Stackpole Books, 2000), 166.

[14] Michael H. Hunt, *Ideology and U.S. Foreign Policy* (New Haven: Yale University Press, 1987), 79.

[15] Frederic M. Wise, *A Marine Tells It to You* (New York: J.H. Sears & Company, 1929), 31.

[16] Mary Hooker, *Behind the Scenes in Peking* (London: John Murray, 1910), 96.

[17] Allan R. Millett, *Semper Fidelis: The History of the United States Marine Corps* (New York: Free Press, 1991), 112. The first motto meant "By Land, By Sea;" the other, "Always Faithful."

[18] Charles McCawley to Lt. Col. J.C. Fields, 13 March 1878, Charles McCawley Papers, Marine Corps University Research Archives (hereafter MCURA).

[19] Richard Brooks, *The Royal Marines: 1664 to the Present* (Annapolis: Naval Institute Press, 2002), 185.

[20] Quoted in Charles Lee Lewis, *Famous American Marines: An Account of the Corps (*Boston: L.C. Page & Company, 1950), 183.

[21] Thomas, 67; Also see Philip Caputo, *A Rumor of War* (New York: Henry Holt, 1996), 22 for his Vietnam-era memories of "Mess Night"—based on the British Army's tradition—at The Basic School, the six-month course for newly-commissioned Marine officers, and for the trophies housed there that were received from the Royal Marines, Royal Welch Fusiliers, and other British regiments.

[22] Heinl, 137.

[23] Winston Churchill, "A Call for the Marine Corps," *New York Times*, 14 June 1917; Brig. Gen. George Richards, "Blood is Thicker than Water: The United States Marine Corps' Recollections of the Royal Welsh Fusiliers," *Gazette*, vol. 3, no. 1 (Mar. 1918), 61. Winston Churchill drew on these connections in a World War I newspaper article that linked the Marine Corps' colonial service to the Fusiliers.

[24] Sharf and Harrington, 218.

[25] Thomas, 52.

[26] On the difficulty of the Boxer Rebellion, see Littleton Waller to Frank Bearss, 28 June 1901, Waller Papers, MCURA. He characterized the duty as "one of the most trying known in modern times." See

Myerly, 115 for how difficult campaigns decreased the differences between officers and men in the British Army.
[27] Thomas, 59.
[28] Ibid.
[29] Thomas, 48.
[30] Thomas, 51.
[31] Sgt. George Herbert, 2 July 1900, George Herbert Personal Papers, MCURA.
[32] Harllee, 65.
[33] Similarly, during the Mexican-American War, Marines chafed at having to guard the pack train as the Army fought its way to Mexico City.
[34] Hooker, 125.
[35] Sharf and Harrington, "Journal of Mary E. Andrews, American Missionary," 195.
[36] Pvt. C. Hundertmark, "Semper Fidelis," *Recruiter's Bulletin*, vol. 1, no. 5 (March 1915), 18.
[37] Sharf and Harrington, "Account of Private Oscar Upham, American Marine," 167.
[38] David M. Shoup, *The Marines in China--1927-1928—The China Expedition which turned out to be the China Exhibition, A Contemporaneous Journal* (Hamden, Connecticut: Archon Books, 1987), 24.
[39] Snively to Brother and All, 19 Feb. 1914; Snively to Parents and All, 21 June 1912; Snively Papers, MCURA.
[40] "Magic China" in the "Marine Corps Travel Series," USMCRPB, 1935, Paul Woyshner Papers, MCURA.
[41] Ibid.
[42] Snively to Parents and All, 22 Nov. 1915, Snively Papers, MCURA.
[43] Shoup, 18.
[44] Roger B. Jeans & Katie Letcher Lyle, eds., *Good-bye to Old Peking: the wartime letters of U.S. Marine Captain John Seymour Letcher, 1937-1939* (Athens: Ohio University Press, 1998), x and 47.
[45] Shoup, 124-125.
[46] Ibid.
[47] Shoup, 93.
[48] Benedict Anderson, *Imagined Communities* (New York: Verso, 1991), 151.
[49] Louis R. Jones, Marine Corps Oral History Collection (hereafter MCOHC), 52-53; Jeans and Lyle, 42.
[50] Myerly, 14; Thomas, 290.
[51] Thomas, 20. See Jeans and Lyle, 65, for Butler's obsession with appearances. For other opinions on whether or not the fixation with appearance came from below, see Shoup, 78.
[52] J. Michael Miller, *My Dear Smedley: Personal Correspondence of John A. Lejeune and Smedley D. Butler, 1927-1928* (Quantico, Virginia: Marine Corps Research Center, 2002), 16 and 177.
[53] Miller, 63.
[54] Shoup, 103.
[55] Merrill L. Bartlett, *A Marine Corps Mess Night*, http://hqinet001.hqmc.usmc.mil/HD/PDF_Files/A%20MARINE%20CORPS%20MESS%20NIGHT.pdf; accessed 25 April 2004.
[56] Kenneth W. Condit and Edwin T. Turnbladh, *Hold High the Torch: A History of the 4th Marines* (Washington D.C.: History and Museums Division, Headquarters, U.S. Marine Corps, 1960), 146-147. Also see John M. Hart, MCOHC, 35, for the diffusion of British traditions.
[57] W.P. Smith, "Here Lies a Good Marine," Scrapbook, n.d., Ralph Greenlee Papers, MCURA.
[58] Preface, *Legation Guard Yearbook*, 1933, MCURA.
[59] Reginald Owen and Paul Lees, *Soochow the Marine* (London: Putnam & Co., 1951), 36.
[60] Unknown author, "The Asiatic Marine," *The Walla Walla*, vol. 2, no. 2 (Jan. 1929), 7-9.
[61] Ibid.

TEDDY ROOSEVELT AND THE CORPS' SEA-GOING MISSION

Jack Shulimson and Graham A. Cosmas

> *As the Navy made its transformation from wooden sailing ships to steel ships with steam propulsion, many within the Navy Department, perhaps justifiably, viewed the traditional role of Marines onboard naval vessels as an anachronism. Dr. Shulimson and Dr. Cosmas detail these failed efforts by the Navy and the White House to remove the Marines from naval vessels in the early twentieth century.*

President Theodore Roosevelt's attempt in November 1908 to remove Marine guards from the warships of the U.S. Navy resulted in a noisy congressional and public controversy. This episode is often depicted as a simple melodrama in which Marines heroically and effectively rose to save their Corps from a cabal of naval officers bent on its destruction. In fact, the issues were more complex and were related to the effort to redefine Marine Corps roles and missions in the 20th century steam-and-steel Navy. In the larger context, the controversy illustrates both the complex bureaucratic infighting that shaped so much of Progressive Era reform and the growing estrangement between the lame-duck Roosevelt and the Old Guard Republican congressional leadership.

In November 1908, the Marine Corps consisted of 267 officers and 9,100 enlisted men. Approximately one-third of this force was stationed afloat, mostly as guard detachments on warships. Another third was on shore duty outside the continental United States with the largest contingent in the Philippines. The remaining third served within the United States as navy yard guards and constituted a reserve from which expeditionary forces could be organized. Since the Spanish-American War, Marine Corps strength had expanded threefold. In the latest increase, in 1908, Congress had added almost 800 officers and men and had advanced the Commandant of the Corps to the rank of major general.

While operating under the Navy Department, the Marine Corps enjoyed the legal status of a separate Service. Its staff in Washington, headed by the Commandant, was closely allied with the powerful Navy Department bureaus and had a reputation for skillful and effective congressional lobbying. Despite this reputation, Headquarters Marine Corps, in the words of one Marine officer, was "not altogether a happy family." Major General Commandant George F. Elliott, known for his blunt and often hasty speech, was partially deaf and rumored to be overly fond of the bottle. His staff was riddled with intrigue as ambitious, politically-connected officers pursued their own bureaucratic aggrandizement. Field Marines often regarded the Washington staff with suspicion. LtCol John A. Lejeune denounced "the politicians stationed at Headquarters" and declared, "Fortunately the real Marine Corps is elsewhere and consists of the 10,000 officers and men who are scattered around the world."

Within the Navy, sharp divisions had emerged between the so-called progressive reformers and the largely conservative bureau chiefs. The reformers, mostly young commanders and captains, favored establishing a Navy general staff, modeled on that recently created for the Army. President Roosevelt generally sympathized with the reformers and had as his personal naval aide one of the most aggressive of them, Cdr William S. Sims, yet the reformers usually met frustration at the hands of the bureau chiefs who enjoyed strong congressional support. The reformers generally viewed the Marine Corps, or at least its Washington headquarters, which usually sided with the bureau chiefs, as an obstacle to their plans. One of the more vociferous Navy progressives, Cdr William F. Fullam, claimed that "the Marines and the bureau system are twins. Both must go before our Navy…can be properly prepared for war."

Since the early 1890s, Fullam had been in the forefront of a movement among naval officers to take Marine guard detachments off the Navy's fighting ships. Fullam and his cohorts especially objected to the use of Marines as ships' policemen, on the grounds that it was an anachronistic holdover from the days of the press gang and was detrimental to the training, discipline, and status of the modern bluejacket.

The Fullamites envisioned a new mission for the Marine Corps within the Navy, once the Corps was freed from its obsolete tasks and was properly organized. The reformers urged that the Marines be formed into permanent battalions and given their own transports, so that they could accompany the fleet either as an expeditionary force or to seize and fortify advance bases. While many Marine officers eagerly embraced the advance base mission, all Marines insisted that the ships' guards be retained. They claimed that service on board warships kept Marines in close day-to-day association with the Navy and provided them with many of the skills needed for expeditionary and advance base duty. By 1908, Fullam's position had gained many adherents among Navy line officers, but Headquarters Marine Corps, with its allies in Congress and the bureaus had defeated repeated efforts to remove the detachments from capital ships.

By mid-1908, naval reform was in the air. The reformers proposed to a sympathetic President Roosevelt the formation of an independent civilian-military commission to study Navy Department reorganization, specifically the breakup of the bureau system. As key instigators of the commission proposal, Fullam, in command of the Navy training station at Newport, and Cdr Sims tried to use Sims' influence with the President to have the Marines removed from ships. Fullam saw success on the Marine question as "an entering wedge" to break the power of the bureaus. "No legislation and no Congressional action are needed," he told Sims, "but it prepares the way for the new gospel – that the men and officers who go to sea and make the ship, the Navy, efficient must control."

On 16 September, Sims, in a long memorandum to the President, outlined the case against the Marines. He reviewed the 20-year history of the issue, emphasizing Fullam's arguments that the use of Marines as ships' policemen undermined the discipline and morale of the blue-jackets. Sims cited the fact that the Bureau of Navigation had twice recommended the removal of the Marines, but that "General Elliott goes to the Secretary and successfully combats the proposition." Sims urged Roosevelt to cut through this political tangle by using his executive authority to order the Marines off the ships. He stated: "The effect of removing the Marines from the ships would be electrical, because the demand is universal."

Besides Sims, Fullam used a number of other formal and informal channels to reach the President and Secretary of the Navy. On 31 August, W.D. Walker, editor of *Army and Navy Life* and a close associate of the naval reformers, urged Roosevelt to remove the Marine guards, employing essentially the same arguments as Fullam and Sims. More important, a close Fullam associate, Cdr William R. Shoemaker, in the Bureau of Navigation, convinced the bureau chief, RAdm John E. Pillsbury, to revive the Bureau's earlier removal recommendation. On 16 October, Pillsbury wrote to Secretary of the Navy Victor H. Metcalf that "the time has arrived when all marine detachments should be removed from . . . naval vessels." Secretary Metcalf brought up the proposal at a Cabinet meeting, and President Roosevelt approved it. On 23 October, Metcalf formally concurred in Pillsbury's recommendation and directed that it be carried out.

Up to this point, all those involved in making the decision had carefully avoided consulting or informing Gen Elliott. Elliott, however, had received hints that the Marines' shipboard position again was under attack. Earlier in October, Adm Pillsbury had issued an order reducing the size of the Marine guard on one of the battleships. Although Elliott had persuaded Metcalf to rescind this order, he realized that the struggle was far from over. On 30 October, he discussed the issue with Sims and stated that he planned to ask Roosevelt directly to "have the pressure stopped." Before Elliott could meet with the President, however, Secretary Metcalf informed the Commandant that the Marines were to come off the ships. Elliott at once counterattacked. After an unsatisfactory meeting with Adm Pillsbury, Elliott, on 7 November, made a final appeal to Metcalf. He presented the Secretary a long memorandum, prepared by his staff, which declared that:

> the proposed removal of Marines from vessels of the Navy is…contrary to the long established and uninterrupted custom of the service, contrary to all precedents and rulings…contrary to the wishes of Congress, and is based upon no argument which is cogent or potent.

Metcalf rejected the Marine plea and informed the Commandant that the President already had decided on removal. Elliott then requested permission to take his case directly to Roosevelt.

On 9 November, in his meeting with the President, Elliott found Roosevelt sympathetic to the Marines but firmly committed to their removal. In the course of the conversation, Elliott emphasized that many Marine officers viewed abolition of the ships' guards as the "death knell" of the Corps. Roosevelt asked whether Elliott shared this opinion. Candidly, the Commandant replied that he did not. Roosevelt then instructed the general to draw up a statement of the Marine Corps mission once the guards were removed from the ships.

Elliott entrusted the preparation of the proposed order to three officers of his personal staff: LtCol James Mahoney, LtCol Eli K. Cole, and Maj Charles G. Long. All three were Naval Academy graduates who had been closely associated with the emerging advance base mission. Their draft order avoided mention of the ships' guards and provided that Marines were to garrison navy yards and naval stations within and beyond the continental limits of the United States. Marines were to "furnish the first line of…mobile defense" for overseas naval stations, and they were to help man the fortifications of such bases. The Corps was to garrison the Panama Canal Zone and furnish other such garrisons and expeditionary forces for duties beyond the seas as necessary. In an enclosure to the memorandum, the three officers recommended organization of the Marine Corps, once the ships' guards were withdrawn, into 9 permanent 1,100-man regiments. Elliott and his staff obviously were making a virtue out of necessity by trying to stake a firm claim to the advance base and expeditionary role, as well as making an expandable expeditionary organization, while conceding the loss of the ships' detachments.

On 12 November, President Roosevelt incorporated the exact wording of Elliott's memorandum in his executive order. The order did not mention ships' guards or call for their removal, although all those concerned understood that to be its intent. During the next several months, the Bureau of Navigation gradually began the removal of the ships' detachments. By early 1909 about 800 of the 2,700 ships' guards had come off.

The immediate reaction to the executive order was predictable. Naval officers generally approved. Upon hearing the news of Roosevelt's decision, Fullam exclaimed: "Hurrah for the President! God Bless him!" and compared the executive order to Lincoln's Emancipation Proclamation.

Marine officers looked upon the executive order with misgivings at best, and most saw it as a first step toward the elimination of their Corps. One Marine officer stated: "The President's order . . . in effect reduces the Marine Corps to the status of watchmen." Rumors circulated in Washington that Marine officers were organizing to lobby Congress for reversal of Roosevelt's decision. Despite the unhappiness among his officers, Gen Elliott loyally supported the executive order in public, claiming that it would be "the making of the Marine Corps." On 16 November, in response to the reported Marine lobbying efforts, Elliott issued a special order forbidding such activity as "contrary to the motto of the Corps – for 'Semper Fidelis' would be but a meaningless term if it shone only on the sunny side of life or duty."

Even as Elliott publicly looked toward a new role for the Marine Corps within the Navy, MajGen Leonard Wood, a confidant of Roosevelt and a leading Army progressive, saw the removal of Marines from ships as an opportunity to incorporate the Corps into the Army. Wood and most other senior Army officers were looking for a way to expand the Army's infantry. The Marine Corps had a prominent place in Army proposals for achieving this objective. During 1907, the Army Chief of Staff, LtGen J. Franklin Bell, floated as a trial balloon a plan to transfer the Army's large coast artillery corps to the Navy (and incorporate it in the Marine Corps). This would leave room in the Army for more infantry regiments. Wood, then commanding general, Division of the Philippines, offered as a counterproposal the simple incorporation of the Marines into the Army. Wood, who had a wide circle of acquaintances within the Navy and Marine Corps, respected Marine military efficiency but had gained the impression that the Navy no longer needed the Corps. Late in 1907, he wrote in a letter intended for Roosevelt's eye that the Marine Corps:

> is an able body, but its desire for enlargement is productive of unrest. A large portion of the navy are in favor of dispensing with Marines on board ship. . . their numbers are . . . far in excess of the actual needs of the navy. We need them in the army

Neither of these plans had gone beyond the talking stage when Roosevelt's executive order reopened the entire issue of the Marines' future. Wood had just returned to the United States to take over the Department of the East. He was already regarded as the leading candidate to succeed Bell as Army Chief of Staff. At Roosevelt's invitation, Wood spent several days in mid-November as a houseguest at the Executive Mansion. During this visit, Wood pressed upon Roosevelt his view that the Marines should be incorporated into the Army. He argued that Elliott, through the executive order, was aiming to establish an expanded Marine infantry under the Navy Department. Wood pointed out that the President, under his executive authority, could order the Marines to duty with the Army, as had been done temporarily several times in the past. Having established such a fait accompli, Roosevelt at a later time could work out with Congress and the Service Departments the legal details of the transfer. Roosevelt was receptive to Wood's proposal. Already irritated with Marine lobbying, he told his military aide, Capt Archie Butt, that the Marines "should be absorbed into the Army, and no vestige of their organization should be allowed to remain."

While in Washington, Wood informally discussed his ideas with Gen Bell and other high-ranking Army officers. He also made an ill-fated overture to two key Marine Corps staff officers, Col Frank L. Denny and LtCol Charles L. McCawley. Both officers were well known in Washington social circles, and both had strong political connections. Denny, the son of a prominent Indiana Republican, had many Army acquaintance and nursed ambitions to become Commandant of the Marine Corps. McCawley was the son of a former Commandant and had been the military social aide to Presidents McKinley and

Roosevelt. In a chance encounter with the two men on the street in front of the White House, Wood told them that he personally favored transfer of the Marine Corps to the Army and confided that the President was inclined to such a course of action. He asked Denny and McCawley to sound out Marine officer sentiment.

On 23 November, Denny and McCawley told the Commandant, who had just returned to Washington, about the proposed merger with the Army and the President's tentative support for the idea. Much to their surprise, Gen Elliott angrily denounced such a move. In a letter of protest to Gen Wood, Elliott claimed that neither he nor the Secretary of the Navy had been told of this proposal and declared: "I would as soon believe there was a lost chord in Heaven" as to believe the President, after redefining the Corps' mission, would contemplate separating the Marines from the Navy. Replying to Elliott, Wood reiterated his own support for Army-Marine amalgamation but denied that he spoke for the President.

In a further exchange of letters, Elliott declared that Wood, as an Army general, had no right to discuss disposition of the Marine Corps, which was a separate Service. The Commandant insisted that "the entire Army and Marine Corps, with the exception of the general officers, would be bitterly opposed to such amalgamation." Wood apologized to Roosevelt for bringing his name into the discussion and forwarded all his correspondence on the subject. On 28 November, Roosevelt, in a letter addressed "Dear Leonard," committed himself on the amalgamation issue. He wrote, "You are quite welcome to quote me on that matter. I think the Marines should be incorporated with the Army." Wood on 2 December flatly informed Elliott that the President supported the transfer. The entire incident convinced Elliott, who up to now had publicly defended removal of the Marine guards, that he and the Marine Corps were being double-crossed. As he later stated, "While we had been following quietly our duties, elimination and absorption were casting unknown to us their shadows at our heels."

Elliott was among the last to learn about Wood's scheme. Almost as soon as Wood had arrived in Washington, the future of the Marine Corps had become a matter of public and private speculation. Fairly accurate counts of Wood's proposals and Roosevelt's reaction appeared in newspapers and journals. While few Marines expressed any enthusiasm about going into the Army, many thought such a course of action inevitable as a result of their removal of ships' guards. In an extreme expression of this point of view, one officer declare "It is imperative that we immediately sever every possible connection with the Navy by transfer to some branch of the Army . . ."

The regular House Naval Affairs Committee hearings on the annual Navy Department appropriation provided the scene for the first political skirmish over both removal of the Marine detachments and the merger of the Marines with the Army. On 9 December, in his testimony, Adm Pillsbury flatly stated the Navy Department position: "I think that it will be a very great mistake to put them [the Marines] in the Army. We want them in the Navy. We do not want them on board ship." Although the Marine officers, including Gen

Elliott, made no mention of the subject in their public testimony. Elliott informed the committee off the record that he now opposed removal of the ships' detachments. In perhaps the shrewdest maneuver of the hearing, LtCol George E. Richards, assistant paymaster of the Corps, responding to a prearranged question from a committee member, presented a memorandum estimating that it would cost the Navy Department an additional $425,000 to replace Marines with sailors on board ships. At the end of the session, the committee voted to hold supplementary hearings by a subcommittee on the entire Marine issue.

In the period between the conclusion of the full House committee hearings in December and the opening of the subcommittee hearings in January, the Marine Corps and its allies mobilized for the struggle. Marine staff officers prepared several detailed memoranda supporting their position. On 20 December, a group of Marine officers from several east coast navy yards met privately at Boston to discuss "the new status of the Marine Corps." While they publicly denied that their meeting had anything to do with attempts to reverse the President's executive order, few observers believed they met for any other purpose. Sims and Fullam exchanged rumors and warnings about the Marines' organizing and lobbying efforts. The Army question, meanwhile, faded into the background. Although Wood continued to discuss the subject privately, neither he nor Roosevelt took any overt action. They and the War Department were apparently unwilling to challenge directly Navy control of the Marines if the Navy wanted to retain the Corps.

When the subcommittee began its hearings on 9 January 1909, it was obvious that pro-Marine forces were in control. Representative Thomas H. Butler, who presided over most of the sessions, had a son in the Marine Corps and was on the record as opposing Roosevelt's executive order. The clerk of the subcommittee was a former Marine officer. Gen Elliott and his staff attended almost the entire hearing, and the subcommittee permitted them to cross-examine witnesses. Cdr Fullam described the atmosphere of the proceedings: "The Marine colonels were ever present. A stranger could not have distinguished them from members of the Committee. They rose at will to exhort, object, and cross-examine." Although one-sided, Fullam's observations were in the main correct. He and the other reformers faced a rigged jury and a hanging judge.

Before the hearings ended on 15 January, a parade of 34 witnesses testified. All of the Marines opposed withdrawal of the guard detachments from ships, while the Navy officers split evenly for and against. Both sides reiterated their traditional arguments for and against keeping Marines on warships. Using rudimentary cost-effectiveness analysis, they presented conflicting estimates of the expense involved in replacing Marines with sailors.

While the subcommittee focused on the cost issue, the question of transferring the Marine Corps to the Army was never far from the surface. Several Marine and Navy opponents of the executive order warned that removal of the guard detachments might lead to the Navy losing the Marine Corps, while supporters of the order affirmed their desire to keep the Marines in the Navy. Fullam, for example, declared: "If I were king here tomorrow, I would preserve the Marine Corps . . . as a splendidly organized mobile force, to serve with the Navy . . ." Secretary Newberry testified that if it were a choice between losing the Marines and putting them back on ship, "I would rather put them back aboard ship." The prospect of absorption of the Marines by the Army was also a stumbling block to congressional supporters of Roosevelt. Representative John W. Weeks, wrote to Fullam: "My mind now inclines to leave in the hands of the Executive the question of where the Marines shall serve, but takes a positive stand against action which will tend to amalgamate the Corps with the Army.

When the full Naval Affairs Committee reported the naval appropriation bill to the House on 16 January, it was clear that the Marine point of view had prevailed. The committee recommended insertion in the bill of a provision that:

> hereafter officers and enlisted men of the Marine Corps shall serve . . . on board all battleships and armored cruisers, . . . in detachments of not less than eight per centum of the strength of the enlisted men of the Navy on said vessels.

When the appropriation bill came up for consideration before the House, administration forces, assisted by vigorous Navy Department and White House lobbying, turned the tables on the Marines. On 21 January the House passed the bill without the proposed amendment to keep Marines on board ships. The fight now shifted to the Senate Naval Affairs Committee, where the Marine Corps could depend on the support of the powerful chairman, Senator Eugene Hale of Maine. Hale, a staunch Roosevelt opponent, was at loggerheads with the President over Navy Department reorganization in general and specifically had come out against the Marines off ships. Without bothering to hold hearings on the question of Marine removal, Hale's committee on 10 February reported the appropriation bill to the Senate with numerous amendments, including reinsertion of the House committee's original provision overturning Roosevelt's executive order.

On the Senate floor, the administration made a major effort to defeat the amendment. Massachusetts Senator Henry Cabot Lodge, a personal friend of Roosevelt and long-time supporter of a big Navy, led the fight, liberally supplied with argument and documents by Sims and Fullam. During the Senate debate on 16 and 17 February, Lodge restated the reformers' arguments about the need to restructure the Marine Corps, but significantly disavowed any intention to put the Marines into the Army and stated that he himself would oppose any such effort. Senator Hale, on the other hand, kept hammering at the point that Congress had equal authority with the President over the Navy Department and warned that "the underlying purpose [of removal] is to take these people away from the navy and in the end turn them over to the army." When the amendment came up for final approval on the 17th, it passed by a vote of 51 to 12. This result reflected more personal and political hostility to Roosevelt than conviction about the status of the Marine Corps. Among the supporters of the amendment were most of the Democrats and a strong contingent of conservative Republicans. All of the opponents of the amendment were either Roosevelt loyalists, such as Lodge, or Republican progressives, including William E. Borah and Robert M. LaFollette.

After Senate passage of the entire bill on the 17th, the legislation went to a conference committee headed by Senator Hale and Representative George E. Foss, Chairman of the House Naval Affairs Committee. As part of the complex bargaining over dozens of amendments, the House initially refused to accept the Senate provision on the Marines. Roosevelt, however, now was willing to surrender on the Marine issue in order to obtain favorable consideration on the other naval issues. On 18 February, he wrote to Representative Foss: "The bill as it passed the Senate will, as regards this point, do a little damage [but] it does not do very much." Roosevelt made no mention of putting the Marines in the Army and declared that he had issued his executive order "with the explicit object of retaining the marines for the purpose of an expeditionary force . . ." With this signal from the President, the House conferees gave way on the Marine issue. On 1 March, both houses passed the naval appropriation bill with the amendment requiring return of the Marine guards to the ships of the fleet.

During the remaining days of his administration, Roosevelt and Secretary Newberry attempted to find loopholes in the language of the appropriation act which would permit the President to keep the Marines off the ships. Newberry declared: "I have issued no orders about the return of Marines to the ships and will not do so."

The new President, William Howard Taft, was not about to challenge Congress and immediately took steps to reverse Roosevelt's final measures. As early as 25 January, the President-elect had taken a conciliatory tone, writing to Senator Hale:

> I intend, so far as possible, to do nothing without full consultation with you managers of the Senate, and while of course it is not expected that we may always agree, it may be asserted that we shall never surprise each other.

On 5 April, Taft's Attorney General, at the Navy Department's request, declared that in his opinion the Congressional requirement that Marines make up eight percent of a ship's crew was constitutional. Very soon thereafter, Marines began marching up the gangplanks of Navy warships, and the controversy was over.

The participants reacted predictably to the outcome. For the Army, it was a case of very little ventured and nothing gained, since Wood's negotiations had been entirely confidential and informal, although quite serious' in intent. Some Army officers, nevertheless, believed that "a great opportunity has been lost by the restoration of the Marines to the ships." Navy reformers such as Fullam railed against the decision, denouncing the "parlor and club colonels" of the Marine Corps and grumbling that the entire Navy was "at the mercy of the shore-staying staff and their political friends." More moderate reformers, for example the respected Radm Stephen B. Luce, founder of the Navy War College, warned that withdrawal of the ships' guards would have led to the "obliteration" of the Marine Corps. Taking Luce's lead, the Navy's General Board in later years would refuse to support the Fullamites in their agitation for removal of the Marine guards on the grounds that such action would lead to the loss of the Corps to the Army. Marines breathed a sigh of relief over what they considered their narrow escape and would cling ever more tenaciously to what was in effect a relatively minor mission. They viewed Fullam and his henchmen with suspicion and often outright hostility and believed they were continually vulnerable to power grabs by ambitious Army and Navy officers. On the occasion of renewed agitation by Fullam in 1913, Maj Smedley D. Butler exploded in a letter to his Quaker father, Representative Thomas Butler, who chaired the special subcommittee in 1909: "I wish somebody would beat the S.O.B. to death. Please try to help us, Father," he pleaded, "for the Lord only knows what will become of the Corps."

Despite Butler's alone-against-the-world outlook, the Marines in 1908-1909 owed their success against Roosevelt's executive order only partially to their own political action. The Marine Corps approached the removal issue with divided councils. Gen Elliott, obviously influenced by the advance base-oriented members of his informal staff, initially tried to trade acquiescence in the removal of the detachments for a reinforced and expanded Corps designed around the advance base and expeditionary missions. There was much justice in the accusation, made by both Adm Luce and Gen Wood, that the Major General Commandant was trying to take advantage of Roosevelt's order to establish an army of his own. Probably a majority of Marine officers in the field, as well as key members of the Headquarters staff, adamantly opposed removal of the guards from the beginning. Still other Marines, typified by Denny and McCawley, simply sought to turn the situation to their own personal advantage and flirted, more or less seriously, with amalgamation into the Army. Whether Elliott was simply swayed by the conflicting currents within the Corps or acting from firm conviction is not entirely clear from the evidence. What is certain is that he swung into active opposition to removal of the Marine guards only after becoming convinced that the President had betrayed him.

President Roosevelt did a great deal to frustrate his own order by, in effect, doublecrossing both the Marine Corps and the Navy reformers through his dealings with Wood. Even these factors and the Marine lobbying would not have been enough to reverse Roosevelt's order, had it not been for the general anti-Roosevelt hostility of the conservative Republican Senate leadership and the particular enmity of Senator Hale for all manifestations of naval reform. Taft's retreat from Roosevelt's policy toward the Marines foreshadowed the new President's gradual drift into alliance with the conservative faction of the Republican party. In the end, then, the ships' detachments owed their salvation at least as much to the cross-purposes of their enemies as to the efforts of their friends. Perhaps a newspaper's amateur poet had the last word:

The guard they stood at attention,
> Like they didn't give a damn,
to hear the word of the Overlord,
> The original great I am.
And he tells us that we ain't wanted,
> That the jackies will go it alone.
But I thought I heard an under word
> From a power behind the throne.

THE CULEBRA MANEUVER AND THE FORMATION OF THE U.S. MARINE CORPS' ADVANCE BASE FORCE, 1913-14

Graham A. Cosmas and Jack Shulimson

Dr. Cosmas and Dr. Shulimson explore the lessons learned from one of the Corps' widely celebrated Culebra maneuvers – traditionally credited as pivotal exercises, if not turning points, in the development of the advance base force that eventually evolved into amphibious assault. In this first exercise, nearly fourteen years after the Navy assigned the advance base force mission to Marines, the Corps finally established the necessary organizational structure to support naval doctrinal theories.

In January 1914, a Marine brigade of 1,723 officers and men defended the tiny Caribbean island of Culebra against a simulated attack by units of the United States Atlantic Fleet. Conducted during the fleet's annual winter maneuvers, this exercise was for the Marine Corps a crucial test of its ability – to perform the advance base mission which was becoming increasingly the principal rationale for the Corps' existence.(1)

The United States Navy, in the efficiency-minded Progressive Era, was trying to orient its permanent peacetime organization, training, equipment, and deployments toward its expected wartime strategy. Influenced by the doctrines of Alfred Thayer Mahan, naval leaders directed their shipbuilding programs and training activities toward creation of a battle fleet able to take command of the sea, at least in the Western Hemisphere. As part of the Navy, the Marine Corps also had to find a specific role toward which it could direct its own organization and training. The Corps' traditional missions of providing ships' policemen and sharpshooters for the fighting tops had been largely eliminated or made superfluous by modern warship technology. Fortunately, for the Marines, the technological limitations of those same warships opened the way for a new mission.

This mission was occupation and defense of an advance base for the fleet. Modern battleships, in contrast to the old sailing ships of the line, required frequent refueling, maintenance, and replenishment of stores and ammunition. Therefore, if the fleet were to operate any distance from its home ports, it had to have either permanent bases in potential overseas theaters of operations or an extensive train of supply and repair vessels. Since the United States had only a few overseas possessions, the large train was the only feasible solution for the American Navy. In any naval campaign, the fleet would have to secure a temporary advance base at which to leave the train while the fighting ships sought the enemy. The fleet, then, required an accompanying land force to seize, fortify, and defend such a base. Further, in defensive operations, for example against a European power invading the Caribbean, land forces would be needed to deny such advance bases to the enemy.

Already part of the naval establishment, the Marine Corps was the logical organization to perform the advance base mission for the Navy and indeed, any landing mission in connection with fleet operations. Traditionally, the Marines had provided ships' landing parties and guarded Navy shore installations. Moreover, during the Spanish-American War, a Marine battalion, deployed with the fleet on board its own transport, had secured Guantanamo Bay as a coaling station for the vessels blockading Santiago de Cuba, in effect establishing an advance base, although it was not called so by name. From its establishment in 1900 as a strategic planning and advisory staff for the Secretary of the Navy, the General Board assigned the advance base mission to the Marine Corps. On 22 November 1900, Brigadier General Charles Heywood, then Commandant, formally accepted the mission and pledged that the Marine Corps would cooperate gladly in carrying it out, although he warned that the effort "will necessitate very careful consideration and considerable time will be necessary for accomplishing it."(2)

In 1900, the General Board visualized the advance base force as consisting of a permanently-organized 400-man Marine battalion trained in field fortification, the landing and emplacement of heavy guns, the installation and operation of mine fields, and other coast defense activities. This battalion was to form the nucleus of a wartime expeditionary force of 1,000 men capable of seizing and holding an advance base. From 1900 through 1912, the General Board, the Navy War College, and the Marine Advance Base School refined and elaborated on the theoretical structure of the advance base force. By 1912, the Navy and Marines had adopted for planning purposes an advance base brigade divided into two 1,300-man regiments and capable of withstanding an attack by light cruisers and an accompanying landing force. One of these regiments, the fixed defense regiment, would consist of artillery, engineer, signal, searchlight, and mining companies and would have as its main armament large-caliber warship guns in temporary shore emplacements, supplemented by harbor-defense mines. The second, or mobile defense, regiment, composed of infantry reinforced by field gun and machine gun units, would repulse enemy landing forces. Both regiments, particularly the fixed defense regiment, were supposed to be kept fully organized, equipped, and trained, ready to embark on their own transports and sail with the fleet in the first days of war.

Despite the elaboration of advance base theory and doctrine during these years, practical obstacles prevented the formation of a permanent advance base force ready for deployment with the fleet. Congress never appropriated funds specifically for equipping the force, which meant that it had to compete for dollars with other programs in the rapidly-expanding Navy. The semi-independent Navy Department bureaus, especially the Bureau of Ordnance, gave the advance base force consistently low priority. As a result, in 1912 only a partial advance base outfit had been assembled, and most of the equipment composing it was obsolete.

Even if the equipment had been available, the Marine Corps would have had difficulty in providing men to use it. Although the Corps nearly doubled in size between 1900 and 1912, from 5,000 men to nearly 10,000, most of these additional Marines were required for ships' detachments and guarding Navy yards, missions which expanded as the Navy did. During most of this period, the Marines maintained a 1,000-man brigade in the Philippines, theoretically an advance base force but in fact little more than a colonial garrison. What manpower the Marines could spare from these missions was committed most of the time to the various Caribbean expeditions and interventions of the era of the "Big Stick" and "Dollar Diplomacy."

The warship detachments, which included about 2,500 Marines, were a bone of contention between the Marine Corps and a group of progressive-minded Navy officers led by Captain William F. Fullam. Fullam and his adherents, who were strong supporters of the advance base mission, argued that the Marines would have enough men to form a permanent advance base force if they would only remove what the Fullam group considered the obsolete and useless warship detachments. Marine Corps leaders, reluctant to surrender any mission, insisted that service on shipboard maintained the naval identity of the Corps as well as providing Marines with majority of the skills required for advance base operations. The Marines advocated further enlargements of the Corps so that it could meet all of its responsibilities. This issue came to a bead in 1908, when Fullam and his cohorts persuaded President Theodore Roosevelt to issue an executive order withdrawing the Marines from battleships and cruisers and redefining the Marine mission in terms of naval base defense and expeditionary duty. After a vigorous lobbying campaign by the Marine Corps, Congress forced Roosevelt in 1909 to put the Marines back on shipboard. The Navy Department subsequently disavowed its initial support for removing the ships' detachments out of fear that taking the Marines off warships would open the way for transfer of the entire Corps to the Army. For the next four years, the problem of Marine manpower distribution remained unresolved.

Although hampered by lack of equipment and conflicting missions, the Marine Corps gradually had begun harnessing its resources to carry out the advance base function. As early as 1901, the Corps temporarily established a small advance base school at Newport, Rhode Island. During the winter of 1902-1903, a Marine battalion of 500 men landed on Culebra island and emplaced some guns during the annual fleet maneuvers. In 1904 and again in 1907, the brigade in the Philippines conducted similar advance base drills. Prodded by the General Board, the Marines and the Navy Department in 1910 renewed and intensified the advance base effort. The Marines re-established their advance base school at Newport and moved it the following year to Philadelphia. Although interrupted periodically by deployment of its staff and students on expeditions, the school developed a systematic curriculum and increasingly focused the professional training and thought of Marine officers on the advance base problem. During 1911 and part of 1912, a Marine battalion of 300 officers and men was stationed at Philadelphia in connection with the school, constituting the nucleus of an Atlantic Coast advance base force. Furthermore, the

Navy Department began collecting all the available advance base material on the East Coast, which had been scattered among a number of navy yards, at Philadelphia, and in 1912 allotted $50,000 to the Bureau of Ordnance for advance base accessories.

In this same period, the Marine Corps began consolidating its shore-based establishment for greater efficiency and expeditionary effectiveness. Taft's Secretary of the Navy, George von L. Meyer, in 1910 set forth as a major objective the concentration of most Marines at one principal station on each coast, that for the Atlantic Coast being Philadelphia. During the following year, the Marine Corps centralized recruit training at four depots and organized Marines stationed at the larger navy yards into permanent 100-man expeditionary companies. The closing of six minor navy yards and naval stations during 1911 allowed some enlargement of the Marine detachments at the remaining yards. In 1911 and 1912, the Marines began routinely forming provisional brigades of up to 2,000 men and regiments of 700 to 1,000 men, from navy yard companies and ships' detachments, for service in Cuba, Nicaragua, and the Dominican Republic.
While these expeditions diverted men from advance base training, they provided Marines with invaluable experience in organizing and maneuvering what were for the Marine Corps unprecedentedly large troop formations.

By the end of 1912, all of the elements for the creation of a permanent advance base force were there to be put together. Despite the continuing diversion of Marine manpower to the Caribbean and the persistent shortages of equipment, the Marines and Navy had perfected advance base doctrine and had conducted much theoretical and some practical training, to the point where it could be put to the test.

In early 1913, the General Board decided that the time had come to conduct an actual advance base maneuver. During January, the board, after inform consultations with Marine Major General Commandant William P. Biddle, Lieutenant Colonel Lewis C. Lucas, the Commandant of the Advance Base School and other Marine officers, drew up a proposal to the Secretary of the Navy for advance base exercise. On 5 February, Admiral of the Navy George Dewey, President of the board, emphasized in a letter to Secretary of the Navy Meyer that the advance base force was an adjunct of the fleet...and its location, as well as its state of preparedness should be such as to enable it to go with the fleet upon short notice." It was time, he declared, to go beyond the "spasmodic efforts during the past 10 years" to organize and equip an advance base force. Dewey recommended that the assemblage of advance base equipment at Philadelphia be completed "without delay" and that an advance base brigade be organized and make an actual landing, emplace guns, and conduct target practice during the Atlantic Fleet's 1913-1914 winter maneuvers. Secretary Meyer on the same day, 5 February, approved Dewey's proposal and instructed Biddle to make the necessary arrangements for the maneuver.(3)

From February through April, the Navy and the Marine Corps worked out the size and organization of the Marine force that would participate in the maneuver. These deliberations were overshadowed by renewed violence in revolution-wracked Mexico, where General Victoriano Huerta had deposed popular President Francisco Madero. As a precautionary move during February, elements of the fleet entered Mexican waters and the Marine Corps formed a 2,000-man provisional brigade which deployed to Guantanamo for possible later commitment to Mexico. With most of his available men assigned to the Guantanamo brigade, Major General Biddle initially expressed doubts about forming a full-scale advance base brigade for the exercise and recommended instead use of only a fixed regiment of about 800 Marines. The General Board, supported by Meyer's successor in the new Wilson administration, Josephus Daniels, rejected Biddle's proposal and insisted that both fixed and mobile regiments be employed, at reduced strength if necessary. By early April, the Marine Corps had agreed to assemble a brigade of about 1,600 men for the maneuver, with two regiments, each of about 800 men. General Biddle also had submitted a detailed statement of his requirements for guns, equipment, and shipping. By this time, the likelihood of American military intervention in Mexico had diminished, and the Marine Corps had completed plans for withdrawing the brigade from Guantanamo, which would free sufficient men for formation of the projected advance base units.(4)

As serious planning for the maneuver began, the Marines' old nemesis, Captain William F. Fullam, now Aide for Inspections, challenged the Corps' ability to perform the advance base mission. Fullam used as his point of departure the report of a Navy board of officers who had inspected the Philadelphia Navy Yard during March, examining, among other functions of the yard, the advance base preparations there. In its report, issued on 19 April, the board found, to no one's surprise, that despite all of the effort since 1900, no effective advance base force yet existed and apportioned the blame for this situation about equally between the Navy Department and the Marines. The board's specific recommendations supported many longstanding Marine Corps proposals, including enlargement of the barracks and facilities at Philadelphia, provision of transports for the advance base force, and the securing of a special appropriation from Congress for completing the advance base equipment and organization. Most important, the inspection board echoed the Marine refrain that the Corps did not have enough men to meet all of its responsibilities.(5)

Beginning on 1 May, Fullam bombarded the Secretary of the Navy and the General Board with a series of memoranda on the inspection board's findings. He largely ignored those parts of the board report detailing Navy Department shortcomings and instead focused on the Marine Corps' failure to maintain permanent advance base battalions. Turning to his favorite hobbyhorse, Fullam argued that the Marines would have enough men for this purpose if they withdrew their ships' detachments. Fullam in his memoranda made several forward-looking proposals, including one for the establishment of what amounted to an amphibious task force of warships and transports with an embarked Marine battalion. Nevertheless, his principal and most controversial theme remained what he considered the maldistribution of Marine manpower, an allegation which the Marine Corps consistently challenged. For every Fullam memorandum, the Marines provided, in effect, the same answer: that the Marine Corps would form at least permanent fixed defense battalions if its manpower were increased or its expeditionary responsibilities reduced.(6)

For the most part, the General Board sided with the Marines against Fullam. On 21 July, the board in its major comments on Fullam's proposals rejected out of hand any removal of Marine ships' detachments, remarking that "this action, if persisted in, may eventually cause the loss of the Marine Corps to the Navy and its absorption by the Army." Like the Marines, the General Board pointed to the lack of equipment as the principal obstacle preventing development of an advance base force without any overall increase in numbers. The board proposed that the brigade in the Philippines, which was serving no real advance base purpose, be withdrawn and that other overseas Marine garrisons be reduced to free men for advance base units. At the same time, the board expressed its confidence in the capability of the Marine Corps to conduct the advance base mission, a capability that the board believed would be "fully demonstrated by the exercises which have been laid out for the Marines . . . this coming winter." The questions raised by Fullam had little impact on the plans and preparations for the forthcoming Caribbean maneuver, but they made the success or failure of that maneuver all the more critical for the Marine Corps. By this time, the joint Army-Navy Board had decided that the major United States Pacific naval bases would be Pearl Harbor and San Diego and that responsibility for garrisoning the Philippines belonged to the Army.(7)

With the return of the Marine brigade from Guantanamo in April and May, the organization of the units which were to take part in the winter maneuver went rapidly. On 30 June, the Commandant informed Secretary Daniels that five of the six companies of the fixed defense regiment had been formed at Philadelphia. These included artillery, mining, engineer, and signal companies, organized according to plans already drawn up by the Advance base School. The Commandant planned to assemble the sixth company of the fixed regiment on 15 July, using men drawn from the recruit depots. Biddle also declared that the three-inch landing gun battery for the mobile regiment had been organized and was being trained at the New York Navy Yard, while the same regiment's automatic rifle company was training at the Marine Barracks in Washington, D.C. The four infantry companies for the mobile regiment, which required no specialized training, would be formed, according to Biddle, "as has heretofore been the case when the Marine Corps has been called on to furnish expeditions; that is, by an equitable reduction in the number of men at the...navy yards on the Atlantic coast, utilizing so far as possible the companies already organized, and adding to each organization a small proportion of those men who have nearest completed their fourteen weeks' course of training at the recruitdepots."(8)

The assembly of supplies and equipment kept pace with the organization of the brigade. Guided by Commandant Biddle's requests, the bureaus issued materiel to the Advance Base School, either from their existing stocks or from new purchases. On 23 May, for example, Rear Admiral Nathan C. Twining, Chief of the Bureau of Ordnance, reported that he had already agreed to spend $50,000 for advance base equipment and now, "will probably be able to supply for advance base purposes approximately $100,000" from available bureau funds.(9)

In spite of these additional purchases, the Marines had to depend heavily on what was on hand, much of which was obsolete, especially for such crucial items as five-inch and three-inch naval guns and mines. Only after much difficulty did the Marines obtain one high-powered five-inch 51-caliber naval gun for experimental purposes and prevail on the Bureau of Ordnance to borrow two 4.7-inch heavy field guns from the Army for testing as possible anti-ship weapons. The fixed regiment's five-inch battery had four five-inch 40-caliber guns, which were less effective against ships. The bureaus flatly refused to purchase draft animals for the mobile regiment's field guns, despite Marine protests that "it is . . . neither desirable nor practical to land men from the fleet to take the place of animals for this purpose."(10)

The Marines had better fortune securing transports and landing craft. At Biddle's suggestion, the Navy Department refitted the receiving ship *Hancock* at the New York Navy Yard, as a Marine transport. The Marines planned to use the *Hancock*, a 6,000-ton former ocean liner, to carry the fixed regiment and the brigade headquarters, while the existing smaller Navy transport, the *Prairie*, would embark the mobile regiment. After jurisdictional wrangling between the Bureaus of Ordnance and Construction and Repair, the Navy Department collected or built an odd assortment of landing craft. These included, in addition to the small boats of the transports, two 24-foot cutters, two motor sailing launches, two steam launches, a large steel fighter with a derrick specially constructed for landing heavy guns, and four Lundin lifeboats which could be rigged together in pairs to support rafts. (11)

By mid-summer, most of the equipment and supplies for the fixed regiment had been assembled at Philadelphia, and the troops had begun their arduous training. Captain Frederick M. Wise, commander of Company I, the three-inch naval gun company, recalled:

> . . . The easy days at Philadelphia were over. With drills and four hours a day schooling, we didn't get out of the yard until four-thirty in the afternoon. Then we had to study at night. . . . Hours every day in the yard we had to haul those three-inch naval guns around. We had to build a portable railroad. We had to dig pits. We had to build gun-platforms. We had to mount the guns. And then, when we had it all done, we had to tear the whole business down and do it all over again!(2)

In September, when the *Hancock* arrived at Philadelphia, the Marines added embarkation and disembarkation drills to their training schedule. By this time, planning for the exercise was well under way. In late July, the General Board and Assistant Secretary Franklin D. Roosevelt selected Culebra, a small island 16 miles east of Puerto Rico, as the advance base site for the maneuver. During the next two months, the General Board worked out the overall schedule and objectives for the problem; Rear Admiral Charles J. Badger, Commander-in-Chief, Atlantic Fleet, prepared detailed plans for the joint activities of the fleet and the brigade; and the Advance Base School drew up the plans for the fortification and defense of Culebra.(13)

The resulting scenario and schedule of activities, approved by Secretary Daniels on 20 October, assumed that a European power, designated RED, would declare war on the United States (BLUE) on 15 December 1913. The BLUE Atlantic Fleet, with its train, would concentrate at Culebra to meet the advancing RED fleet. On 7 January 1914, the BLUE fleet would return to the U.S. east coast to counter a sudden threatened attack by a RED detachment. The BLUE train would remain at Culebra, and on 8 January the Blue advance base force, the actual Marine brigade, would arrive on. Culebra and establish its defenses. On 18 January, a presumed RED light cruiser task force, accompanied by a fast transport carrying about 1,000 troops, would appear off Culebra, its mission to destroy the BLUE advance base and capture the train. From 18 to 23 January, the U.S. Atlantic Fleet, playing the role of the RED aggressor force, would conduct a series of simulated attacks on the advance base brigade, including a landing of sailors and Marines. These joint exercises would end on the twenty-third and the Marines then would remain on the island for target practice and other training, and a possible second attack by the fleet, re-embarking for home on 9 February.(14)

Although the aggressor force in this exercise was code-named RED, the scenario was clearly derived from the Navy's BLACK plan for war with Germany. Since the turn-of the century, a long series of Navy War College studies and plans had assumed that in a naval war with Germany, "Culebra is the key to the Western Atlantic and Caribbean regions," either as a concentration point for the U.S. fleet or an advance base for the attacking German fleet. In fact, as is now known, German war plans for naval operations against the United States called for the early seizure of Culebra. For the Marines, then, the forthcoming maneuver was a rehearsal for probable wartime operations as well as a test of their organization and capability to carry out the advance base mission.(15)

Marine preliminary activities for the maneuver began on 1 November when Captain Earl H. Ellis, who had recently completed a study of advance base problems at the Navy War College, left for Culebra to reconnoiter the artillery positions and camp sites designated in the Advance Base School defense plan. Upon his return, Ellis confirmed the feasibility of the planned deployments. While Ellis was still at Culebra, the Navy Department, as a result of renewed diplomatic pressure by the Wilson administration on the Huerta regime in Mexico, pushed forward by a month the formation of the mobile regiment. On 27 November, the regiment commanded by Lieutenant Colonel John A. Lejeune, sailed from Philadelphia on the *Prairie* for Pensacola. From Pensacola, the regiment could deploy either to Mexico or to Culebra.(16)

At Philadelphia, the fixed regiment commanded by Lieutenant Colonel Charles G. Long, began loading its equipment on board the *Hancock* on 18 December. This embarkation had many modern features, including the appointment of a single embarkation officer and a fairly sophisticated combat loading plan, which was partially disrupted by the last-minute arrival of some of the supplies. Despite difficulties in moving the heavy equipment from the warehouse to the pier, the regiment had finished embarking all of its men and materiel by noon on 3 January. Besides the six companies and staff of the fixed regiment the *Hancock* carried the brigade commander, Colonel George Barnett, and his staff and the brigade hospital. Also attached to brigade headquarters and embarked on the *Hancock* was a Marine aviation detachment of two officer-pilots and 10 enlisted mechanics with two primitive wood and fabric pusher biplanes borrowed from the Navy.(17)

At Pensacola, the mobile regiment had spent a cold, damp December, warmed for some of the younger officers by what Lieutenant Colonel Lejeune characterized as "a very gay time with the girls." On 19 December, Lejeune received orders from Headquarters Marine Corps to embark his men so as to sail on 3 January. In contrast to the fixed regiment with its heavy equipment, the more lightly armed mobile regiment had little difficulty in loading on board the *Prairie*. By 7 P.M. on 3 January, Lejeune could report his four infantry companies, automatic rifle company, and landing gun company all embarked.(18)

By 4 January, both the *Hancock* and *Prairie* were steaming toward Culebra. Conditions on both ships were crowded and uncomfortable. The appropriations for refitting the *Hancock* had run out, and the job was only partially completed. Compounding the difficulties, and despite the Marine Corps' emphasis on serving on board Navy ships, the majority of the fixed regiment had not been to sea before. Most of the men suffered from seasickness. Long remarked, "The carelessness of seasick men resulted in bad odors," but observed that the ship's food was well prepared and served "considering the circumstances." Life on the *Prairie*, if anything, was even worse. Lejeune bluntly stated that the ship "is unfitted for use as a transport." His 2d Battalion commander, Major Wendell C. Neville, compared the Marine junior officers' quarters to "a cheap Bowery lodging house."(19)

Except for the creature discomforts, the voyage was uneventful. Most of the higher-ranking officers spent much of their free time speculating on who would be chosen the new Commandant. In November, Major General Biddle had announced his intention to retire, and Colonel Barnett and Lieutenant Colonel Lejeune, both of whom had powerful political support, were active candidates for the position. Secretary Daniels had delayed naming Biddle's successor until Congress passed a law limiting the Commandant's term in office to four years. As the transports steamed toward Culebra, all Marines knew that Daniel's decision was imminent. Most informed observers, including Lejeune, who was aware of his own relatively junior rank, believed Colonel Barnett to be the frontrunner.

Nevertheless, for both Barnett and Lejeune, successful performance in the Culebra maneuver was all the more imperative.(20)

On 9 January, a day later than scheduled, the *Hancock* and *Prairie* dropped anchor off Culebra. Both regiments began disembarking the following day. Because the *Hancock* was too large to safely enter the principal anchorages of Culebra, the Marines of the fixed regiment had to transfer themselves and their equipment onto their landing craft in the open sea. Although hampered by contrary winds and the unsuitability of some of the craft, the regiment by 18 January had managed to move its men and equipment to shore, haul its guns and materiel to the headlands where its batteries were to be located, blast out gun pits, and mount the guns, as well as setting up camp and completing mine firing stations and other installations. The fixed defense regiment was deployed along the southwestern and southern shores of the small, mountainous island, with the five-inch and three-inch naval gun batteries and the mine fields positioned to protect Great Harbor, a deep indentation in the southern shore where the hypothetical fleet train was presumed to have taken refuge.

As with the embarkation, the disembarkation of the mobile regiment went more easily. Lejeune positioned one of his infantry battalions on the southeastern tip of Culebra to protect the flank of Great Harbor, with one company located on the offshore islet of Culebrita. The other infantry battalion, supported by the automatic rifle company, deployed along the western and northwestern shores of Culebra, covering the most likely landing beaches. Lejeune placed his three-inch landing gun company on a 480-foot hill from which it could support the infantry defenses. The Marines of the mobile regiment dug trenches commanding the beaches, cleared fields of fire, and cut trails connecting their various defensive positions. They installed barbed wire entanglements, and the automatic rifle company, applying a lesson from the Russo-Japanese War, erected bomb-proof roofs over several of its gun positions. The Marines were hampered in their work by the hard rocky soil, the tough tropical vegetation, and inadequate tools. Lejeune complained:

> Machetes were of no value, the edges turning after slight use and the handles cracking. The picks were made of soft metal, and the scythes were useless for the same reason. The metal of the drills was too soft, the wire cutters did not cut. (21)

While the two regiments established their positions on shore, Barnett set up brigade headquarters at the abandoned U.S. naval station near the head of Great Harbor. By the eighteenth, the Marine defenses were ready. Everyone heaped praise on the way the men had worked. Barnett later recalled:

> . . . It was a never-ending joy to be associated with men and officers who worked night and day as loyally, as incessantly under great difficulties and with as much *esprit de corps* as these men did. It was certainly a perfect joy to see them work.

They dug and they blasted and pulled and dragged these guns up those mountains in a perfectly phenomenal manner.(22)

On the night of the 18th, ships of the Atlantic Fleet which had arrived off Culebra two days earlier, began the joint exercise. For the next two days and nights, the fleet conducted a series of simulated attacks on the Marine defenses. The destroyers made day and night reconnaissances and attempted to sweep the mine fields. Acting the part of enemy light cruisers, the battleships simulated the bombardment of the Marine shore batteries. Simultaneously, the Marine mining company tracked the enemy ships and pretended to detonate mines under them. During the day, the Marine aviators flew reconnaissance and spotting missions over the attacking ships. Marine gunners blazed away with such enthusiasm that Barnett found it necessary to order that:

> Owing to the expenditure of the very limited supply of blank ammunition for the Five-Inch Batteries, . . . those batteries will . . . simulate fire by firing one blank charge as the first round. To simulate succeeding rounds they will fire smoke pots in the afternoon and green stars from Very's pistol at night.(23)

The climax of the joint exercise occurred in the early morning hours of 21 January, when the mixed regiment of 1,200 sailors and Marines from the fleet attempted a landing. For this part of the maneuver, Rear Admiral Badger departed from his general policy for the exercise of not assigning umpires or determining victory or defeat in any particular engagement. Badger appointed Captain William S. Sims of the destroyer flotilla and eight other Navy officers umpires for the landing.

Shortly before dawn on the 21st, the assault regiment, supported by the guns of the destroyers of the 6th Division, began its landing at Firewood Bay, on the western side of Culebra. The Marines reacted rapidly. They placed heavy rifle, machine gun, and artillery fire on the approaching boatloads of sailors and Marines. Observing the action with Lejeune, Sims reported that the landing boats "were plainly visible . . . from all occupied positions . . . due partly to the moon, which was one-quarter full, to the searchlights of the bombarding vessels playing on the hills above, to a bonfire fired by the defense, and to the fact that bluejackets were in white uniform." As the boats reached shore, Lejeune reported, the attackers "huddled together in masses along the narrow strip of beach, . . . literally surrounded by a semi-circle of fire." The destroyers simulated a heavy bombardment that, in Sims' judgment, would have possibly silenced the Marine landing gun battery, which was firing from a dangerously exposed position; but the Chief Umpire concluded that "it is improbable that the landing force could have effected a successful landing in sufficient numbers to have made any impression on the defense . . ." Nevertheless, as the result of a prior agreement with Barnett, Sims allowed the naval force to continue its attack from the beach. At 0700 he ordered a ceasefire and declared a victory for the defense, which had held its main line of resistance and maneuvered its reserves effectively to contain enemy breakthroughs.(24)

Although the landing and its repulse were the highlights of the maneuver, the Marines of the advance base brigade remained on Culebra for two more weeks. The joint exercise with the fleet continued through the twenty-third with additional simulated bombardments and mine sweepings. Also on the twenty-third, a 350-man fleet Marine battalion, in a second landing attempt, overran the mobile regiment company on Culebrita. After the end of the joint exercise and the departure of the fleet, the fixed regiment conducted target practice and experimental firings of the five-inch 51-caliber naval gun and the Army 4.7-inch field gun. The Marines concluded from these tests that both guns deserved further consideration as advance base weapons. The mining company attempted to fire its mines, but only succeeded in detonating one; the connecting cables to most of the mines had leaked and short-circuited the firing mechanism.

During the same period, the mobile regiment conducted infantry maneuvers and field artillery target practice. Two special boards of Marine and naval officers made studies of alternate advance base sites in the Culebra area and reviewed and elaborated on the existing Culebra defense plan. Early in February, good news arrived for Barnett. At three o'clock one morning, he recalled later, his aide "came running into my room yelling like a wild Indian, telling me I had been appointed Major General Commandant of the Marine Corps." An impromptu celebration parade by pajama-clad officers and men followed in the hot and rainy darkness, concluding with champagne from the *Prairie*'s mess.(25)

Even as the target-practice and training continued, the Marines began dismantling their batteries and moving their heavy equipment back on board the transports. By 9 February, as originally planned, both regiments had completed re-embarkation, and the *Hancock* and *Prairie* sailed for the United States. The brigade arrived at Pensacola on 15 February. Barnett then left the brigade to assume his new duties as Commandant in Washington, turning over command to Lejeune.

The various elements of the brigade went in different directions from Pensacola, due to the continuing tension with Mexico. Part of the mobile regiment soon sailed on the *Prairie* for Vera Cruz, where, as Lejeune wryly put it, "they will wait for something to happen."(26) The fixed regiment went to Mobile and New Orleans to take part in Mardi Gras festivities. Captain Frederick H. Delano, adjutant of the mobile regiment, looked on these visits as "not good for discipline, but suppose they have to be done to keep the service in the public eye."(27)

For the Marine Corps, the Culebra maneuver was significant from many points of view. The maneuver demonstrated that the Marines could organize an advance base force on short notice and carry out all the complex steps of an advance base operation. The Marines had learned many practical lessons, including the need for expeditionary packaging of supplies and equipment, a more accurate assessment of the proper number and types of landing craft, the importance of adequate" ground transportation once on shore, and the value of aircraft for reconnaissance and possibly bombing enemy ships. Many of the practices employed by the Marines in the maneuver, such as combat loading of vessels, would become mainstays of later amphibious doctrine. Participating in the Culebra maneuver, besides Commandant-designate Barnett, were two other future Commandants of the Marine Corps: Lieutenant Colonel Lejeune, commanding the mobile regiment, and Major Wendell C. Neville, commander of one of Lejeune's battalions. Captain Earl H. Ellis, the brigade intelligence officer, would become one of the Marine Corps' most influential early articulators of amphibious doctrine.

Most important, a Marine advance base force at last came into being. The two regiments of the brigade, although diverted to expeditionary duty at Vera Cruz and later in Haiti, the Dominican Republic, and Cuba, maintained a continuous existence until replaced by the East Coast Expeditionary Force following World War I. It can be said, then, that the advance base brigade at Culebra was the forerunner of the modern Fleet Marine Force.

NOTES

1. This paper is based on the following sources: Records of the General Board of the Navy, Operational Archives Branch, Naval Historical Division, Washington; D.C., particularly Files 408 and 432 for the years 1900-1915; Records of the U.S. Marine Corps, RG 127, U.S. National Archives, especially File 1975 for the years 1900-1915; Black War Plan, Ref. No. 5y, War Portfolio No.1, General Board Records, hereafter Black War Plan; General Records of the Navy Department, RG 80, U.S. National Archives; Capt. Earl H. Ellis, Report of a Reconnaissance Made of Culebra Island and Adjacent Cays, 8-23 Nov 1913, with Enclosures, USMC Records, FRC, Suitland, Md., hereafter Ellis, Reconnaissance Report; Biographical and Subject Files, Reference Section, History and Museums Division, Headquarters Marine Corps; George Barnett Papers in Personal Papers Collection, History and Museums Division, Headquarters Marine Corps; John A. Lejeune Papers, William F. Fullam Papers, William S. Sims Papers, and Josephus Daniels Papers, Library of Congress; Annual Published Reports of the Secretary of the Navy and the Commandant of the Marine Corps, 1900-1915; *Army and Navy Journal*, 1900-1915. The following secondary sources have been consulted: Robert Debs Heinl, Jr., *Soldiers of the Sea* (Annapolis, 1962); Frank O. Hough, Verle E. Ludwig, and Henry I. Shaw, Jr., *Pearl Harbor to Guadalcanal, Vol.1 of History of U.S. Marine Operations in World War II* (Washington, 1958); Jeter A. Isely, and Philip A. Crowl, *The United States Marines, 1775-1975* (New York, 1976); Raymond G. O'Connor, "The U.S. Marines in the Twentieth Century: Amphibious Warfare and Doctrinal Debates," *Military Affairs*, 38:3 (Oct 1974), pp. 97-103. We are grateful to Dr. Allan R. Millett for permitting us to examine the pertinent draft chapters of his forthcoming history of the U.S. Marine Corps.
2. President, General Board, ltr to Secretary of the Navy, dtd 6 Oct 1900, and BGen Comdt, USMC, ltr to President, General Board, dtd 22 Nov, 1900, File 408, GB Records. For general development of the early advance base force, see Graham A. Cosmas and Jack Shulimson, "Continuity and Consensus: the Evolution of the Marine Advance Base Force, 1900-1924" (paper Delivered at Citadel Conference on War and Diplomacy, 1977).
3. Proceedings of the General Board, Vol. 5 (1913), pp. 10, 18, 22, 32; President, General Board, Ltr to Secretary of the Navy, dtd 5 Feb 1913, and Secretary of the Navy, 1st Endorsement, to MGen Cmdt, dtd 5 Feb 1913, File 1975-10, RG 127.
4. MGen Cmdt, USMC, Ltr to Secretary of the Navy, dtd 24 Feb 1913. File 5503, RG 80; President, General Board, ltr to Secretary of the Navy, dtd 8 Mar 1913, File 432, GB Records; MGen Cmdt USMC, ltr to Secretary of the Navy, dtd 10 Apr 1913, File 1975-10, RG 127.
5. Report of Inspection of Navy Yard, Philadelphia, conducted 25-28 Mar 1913, from Board of Inspection, Navy Yard, Philadelphia, to Secretary of the Navy, dtd 19 Apr 1913, File 1975-10, RG 127, and Permanent File Binder No.27, RG 38, Board of inspection for Shore Stations.
6. See Aide for Inspections, memos to Secretary of the Navy, dtd 1 May, 23 June, and 28 June 1913, File 432, GB Records; MGen Cmdt, USMC, ltr to Secretary of the Navy, dtd 17 May 1913, File 1975-10, RG 127; Gen Cmdt, ltr to Secretary of the Navy, dtd 7 June 1913, File 432, GB Records.
7. President, General Board, memo to Secretary of the Navy, dtd 21 July 1913, File 432, GB Records.
8. MGen Cmdt, USMC, memo to Secretary of the Navy, dtd 30 June 1913, File 408, CB Records.
9. Chief, Bureau of Ordnance, memo to Navy Department (Materiel), dtd 23 May 1913, File 1975-10, RG 127.
10. Chief, Bureau of Ordnance, memo to Navy Department (Materiel), dtd 26 May 1913, and HQMC, Memo to Secretary of the Navy (Personnel), dtd 11 July 1913, File 1975-10, RG 127; Senior Member, General Board, ltr to Secretary of the Navy, dtd 26 July 1913, File 408, GB Records.
11. MGen Cmdt, USMC, memo to Secretary of the Navy, dtd 10 April 1913; Chief, Bureau of Navigation, memo to Council of Aides, dtd 24 April 1913; and Navy Department, memo to Bureau of Ordnance, dtd 21 May 1913: File 1975-10, RG 127. Senior Member Present, General Board, memo to Secretary of the Navy, dtd 26 July 1913, File 432. GB Records; Bureau of Construction and Repair, memo to Navy Department (Materiel), dtd 15 Aug 1913, File 5103, RG 80.
12. Frederic M. Wise, *A Marine Tells it to You* (New York, 1929), p.119.
13. Acting Secretary of the Navy, ltr to President, General Board, dtd 35 July 1913, File 1975-10, RG 127; 2d Senior Member, General Board, ltr to Secretary of the Navy, dtd 26 July 1913, with Navy Department

Approval, dtd 29 July 1913, File 432, GB Records; C. E. Vteeland, memo to Secretary of the Navy, dtd 13 Sept 1913, Subj: Comprehensive Plan for THE CULEBRA MANEUVER 177 Work of Advance Base Expedition from date of Embarkation to Completion of Work, File 1975-80-20, RG 127; Charles G. Long, memo to MGen Cmdt, dtd 5 Oct 1913, forwarding Advance Base School plan for defense of the island of Culebra, in Ellis Reconnaissance Report; U.S. Atlantic Fleet, memo, dtd 13 Oct 1913, re: Joint Exercise of Fleet and Advance Base Detachment, Winter 1914, in Ellis Reconnaissance Report, hereafter Atlantic Fleet Plan.

14. Atlantic Fleet Plan.
15. Black War Plan, p. 1, and "Studies and Conclusions of Naval War College, 1901-13," App. D, Black War Plan. For references to the German plans, see Richard W. Turk, "The United States Navy and the Taking of Panama, 1901-03," *Military Affairs* 38 (October 74); pp. 92-96, and John A.S. Grenville and George Berkeley Young, *Politics, Strategy, and American Diplomacy: Studies in Foreign Policy, 1873-1917* (New Haven, Conn., 1966), pp. 305-307.
16. Ellis Reconnaissance Report and LtCol John A. Lejeune, Report to Brigade Comdr, subj: Maneuvers and Operations, dtd 31 Jan 1914, File 1975-80-20, RG 127, hereafter Lejeune, 2d Regiment Report.
17. 1st Adv Base Regt, Order No.1, dtd 17 Dec 1913, File 1975-80-20, RG 127, and LtCol Charles G. Long, Report to Brigade Comdr, Subj: Operations of 1st Regiment from Dec 18, 1913 to January 25, 1914, dtd 30 Jan 1914, File 1975-80-20, RG 127, hereafter Long, 1st Regt Report.
18. Lejeune, 2d Regt Report and LtCol John A. Lejeune, ltr to Augustine Lejeune, dtd 30 Dec 1913, Lejeune Papers.
19. Long, 1st Regt Report; Lejeune, la Regiment Report; CO 2d Battalion, 2d Advance Base Regiment, Report to CO, 2d Regiment, subj: Maneuvers and Operations, dtd 27 Jan 1914, File 1975-W20, RG 127.
20. Josephus Daniels, *The Wilson Era: Years of Peace, 1910-1911* (Chapel Hill, 1944), pp. 322-324; *Army and Navy Journal* (Dec 1913), p. 437; Folder, "Candidacy for Commandant, 1900-1913," Lejeune Papers.
21. Lejeune, la Regiment Report.
22. U.S. Congress, House, Committee on Naval Affairs, Hearings on Estimates Submitted by the Secretary of the Navy, 1915, 63d Congress, 1st Session, 7 Dec 1914, p. 446.
23. 1st Advance Base Brigade, Brigade Order No.6, dtd 19 Jan 1914, File 1975-80-20, RG 127.
24. Chief Observer, memo to CinC Atlantic Fleet, Subj: Report of Chief Observer on Landing Operations by the Fleet on 21 January 1914, dtd 23 Jan 1914, File 1975-80-30, RG 127; LtCol John A. Lejeune, Report to Brigade Commander, "Battle of Firewood Bay," dtd 24 Jan 1914, File 1975-80-20, RG 121.
25. Col George Barnett, memo to CinC Atlantic Fleet, subj: Report of Maneuvers and Operations from January 3-to January 24,1914, dtd 3 Feb 1914, File 1975-80-20, RG 127; Lt Col Charles G. Long, Report to Brigade Comdr, Subj: Target and Mine Practice and Reembarkation of 1st Regiment; Jan 24 to Feb 8, 1914, File 1975-80-20, RG 127. Quote is from MGen George Barnett, "Soldier and Sailor Too" (Unpublished MS, History and Museums Division, HQMC), Chapt. 24, p. 8.
26. LtCol John A. Lejeune, ltr to Augustine Lejeune, dtd 5 Feb 1914, Lejeune Papers.
27. Frederick H. Delano, ltr to Mrs. Delano, dtd 14 Feb 1914, Frederick H. Delano Papers, Military History Research Collection, Carlisle Barracks, Carlisle, Pa.

SEA SOLDIERS ASHORE: U.S. MARINES IN WWI

Joseph H. Alexander

In the long history of the Marines, their use in World War I, ironically, stands out as both an anomaly in terms of mission and as a watershed event in terms of performance. Colonel Alexander, a retired Marine and award-winning historian, demonstrates how this sea service proved so capable in France when used redundantly as a land army. He then describes the long-term institutional effects of the campaign on the Marine Corps. At the end of the essay, the author speculates about the Corps' use in another protracted land campaign alongside the Army, specifically in the Middle East. Remarkably, he did so prior to both American wars in the Persian Gulf.

Col John A. Lejeune landed in VeraCruz on 22 April 1914 to take command of the Marine brigade engaged in President Wilson's bloody show of force against the Mexican Government of Victoriano Huerta. The brigade was truly a composite force, a hasty assembly of ships' detachments, the embryonic advance base force, and the gleanings of a dozen Marine Barracks from across the country. Four Marines died in the sharp street fighting that occurred in the initial days of the VeraCruz occupation. In all, however, it was a routine expeditionary landing for the Marines, one of many such deployments as "colonial infantry" during America's unabashed imperialistic era.

Four years later, in November 1918, Lejeune was a major general commanding the 2d U.S. Division in France during the climactic campaign to force the crossing of the Meuse River under a hellish German bombardment. Lejeune's soldiers and Marines were halfway across the Meuse at the hour of the final Armistice. When the shooting stopped, his Marines counted well over 11,000 casualties in the Great War, a figure considerably greater than the total size of the entire Corps at the time of the VeraCruz landing.

World War I was a watershed for many institutions throughout the world. The U.S. Marine Corps was no exception. The contrast between Lejeune's patchwork expeditionary force in Vera Cruz and his veteran infantrymen in France is illustrative of this watershed within the Marine Corps. After 142 years of service with the fleet, the Marines abruptly opted for a protracted campaign ashore with the Army, a significant employment almost completely devoid of naval contact. And although the post war pendulum did swing back toward integration with the fleet, the precedent had been set. Today, operating under an omnibus proviso in its mission statement to be ready to "conduct such other duties as the President may direct," the Marine Corps well recognizes it could find itself involved in another protracted campaign ashore with the Army.

This article will analyze the employment of U.S. Marines during World War I and assess the institutional impact of the maritime/continental shift on the postwar Marine Corps, to include implications for joint employment ashore in the future.

The Marine Corps at the outbreak of World War I was truly a Service at the crossroads. Its traditional role of manning the "fighting tops" and boarding parties of the frigate Navy had long been eclipsed by technology. Its expeditionary landings in the various "Banana Wars" of the early 1900s, while useful, were arguably not worth the operating expense of a separate Service. Although the Marines could point with pride to the generous publicity they received in the VeraCruz fighting, they had in truth been subordinate all along to the operational command of, sequentially, the Navy and the Army in that seven-month affair. And while Marines have traditionally worried about losing their functional identity to another Service, that worry was acute and well founded in 1917. The Marines were in a backwater, and they knew it.

The solution to the Marines' institutional dilemma was perceived by some to be the undertaking of the advance base mission. A characteristic of the post-frigate Navy was its new dependence on overseas coaling (later fuel oil) stations necessary to sustain a naval campaign. For years, the General Board of the Navy had recommended the mission of seizing and defending advance naval bases for the Marine Corps. The Corps was at first reluctant to accept the concept. It would involve specialized training and equipment that could only be provided at the expense of other, more traditional, roles. Fortunately for the Corps, a pair of open-minded field grade officers, George Barnett and John A. Lejeune, appeared at key leadership levels and enthusiastically supported the advance base concept. Barnett commanded the experimental advance base force in the Culebra maneuvers of 1914 and was directly selected as Major General Commandant. The advance base mission was formally adopted, forces assigned, and equipment procured. This was a healthy measure, a distinct progression toward the amphibious doctrine of World War II, but it was a premature development for the first war.

Thus, when Congress on 6 April 1917 declared "that a state of war exists between the United States and the Imperial German Government," the Marine Corps had the following roles and missions on the books:

> to provide detachments for certain vessels of the Navy; to garrison regular navy yards and naval stations; to defend when necessary naval stations beyond the continental limits of the United States; to provide a force of Marines for seizing and defending advanced naval bases in time of war; to help garrison the Canal Zone; and to furnish such garrisons and expeditionary forces for duties beyond the seas as might be necessary in time of peace.

The absence of verbiage to specify protracted service ashore with the Army or "such other duties as the President may direct" is obvious in the foregoing – in spite of the fact that President Wilson was authorized by law to detach Marine forces from the Navy Department for operations under command of the Army. This was not an uncommon occurrence; it had, in fact, been utilized as recently as the Vera Cruz crisis. The Marine Corps was simply not anticipating a commitment to the Western Front in the pending war, despite the evidence in the daily newspapers. The Corps did not possess a war planning staff and showed little ability to project a meaningful role for itself in the future conflict. Lejeune came the closest in a 1916 article on the advance base concept in the first issue of the *Marine Corps Gazette*:

> In the event of a war with a non-naval power, our duties would be that of the advance guard of an army. The Marine Corps would be the first to set foot on hostile soil in order to seize, fortify and hold a port from which, as a base, the Army would prosecute its campaign. Here again being first on the scene, the Corps . . . would be ready to join the Army in its march against the enemy.

Lejeune had the right concept but the wrong war. The American fighting role in France was to be almost exclusively a continental campaign without significant, offensive maritime support. All the ports of debarkation were firmly within allied hands. It was time for Barnett and Lejeune to resort to politics and improvisation.

Once the United States had entered the war, it became Barnett's goal as Major General Commandant to see that his Marines got a "piece of the action." He was aware that the Corps would probably not survive a national experience like the Great War if it were relegated to a minor maritime role in a classic continental struggle. He was also acutely aware of the slogan "First to Fight," which had adorned Marine Corps recruiting posters ever since Lejeune's Marines had beaten the Army ashore at Vera Cruz in 1914. The slogan had been paying handsome dividends in recruiting stations across the country; Barnett was determined to make it a reality by getting a Marine unit to France in the first convoy.

It was not to be an easy task. Practically every red-blooded male in the country wanted to sail with Gen John J. Pershing, the commander of the new American Expeditionary Force (AEF). Pershing was swamped with applications from veterans, adventurers, and patriots of every configuration. What he did not have, however, were sufficient regular infantrymen, trained and ready for deployment. The Marines could fill that bill, to a degree. Barnett sensed the opening, avoided Pershing, and instead lobbied Secretary of the Navy Josephus Daniels and Secretary of War Newton Baker. Daniels later recorded his role in this effort, stating:

> When the war was declared, I tendered, ready and equipped, two regiments of Marines to be incorporated in the Army . . . some Army officers were not keen to accept them.

The Army itself did not have much of a vote in the matter. Barnett and Daniels effectively pressured Baker into asking President Wilson for a Marine contingent to deploy to France. The 5th Marine Regiment was ready in Philadelphia. Thus, on 27 May 1917, Wilson delivered this message to Daniels:

> In pursuance of the authority vested in me by law, it is hereby directed that you issue the necessary orders detaching for service with the Army a force of Marines to be known as the 5th Regiment of Marines.

The Army had other means of blocking what they perceived to be a Marine Corps encroachment into their functional responsibilities. The day before the first convoy was to sail, the Secretary of War wrote Barnett stating that it would be "utterly impossible for the War Department to furnish transportation for the Marine regiment." Barnett, however was up to the occasion: "Please give yourself no further trouble in this matter," he replied, "as transportation for the Marines has been arranged on board naval ships." Barnett had foreseen the development and arranged with the Chief of Naval Operations to provide substitute ships for the deployment. On 14 June 1917, Col. Charles A. Doyen's 5th Marines embarked aboard the naval transports *Hancock*, *Henderson*, and the auxiliary cruiser *DeKalb* (formerly the German liner *Printz Eitel Friedrich*) and set sail for France, thus preserving Barnett's recruiting slogan and his first goal.

The Marines officially came under the operational command of the Army as soon as they arrived in France. No individualism, or "Marine ethnicity," was to be tolerated. The Marines had to discard their green uniforms and don Army olive drab. No distinctive emblems or insignia were authorized. Army drill, organization, and logistic support prevailed. The Marines also had to exchange their Lewis machine guns for French Chauchat automatic rifles and Hotchkiss machineguns.

The Marines were more concerned with the potential loss of their unit integrity than with their distinctive uniforms. Pershing considered the 5th Marines to be in excess of the first U.S. Division and employed them as "line of communication" troops – stevedores, military police, provost marshals, couriers – at the expense of the concentrated training underway with the rest of the U.S. troops. When Barnett complained, Pershing wrote the Major General Commandant, complimenting the "high state of discipline and excellent soldierly appearance" of the Marines, but stating in effect that if any unit had to be scattered for service in the rear, it was best not to use regular Army troops. Barnett chafed under the arbitrary ruling, but by this time he was powerless to influence the action overseas. Pershing had grown adept at withstanding Washington pressures of all kinds; Barnett's influence with the Navy and War Department was not effective in France.

In retrospect, Barnett's fears were groundless. As bona fide Army rear-echelon troops eventually arrived in France, the Marines were relieved of these onerous duties and reassembled for final training. They certainly did not miss any of the fighting. Pershing, to his credit, refused to allow any piecemeal commitment of the AEF to combat until he was satisfied its training was completed. And when the 6th Marines and the 6th Machinegun Battalion arrived in February 1918, Pershing allowed the consolidation of the Marine units into the "4th Brigade (Marines)," even allowing the parenthetical designator to remain – a decision he probably regretted that summer.

Col Doyen, promoted to brigadier general, took command of the 4th Brigade, but his health failed him and he was sent home by Pershing. Barnett moved to get Lejeune to France, but he was not fast enough. Pershing assigned his own chief of staff, BGen James G. Harbord, to command the brigade. The Marines in Washington may have gnashed their teeth in outrage, but to the Marines in France it was love at first sight. Harbord led the Marines through the thickest of the fighting at Belleau Wood and Soissons, and he was a competent, inspirational commander. Even the dour Maj Holland M, ("Howling Mad" in World War II) Smith was impressed, finding Harbord to be "one of America's great soldiers." Harbord's own feelings toward the Marines were mutual; "They never failed me," he wrote in his autobiography, "and I look back upon my service with the Marine Brigade with more pride and satisfaction than on any other equal period of my long Army career."

The combat exploits of the 4th Marine Brigade have been well-chronicled and need not be duplicated here. The Marines were obviously anxious to give a good accounting of themselves, and they did. Army historian S. L. A. "SLAM" Marshall summarized the Marines' sense of motivation rather neatly:

> The Marine Brigade because it was unique – a little raft of sea soldiers in an ocean of Army – was without doubt the most aggressive body of diehards on the Western Front.

Such valor was never displayed on the Western Front without a high price in casualties. A thousand Marines fell at Belleau Wood on the first day alone – more casualties than the Corps had lost in its entire history up to that point. Nor were its tactics noteworthy. As reported by a German officer on the other side of the firing line within Belleau Wood, the Marines approached "in thick lines of skirmishers, supported by columns following immediately behind . . . The Germans could not have desired better targets."

The Marines held no corner on the market on combat valor or high casualties. Most U.S. Army units also fought hard and bled profusely. The problem came in the publicity that the Marines received to the relative exclusion of their Army contemporaries. The war in France was tightly censored by the AEF. Individual units were rarely identified. The parenthetical nametag Pershing had acceded to [the "4th Brigade (Marines)"] gave exception to the rule, and the Marines were frequently lauded in the press when Army units could not be mentioned. This irritant was exacerbated by the Floyd Gibbons incident. Gibbons was a Chicago Tribune writer who was severely wounded accompanying the Marines in Belleau Wood. The first rumor had him killed in action. By coincidence the press censor in Paris was a friend of Gibbons who, believing him dead, decided to let "Floyd's last release" go through uncensored. The report – emotional, exaggerated, and inaccurate – was devoured by the American press, hungry for war news. The Gibbons report conveyed the impression that the Marine brigade alone had saved Paris from the Huns, derailed Ludendorff's final offensive, and won the war for democracy. The Marines, of course, loved it, but it was a bitter pill for the Army to swallow. Eighteen years after the event, Harbord noted that the Gibbons dispatch "lit fires of professional jealousy that still smolder."

Thus, a Marine unit was gainfully employed in combat in France. Yet Barnett and Lejeune were not satisfied. They saw the war on the Western Front as being fought and decided by divisions, not by regiments or brigades. They saw a need to deploy a combined arms team in order to utilize their newly formed artillery regiment in combat. The next goal for Barnett and Lejeune was to form an entire Marine division for employment with the AEF. There were to be formidable institutional barriers to this goal.

For one thing, Barnett had his hands full in keeping his commitments for other missions in support of the Navy. Even though he was quite successful in lobbying for expansion of the Corps, he was at the same time beset by increasing demands for security forces from his jealous sister Service. For example, of 75,000 Marines in service at the war's end, less than 25,000 were assigned to the AEF. Nearly 8,000 were manning overseas naval stations or serving in the ongoing occupations of Cuba, Haiti, and the Dominican Republic. Another 2,000 Marines served aboard warships, including those U.S. ships assigned to the Grand Fleet (and those who landed in Vladivostok in 1918). A full 37,000 were in the United States, either filling the pipeline for the AEF or assigned to a legitimate advanced base force stationed in Galveston, Texas, prepared to protect the Mexican oilfields near Tampico.

Barnett had testified before the House Committee on Naval Affairs early in 1918 that he needed additional troops in order to field and maintain a Marine division with the AEF. The committee was generally sympathetic; Congress enacted the proposed expansion that July. But Congress was not the hurdle; neither was it the War Department. It was Black Jack Pershing. Barnett went ahead and formed the 5th Marine Brigade and the 10th Marine Regiment (Artillery) in Quantico, but there were unmistakable signals from France that neither organization would be welcome on the frontlines.

Barnett then sent Lejeune to France as his personal ambassador to Pershing. Lejeune was a good choice for the assignment. A graduate of both the Naval Academy and the Army War College, Lejeune was perhaps the most ecumenical of all the senior Marines. Calling on Pershing in the AEF Headquarters at Chaumont, Lejeune presented an eloquent plea for authorization to form a Marine division within the theater of operations in France. According to Lejeune, Pershing's negative response was equally eloquent, giving as reasons that the presence of a Marine division:

> . . . would interfere with his plan for a homogeneous Army and would add greatly to the many complications incident to providing replacements. . . . He pointed out that it was scarcely possible to always provide the 4th Brigade with Marine replacements, and a Division would require such a large variety of Marine replacements as to make the problem altogether insoluble.

Pershing's diary account of the meeting with Lejeune was more succinct:

> General Barnett, Chief of Marine Corps, recommends formation entire Marine division, but the Second Division [of which 4th Brigade was part] cannot be broken up after its fine record.

The next day he cabled the Secretary of War: "While the Marines are splendid troops, their use as a separate division is inadvisable."

Various historians of the Marine Corps have imputed dark motives to Pershing's rejection of the Barnett/Lejeune offer of a combined arms division. Allan R. Millett believed that the basis for Pershing's rejection was touchiness about increased Navy Department interference in France. Robert Debs Heinl saw Pershing's decision as an example of a "deliberate Army policy to minimize, if not prevent, Marine participation in the AEF."

Pershing's real motivation for his decision was probably composed of several elements. First, since the meeting with Lejeune occurred less than two weeks after the Floyd Gibbons dispatches about Belleau Wood, he was quite likely still miffed over the excess and unauthorized publicity the Marines had received at the exclusion of his other components. Second, the problem of Marine replacements was indeed a strain on his staff. The AEF reported the requirement for more than 20,000 Marines in the replacement system just to support the 4th Brigade. Barnett sent seven replacement battalions between February and August, but the sum did not even match the brigade's total casualties. A full division would have compounded the problem severely. Third, and more fundamental, Pershing probably had no real need for any further Marines. The 5th Regiment had comprised 20 percent of the initial deployment of the AEF to France. The well-trained, combat veterans had been most welcome a year earlier. But by mid-1918 Pershing had 150,000 "veterans" and a pipeline expanding to the point where an anticipated 3 million American troops in 80-100 divisions would be in France by 1919. The Marine brigade had been a valuable asset at first, but an expanded force was not worth the administrative hassle. Hence, Lejeune was assigned to an Army unit, the 5th Marine Brigade was scattered to rear area assignments on arrival in France and the 10th Marines remained in Quantico for the duration. The Marine division concept died stillborn.

Was there perhaps another role for a Marine combined arms unit in the war? The opportunities were scant. The Marines did provide an artillery battery and an "aeronautical company" as kind of a primitive advance base force in the Azores during the final year of the war, but they never engaged the enemy. A larger possibility emerged in the form of "Memorandum #9" developed by Adm William S. Sims' Naval Planning Section in London in January 1918. The plan proposed offensive naval action in the Adriatic to eliminate the Central Powers' submarine bases. A force of 20,000 American Marines was deemed necessary to seize and defend the Sabbioncello Peninsula and raid the other Adriatic ports. The plan had potential, but it got bogged down in protocol (similar to NATO today). It was submitted too late to make the agenda for the February meeting of the Inter-Allied Council. Approved by that council in March, the plan was then forwarded for consideration by the military representatives of the Versailles Council. By then Ludendorff had unleashed his spring offensives, and all attention was focused on the Western Front. Besides, the political consequences of the Gallipoli disaster were still fresh in the decision makers' minds. The successful German landing at Riga was discounted. Amphibious operations by the Allies would have to wait another quarter of a century. The Marines stayed in France. Lejeune commanded the 4th Brigade briefly, then rose to command the 2d Division throughout the remainder of the war.

Thus, the Marine Corps broke the mold and got at least a piece of the peculiar action in France. Like other U.S. units, it earned its spurs under fire against a formidable opponent. If frightful casualty rates can ever "prove" anything positive, the Marines in France "proved" to possess a propensity for violent combat certainly equal to: any other American outfit on the Western Front. But what was the overall impact of this bloody excursion?

The Marine Corps experience in World War I – sevenfold expansion, protracted service ashore with the Army, close combat against a sophisticated enemy, unprecedented casualties, generous publicity, a growing estrangement from other services – had significant institutional effects. First and foremost, the experience guaranteed the survival of the Corps. It is not difficult to imagine the fate of the Marines had Barnett and Lejeune failed to get a fighting force to France: a residual band of ceremonial troops, all spit and polish but without any warfighting capabilities; in effect, military eunuchs. Second, the experience of the war and the near extinction of their Corps created an intellectual revolution in the officer ranks – led by Lejeune and the enigmatic Pete Ellis – which caused an organizational search for a unique mission, one that would capitalize on both the Marines' traditional maritime roots and their newly proven combat capabilities ashore. The development of amphibious warfare doctrine in the 1920s and 1930s was a natural development of that intellectual stimulus. Third, the war caused a much needed reorganization within the Marine Corps. Infantry was still the central force, but now the emphasis was more on combined arms operations, including Marine aviation. Marine Corps Headquarters was expanded and organized along the lines of the Army General Staff and the Office of the Chief of Naval Operations. A War Plans Section was finally established. Fourth, the Marine Corps acquired legitimate training bases of its own at Quantico, San Diego, and Parris Island, and no longer had to function in a corner of some urban Navy Yard. Fifth, sadly, the Marine Corps incurred the enmity of a generation of Army officers, largely due to the Belleau Wood hoo-haw. Sixth, in contrast, the Marine Corps enjoyed a windfall public acceptance for its well documented exploits in combat which would sustain it in many a bureaucratic fight in Washington in the lean years to come.

Today our national media contains frequent reference to a potential crisis scenario in, say, the Persian Gulf in which Marine Corps forces would once again be deployed alongside the Army in a protracted campaign ashore against a sophisticated, expansionist power. There are some similarities and some distinct differences in comparing the situation in 1918 with the one projected for the 1980s. Among the similarities would be the Army's continual need for well-trained, combat ready forces from any source to augment its own peacetime force; the institutional specter of a "second land army," with its budgetary duplication connotations; the continuing inter-service rivalry regarding the "First to Fight" slogan; and the probable need for Army logistic support for Marine forces beyond a certain point in time and space. Chief among the differences would be the new emphasis by the Marines on unit integrity. No longer would Marine units be detached for service with the Army as pure infantry outfits. Marines would now be employed as Marine air-ground task forces (MAGTFs). The MAGTF commander would, by doctrine, retain operational control of all his assets, even after termination of the amphibious operation. In a protracted land campaign, the Army would probably demand consolidation of all air defense and combat service support units; the Air Force would predictably demand control of all fixed-wing aviation assets. The fight would be legendary.

The larger issue, of course, involves command relations. In World War I, Pershing commanded all elements of the AEF. In a current crisis, a joint task force commander would be designated. If this comes to pass, the MAGTF commander should become a component commander, "ComMarFor" in the vernacular, and MAGTF integrity would be preserved. The ideal is yet to be achieved.

Could USMC forces operate successfully in a protracted land campaign with the Army today? Yes, given certain understandings on command relations, unit integrity and logistic support. Would this joint employment be in the best interest of the Marine Corps and the Nation? On one hand, arguably not; the Marine Corps can conceivably serve the Nation best by providing a ready amphibious assault force of combined arms, a force that can define much of its mobility, flexibility, logistic support, and overall political value from the sea. On the other hand, the point could well be moot. The enduring lesson of the Marine Corps' service in World War I was its essential usefulness to the Nation. Perhaps the existence of a ready combat force, equally adept ashore or afloat, is the best possible legacy of the Corps' watershed performance in the Great War.

CACOS AND *CAUDILLOS*: MARINES AND COUNTERINSURGENCY IN HISPANIOLA, 1915-1924

Graham A. Cosmas

> *In this essay, Dr. Cosmas, a highly praised historian at the Army Center of Military History, analyzes the complexities of a decade-long occupation of Haiti and the Dominican Republic. Fighting an elusive guerrilla enemy with conventional forces proved difficult, especially when World War I detracted resources from these secondary operations. Ultimately, Cosmos provides a balanced perspective on the positive and negative lessons learned in Hispaniola.*

The marines who occupied Haiti and the Dominican Republic during and after World War I possessed little specific preparation for counterinsurgency or other types of low-intensity conflict. During the decades preceding these interventions, the corps had concentrated its attention on developing an advance base force for use with the fleet in conventional naval warfare. Marine leaders viewed expeditionary duty as a secondary mission of the advance base infantry regiments. Nevertheless, when the marines sent an expeditionary brigade to Haiti in 1915 and another to the Dominican Republic in 1916, they confronted challenges across the entire spectrum of low-intensity conflict, from semi-conventional and guerrilla warfare by organized military forces through terrorism, banditry, and rural crime and social disorder. The marines in response employed a wide variety of counterinsurgency tactics and techniques. They also experienced the dilemmas and frustrations often encountered by troops sent overseas to battle an elusive, resourceful enemy on the enemy's own ground.(1)

In Haiti the First Provisional Marine Brigade encountered the *cacos*, peasant warriors from the wild, mountainous northern and central regions of the country. These men, recruited by local chieftains on the basis of personal loyalty and the promise of loot, fought in the mercenary armies of a succession of presidential aspirants from Haiti's urban, elite political class. During the years preceding the American intervention, *caco* revolts had made and broken governments at a rate of about one per year. The American landings in July 1915 aborted still another *caco*-enforced change of presidents. The marines quickly suppressed initial resistance to the occupation, and the *cacos* remained quiet for nearly three years. During that interval the marines organized and trained a Haitian Gendarmerie, which took over most of the day-to-day work of garrisoning and policing the interior of the country.

Misconduct by the gendarmes and some of their marine commanders brought the *cacos* to arms again in late 1918. To secure labor for building roads, the Gendarmerie reinstituted the unpopular *corvée,* an old Haitian practice of drafting peasants for short terms of construction work near their homes. In the northern district, heart of *caco* country, gendarmes under marine Major Clark W. Wells administered the *corvée* in a brutal and corrupt fashion. Correction of these abuses by the First Brigade commander came too late to prevent thousands of *cacos* from taking to the hills and to arms. The insurgency found a charismatic leader in Charlemagne Massena Peralte, a politician from the fringes of the black elite. Charlemagne, recognized by lesser *caco* chiefs as the head of a revolutionary government, proclaimed the objective of expelling the Americans from Haiti; but he seemed equally interested in ousting the Americans' client, President Sudre Dartiguenave, and replacing Dartiguenave with a candidate from Charlemagne's own faction. Whatever his political goals, Charlemagne was a formidable threat to the occupation. His *cacos*, who began attacking Gendarmerie outposts in October 1918, numbered, by American estimate, almost five thousand full-time fighters. Perhaps fifteen thousand additional peasant supporters turned out for operations near their homes or kept the insurgents supplied with food and intelligence. In the capital, Port au Prince, anti-American and anti-Dartiguenave politicians organized a rudimentary underground on Charlemagne's behalf. Fortunately for the marines and gendarmes, the *cacos* were poorly armed. A minority of them carried old-model black-powder rifles; the majority went into battle with swords, machetes, and pikes.

When marines landed in the Dominican Republic in May 1916, they had little difficulty in securing the capital and the central and western regions of the republic. In the eastern provinces of Seibo and Macoris, however, they encountered armed opposition which, while less militarily formidable than the *cacos*, proved more difficult to suppress. Rural Haiti, while extremely poor, was a stable and comparatively harmonious society of peasant freeholders. The eastern Dominican Republic, by contrast, was a region in transition from subsistence agriculture to an export economy dominated by foreign-owned sugar estates. The region was geographically isolated from the rest of the republic. It possessed only weak local governments and police forces and long had been ruled by *caudillos*, military strongmen whose power rested on their ability to maintain armed bands recruited, like the *cacos*, on the basis of personality and plunder. The *caudillos* participated in the country's periodic revolutions, often receiving local political offices for their services. Between revolutions both the *caudillos* and professional bandits called *gavilleros* sustained themselves and their followers by robbery and extortion at the expense of whomever in the region possessed any surplus wealth, mostly rural storekeepers, sugar estate owners, and the citizens of smaller municipalities. The stronger chieftains maintained informal alliances with the political elites of the few existing towns and cities as protection against the central government's rare, feeble attempts to assert its authority. Some chiefs also accepted regular cash payments from the sugar companies in return for keeping company properties safe from attack by lesser *caudillos* and *gavilleros*.

The American military government in Santo Domingo City,(2) unlike its Dominican predecessors, was determined to assert its authority and to restore law and order in the eastern provinces. Hence, from 1917 to 1922 marines of the Second Provisional Brigade waged armed conflict against the *caudillos*. The Dominican leaders were inspired in some instances by nationalist political motives, but more often fought to maintain their regional authority and military reputations. Their followers were fewer in number than the *cacos*, amounting to a maximum of perhaps 600 full-time fighters and an indeterminate number of occasional or seasonal adherents, many of whom were economically motivated. Indeed, rural disorder waxed and waned with the annual sugar industry employment cycle. The Dominican insurgents acknowledged no supreme leader comparable to Charlemagne Peralte and usually operated in groups of less than 150 men. After late 1919 these bands rarely engaged even the smallest marine patrols. Like the *cacos*, the Dominicans possessed mainly antiquated rifles and, more commonly, were armed only with pistols and shotguns. *Caudillos* and *gavilleros*, however, could count on at least the passive support of much of the rural population, support based in part on fear reprisal, in part on local and personal loyalties, and in part resentment of the marines as occasionally brutal and heavy-hand foreign intruders.

The marines, in operating against both *cacos* and *caudillo* assumed as the foundation of their strategy the necessity minimizing the use of force and devoting maximum attention to winning the friendship, or at least the tolerance, of local civilians. Marine leaders continually informed their troops that they were not at war with the Dominicans or the Haitians, but in each instance were instead protecting a law-abiding majority against a minority of troublemakers. To reinforce this image, the marines deliberately labeled their opponents "bandits." In July 1919 the First Brigade for example, instructed its troops to use that term, rather than "*caco*," when referring to "natives, who, in certain sections are menacing the peace of the country." The marines in both countries tried to avoid seizing or destroying civilian property and attempted to minimize disruption of the normal routine of the rural population. Brigadier General Harry Lee, the last commander of the marines in the Dominican Republic, summed up the basic principles of marine counterinsurgency in Hispaniola:

> There are records where civilized powers, whose armed forces were engaged in the suppression of banditry, countenanced the most drastic methods. These . . . included the destruction of stocks and crops . . . , the burning of homes and villages, the laying to waste of entire sections, where the inhabitants harbored brigands. However, such drastic measures were never employed in Santo Domingo, because there exists one great disadvantage of their use: the moral effect upon the peaceful inhabitants, who become so exasperated as to forfeit their friendship for generations. That the friendship of the people of an occupied state should be sacrificed by any unnecessary measure was avowedly contrary to the policy of the United States.(3)

Efforts to implement these enlightened principles were hampered by deficiencies in the number and quality of available marines. Counterinsurgency theorists of the 1960s contended that a troop ratio of ten to one or better was necessary for victory over guerrillas; the marine brigades in Haiti and the Dominica Republic never approached that advantage. The First Brigade numbered about 900 officers and men when the *caco* revolt began and nearly 1,200 when it ended. In the Dominican Republic the Second Brigade could spare only 500 or so officers and men to pacify the eastern provinces until early 1919, when the arrival of an additional regiment increased marine strength in the area to about 1,200. Both brigades were supplemented by native constabularies organized and officered by marines. The 2,700-man Haitian Gendarmerie, although inferior to the marines in training and armament, bore much of the burden of combat and freed the marines of garrison duty in secure areas. By contrast, the *Guardia* (later *Policia*) *Nacional Dominicana*, counterpart of the Haitian Gendarmerie, provided the marines little reinforcement. Delays in organizing the *Guardia*, rapid turnover in its marine commanders, and a lack of money and equipment kept the Haitian force weak, ineffective, and well under its authorized strength of about 1,200 men throughout the period of hostilities. During final operations in the east, only two small *Guardia* companies performed auxiliary duties, leaving the field campaigning largely to the marines.(4)

In 1917 and 1918 both occupation brigades gave up many of their most experienced and most capable officers and men to the brigade in France and to other elements of the expanding Marine Corps. Mobilization, followed rapidly by demobilization, brought wholesale personnel turnover to the two brigades in Hispaniola as they received large infusions of newly promoted officers and NCOs and first-term enlisted men. The resulting deterioration in small-unit leadership and troop quality, combined with racial and cultural antagonisms and the strains of operating against guerrillas, contributed to repeated incidents of misconduct by marines in command of constabulary units as well as their own organizations. These incidents included the torture and execution of prisoners, indiscriminate firing on civilians by patrols, arbitrary seizure of peasants' food and livestock, and off-duty crimes and acts of violence and discourtesy toward ordinary Haitians and Dominicans. Such abuses occurred in both countries; however, they appear to have been more numerous and damaging to the occupation in the Dominican Republic, where small marine units were dispersed more widely and where the counterinsurgency campaign was more prolonged and indecisive.(5)

Marine misconduct, often exaggerated and sensationalized by critics of the interventions, became an issue in the 1920 American presidential campaign and was the subject of U.S. Navy, Marine Corps, and Senate investigations. In response to such exposure, both brigades during the early 1920s attempted to improve troop conduct and attitudes. Marine offenses against local citizens were investigated more thoroughly and punished more rapidly and sternly than before. Brigade leaders also intensively indoctrinated their men in the peaceable nature of their mission and the necessity of winning the friendship of the population. These efforts, combined with the end of active operations and the concentration of most marines in fewer, larger garrisons, eliminated the worst abuses. By that time, however, much damage had been done. *Corvée* abuses in Haiti had helped set off the *caco* uprising, and widespread hatred of the marines among rural Dominicans swelled guerrilla ranks and hindered marine efforts to end the insurgency and banditry.(6)

The marines directed the preponderance of their military effort to the pursuit and destruction, or at least the dispersal, of organized rebel bands. They attempted to do this by saturating the countryside with small patrols, rarely larger than twenty men, which operated from permanent posts or temporary bases. Patrols followed up attacks or engagements, intensively searched fixed zones, and set ambushes on known enemy movement routes. Marine patrols also went after particular enemy bands or leaders when reliable information as to their location could be obtained. The brigades directed these operations through regimental and battalion headquarters, each of which was responsible for a section of territory and a varying number of garrisons. Patrols normally went out under lieutenants and senior NCOs; but company, battalion, and even regimental commanders at times took the field to familiarize themselves with the terrain, to respond to major enemy raids, or to follow up especially promising intelligence leads. Command and control were difficult, especially before portable field radios became available in the early 1920s. Headquarters often lost track of patrol routes and positions. Clashes inevitably occurred between friendly forces; in the most costly of these, marines in Haiti killed a gendarme, a civilian scout, and a *caco* prisoner in an ambush of one patrol by another.

Marine commanders distilled their patrolling experience into standard operating procedures. These covered such basics as employment of point men, the conduct of stream crossings and house searches, security at halts and bivouacs, hand signals for silent control of movement, telltale signs of enemy ambushes, and mundane but vital details such as foot care. In the Dominican Republic, where much territory had to be covered and horses were available locally, the marines often patrolled mounted; the Second Brigade stationed a full company of such "horse marines" in the eastern provinces. Supply was simple. Patrols in the field carried iron rations with them on their persons or on pack animals; when these ran out, they lived off the country – a practice unavoidable in many cases, but one also productive of some of the abuses noted previously.(7)

Even the smallest marine patrols had little to fear in combat from enemies poorly armed and untrained in small-unit tactics. When *cacos* and guerrillas sprang successful ambushes, as they frequently did, the insurgents' poor weapons and worse marksmanship usually rendered their fire ineffective. Insurgent attempts to close for hand-to-hand combat, more frequent in Haiti than in the Dominican Republic, occasionally cost marine and constabulary forces heavily, but more often simply gave them easier targets to shoot.

The marines' problem was finding the enemy. In the roadless, heavily wooded hills and mountains of Hispaniola, the insurgents were difficult to bring to battle unless they chose to fight or the marines and constabulary surprised them in their camps. The *cacos*, accustomed to waging more or less conventional warfare in their various revolutions, made the marines' work easier by launching frequent attacks on Gendarmerie posts, not to mention two mass assaults on Port au Prince and an abortive storming of Grande

Riviere du Nord during which Charlemagne Peralte was killed in a Gendarmerie raid on his command post. Even in the hills, the *cacos* tended to move in large groups and to remain too long at customary concentration points, often old forts dating back to the French occupation. The Dominicans, by contrast, though ineffective in combat, were masters of evasion and never attacked posts or defended towns. Bringing them to battle, a marine commander admitted,

> to a large extent, depends on the bandit leader. If he wants to fight, and sometimes he does, he will open fire on the detachment, mostly on the point, and then disappears in the brush, where his retreat . . . is facilitated by the dense vegetation, intimate knowledge of the numerous trails . . . and . . . fleetness of foot. If the bandit does not want a fight he simply lets the detachment pass by undisturbed.(8)

To help find the enemy and also to assist in governing the occupied republics, the marine brigades built up elaborate intelligence services. Patrols in the field, interrogation of *caco* and guerrilla prisoners and defectors, as well as networks of voluntary and paid local informants were the marines' principal sources of information about the enemy. After air squadrons were attached to the brigades in early 1919, the marines used aerial reconnaissance to improve their knowledge of the countryside and occasionally to find enemy bands and camps. At brigade and lower headquarters, intelligence officers collated, evaluated, and distributed information from all sources. They paid attention to more than purely military matters, assembling as well material on social and political conditions and the indigenous culture. Timely, accurate intelligence contributed substantially to the deaths of Charlemagne Peralte and Benoit Batreville in Haiti; but marine intelligence also had its failures. During 1917-1918, for example, commanders and intelligence officers wasted much effort in futile attempts to establish that local German businessmen and landowners were stirring up and arming *cacos* and guerrillas. The marines also were more efficient at accumulating a large volume of information than they were at evaluating and distributing that information. A regimental commander in the Dominican Republic declared: "Though a vast amount of information is secured, the greater part of it is of no value, either by reason of absolute inaccuracy . . . or by reason of delay in delivery"(9)

New technologies – principally aircraft and radios – assisted marine operations after the end of World War I. In both Haiti and the Dominican Republic, marine aircraft occasionally bombed and strafed enemy camps or fleeing troops, inflicting casualties and causing temporary panic. Such incidents, however, were rare, due to the inability of marines on the ground to communicate rapidly with the aviators. Of more substantial value was the air squadrons' work in reconnaissance; in transporting mail, supplies, and personnel; and in evacuating the sick and wounded from remote posts. In the Dominican Republic aircraft also helped to coordinate patrol activity by dropping messages to the infantry. Meanwhile stationary radio sets at unit headquarters and a limited number of portable field radios speeded response to incidents, simplified the task of coordinating widespread patrols, and reduced the need to tie up scarce mounted personnel in escorting couriers.(10)

In both Haiti and the Dominican Republic, the insurgents drew recruits, supplies, and information from the rural population and, especially in the latter stages of the Dominican disorders, lived with the peasants between occasional forays. The marines therefore experimented with measures for separating their armed enemies from the people and for enlisting local help against the insurgents.

Such efforts in Haiti were comparatively modest. The marine brigade and the Gendarmerie revived an earlier Haitian system of internal passports to restrict civilian movement in *caco* areas. In 1919 the marines and gendarmes began recruiting and paying citizens called *vigilantes* to guide patrols within their home areas and to help identify *cacos* and their sympathizers. The marines also set *cacos* against *cacos*. They enlisted a well-to-do Haitian, Jean Conze, to organize a Gendarmerie-sponsored band and allowed him to win several noisy mock battles to enhance his military reputation. Conze succeeded in establishing himself as a principal lieutenant of Charlemagne Peralte and used this position to lure Peralte into the fatal expedition against Grande Riviere, an action for which Conze received a large cash reward.

Population control efforts by the marines in the Dominican Republic were much more extensive and elaborate. Guerrilla warfare and banditry in the eastern provinces centered about areas of thick woods, interspersed with small farming settlements called *canucos*, which abutted the large sugar estates. There guerrilla leaders maintained their hideouts. Between raids, many of their followers lived in the *canucos* or in the company-owned villages on the sugar plantations, where they were seasonally employed.

After several limited population control and screening efforts during 1918 and 1919 produced few results, the Fifteenth Regiment under its new commander, Lieutenant Colonel William C. Harllee, launched a systematic effort in the autumn of 1921 to drive the guerrillas from their hideouts. Between 24 October 1921 and 11 March 1922, Harllee conducted nine large-scale cordon and search operations against guerrilla base areas. In these drives, which involved most of the Fifteenth Regiment and elements of the *Policia Nacional*, marine patrols, directed by radio and air-dropped messages, encircled an objective area and then moved inward, rounding up most of the adult population at a central collecting point. There a specially assembled corps of Dominican informers, supervised by marine intelligence personnel and screened from sight of the detainees, picked alleged bandits out of the multitude. The suspects were held for further investigation and trial by marine provost courts. Colonel Harllee provided food and medical assistance for the remaining detainees and, after personally explaining that the operation had been for the purpose of removing the criminals who had preyed upon the people, allowed them to return home. The marines thoroughly mapped the areas in which they operated and used prisoners convicted by the provost courts as work gangs to cut networks of trails through the woods in order to make them more readily penetrable by military patrols. The operations met no armed resistance and resulted in few Dominican casualties. After one of the first of these drives, however, the Second Brigade, in response to civilian complaints, ordered that citizens "will not be collected, tied, and marched to distant points" for screening, an indication that the Fifteenth Regiment's roundup methods were other than gentle.

The effectiveness of Harllee's operations became a matter of controversy. No major guerrilla leaders were caught in these dragnets, but several hundred part-time fighters and supporters were captured and the groups still, at large were forced out of their accustomed areas of operation. Harllee himself contended that his operations disrupted the guerrilla infrastructure and taught the people "that the bandit chiefs are no longer masters in their areas." Pro-occupation Dominican municipal officials and sugar estate managers alike complained, however, that the cordons terrorized the people and upset normal economic activity without halting the guerrillas. The cordons probably did bring effective pressure to bear on the insurgents' civilian support network and greatly increased the marines' ability to operate in what formerly had been almost impenetrable forest redoubts. Nevertheless, the Second Brigade commander, Brigadier General Harry Lee, who had orders from Washington to conciliate the Dominicans, sided with Harllee's critics. On 5 March 1922 the general ordered an end to the concentrations.(11)

Lee abandoned cordon operations in part because he believed he had a more effective weapon in hand: combined patrols of marines and Dominican counterinsurgents. The marine brigade had experimented with the use of indigenous irregulars early in the occupation, at one point employing one *caudillo* and his band to attack another. The military government, however, devoted most of its effort to the maintenance of law and order. It sought to disarm Dominican civilians, to suppress the private security forces of the sugar companies, and to confine military activity on the part of the Dominicans to the *Policia* and small municipal police forces. Throughout most of the occupation, relations remained contentious between the marines and the sugar estate managers, who had access to much valuable intelligence and whose employees offered a potential source of both antiguerrilla and guerrilla manpower (to include the guerrilla chiefs themselves). Marine commanders justifiably complained that the company managers withheld information, especially about guerrilla leaders whom they paid off. The marines also contended that the estate managers and large landowners often fabricated reports of guerrilla activity in order to encourage the establishment of marine garrisons near their property less to fight the insurgents than to intimidate their own workers. The estate managers for their part freely criticized marine tactics and accused the American military government of failing to protect their properties.(12)

Brigadier General Lee set out to co-opt the estate managers. After listening sympathetically to their protests against Harllee's cordons, he adopted a suggestion made by the managers and local Dominican officials that civilian irregulars who knew both the terrain and the enemy be enlisted to hunt down the insurgents. Planning for the irregular force began in November 1921, and by early the following April, five groups of so-called

Civil Guards were ready to take the field. Each consisted of fifteen Dominicans who were selected by their municipal governments or estate managers, armed and trained by the marines, and commanded by a marine officer assisted by two or three marine NCOs. Operating in their own neighborhoods and backed by marine firepower, the irregulars proved able to find insurgent groups, engage them, and inflict casualties. Their operations during April, according to Lee, "fairly broke and led to the disintegration of the bandit groups." The principal chiefs as a result all surrendered in the following month.(13)

To secure these surrenders, Lee employed still another counter-insurgency weapon: amnesty. The marines treated their foes legally as criminal offenders either against the American forces in the Dominican Republic or against the client government in Haiti. Once they established military superiority over their adversaries, however, the marines offered exemption from prosecution and punishment to the guerrilla leaders and any of their men who surrendered voluntarily with their weapons. In Haiti the First Brigade provided not only amnesty but also cash rewards and civilian jobs to *cacos* who gave up. In return for leniency, *caco* chiefs were required to tour the countryside with marine and Gendarmerie patrols, to urge other *cacos* to surrender, and to speak in favor of the government and the occupation. Chiefs who thus identified themselves with the Americans, the brigade commander reasoned, "would not again be accepted by the bandits." Accepting these terms, 165 *caco* commanders and more than 11,000 of their soldiers reportedly turned themselves in during late 1919 and early 1920.(14)

In the Dominican Republic in 1917, the Second Brigade employed negotiation and offers of amnesty to secure the surrender of several major *caudillos* and their bands. The military government, however, subsequently prosecuted one of these leaders and several of his lieutenants for the murder of two American civilians. The long sentences these men received, followed by the killing of their leader while reportedly attempting to escape from prison, diminished the value of offering amnesty for some time.

In early 1922 General Lee took advantage of the intensified military pressure of the cordon operations and the Civil Guards to revive the offer of amnesty. Using the sugar estate managers and local Dominican politicians as go-betweens, Lee declared a temporary cessation of hostilities and in May secured the surrender of seven major insurgent chiefs and some 140 of their followers – a majority of the guerrillas still fighting at the time. Lee's terms were strict. Insurgents who surrendered were required to give up their weapons and stay near their homes or a marine or *Policia* post where they could be kept under surveillance. The leaders had to stand trial before military commissions that imposed fifteen-year prison sentences, suspended during good behavior. Supplementing the amnesty program, Lee and his superior Rear Admiral Samual S. Robison, the military governor, sought with only limited success to persuade the sugar estates to employ more workers during the normally slack season in an effort to reduce the common economic incentive for banditry.(15)

Even before the last Dominican rebels had surrendered, marine officers began digesting their campaign experience in Hispaniola and using what they had learned there to devise a doctrine for the conduct of what they called "small wars." The results of their work appeared in their professional journal, the *Marine Corps Gazette*, as well as in classes taught at the Marine Corps schools at Quantico, Virginia. Much of this early doctrine simply restated what had been practiced in Hispaniola and included such obvious lessons as the indispensability of accurate, timely intelligence; the importance of top-caliber small-unit leadership and individual training; the desirability of restraint in the employment of firepower; and the necessity of not offending the inhabitants of small countries being "cleaned up." The scandals and investigations accompanying the occupation of Hispaniola had left at least some marines aware of the difficulties of waging war under the eye of public opinion. Major Earl H. Ellis, a former Second Brigade intelligence officer, noted that in pacification the United States government must appear as "the good angel"; hence, its military agents must behave in ways that would not "cause undue comment among [their] own people or among foreign governments."(16)

The marines, despite some lapses in their conduct, were successful counterinsurgents in Haiti and the Dominican Republic. They engaged traditional military forces that had defied or disrupted national governments for generations. When the marines finally withdrew, they had defeated those forces thoroughly enough and had left the central authorities strong enough that *cacos* and *caudillos* never regained their pre-intervention influence.(17)

It should be noted, however, that the marines' antagonists in these wars lacked not only modern weaponry but also a modern political ideology and organization. Indeed, in the Dominican Republic the *caudillos* and their followers resembled criminal gangs more closely than they did guerrilla revolutionaries. As a result, the enemy leaders in Hispaniola were driven by thoroughly pragmatic considerations of power and ambition; they stopped fighting for equally pragmatic reasons when it became too dangerous and difficult to resist further and when the Americans made it worth their while to quit. Even these forces might have proved more than the marines could handle had the guerrillas been equipped with bolt-action rifles and plentiful ammunition. Nevertheless, the marines learned many useful lessons from what was up to that time their most ambitious counterinsurgency effort, and a generation of marine officers acquired hard-won experience. Both would stand them in good stead later in Nicaragua, where the marines would encounter an enemy both politically and militarily more formidable than the *cacos* and *caudillos*.

NOTES

1. The evolution of the advance base mission is covered in Graham A. Cosmas and Jack Shulimson, "Continuity and Consensus: The Evolution of the Marine Advance Base Force, 1900-1920," *Proceedings of the Citadel Conference on War and Diplomacy, 1977* (Charleston, S.C., 1979), 31-36.

Unless otherwise noted, the discussion of the Haitian occupation in this paper is based on the following sources: Hans Schmidt, *The United States Occupation of Haiti, 1915-1934* (New Brunswick, 1971), 43-91, 100-107, 119-23; Robert D. Heinl, Jr., and Nancy Gordon Heinl, *Written in Blood: The Story of the Haitian People, 1492-1971* (Boston, 1978), 449-73; and Headquarters, Garde d'Haiti, *The History of the Garde d'Haiti*, April-July 1934, Geographical Files, Reference Branch, U.S. Marine Corps Historical Center, Washington, D.C., 339734, 499767. This comprehensive history of the Haitian Gendarmerie, later renamed Garde d'Haiti, was prepared by a board of marine officers headed by Major Franklin A. Hart and will hereafter be cited as the "Hart Report." Unless otherwise noted, the discussion of the occupation of the Dominican Republic is based on Bruce J. Calder, *The Impact of Intervention: The Dominican Republic during the U.S. Occupation of 1916-1924* (Austin, 1984), chap. 4-5, esp. 123-32, 140-43, 151-53, 162-63, 168-78; and Capt. Stephen M. Fuller, USMC, and Graham A. Cosmas, *Marines in the Dominican Republic, 1916-1924* (Washington, 1974), 13-22, 28-43, 45-48, 57-58, 65. Material has been drawn also from the Records of the Military Government of Santo Domingo, Record Group 38, Entry 6, Boxes 13, 23, 24, 36, 37, 48, 50, 64, and 74, National Archives, Washington, D.C. (hereafter cited as RG 38, E6), and from the Naval Records Collection of the Office of Naval Records and Library, Record Group 45, WA-7, Boxes 755-57 and 761, National Archives, Washington, D.C. (hereafter cited as RG 45, WA-7).

2. In the Dominican Republic, in contrast to Haiti, the United States in 1916 installed a military government, which was normally headed by a navy rear admiral as military governor. The Second Marine Brigade came under the military governor's command, and the brigade commander headed the combined ministries of War and Marine and Interior and Police, in effect making him responsible for the provincial and municipal governments, law enforcement, and national defense.

3. First quotation is from Headquarters, First Provisional Brigade, General Order 17, 18 July 1919; the second is from Report, Military Governor of Santo Domingo to the Secretary of the Navy, subject: Claim of Dugal McPhail . . . , 19 May 1924; both of these documents are in RG 38, E6, Boxes 13 and 74.

4. The manpower needs of counterinsurgency are emphasized in Message, Flag San Domingo to OpNav, 24 November 1918, and Report, Commanding Officer, Third Provisional Regiment, to Brigade Commander, subject: Field Operations, etc., 27 February 1919, RG 45, WA-7, Boxes 756-57. For the size of the marine brigades, see Robert D. Heinl, Jr., *Soldiers of the Sea: The United States Marine Corps, 1775-1962* (Annapolis, 1962), 237, 241-42.

5. For typical comments on manpower turbulence and its effects, see Quarterly Reports of the Military Governor of Santo Domingo, 1 October through 31 December 1919 and 1 January through 31 March 1921, RG 38, Entry 15, Box 1.

6. Commanding General, Second Brigade, to All Officers of the Brigade, subject: General Instructions, 19 August 1921; Commanding General, Second Brigade, to All Officers of the Brigade, subject: The Brigade attitude toward the inhabitants and its place in the occupation, 15 November 1921; both letters are in RG 45, WA-7, Boxes 761 and 757. See also Headquarters, Second Brigade, Brigade Order No. 9, 20 August 1921, RG 38, E6, Box 37.

7. Lt. Col. G. C. Thorpe, Third Provisional Regiment, Campaign Order No. 2, 4 September 1918; Order, Regimental Commander to Capt. Thomas J. Watson, 9 January 1919; both orders are in RG 45, WA-7, Box 757, and illustrate patrolling procedures in the Dominican Republic.

8. Col. C. Gamborg-Andresen, Third Provisional Regiment, Report to Brigade Commander, Second Brigade, subject: Field Operations, etc., 27 February 1919, RG 45, WA-7, Box 757.

9. Quotation is from Col. C. Gamborg-Andresen, Third Provisional Regiment, Report to Brigade Commander, subject: Field Operations, etc., 27 February 1919, RG 45, WA-7, Box 757. For an example of concern with the Germans, see study by Lt. Col. G. C. Thorpe, 11 June 1918, RG 45, WA-7, Box 756. For

an appreciation of the vital importance of intelligence, see Maj. Earl H. Ellis, "Bush Brigades," *Marine Corps Gazette* 6 (March 1921): 12-14.

10. Air operations are summarized conveniently in Lt. Col. Edward C. Johnson, USMC, *Marine Corps Aviation: The Early Years, 1912-1940* (Washington, 1974), 499753. The value of radios in Dominican operations is indicated in Col. C. Gamborg-Andresen, Third Provisional Regiment, Report to Brigade Commander, subject: Field Operations, etc., 27 February 1919, RG 45, WA-7, Box 757.

11. Harllee described and defended his operations in his Report to the Commanding General, Second Brigade, subject: Operations of 15th Regiment..., 2 January 1922, RG 38, E6, Box 48. See also John Harllee, *The Marine from Manatee: A Tradition of Rifle Marksmanship* (Washington, 1984), 258 and chap. 28. Brig. Gen. Harry Lee, Report to the Major General Commandant..., subject: Report of activities of the 2nd Brigade..., for the year ending June 30th, 1922, RG 45, WA-7, Box 757, gives the brigade commander's evaluation. See also unsigned memorandum of conversation with sugar estate managers, 2 November 1921, RG 38, E6, Box 37. For the brigade order on roping suspects, see Lt. Col. W. C. Harllee, 6th endorsement to report from Department of Justice and Public Instruction, 8 December 1921, and accompanying documents in RG 38, E6, Box 37. Harllee had served in the U.S. Army in the Philippine War before joining the Marine Corps. He was a veteran of marine expeditionary service and one of the leading promoters of rifle practice in the corps.

12. Harllee, *Marine from Manatee*, 260-61, illustrates the suspicion with which marine commanders viewed the estate managers.

13. Brig. Gen. Harry Lee, Report to Major General Commandant subject: Report of activities of the 2nd Brigade... for the year ending 30th, 1922, 24 August 1922, RG 45, WA-7, Box 757.

14. Headquarters, First Brigade Daily Diary Report, 1 April 1920, RC E6, Box 24.

15. For Lee's terms and disposition of cases, see Brig. Gen. Lee, Rep Major General Commandant..., subject: Report of activities of the 2nd Brigade... for the year ending June 30th, 1922, 24 August 1922, R(WA-7, Box 757; Rear Adm. Samual Robison to Sugar Estate Managers, 13 June 1922; Lee, Report to Military Governor, subject: Bandits and b leaders, status of, 22 May 1923, RG 38, E6, Boxes 36 and 64.

16. The evolution of small wars doctrine in the Marine Corps during 1920s and 1930s is described in Ronald Schaffer, "The 1940 Small Manual and the 'Lessons of History,'" *Military Affairs* 36 (April 1 46-51. For marine views in the early 1920s, see Ellis, "Bush Brigades," 1-16, from which the quotation is taken, and Maj. Samuel M. Harrington, "The Strategy and Tactics of Small Wars," *Marine Corps Gazette* 6 (December 1921): 474-91; and 7 (March 1922): 84-93. Both these authors devote as much or more attention to urban street fighting as they do to rural operations against guerrillas.

17. Calder, *Impact of Intervention*, 181-82, notes the *caudillos*' intervention loss of local influence.

U.S. MARINES AND MISKITO INDIANS: THE RIO COCO PATROL OF 1928

David C. Brooks

> *After nearly three decades conducting counterinsurgency operations, the Marine Corps clearly established a learned expertise in waging war of this kind in Nicaragua. Perhaps the clearest example of this progress can be garnered from Merritt A. Edson's remarkable leadership in the Rio Coco patrol of 1928. In this endeavor, Edson demonstrated a maturity in obtaining political objectives through force of arms as well as a healthy appreciation of the indigenous cultures encountered. Rising scholar David Brooks provides a rare anthropological perspective on these events.*

When it comes to the history of the U S. Marine Corps, few names stand out more than MajGen Merritt A. "Red Mike" Edson's. Famous for winning the Medal of Honor on Guadalcanal, Edson is also recognized for his leadership during the Rio Coco patrol during the Second Nicaragua Campaign (1926-33). Although several historians have treated the Rio Coco patrol, they mostly have emphasized Edson's composure in the face of natural hazards and determined opposition from Sandinista guerrillas or his creativity in employing light infantry tactics.(1) Most of these accounts have not dealt with the unique political aspect of the mission. Yet this "other side" of the Rio Coco patrol is perhaps the more significant for today's Marines. Edson's story illustrates how the many campaigns of that era, together known by the trivializing term "Banana Wars," may have much to say to the Marines of today.

Though the link between the 1920s and 1990s may not be obvious, the two eras basic similarity: The collapse of the United States' great power rival (in the earlier case penal Germany, in the latter the Soviet empire) has led to a period of prolonged peace characterized by limited war and multiple forms of small-scale military engagement. Historically, the burden of these messy kinds of political military missions has fallen heavily upon U.S. Marines. Like their Banana Wars' ancestors, today's Marines have to carry out a variety of complex tasks – peacekeeping, hostage rescue, refugee support, drug interdiction, counterinsurgency, and combinations thereof – on the shoestring budgets typical of these periods of military retrenchment. In its own way, Edson's Rio Coco patrol illustrates how Marines in the past successfully adapted to similar exigencies. The full story of the patrol, however also shows some of the stickier and unanticipated difficulties that accompany any effort at foreign intervention, even a relatively successful one.

Background to Intervention

Before discussing Edson's mission, it is important to recall the circumstances that brought about the Second Nicaragua Campaign. In 1926, vicious civil war broke out in Nicaragua between the country's two rival political parties, the Liberals and the Conservatives. Washington responded as it so often had in the past, by sending Marines to Nicaragua to establish neutral zones and protect U.S. lives and property.

Along with the Marines came Special Presidential Envoy Henry Stimson in May 1927. Stimson put forward a plan to get the warring factions to move their struggle from the battlefield to the ballot box. U.S. Marines would both train a new, nonpartisan Nicaraguan army, the Guardia Nacional, and would supervise a free election. Under pressure from Stimson, Liberal and Conservative leaders agreed to the American representative's plan – all save one. In May of that year, Liberal General Augusto C. Sandino rejected the U.S. sponsored scheme as unwarranted Yankee interference in his country's affairs and retreated into the mountains of the Nicaraguan north with about 200 men to launch an early "war of national liberation" against what he called Nicaragua's *vendepatria* (country-selling) elites and the U.S. Marines.

Within a year, the conflict had become a stalemate, locking itself into a pattern familiar to students of counterinsurgency. The Marines easily controlled the cities and towns of western Nicaragua. Sandino and his men, however, were masters of the rugged hills of Nueva Segovia. In addition, when pressed from Marine patrols, the Sandinistas could cross the mountains that divide Nicaragua and descend the Coco River, or Rio Coco as it is known in Spanish, which forms the border between Honduras and Nicaragua, and attack the country's Caribbean side – the site of many important U.S. and foreign investments. This region of Nicaragua, known locally as the Atlantic Coast, served as a kind of strategic rear for the insurgents.

The Marines recognized the military significance of the Atlantic Coast and moved into this zone in 1928, establishing the Eastern Area, under the command of Maj Harold H. Utley. Working under Utley was an innovative young captain named "Red Mike" Edson. In the weeks before landing, Edson and his shipmates aboard the USS *Denver* eagerly followed the campaign in Nicaragua by studying a Christian Brothers map of the country that hung from the bulkhead of the ship's mess. At that time, Edson noted how the Rio Coco dominated the northern part of the country. A kind of Nicaraguan Mississippi, the Coco begins in Nueva Segovia, in the heart of what was then Sandinista territory, and runs more than 300 miles to empty into the Caribbean Sea at Cabo Gracias a Dios. Edson reasoned that the Marines might use the mighty Central American waterway to penetrate Nicaragua's difficult terrain and blindside Sandino, hitting him from a previously secure flank.

The Marines Land on the Atlantic Coast

Utley, Edson, and about 150 other Marines came ashore in January 1928. Almost immediately, Edson and several of Utley's other officers began a series of riverine penetrations, an experience that gave Edson the chance to try out his ideas about navigating the Coco. These first efforts became a test that his Marines would fail decisively. Edson himself later recalled what happened when the "can –do" attitudes of his men clashed with the realities of Central America's most formidable river. As he wrote:

> While here [at Livings Creek on the Rio Coco] two men of the patrol made their first attempt at navigating a native dugout with a pole and paddle as they had seen the Indians do. [The two Marines] pushed out into the river, both paddling frantically, first on one side then the other. The boat went round and round in circles until finally the current washed it ashore a mile or so down stream and the two men gave up the attempt and walked back. It was ludicrous enough but it was a fair example of what might be expected from men whose only experience with water craft had been as passengers in a ship's motor sailer.(2)

In contrast to the early and rather bumbling efforts of the Marines, the Indians were masters of the Rio Coco. As Edson described them:

> [They] were taught to swim as soon as they were taught to walk, and once they could stand erect they found a pole and paddle thrust into their hands so that they could learn to navigate the native pitpan [dugout canoe].(3)

The natives that Edson referred to were Miskito Indians, members of an indigenous group that, along with their neighbors, the Sumu and the English-speaking black Creoles, made up the population of Nicaragua's Atlantic Coast. These different peoples constituted more than just a series of Nicaraguan ethnic groups. In fact, the Atlantic Coast was (and, some would argue, remains) a kind of submerged nation within Nicaragua that possessed distinct history, languages, and cultural rhythms from the rest of the country.

A Nation Within a Nation-State

At the time of the intervention, the Miskito made up the largest and most important population group along the Rio Coco. As a people, they have a singular and proud history. Unlike other Central American Indian groups, the Miskito successfully resisted Spanish conquest in the 16th century. Later, in the 1600s they made common cause with British buccaneers who found them useful allies in raids against the Spanish for their canoeing and maritime skills. This de facto Indian-English alliance would receive official expression in 1687 when British naval officers in Jamaica crowned the Miskitos' most prominent chief, Jeremy I, King of the Mosquito (the spelling commonly used by British of that time, as in Mosquito Coast).

For a little over two centuries, the Mosquitia, a separate kingdom with its own monarch, would remain independent from Nicaragua. Over time, the Indian society lost its military coloration as Moravian missionaries from Bethlehem, PA, and American and British companies like Standard Fruit moved into the area. Along with the foreign companies and the missionaries came small businessmen – many of them Britons, Germans, and Americans – who settled in the interior of the Rio Coco. They settled into the region, married Indian women, and set up trading posts, ranches, boatyards, and lumber supply areas along the river. These people, calls "bamboo whites" by the Marines, shipped raw wood from inside Nicaragua to sawmills located at Puerto Cabezas on the coast. Both politically and economically, they would prove critical in the war with Sandino.

As a result of all these developments – missionary activity, the development of foreign owned "big businesses" along the coast, and the addition of a new strata of "bamboo businessmen" to the area's social structure – the Mosquitia remained more connected to the United States and the English-speaking Caribbean than to Hispanic Nicaragua. But if local history and economics pushed the coast in one direction, geopolitics moved it in another. Backed by pressure from the United States, Great Britain dropped the coast from protectorate status and officially ceded the area to Nicaragua in 1860. Since Nicaragua was too weak to exercise its claim, the coast remained in political limbo for decades until Nicaraguan President Jose Santos Zelaya sent troops into the area to capture Bluefields in 1894.

Despite military occupation by Spanish-speaking troops, the Indians continued to resent the Nicaraguans. The inhabitants of the coast also kept looking to Great Britain for support. In the years following the 1894 takeover, Black Creoles and Miskito Indians would pepper the British Foreign Office with petitions that asked the British to retake their territory, a tradition that would continue until the late 1950s.

Competing for Contacts

From the first, Edson worked hard to create a network of contacts that could help him win the cooperation of the local people. Fortunately, the area's social structure provided him with a natural "in" with the natives. Benny Muller, a bamboo businessman, was an American logger who had lived in the area since 1895. Through Muller, Edson:

> met all of the influential people in this section and the chiefs of the larger settlements, and they in turn assisted in inculcating the ordinary Indian with the idea that we meant them no harm . . . (4)

These same local notables also related to Edson the essentials of the Indians' history and culture, and he was quick to appreciate their implications for his own mission. As he wrote years later in the *Marine Corps Gazette*:

> The Miskitos were inculcated from the rime of their birth with a hatred of the Nicaraguans whom they called Spaniards' and so were potential allies if properly approached and handled.... By learning enough native words to make my wants known to them; by showing an interest in their mode of living; and by always treating them fairly, I believe that I succeeded in that part of my mission to establish cordial relations with the inhabitants.(5)

Despite his advantages, Edson's task would not be an easy one. Sandino, too, had recognized Indian's importance and had taken steps to win their trust. In addition, the people of the coast historically supported the Liberal Party, Sandino was a member, albeit a dissenter. Edson later recalled:

> In his journey up the river in 1927, Sandino treated the inhabitants of the river in a friendly and conciliatory manner so that the feeling, not anti-American, was certainly not anti-Sandinista. Through his agents, Sandino exerted a distinct influence throughout the whole valley and received tribute of both money and food from as far east as Bocay.(6)

Sandino, like the Marines, depended on Miskitos to help to move up and down the Rio Coco. One sign of the importance that the Nicaraguan guerilla attached to the Indians' assistance was lieutenants whom he appointed to oversea operations in this part of Nicaragua – Abraham Rivers and Adolfo Cockburn. Both were intimately familiar with the Rio Coco and performed services for Sandino that resembled those carried out for Edson. Thus, the miniwar for the Rio Coco quickly became less a contest for territory and more a political one for the loyalty of people whose skills either side would need to control the region.

When in the Mosquitia, Do as the Indians Do

Soon after arriving on the Atlantic Coast, Edson suggested his idea for a long-range patrol up the Rio Coco, but this was at first rejected by the Marine command. In the meantime, he worked to extend his relations with the local people. Perhaps the most interesting facet of his efforts at this stage was his attempt to imitate the Indians and get other Marines to do the same. When he had the opportunity, Edson traveled with the Miskito in their canoes. In letters home, he recounted how he enjoyed shooting the Rio Coco's white water rapids with the Miskito. As his correspondence shows, however, canoeing with the Indians constituted more than mere sport. By learning to handle a fast-moving *pipante*, Edson and his men were later prepared when local help proved hard to find. As he wrote to his wife in early June 1928:

> On the 2d ... Linscort, eight enlisted and myself left Kalasanoki by boat and came down to Bocay. There is no trail down the river, so we came down to look it

over. Due to the shortage of Indians, a corporal of my outfit and I paddled down in a small boat. . . . You should have seen us shooting rapids – almost as good as Indians. It was great trip and rather thrilling in spots.(7)

Patrols overland also benefited from the Miskito example. In a letter to his son, written in May 1928, Edson described how the Marines had adopted camping techniques from the Indians:

> You are probably asking if these Indians live in tents, aren't you? They do not use tents, but lean-toos (sic) when stopping for only a few days. These lean-toos are made like this. Four bamboo poles are cut and tied together at the top. Then on the side towards the wind where the rain will come, they put up a roof or a wall of leaves something like this. [Illustrated in letter.] The floor is the sand, and their beds are made of big green banana leaves laid on the sand. Then they put down a blanket from the bark of a tree, and that is their sleeping plan. It is not a bad bed either, for your Daddy has slept several nights just like that.(8)

The Rio Coco Patrol

In July 1928, the Marine command decided to launch a patrol up the Rio Coco to take Poteca, Sandino's headquarters 350 miles into the interior of Nicaragua. This was a formidable task. First, the mission would take place at the height of the rainy season, when the Coco becomes a raging torrent that can rise as much as 20 feet, often tearing trees from its banks and hurtling them downstream with deadly force. All supply would be cut off except by air, and even that contact would be intermittent during stormy weather. In addition to natural obstacles, the Marines would also face the prospect of ambush by Sandinista guerrillas in the interior. On 26 July 1928, Edson set out with 46 other Marines and their Indian guides and oars men from Bocay to take Poteca.

Under these conditions it became essential to win local cooperation if the mission was to succeed. Edson found that despite his successes with the Indians down the river, those who lived closer to Poteca were more wary of the Marines. This often resulted in a shortage of willing Indian boatmen, and forced the Marines into a "stop and go" pattern in their advance.(9) Still, Edson instructed his men to approach the river people in a friendly way, even though some had aided Sandino in the past.(10)

Utley backed Edson's patient approach. Although this slowed the advance, he realized that the Marines had to consider the Miskitos' delicate political situation, sandwiched as the Indians were between the forces of the intervention and those of Sandino. In a letter to the Marine command in Managua written in August 1928, he justified Edson's slow pace in political terms:

> It appears that we are approaching one of the delays due to lack of transportation which while I anticipated, are nevertheless heartbreaking. . . . We are . . .

handicapped by two factors; the lack of boats and the disinclination of the indians (sic) to go into the zone of operations. We can get enough to operate all the boats we have as far up as Bocay but it is difficult to get them to go farther then that. Impressment only serves to kill the goose that laid the golden egg, as it means that in the future the approach of Marines is the signal for abandoning of the towns and houses. We have been at some pains to establish a feeling of confidence among the indians (sic) and hope that the situation will improve. The fact that Edson did not have any of his indians hurt was an important factor and I took pains to broadcast that information down the river as well as at Bocay.(11)

Delay was a small price to pay for good relations. Edson did resort to impressment on occasion, but his general treatment of the Indians appears to have been good. As he moved into the interior and captured Indians who had worked for Sandino, he had them disarmed, questioned, and then released in keeping with his attempts to win their favor.(12)

Edson and Utley's gradual and humane approach to the Indians of the Rio Coco contrasted markedly with the way that at least some Marines treated Sandinista "collaborators" in Nueva Segovia on the other side of Nicaragua. There, the burning of the houses of guerrilla sympathizers and the loss of many prisoners "shot while attempting to escape" took place frequently enough that it compelled the Marine command to issue orders in 1928 and 1931 asking for restraint in dealing with the locals and prohibiting the destruction of homes.(13) In 1930 the Marines in this region also tried to resettle villagers by force into secured zones, an effort that was called off when Matagalpa and Jinotega became flooded with refugees.(14) In part, the Marines in Nueva Segovia resorted to harsher policies because they were engaged in a shooting war when Edson and Utley faced primarily a political situation. Nonetheless, the contrast between the Marine approaches to these two different regions of Nicaragua is noteworthy. Although the differences in Marine methods used is only one variable in a complex situation, it seems that Edson's patience contributed importantly to his ultimate success along the Rio Coco and that the harsher measures used in Nueva Segovia probably aggravated an already bad situation in the Sandinistas' home area.(15)

The patience of the Eastern Area Marines would pay off handsomely in strategic terms. After foiling an ambush by Sandinista guerrillas on 7 August, Edson and his men captured Sandino's headquarters at Poteca 10 days later and sent the Nicaraguan guerrilla forces scattering into the interior of the country. This action not only threw the Sandinistas off balance, it also prevented them from massing to disrupt the U.S. supervised election in the fall of 1928.

Edson's Rio Coco patrol would represent, in the words of Maj Utley, the "elastic limit" of the Marines' penetration of Nicaragua from its eastern shore.(16) Along the river, behind Edson's base, Marines began to set up strong points that secured the area from further Sandinista attacks. Both the Miskito and the region's bamboo whites benefited from the added security. The Marine presence and careful treatment of the locals had won the Indians' trust. After an initial period of wariness, more Indians began to cooperate freely with the Marines and many returned to their villages from the woods where they had hidden.(17)

The stability achieved along the upper reaches of the Rio Coco did not endure, however. In March 1929, the Marine command in Managua ordered a pullback from the interior of the Rio Coco for later that year. Maj Utley protested these orders in the name of a people whose friendliness he had cultivated. As he put it, the Indians of the interior:

> . . . have gained confidence in our ability and willingness to afford them protection. To abandon Bocay will leave the entire north eastern (sic) part of the province of Jinorega open to any small band of marauders who – when organized bands are broken up – may be expected to continue their depredations.(18)

In fact, the Indians had gained more than just confidence in the Marines. Some decided to fight alongside the Marines by joining the Guardia Nacional. Although it has proven impossible to pin down exact numbers, one Marine report from 1930 that describes Guardia recruiting stated that, "On the Atlantic Coast a considerable Mosquito Indians are enlisted."(19) Evidence exists that Marine trainers appreciated the special abilities of their Indian recruits. As one instructor working at Bluefields in 1929 commented:

> I can conceive of no more valuable soldier than a properly trained and disciplined Mosquito boy with his knowledge of woodcraft and tracking at the same time an ability to read a simple map and perhaps make a simple sketch.(20)

While young Indians joined the Guardia Nacional, their community leaders looked at Americans in new ways as well. In particular, they saw them as potential deliverers from the abuses and depredations of the "Spaniard" regimes in Managua, a development that added a wrinkle of complexity to the Marine-Miskito connection. Indians involved in land disputes with the Nicaraguan Government protested to Maj Utley in 1929, and to a Marine Col Wynn in the Guardia Nacional in 1931.(21) The concluding words to the petition sent to Col Wynn show how at least some Miskito had come to view the Marines and, by extension, the United States. It read:

> We Miskito Indians are clamoring for the Americans to sever us from our bonds, from this Nicaraguan yoke, [to] give us as before our reservation, and hold the sole rights of protectorate, given by us.(22)

Washington, however, viewed the problem from a different perspective. The administration hoped to wrap up an unpopular intervention as soon as possible and so the planned withdrawal of the Marines took place. Soon after, the Sandinistas regained control of Bocay and used this as a staging area to rebuild their position along the upper reaches of the Rio Coco. In February 1931, Indian spies told Guardia Nacional

Intelligence that the Sandinistas were once again gathering forces at their old headquarters. Driven from Jinotega and Maragalpa in the west by aggressive Marine patrols, they were preparing a strike downriver with the aid of agents located as far down as Puerto Cabezas. A critical part of the insurgents' preparations had involved successful political work among the Bocay Indians. As the report said:

> A deliberate effort has been made to gain favor with the Bocay Indians with a view to having their support, and has met with considerable success. The Indians in this reason professing (sic) themselves ready to take part in any attack on Guardia or expedition to Puerto Cabezas or Cabo Gracias [a Dios]. What means, exactly, has been used to gain the confidence of the Bocay Indians is not known, but their feelings and sympathies have been clearly brought over to the side of the bandits.(23)

The United States' precipitous pullback combined with the effects of the global economic depression set the stage for a devastating guerrilla retaliation. In April 1931, the Sandinistas launched an offensive against the Atlantic Coast. Striking down the Rio Coco, they captured Cabo Gracias a Dios and assaulted Puerto Cabezas, the headquarters of the Standard Fruit Company and the home of hundreds of its American employees. The Sandinista raids caused panic within the city and disrupted Indian communities all along the river.(24)

Despite these later reversals, Edson's and Utley's careful work would not be completely undone. Miskito Indians, particularly those located on the lower Rio Coco and those along the Caribbean coast, served in the Guardia Nacional alongside Marine officers and helped thwart these same attacks.(25) At least one reason for the Miskitos' continued loyalty to the Marine-led Guardia was a new found fear of the Sandinistas. Although Sandino's lieutenants would still enjoy the help of some Indians from deep inside the Rio Coco region,(26) they abandoned the guerrilla general's earlier careful treatment of the inhabitants and resorted to terrorism in dealing with the Indians and bamboo whites. They beheaded a Moravian missionary for allegedly operating as a Guardia spy and burned his village because its inhabitants had helped Edson. In addition, Sandinista guerrillas roved the Rio Coco with hit lists of bamboo whites condemned to death for having aided the Marines. Finally, the insurgents captured and killed a number of employees of Standard Fruit, dismembering their bodies with machetes.

Despite their violence, these measures would do the guerrillas little good. Far from their logistical base, they became vulnerable to Marine counterattacks by aircraft and by ground patrols. After one of Sandino's top lieutenants, Pedro Blandon was killed in the attack on Puerro Cabezas, the insurgents had to retreat back up the river. In the end, the depredations they carried out only turned the inhabitants against the insurgents and earned the earlier Sandinistas a reputation as "bandits " among the Indians, a perception that persists to this day and helps explain Miskito resistance to the Sandinista Government of the 1980s.(27)

Lessons Learned

Soldiers are inclined to view history in a very technical fashion. Frequently, they want to know what tactic or gambit can be borrowed from the past and used in the future. This view, however, better fits large, conventional battles than it does small wars, interventions, and counterinsurgency campaigns, which rarely turn on a single dazzling maneuver. Instead, such endeavors prove the truth of the old cliché about presidential campaigns in the United States that, "All politics is local." Small wars most often turn on local factors, and they are consummately political contests.

On this score both Edson and Sandino have to be given high marks. Each possessed an ability to "read" the local situation and put that knowledge to effective use. If, in the end, Sandino "lost" the Atlantic Coast, this would appear to have happened not through any blunder of his own, but rather because he failed to control his lieutenants – a problem not uncommon to armies fighting guerrilla wars, as the examples of Marine tactics in Nueva Segovia cited above indicate. As the conflict with the Americans dragged on and as their frustration mounted, Sandino's lieutenants seemed to view the complex bamboo white social structure of the Atlantic Coast through the lens of their own militant Hispanic nationalism. Thus, missionaries and bamboo whites friendly to the Marines, many of them American, appeared as foreigners or *vendepatrias*, deserving only death. These actions only alienated the Miskito who looked upon these foreigners as friends, employers, and even kinsmen.

But beyond Edson's (or Sandino's) effectiveness as a "soldier-diplomat," the Rio Coco case study also shows, in an overall sense, how interventions are shaped by the complex, many-sided politics of underdeveloped countries. Since Vietnam, it has become fashionable in some circles to interpret interventions as primarily conflicts between the resented forces of foreign powers and outraged nationalists, between "imperialists" and local patriots. From the perspective of post-World War I decolonization, such a view seemed natural. Yet in the case discussed here the conflict was not a two-sided military one, but a three-sided relationship between Indians, Marines, and insurgents – an association that was shaped as much by the politics of adhesion as by some reflex on the part of the locals to reject the outsider.

As Edson and Utley understood, special factors made the Miskito "potential allies if properly approached and handled." Yet, this added new complications to the Marines' task, for to have remained effective along the Rio Coco the Americans would have had to stay in the area. Overall, the Indians preferred the Marines to the largely Spanish-speaking Guardia Nacional. Still, to have created a purely Miskito army would have been locally logical but also would have undercut U.S. "nation-building" agenda in Nicaragua, its plan to bolster the elected regime of friendly "Spaniards" in Managua. Yet to fail to do either of these things left the Indians open to the angry Sandinista backlash of 1931. Thus, the Indians were not just "potential allies" but also potential victims, as Utley recognized, when Washington's shifts undercut the actions of creative Marines in the field.

In this way, the Rio Coco case study speaks to what happens when U.S. forces encounter a frustrated national group of the type that appears to be emerging in a variety of areas today. The Miskito example discussed here brings to mind the Montagnards in Vietnam and, more recently, Kurds of northern Iraq. Alliances with communities like these quickly become very tricky and are charged with ethical implications because such peoples frequently become dependent on the forces of an occupation for protection and support or, more importantly, because they may want to use the intervention as a springboard for further political action. When these considerations do not parallel Washington's agenda, it is often up to the military to resolve the differences in the field, something that can be a difficult and messy task.

In conclusion, the Rio Coco patrol serves as more than just an apt illustration of how some members of an earlier generation of Marines modified their tactics to fit the politics of the areas in which they served. Ultimately, it also shows why counterinsurgency remains the most difficult military tasks even when well executed under favorable circumstances. In the end, this may be the most important lesson that today's Marines can learn from the story of Edson's mission and the Marine-Sandinista struggle to control the Rio-Coco from 1928-1931.

NOTES

1. For an insightful discussion of Edson's use of light infantry tactics, see Maj Jon T. Hoffman, "Edson's First Raiders,"' Vol. 5, No. 3, Fall 1991, pp. 20-25.
2. Edson, "Coco Patrol," *Marine Corps Gazette*, (August 1936).
3. Edson, Coco Patrol," *Marine Corps Gazette*, (August 1936), p. 41.
4. Edson, "Coco Patrol," *Marine Corps Gazette*, (August 1936), p. 40.
5. Edson, "Coco Patrol," *Marine Corps Gazette*, (August 1936), p. 41.
6. Edson, "Coco Patrol," *Marine Corps Gazette*, (August 1936), p. 40.
7. Letter to Ethel R. Edson, Bocay, Nicaragua, 4 June 1928. File: "letters Nicaragua. MAF to IRE. 5 April 1928 to 8 July 1928." Container 2. Edson Papers. Library of Congress (LC).
8. Letter to M. Austin Edson, Musawas, Nicaragua, 22 May 1928. File: "Letters Nicaragua. MAF to ERE. 5 April 1928 to 8 July 1928." #16 Container 2. Edson Papers. LC
9. A telegram from "Commanding Officer, Puerto Cabezas," (Utley) to "Brigade Commander," (Managua), 4 June 1928 reports that as Marine patrols penetrated the Bocay-Poteca region deep in Nicaragua's interior, "All reports indicate natives and Indians show fear of Marines." NA, RG 127, Entry 221, File 923 (Information from Eastern Area 1928).
10. Headquarters, Eastern Area, Nicaragua, Marine Barracks. Puerto Cabezas, Nic., 17 June 1928. Special Intelligence Report – Wanks River – Waspuc River – Bocay Area. Signed, "MA. Edson." The report notes that most of the people in the area have aided Sandino at one time or another but that, "If properly handled, a great deal of assistance may be expect (sic) as boatmen, guides and laborers." The key, Edson asserts, is, "to maintain a friendly attitude towards them." Folder 20, Entry 204 RG 127 National Archives.
11. United States Marine Corps, Headquarters, Eastern Area, Puerto Cabezas Nicaragua, 16 August 1928. Letter from Maj Harold H. Utley to the Commanding General. NA, RG 127, Entry 221, File 922 (East Coast).
12. Headquarters, Second Brigade, Marine Corps, Managua, Nicaragua, 17 August 1928, "Dispatch – Outgoing – Code Underlined Words."
13. Headquarters, Northern Area, Western Nicaragua, U.S. Marines, Ocotal, Nicaragua, 23 Mayo 1928, Memorandum for all Officers and Men of the Marine Corps and Guardia Nacional in the Northern Area from Col R.H. Dunlap, USMC, Commanding Officer, RG 127, Entry 220, File 811.0(2), 11th Regiment Correspondence. Therein, Col Dunlap reminds Marines that rural inhabitants are the victims of bandit depredations and so, "they hide out, act suspicious and . . . become hunted creatures by both bandits and Marines." The Memorandum asks that Marines make sure that the houses they destroy belong to bandits. Two years later the commander of the Guardia Nacional, Col Julian C. Smith, would forbid all house-burning and prohibit the Guardia from exercising arbitrary authority under martial law, although such was technically permitted in northern areas of the country at the rime. See: Headquarters Central Area, Guardia Nacional de Nicaragua, Jinotega, Nicaragua, 26 May 1931, Area Order from Col Julian C. Smith, Guardia Nacional de Nicaragua, Commanding Central Area, RG 127, Entry 202, File 32.0.
14. Telegram from the CO, GN Northern Area to Jefe Director GN Managua; All GN Northern Area, 9 June 1930. See also: Telegram, Dept Comdr Matagalpa to D.C. McDougal. Both located in RG 127, Entry 220, File 815: Commander of the Special Service Squadron.
15. For examples of the harder-edged approach that the Marines took toward pro-Sandinista peasants in Nueva Segovia, see: Guardia Nacional, San Juan, 22 February 1931, Patrol Report [by 1stLt J.H. Sanerfield, G.N.] which describes how a "bandit" was wounded and left where he fell, "jaw broken, right arm broken also shot thin (sic) back" after attempts at interrogation. House burning is described in: Headquarters, District of Palacaguina, Guardia Nacional, 9 March 1931, Patrol Report from J. Ogden Brauer, District Commander, which describes burning of houses. For an example of prisoner "shot while attempting to escape," see: Guardia Nacional de Nicaragua, San Juan de Telpaneca, Nic., 13 March 1932, Patrol Report from 2dLt Donald G. Truesdale, Guardia Nacional. All of the above references are RG 127, Entry 202. The first two are from File: 52.0 and the last from File: 54.0. Further such information can be found in the same Entry (202) in File: 57.0 and among loose materials near File: 55 in the front of Box 13.
16. Headquarters, Eastern Area, Nicaragua, Marine Barracks, Puerto Cabezas, Nicaragua, 1 June 1928,

Letter from Maj Utley to the Commanding General. Utley's estimate of the situation attached. p. 1 of Estimate.

17. On Indians returning to their homes, see: Headquarters, Eastern Area, Nicaragua, Marine Barracks, Puerto Cabezas, Nicaragua, Intelligence Reports for 1 April 1928 and 3 June 1928, RG 127, Entry 204, Folder: 20.

18. Letter from the Commander Eastern Area to the Commanding General, Second Brigade, 26 March 1929, PC 127, Box IV, Utley Papers, Marine COTS Historical Center, Building 58, Washington Navy Yard, Washington, DC.

19. "Estimate of the Situation in Nicaragua," Sec. Nav. Gen. Corresp. 1925, "EF-49" Box 2009 Folder: EF 49/P9-2 (291112 to 30033).

20. Letter from H.D. Linscort, Department Commander, to The Area Commander, Area of the East, Guardia Nacional, Bluefields, Department of Northern Bluefields, Guardia Nacional, Puerto Cabezas, Nicaragua, 6 September 1929 RG 127 Entry 202, File 92.0.

21. Letter from Maj Harold H. Utley, Headquarters, Eastern Area, Nicaragua, Marine Barracks, Puerto Cabezas, Nicaragua, 18 February 1928, to H. Sanford London, Esquire, His British Majesty's Charge D'Affaires, Managua, Nicaragua, Folder: Utley's Personal 3 Jan '28 to Jul 31, Box, 3, Utley Papers, Marine Corps Historical Center, Building 58, Washington Navy Yard.

22. Letter from the Miskito Indians of Bilwi to the Honorable Colonel Wynn, Commander, Guardia Nacional, Eastern Area, Bluefields, Nicaragua, 15 May 1931, File E, Bilwi, Entry 206, RG 127, National Archives.

23. Letter from H.N. Sent to The Department Commander, Department of Northern Bluefields, Guardia Nacional Dc Nicaragua, 20 February 1931, RG 127, Entry 43-A, File: 2d Brig B-3 Repts & Mess 1Jan-24Mar31.

24. Months later, Marine Inspectors would report how previously-secured areas remained in chaos as a result of the Sandinistas' resurgence. In describing the situation around Waspuc, one Marine author (unidentified) commented on how, as a result of Sandinista raids, "Several hundred Indians who previously lived in that region [the area around Waspuc, a town far behind the areas originally secured by Edson] have come into the town below Kisalaya, over crowding them (sic) and making living conditions almost impossible." Inspection Report (apparently a rough draft), Guardia Nacional de Nicaragua, 9th Company, Puerto Cabezas, 31 August 1932, located on back of last page of said report.

25. See: "Estimate of the Situation in Nicaragua," Sec. Nay. Gen. Corrsp. 1925, "EF-49" Box 2009 Folder EF 49/P9-297 (291112 to 30033); Letter from H.D. Linscott, Department Commander, to The Area Commander, Area of the East, Guardia Nacional, Bluefields, Department of Northern Bluefields, Guardia Nacional, Puerto Cabezas, Nicaragua, 6 September 1929, RG 127, Entry 202, File 92.0.

26. See Patrol Report from 2dLt E.J. Suprenant, G.N. to The Area Commander, Eastern Area, Bluefields, Nic., District of Kisalaya, Department of Northern Bluefields, Kisalaya, Nicaragua, 2 February 1932. NA, RG 127, Entry 202, File 58.0.

27. See Patrol Report by E.J. Suprenant, District Commander, to The Area Commander, Eastern Area, Bluefields, District of Kisalaya, Department of Northern Bluefields, Kisalaya, Nicaragua, 29 February 1932, RG 127 Entry 202, File: 54.0 Therein, Suprenant describes the enthusiastic participation of aggrieved Miskitos in a Marine-led, Guardia Nacional patrol directed against Sandinistas who had recently raided several villages in the Kisalaya area. Suprenant conclusion relates his own frustration at nor having enough men to "clean up" the area above Kisalaya and his inability to explain this deficiency to "the land owners [Miskito Indians, for land along the Rio Coco is plentiful] that (sic) have property above Kisalava. On a similar sacking of Sacklin, a town with pro-Sandinista connections, for example, see: patrol Report from: Department Commander O.A. Inman, to: Area Commander, Area of the East, Guardia Nacional, Bluefields, Nicaragua, Department of Northern Bluefields, Guardia Nacional de Nicaragua, Puerto Cabezas, Nicaragua, 29 April 1931, RD 127, Entry 202, File: 57.0. In other areas, particularly along the Prineapolka River, at least some Miskito sought more of a Marine presence to maintain order and protect them from elements they saw as lawless. For an example, see Letter from Stephen Boudien (?), Head of Community Mosquitos (sic) Tungla to Commander in Chief of the U.S.M.C., Tungla (Nicaragua), 7 January 1929 RG 127 Entry 204, Folder 26.2. Numerous other reports document consistent Miskito cooperation with the Marines in terms of providing a rich flow of information about Sandinista or "bandit"

movements. This contrasts with the often unreliable information Marines received in Nueva Segovia, Sandino's major area of support.

SANDINO AGAINST THE MARINES: THE DEVELOPMENT OF AIR POWER FOR CONDUCTING COUNTERINSURGENCY OPERATIONS IN CENTRAL AMERICA

Kenneth A. Jennings

Captain Jennings, U.S. Air Force, explains the remarkable ingenuity of Marine Corps aviation in Nicaragua in the late 1920s and early 1930s, as Marine pilots made historic developments in the use of close air support as well as other missions in support of the infantry. Jennings gives a rather glowing report of the operations but also makes clear that the case study of Nicaragua offers a number of constructive lessons about utilizing air in support of counter-insurgency operations.

Although Project Warrior studies often concentrate on the role of Army Air Corps, the U.S. Marine occupation of Nicaragua during the late 1920s and early 1930s made significant contributions to the development of air power. After Marine Corps units had occupied Nicaragua for more than a decade and were withdrawn in 1925, U.S. adventurers flew in the Nicaraguan Civil War in 1926, and Marine aviators participated in the counterinsurgency campaign against Augusto Sandino when Marines were redeployed to the troubled nation.

As one examines Marine air activities and the legacy of ironies that the Marines left behind when they finally departed in 1933, two important lessons emerge from the Nicaraguan counterinsurgency experience: air power should be used with sufficient ground forces and a comprehensive effort to "win the hearts and minds" of the people, and air power must be used selectively to avoid generating support for the insurgents. These lessons remain applicable to today's Central American insurgencies.

1926-27: Free-Lancing in the Liberal-Conservative Civil War

The first major use of the airplane as an instrument of war in Central America took place during the mid-1920s in Nicaragua as a result of internal political strife. The roots of this conflict went back to the 1800s when Liberal and Conservative Party factions engaged in civil wars and rebellions against each other. In response to this turmoil, the United States sent in the Marines to protect its political and economic interests. The longest period of occupation lasted from 1912 until 1925 and involved as many as 2,700 Marines.(1)

When the Marines left in 1925, the United States helped to establish a Nicaraguan constabulary (under a retired U.S. Army major) in an attempt to promote stability. The United States provided arms to the constabulary and hoped that it would remain a nonpartisan military force serving the coalition government agreed on by the Liberals and Conservatives. Soon the Conservatives seized power, however, and the constabulary became an instrument for the Conservatives. The Liberals resorted to arms in 1926 to oppose the Conservatives and obtained support from Mexico.(2)

Former U.S. aviators received commissions in the Nicaraguan Military Air Service and started flying a variety of missions in support of the Conservative forces, including seaborne interdiction missions against Mexican gunrunning vessels. Their best-remembered air operation took place in February 1927 in Chinandega, located about sixty miles northwest of the capital of Managua. The pilots bombed Liberal positions to support a Conservative attack to regain possession of the city. When the Conservatives recaptured the city, more than ten blocks of the town had been destroyed by a fire. The pilots were criticized for setting off the blaze with their bombs, but the fire had probably been started by the Liberal forces.(3)

These early pilots were often forced to improvise. Because there were no bombs in Managua for the Chinandega operation, the pilots made three homemade devices. The four-foot-long, eighteen-pound bombs consisted of "dynamite and percussion caps set in containers and weighted with metal."(4) In addition to this type of homemade bomb, the pilots used assorted kinds of bombs for other operations, including shrapnel shells and homemade incendiary bombs made out of noxious-smelling ant poison, iron balls, and explosive powder. According to one of the pilots, "it looks bad and falls awry but makes lots of noise, dust, and odors when it goes off."(5)

These early air operations demonstrated that the airplane was an especially valuable asset in Nicaragua for conducting reconnaissance, sending messages, and disrupting enemy concentrations through air support and interdiction operations. The effectiveness of the airplane was further demonstrated by the U.S. Marines when they returned for their second occupation in 1927.

U.S. Marines in Nicaragua, 1927-33: The Second Time Around

The Marines increased their troop strength in Nicaragua throughout January 1927; by late February, there were more than 5,400 Marines occupying all the principal cities.(6) While the Marines deployed throughout Nicaragua and the United States provided massive aid to the Conservative government and Nicaraguan National Guard, the United States did not intend to enter the fighting directly. In May 1927, the United States negotiated an end to the hostilities, reportedly threatening the Liberals that the Marines would take to the field against them if the Liberals did not come to terms.(7)

Although this agreement ended the Liberal-Conservative conflict, one of the Liberal leaders, Augusto Sandino, felt that the Liberals had sold out to the Americans. He vowed to continue to fight against the U.S. occupation. On 16 July 1927, Sandino and his forces attacked the Marine garrison at Ocotal.

The Battle for Ocotal: First Dive Bombing in History

Sandino's attack against Ocotal in mid-July would no doubt have been successful, were it not for Marine air power. The Marines had started organizing their air assets in February 1927 when they received their first aircraft under the command of Major Ross Rowell. Six two-seater de Havilland biplanes arrived, as well as four two-seater scouting planes. The de Havillands could carry twenty-five-pound bombs and were equipped with both a forward fixed machine gun fired by the pilot and a rear swivel machine gun controlled by the observer.(8)

Ocotal, approximately 110 miles north of Managua, was defended by forty-one Marines and forty-eight Nicaraguan National Guardsmen when Sandino's attack began at 0115 on 16 July. A Marine sentry discovered the attack, as approximately 300 of Sandino's men in three columns were closing in on the Marine's position under the cover of darkness. The Marines beat back several attacks during the night and refused several summons by Sandino to surrender during the morning. By mid-morning, two Marine reconnaissance planes arrived on their daily patrol and read an aerial panel message laid out by the Ocotal garrison requesting help. One pilot strafed the rebel positions, while the other landed briefly outside of town to get an assessment of the situation from a local peasant.(9) The pilots departed for Managua to obtain reinforcements, and the first major Marine air operation in Nicaragua began when five de Havilland bombers under the command of Major Rowell arrived at 1435 hours.(10) After conducting reconnaissance flights to locate the concentrations of Sandino's forces, "one after the other, the planes peeled out of formations at 1500 feet, fixed machine guns blazing as they dived to 300 feet, where they dropped their bombs."(11) The observers used the rear swivel machine guns to shoot additional Sandinistas as the planes climbed back up to altitude.(12) A ground observer of the air attack stated that it "was as if hell broke loose. Quick explosions, then a heavy thundering one, sometimes indescribable."(13) During the forty-five-minute aerial attack, the aircraft strafed the rebels with 4,000 rounds of ammunition and dropped twenty-seven bombs, killing more than 100 of Sandino's men.(14)

Most of the rebels fled from the bombing attack, but a small number continued to fight. The ground battle continued until after 1700 hours. When it was over, Sandino had lost as many as 300 of his estimated 400-500 men who participated in the battle; Marine and Guard losses were placed at one dead and five wounded.(15)

The battle at Ocotal proved significant for air power by introducing several innovations to air warfare. As Neill Macaulay, a historian and expert on Sandino, observes, the Marine aviators conducted "the first organized dive-bombing attack in history—long before the Nazi Luftwaffe was popularly credited with the 'innovation'."(16) Another authority on the Marine campaign, Lejeune Cummins, adds that the battle marked "the first time in military annals that the relief of a beleaguered town was effected through the air."(17)

The battle at Ocotal made a definite impression on Sandino also. Before the battle, he reportedly belittled the airplanes and bombs and was quoted in the *New York Times* as telling his men that "they only made noise."(18) Once the air attack began, his followers were concentrated in groups, making them better targets for the Marine pilots. Richard Millett, a historian on Central America, states that Sandino "admittedly, had completely omitted from his pre-battle calculations" the activity of the Marine aircraft.(19) The defeat was costly, but Sandino learned from his mistakes; after Ocotal, Sandino "concentrated on ambushes and sudden raids instead of open attacks on a strong and fortified enemy."(20)

The Siege of El Chipote: Broadening the Scope of Air Operations

As demonstrated at Ocotal, the airplanes conducted air support operations for the ground forces and "performed the functions of artillery with their concentrated bomb attacks."(21) In November 1927, the concept of air operations broadened from just supporting ground forces to independent air actions. On 23 November, Marine aircraft located Sandino's mountain headquarters of El Chipote in northern Nicaragua and started bombing it almost daily. In January, the bombing campaign became more effective when the de Havilland planes were replaced with new Vought Corsairs and Curtiss Falcons having greater bomb-carrying capabilities.(22) The bombing campaign against El Chipote reached the conclusive stage on 14 January 1928 when Major Rowell led an air attack with four of the new two-seater Vought Corsair planes. Each plane was armed with machine guns, and together they bombed El Chipote with eighteen seventeen-pound and four fifty-pound demolition bombs.(23) The aviators, as Major Rowell stated in an interview, "finished the party up with [eighteen] infantry [white phosphorous] hand grenades."(24)

This operation proved to be significant in the development of air power. Jane's *All the World's Aircraft*, acknowledged for its expertise on military affairs, stated in its 1928 edition that the independent air attack against El Chipote was believed to be "the first aeroplane attack, unsupported by ground troops, ever made against a fortified position."(25) While it succeeded in driving Sandino and his force of 1,000 to 1,500 combatants out of the base, they escaped before U.S. ground forces could engage them.(26)

Expanding Air Power: Observation and Reconnaissance Missions

By 1928, the Marine aircraft inventory included twelve Falcon and Corsair observation-bombers, as well as seven Loening amphibian observation-bombers. Five trimotor Fokker transports also supported Marine operations. All of these were based at Managua initially, but several of the Loenings were later transferred to an airfield at Puerto Cabezas on the east coast.(27)

This aircraft inventory played several vital roles throughout the occupation. In addition to ground-attack operations, the pilots also conducted observation, communication, and transportation missions. Observation, or aerial reconnaissance, missions met with some difficulty as a result of the terrain and Sandino's guerrilla tactics. Many of the Marine operations were conducted in the northern Department of Nueva Segovia, along the Honduran border. Cover and concealment provided opportunities for Sandino's forces to move or set up ambushes without being noticed from the air. A *New York Times* correspondent flew over the area in 1928 and described the terrain as "thickly wooded mountains . . . tortured into a patternless wilderness of peaks, ridges, and rock-strewn cliffs. . . . Its infrequent trails are almost invisible from the air."(28)

Sandino's new tactics added to the terrain problems for those conducting observation missions. Bernard Nalty, author of the U.S. Marine Corps historical study on the Nicaraguan campaign, points out that "Sandino's men were adept at camouflage. Seldom did they move in large groups, and, if at all possible, they marched at night."(29) Carleton Beals, a correspondent visiting Sandino's forces in March 1928, made similar comments. Beals noticed that Sandino's forces traveled in the early morning before the planes made their patrols or late in the afternoon/evenings after the planes returned to base. Sandino's troops learned the habit patterns of the Marine aerial reconnaissance flights and took advantage of them; when his forces moved at other times during the day, they used the jungles for concealment.(30)

The Marine aviators refined their techniques of reconnaissance to achieve the best possible results. Usually flying patrols with two planes, the pilots would "throttle their engines and glide in over suspicious places from behind hills or mountains, flying low enough to look into windows and doors." The Marines looked for signs of Sandino's forces, "taking into account the proportion of men to women visible, the amount of wash on clotheslines, the number of animals present, and the general bearing of the people."(31)

Air observation missions provided essential support for both ground patrols and isolated outposts. Marine aircraft could sometimes detect ambushes for ground patrols, but the planes also alerted the Sandinistas to the possibility of Marine patrols in the area. In addition, the planes flew over every outpost almost daily. Since Sandino's forces would not expose themselves to air attack in a prolonged siege of one of these outposts, if "a garrison could hold out for twenty-four hours, it was usually safe."(32)

Combat aerial patrols for supply trains made up of bull carts also played an important role. For example, in February 1928 officials in Ocotal sent supply trains (one consisting of 185 oxcarts) to support Marine operations farther to the north in Nueva Segovia. The airplanes accompanied them until nightfall to watch out for ambushes after the trains cleared the outskirts of the city everyday.(33)

At times, these patrols were dangerous. On 8 October 1927, two planes were patrolling near Quilali when they discovered and attacked one of Sandino's pack trains. The rebels returned fire with rifles and hit one of the planes. It crashed, but the pilot and gunner survived and the other plane dropped them a map and notified several garrisons to send help. Search parties looked for the two men, but they were too late. Sandinista forces had captured and shot the aviators the same day of the crash. The rebels had also hanged the body of the pilot from a tree and photographed it; the picture was later published in Mexican and Honduran newspapers.(34)

Communication Missions: "On the Fly"

The airplanes also played an important role in facilitating communication between dispersed units and headquarters. During the early phases of the occupation, when an aircraft was unable to land, air-to-ground communication usually consisted of messages that pilots dropped from their airplanes. Ground-to-air communication involved several methods. White cloth signal panels laid out on the ground indicated the status of the unit or requests for supplies, air support, or medical assistance. Hand semaphore and catching messages "on the fly" were also used. "On the fly" meant that an airplane with a line suspended from its fuselage would pick up a message that was suspended in a pouch on a wire or string between two poles. Later in the occupation, both the amphibian and transport planes used radios, but radios were not used in the observation-bombers because of their unreliability.(35)

Transportation Missions: The First Air Ambulance and "Autogiro" Tests

Aviation made the difference in transportation as well. The rough terrain, dense brush, and possibility of ambush made transportation and supply difficult in "this impenetrable jungle where bull carts, the normal means of transportation, often make three to six miles a day."(36) Initially, the pilots were unable to provide much help in transport missions because their de Havillands were not big enough. In December 1927, however, they received a trimotor Fokker transport that was capable of carrying either two thousand pounds of cargo or eight fully equipped soldiers. By August 1928, the Marines were flying five Fokkers on supply and transport missions. According to Bernard Nalty, "everything from cigarettes to mules was delivered by air; in fact, some remote outposts received payrolls by airdrop."(37)

Another "first" in aviation occurred in the field of airborne transportation in January 1928. Never before had a pilot used his aircraft as an air ambulance in combat. First Lieutenant Christian Schilt became one of the aviation heroes of the Nicaraguan campaign and was awarded the Congressional Medal of Honor for his air evacuation of wounded men under fire from a makeshift airfield in Quilali. After an attack by

Sandino's forces, the Marine commander at Quilali requested an airplane to evacuate the wounded. Quilali had no airfield, however, so the necessary tools had to be air-dropped in. In three days, the Marines constructed a landing field 200 yards long in Quilali by cutting down trees and burning some of the Nicaraguan residents' houses.(38)

Between 6 and 8 January, Lieutenant Schilt made ten trips in a Vought Corsair to bring in medicine and supplies and pick up the wounded, while another plane acted as an escort, flying figure eights to suppress rebel fire. The landings were risky because Schilt's plane had been reequipped with wheels from a de Havilland and had no brakes. Each time the plane landed, the Marines ran forward to seize the wings and slow the plane down with their weight to prevent it from crashing off the runway. For takeoffs, the Marines would hold the plane in place until Schilt reached full throttle and then let go, enabling him to achieve short takeoffs.(39)

By 1931, the Nicaraguan National Guard had replaced the Marines throughout the country, but the Guard still relied on Marine aviation for supplies and transporting troops, especially when Sandino intensified his operations. Entire units were occasionally moved by air. In 1931, for example, the entire cadet corps of the Nicaraguan Military Academy was airlifted from Managua to reinforce Estelí.(40)

A basic problem for aerial transportation in Nicaragua was that adequate landing strips were not always available where they were needed. Recognizing this problem, the Marines started field-testing the predecessor to the helicopter in Managua in 1932. The "autogiro" had short wings and a forward propeller in addition to the rotor. On takeoff, the pilot would switch the engine from the rotor to the forward propeller after the rotor was spinning. While the takeoff was not vertical, it used much less runway than conventional aircraft. When the pilot disengaged the forward propeller, the rotor would autorotate and the pilot would land. The Marines were disappointed, however, because the aircraft could carry only two people and fifty pounds of cargo efficiently.(41)

Special Operations Missions: Long-Range Patrols and Leaflets

The role of aviation in assisting transportation and supply overlapped into what can be called special operations missions. In 1928, First Lieutenant Merritt Edson conducted several long-range reconnaissance ground patrols from the east coast into central Nicaragua. His objective was to plan for an operation to catch Sandino's forces in a pincers movement. Edson and his patrol operated for several months behind enemy lines, with planes occasionally bringing him reinforcements, supplies, and the mail from their new east coast air base at Puerto Cabezas. Initially, some of Major Rowell's Corsairs operated from this base. In May, however, five amphibian planes arrived on station. Amphibian planes were preferable because sudden rain squalls were common in the northeast and these planes could land on one of the lakes or rivers in the region to ride out the storms. They could also use these waterways to evacuate the "sitting wounded."(42)

In another aspect of special operations, the Marines conducted leaflet drops to influence the will of the Sandinistas. In November 1928, Marine aircraft dropped thousands of leaflets over the area of Sandino's headquarters. Some leaflets carried the message that preparations were under way to finish off the Sandinistas, while others were signed by Sandino's father and asked Sandino to go see his sick mother before she died.(43)

End of the Occupation: A Legacy of Ironies

When the last contingent of Marine aviators left Nicaragua in January 1933, they left behind a legacy of ironies about the Marine occupation. The Marines had supervised the 1932 presidential election and the 1 January 1933 inauguration of Liberal President Juan Sacasa. Sacasa had been the popularly elected vice-president in the 1926 elections, whose opposition to the Conservative takeover of the government had sparked the civil war that provoked the second U.S. intervention. There is speculation that the entire civil war and Sandino's insurrection could have been avoided if the United States had supported Sacasa's efforts to prevent the Conservative takeover in 1926.(44)

Another irony was the buildup of the National Guard to replace the Marines when they left, with the objective of making this military force a professional, nonpolitical institution. Since the U.S. ambassador pushed for Anastasio Somoza (who was also Sacasa's nephew) to be designated as the National Guard commander, President Sacasa appointed him as such after winning the election.(45) Somoza then subverted U.S. efforts to make the Guard nonpolitical. He developed the Guard as his power base and, in 1936, consolidated his control over Nicaragua to begin the forty-three-year Somoza family dynasty.

The final irony is the legacy of Sandino. As Richard Millett has pointed out, after five years of fighting Sandino, the Marines left him "as great a threat in January 1933 as he had been at any previous point in his career."(46) A month after the Marines left, however, he met with Sacasa and agreed to end the insurrection. In February 1934, Sandino was killed by members of the National Guard, apparently acting under Somoza's orders.(47)

Sandino's assassination and legacy served as inspiration to the new Sandinistas who fought Somoza's son and National Guard in the 1970s. The National Guard's indiscriminate use of air power against civilians increased popular support for the Sandinistas and played an important part in the July 1979 Sandinista victory. Today, the counterrevolutionary insurgents (contras) are confronting the Sandinista air and ground forces by using many of the same strategies and operating in the same areas as Sandino did.

Benefits of Marine Air Activities: Experience for World War II

What were the benefits of air power during the Nicaraguan intervention? Lejeune Cummins asserts a theme that several other observers echo: while there was a loss to U.S. military prestige in failing to catch Sandino, the armed forces received invaluable training in "such significant developments as the 'invention' of dive bombing and large-scale aerial logistical support."(48) Bernard Nalty concludes his Marine study on the same note, mentioning the importance of the Marines' gaining experience, but adding that more important ". . . was the fact that Marine aviators and infantrymen functioned smoothly as a unified team."(49) These observations, written some thirty years after the conflict, are interesting when compared to those of a correspondent writing in the *New York Times* on 21 January 1928; he points out that, from a tactical standpoint, the operations "furnish the first practical laboratory for the development of postwar [World War I] aviation in coordination with ground troops."(50)

Results of Marine Air Power: Impact on Sandino's Strategy

What impact did air power have on Sandino's insurgency strategy? The airplane saved the day at Ocotal, but it also convinced Sandino to start using innovative tactics in the face of this new weapon. As a result, he initiated hit-and-run attacks, operating in small patrols, utilizing cover and concealment, and building support among the local populace.

In addition, the air attack on El Chipote demonstrated that "Sandino had learned at last the rudiments of antiaircraft defense."(51) During the El Chipote bombings, the pilots faced not only rifle and machine gun fire but also a "barrage of incendiary sky rockets," which Sandino's troops called dynamite rockets; these were probably launched from the iron pipes affixed to tripods they had reportedly been making. Realizing the folly of fighting the planes, Sandino ordered his men to gather piles of wood on his fortress so that large fires would cover their escape during the bombing.(52) Several days after the air attack, aerial observers reported that there were no signs of life at the mountain stronghold "except two men and a mule, where formerly the place was swarming with men."(53) In a 1928 interview with Sandino after he escaped from El Chipote, Sandino asserted that his strategy was to sit and wait for the Marines to mobilize and come to him—and then to slip out of the trap into another part of the country.(54)

Lessons Learned: Central America Today

What are the lessons to be learned about air power in the campaign against Sandino, and how do they relate to today's counterinsurgency operations in El Salvador, Guatemala, and Nicaragua? The first lesson is that a combined effort of both sufficient air and ground forces, with a program designed to win the allegiance of the people, is required to conduct a successful counterinsurgency campaign.

Despite the fact that Sandino was still a threat, the United States reduced its ground forces during the latter stages of the occupation in an attempt to disengage from the prolonged conflict. By 1931, there was an overdependence on the Marine air assets to support the remaining U.S. and Nicaraguan ground forces. The result was a stalemate: the air assets restricted Sandino's activities, but there were not enough ground troops to defeat Sandino's insurgency. Critical of President Hoover's Nicaraguan policy, Senator Hiram Johnson from California asserted in 1931 that the United States "should pursue one of two courses: either withdraw the Marines entirely, or send enough there to do the job."(55)

In addition to relying on air assets to make up for not employing sufficient ground forces, there was not enough done during the campaign to attract popular support to the Nicaraguan government. Sandino's major asset was popular support. Sandino recognized the value of good public relations early during his struggle: "The people of the countryside kept him supplied with provisions, sheltered his soldiers, and, most important of all, kept him informed of every move the Marines and Guard made." As a result, Sandino "proved to the world that a 'people's army' could resist every effort of the most modern military machine."(56) Sandino's effort of using old rifles, machetes, and even bombs made from discarded Marine sardine cans to confront U.S. machine guns and dive bombers was "one of the first modern examples of what a guerrilla army with mass popular support could do against a technologically superior army."(57)

This lesson is still important, as demonstrated in the 1979 Sandinista Revolution. Somoza's heavy emphasis on air assets, along with inadequate ground forces and few attempts to improve the legitimacy or popular appeal of his government, contributed to his downfall. Today the governments of El Salvador, Guatemala, and Nicaragua are using air power to combat their insurgents, but as yet they have been unable to translate their superior firepower into a total victory. Additional ground forces and greater efforts to secure popular loyalty are required to consolidate the advantages that their air power provides them on the battlefield.

The second lesson learned from the campaign against Sandino is that air assets must be employed selectively to avoid creating popular support for the insurgents. Thomas Walker, a political scientist and authority on Nicaragua, illustrates this point: "Practices such as the aerial bombardment of 'hostile' towns and hamlets and the forced resettlement of peasant populations only intensified popular identification with the guerrilla cause."(58) George Black, an author on Nicaragua, follows Walker's line of reasoning and points out that Marine airstrikes "only served to swell Sandino's forces, by increasing peasant hostility to the U.S. presence and failing miserably in their military objectives." Black asserts that Sandino specialized in diversionary attacks to provoke useless bombing raids as "the only American response to the impotence of their ground forces, bogged down in unfamiliar territory."(59) As historian Richard Millett points out, in the final analysis, the counterinsurgency campaign against Sandino "clearly demonstrated that the Guardia, even with Marine air support, was hard pressed to contain, let alone destroy, Sandino's forces."(60)

In recognition of the responsibility for protecting civilian populations, rules of engagement did exist as guidelines for the Marine aviators. Orders prevented the aviators from attacking groups unless they were carrying weapons, were located in the vicinity of a recent guerrilla action, or behaved suspiciously by running for cover. Although under orders not to bomb towns, the aviators bombed and strafed houses and animals believed to be used by the Sandinistas. The "fog of war" no doubt caused some civilian casualties and created the basis for Sandinista charges of aerial atrocities. On the other hand, Major Rowell complained about the "restrictions of a political nature" that hurt the morale and efficiency of his air power forces, particularly given the fact that some towns were used as sanctuaries by the Sandinistas.(61)

Fifty years later, Somoza isolated himself from both domestic and international support by bombing his own cities during the Sandinista Revolution. Today's guerrillas in each country have been effective at either criticizing actual attacks against civilians or lying about them through propaganda. While the ability to distinguish between civilians and guerrillas is very difficult at times in a counterinsurgency conflict, the insurgents capitalize on excesses in the use of air power. They publicize each occurrence not only to build popular support at home for their cause but also to exploit the propaganda value abroad against their country's government.

The U.S. Marine occupation of Nicaragua made significant contributions to the development of air power. Marine aviators expanded the concepts of close air support and independent aerial bombardment. They refined other uses of air power by conducting reconnaissance, communication, transportation, and even special operations missions. In addition to these developments, the coordination between air and ground forces provided valuable experience prior to World War II. The Marine campaign against Sandino provided several lessons about the role of air power in counterinsurgency conflicts—lessons that are still applicable today to current and possible future turmoil in Central America. The governments of El Salvador, Guatemala, and Nicaragua can improve their chances of defeating the insurgents if they follow these lessons and use their air power both selectively and in conjunction with an integrated ground force and popular support campaign. While these lessons cannot guarantee success, Nicaraguan history has demonstrated that refusing to follow these lessons can result in failure. The results of today's conflicts will be determined in large part by how well the lessons learned in the Nicaraguan counterinsurgency conflict more than fifty years ago are applied to today's insurgencies.

NOTES

1. John A. Booth, *The End and the Beginning: The Nicaraguan Revolution* (Boulder, Colorado: Westview, 1982), p. 31.
2. Ibid., pp. 37-38.
3. See "American Fliers Fight for Nicaragua, Two Bombing a Mexican Gun-Runner," *New York Times*, 27 August 1926, sec. 1, p. 3; "Says Chinandega Has Been Retaken," *New York Times*, 8 February 1927, sec. 1. p. 25; and Neill Macaulay, *The Sandino Affair* (Durham, North Carolina: Duke University Press, 1985), p. 33.
4. William S. Brooks, "Chinandenga Battle as Seen from Plane," *New York Times*, 5 March 1927, sec. 1, p. 3.
5. William S. Brooks, "Bombing Liberals in Nicaraguan War," *New York Times*, 29 May 1927, sec. 1, p. 10.
6. Booth, p. 40.
7. "800 Marines Board Ships for Nicaragua," *New York Times*, 12 May 1927, sec.1, p. 29.
8. See Bernard C. Nalty, *The United States Marines in Nicaragua*, revised edition (Washington: Government Printing Office, 1962), p. 14; "Our Marines Fired On," *New York Times*, 28 February 1927, sec 1, p. 5; "Planes and Marines Sent to Nicaragua," *New York Times*, 17 February 1927, sec. 1, p. 6; and Macaulay, p. 80.
9. See Nalty, pp. 16-17; and Lejeune Cummins, *Quijote on a Burro: Sandino and the Marines*, subtitled *A Study in the Formulation of Foreign Policy* (Mexico, Distrito Federal: La Impresora Azteca, 1958), p. 53.
10. Nalty, p. 17.
11. Bernard Diederich, *Somoza: The Legacy of US Involvement in Central America* (New York: E. P. Dutton, 1981). p. 17.
12. Macaulay, p. 81.
13. Cummins, p. 54.
14. Oswald G. Villard, "Editorial Paragraphs," *The Nation*, 27 July 1927, p. 75.
15. See "Sandino in Hiding, 'Army' Deserts Him," *New York Times*, 20 July 1927, sec. 1. pp. 1-2; Richard Millett, *Guardians of the Dynasty: A History of the U.S.-Created Guardia de Nacional and the Somoza Family* (New York: Orbis Books, 1977), p. 67; and Nalty, p. 17.
16. Macaulay, p. 81.
17. Cummins, p. 55.
18. "Sandino in Hiding," p. 2.
19. Millett, p. 67.
20. Ibid.
21. Harold N. Denny, "Marines Push Drive in Nicaragua Wilds," *New York Times*, 21 January 1928, sec. 1, p. 3.
22. Macaulay, pp. 96, 103.
23. Nalty, p. 22.
24. Russell Owen, "The Airplane Plays a Leading Part in Nicaragua," *New York Times*, 25 May 1928, sec. 9, p. 16.
25. C. G. Grey, editor, *Jane's All the World's Aircraft of 1928* (London: Low and Martson, 1928), p. 30b, as cited in Cummins, p. 64.
26. Owen, op. cit.
27. Macaulay, p. 118.
28. Denny, sec. 1, p. 1.
29. Nalty, p. 19.
30. Carleton Beals, "With Sandino in Nicaragua, Part V: Send the Bill to Mr. Coolidge," *The Nation*, 21 March 1928, p. 315.
31. Macaulay, p. 117.
32. Ibid., p. 153.
33. Harold N. Denny, "New Marine Forces Begin Sandino Hunt," *New York Times*, 16 February 1928, sec. 1, p. 4.

34. See Nalty, p. 19; "Marine Fliers Slain Fighting to the End," *New York Times*, 9 November 1927, sec. 1, p. 14; and Macaulay, pp. 93, 103.
35. See Harold Denny, "Five Marines Are Killed and 23 Wounded in Battle with Nicaraguan Rebels," *New York Times*, 2 January 1928, sec. 1, p. 20; Macaulay, pp. 68, 118; Nalty, p. 19; and "Marine Plane Flies without Stop from Miami to Managua," *New York Times*, 15 January 1928, sec. 1, p. 1.
36. Denny, "Marines Push Drive in Nicaragua Wilds," sec. 1, p. 3.
37. See Nalty, p. 18; and Macaulay, p. 118.
38. See Cummins, p. 62; and Harold N. Denny, "Plane Brings out Wounded Marines under Enemy Fire," *New York Times*, 8 January 1928, sec. 1, p. 1.
39. See Lauren D. Lyman, "Marines Use Planes as War Ambulances," *New York Times*, 15 January 1928, sec. 9, p. 9; Nalty, p. 21; and Macaulay, p. 101.
40. See Cummins, pp. 91-92; and Millett, p. 75.
41. Macaulay, pp. 227-28.
42. See Nalty, pp. 23, 24-25; Cummins, p. 72; and Macaulay, p. 124.
43. Macaulay, pp. 131-32.
44. Cummins, p. 95.
45. Booth, p. 46.
46. Millett, p. 98
47. Booth, pp. 48, 51.
48. Cummins, p. 98.
49. Nalty, p. 34.
50. Denny, "Marines Push Drive in Nicaragua Wilds," sec. 1, p. 3.
51. Nalty, p. 22.
52. See Owen, sec. 9, p. 16; Harold N. Denny, "Sandino Directed Men from Fox Hole," *New York Times*, 10 January 1928, sec. 1, p. 33; Carleton Beals, "With Sandino in Nicaragua, Part VI; Sandino—Bandit or Patriot?" *The Nation*, 28 March 1928, p. 340; and Cummins, p. 64.
53. Harold N. Denny, "Sandino Reported Killed in Bombing by Marine Planes," *New York Times*, 19 January 1928, sec. 1, p. 1.
54. Beals, "With Sandino in Nicaragua, Part V; Send the Bill to Mr. Coolidge," p. 314.
55. "Johnson Condemns Policy on Nicaragua," *New York Times*, 30 April 1931, sec. 1, p. 3.
56. Diederich, op. cit.
57. Harry E. Vanden, "The Ideology of the Insurrection," in *Nicaragua in Revolution*, edited by Thomas W. Walker (New York: Praeger, 1982), p. 45.
58. Thomas W. Walker, *Nicaragua: The Land of Sandino* (Boulder, Colorado: Westview, 1981), p. 22.
59. George Black, *Triumph of the People: The Sandinista Revolution in Nicaragua* (London: Zed Press, 1981), p. 19.
60. Millett, p. 97.
61. Macaulay, pp. 116, 228.

PETE ELLIS: AMPHIBIOUS WARFARE PROPHET

John J. Reber

> *Paradoxically, the legendary Pete Ellis personified a diverse assortment of personas – intellectual, warrior, professional, and eccentric. Retired Lieutenant Colonel John J. Reber candidly clarifies the clandestine actions of Ellis in the Pacific. Traditionally, historians have given Ellis great credit for his contributions to amphibious assault doctrine, but his demise is fraught with speculation.*

At 0620, 21 May 1923, a State Department clerk in Washington logged in the following cable from the American Embassy in Tokyo:

> I am informed by governor general of Japanese south sea islands that R. H. Ellis, representative of Hughes Trading Company, #2 Rector St., New York City, holder of department passport No. 4249, died at Parao, Caroline Islands on May 12th. Remains and effects in possession of government awaiting instructions.
> Wilson

A routine follow-up with the Hughes company by a State Department investigator revealed that the president was a retired Marine Corps colonel who appeared uneasy as the questioning began. Finally, the colonel blurted out that Earl H. Ellis was never his employee but was an active-duty Marine Corps lieutenant colonel on an intelligence mission. At the request of Marine Corps authorities, he had permitted his company to be used as a cover for Ellis.

A copy of the State Department cable was passed via Captain Luke McNamee, director of naval intelligence, to the major general commandant of the Marine Corps, John Archer Lejeune. Lejeune had been "Pete" Ellis's friend and patron since they first served together in the Philippines in 1908. At first, Lejeune tried to protect the nation, the Marine Corps, and Ellis by saying nothing. But the story soon leaked and hit front pages all over the country. Reporters demanded to know what a Marine Corps officer was doing in the Japanese islands of Micronesia.

General Lejeune kept silent for as long as possible. Then, at the prodding of Admiral Robert E. Coontz, chief of naval operations, he issued the only statement he ever made on the subject, saying that Ellis was absent without leave. Colonel Ellis, he said, had been a patient at the Naval Hospital, Yokohama, Japan, suffering from nephritis (inflammation of the kidneys) and was last seen on 6 October 1922. He had been on leave touring the

Orient. That leave had been revoked before Ellis vanished from the hospital. The official records backed up the general's statement.

The commandant's cold official statement was probably meant only to protect the Marine Corps and the nation from an embarrassing international scandal. His official statement is belied by the warmth with which he corresponded with Ellis's brother Ralph. One year older than Pete, Ralph was the managing editor of the *Kansas City Journal* and the family spokesman. That Pete Ellis himself certainly would have approved of Lejeune's action is evidenced by the contents of an envelope he left with Lejeune. When opened soon after Ellis's death, it contained the colonel's signed but undated letter of resignation from the Marine Corps. Lejeune destroyed it.

The reporters would have had a more startling angle if they had known that two years earlier Ellis had written a secret operation plan for the invasion of Japan's mandated islands. His thirty thousand-word document was entitled *Advanced Base Operations In Micronesia*.[1] It is one of the most amazingly prophetic documents in military history. Approved by General Lejeune on 25 July 1921, it became the keystone of Marine Corps strategic plans for a Pacific war. It formed the basis for the first Orange Plan approved in 1924 by the joint board of the army and navy for offensive operations against Japan in the event of war.

Ellis's predictions as to the general course of a future war against Japan and his recommendations for the prosecution of that war reveal rare insight. "Japan is a World Power," he wrote. "Considering our consistent policy of non-aggression, she will probably initiate the war which will indicate that she believes that . . . she has sufficient military strength to defeat our fleet." He prophesied the progress of the war in the Pacific and the swift Japanese onslaught. He planned that the U.S. drive should be straight through the Marshalls and Carolinas, then northward toward the homeland. This might well have been the actual route in World War Two had not the initial enemy success compelled us to fight in the South and Southwest Pacific, and if General Douglas MacArthur and political considerations had not made recapture of the Philippines obligatory in 1944.

Ellis went even further than strategic operations he got into the details of new tactical concepts. Night amphibious operations were discouraged, but Ellis concluded that transports with assault troops should approach under cover of darkness and attack in the early morning to have the advantage of the maximum number of daylight hours. He foresaw future requirements such as underwater demolition teams, the shore party organization, naval gunfire spotters with troops, and other special purpose units. "Task forces must be formed before leaving base port," he wrote, "and must be embarked as such. No shifting of troops or material between ships on blue waters is practicable." Foreseeing the requirement for task organization and combat loading, he wrote, "Signal troops, field artillery, demolition experts and other specialists will accompany the first waves of assault." He described the employment of boatheads [beachheads], beach markers with large placards or flags for beach identification and control, aerial bombing support, naval gunfire, feints and the other ABCs of World War Two-type amphibious operations. More realistic than later military planners, he foresaw that we probably would lose the Philippines at the start of the war. Some of his estimates were upheld with amazing accuracy. He listed four thousand assault troops in his tactical plan for Eniwetok in the Marshalls, and this was approximately the number of Army and Marine troops who secured the atoll in 1944.

His document was revolutionary in many respects, but his main theme – which later proved to be the salvation of the Marine Corps and paved the way for victory in the Pacific – was his conviction that the Marines's primary role should be offensive amphibious operations. Many outlying bases would have to be seized from the Japanese. The seizure of such bases naturally would fall on the Marine Corps as the advanced base force of the Navy. This was right on the heels of the failure of the British offensive amphibious operation at Gallipoli during World War One.

Most military leaders of the 1920s, including many senior Marine Corps officers, were still thinking in terms of World War I trench warfare. At best, the Marine Corps's role was thought to be that of advanced base defense, primarily coastal artillery units. But there was no widespread interest in this advanced base defense work even in its pure defensive aspects among officers in the Marine Corps immediately after World War I.[2] And they surely were not thinking about landing against defended shores in the World War Two sense.

In addition to being a master military planner, strategist, and tactician, Pete Ellis was also a very complicated, sick, and neurotic man. Prone to melancholia, he was hospitalized many times for neurasthenia and psychasthenia.[3] He was hyperactive, and his record is replete with accounts of his working around the clock to finish a project, then ending up in a hospital with shattered nerves.

Ellis began his career by enlisting as a private on 3 September 1900 at Chicago. At a time when many enlisted men could neither read nor write, he was a high school graduate. While an enlisted man, he performed guard duty at the Washington Navy Yard. He won a commission on 21 December 1901, two days after his twenty-first birthday. His abilities were recognized early in his career. Consequently, he was given choice assignments usually reserved for more senior officers. General Lejeune had this to say in a letter to Ellis' mother, "He had a brilliant mind and by reason of continued study and application he became one of the best informed officers on military and naval subjects in any branch of the service." A lifelong bachelor, Ellis devoted his life to the Marine Corps.

Young Lieutenant Ellis landed at Cavite in the Philippines on 13 April 1902 for his first duty assignment as an officer. There he came under the influence of such Marine Corps notables as Major Littleton W. T. "Tony" Waller, Marine Captain Smedley D. Butler, and others who helped him form his attitudes and objectives. On 21 January 1903, Lieutenant Ellis reported aboard the USS *Kentucky* (later BB-6), the flagship of the Asiatic Fleet. For the next year and a half, he visited the principal ports of China and Japan. The *Kentucky* frequently stopped at Yokohama, thus providing Ellis an excellent opportunity to begin his study of Japan. A second tour in the Philippines (1907-11) as a first lieutenant and captain found him assigned to such duties as the litigation of land cases at Olongapo, serving as officer in charge of the advanced base material (chiefly guns taken off U.S. warships) and commanding fortifications on Grande Island in the defense of Subic Bay. During this tour in the Philippines, Ellis began his long friendship with Lejeune, then a major, and with Joseph H. Pendleton, then a lieutenant colonel.

It was in the Philippines that the unbalanced side of Ellis's personality first came to the attention of his superiors. The brigade chaplain called on him while he was living in a palm frond house on Grande Island with two marine lieutenants. The chaplain's overly righteous attitude discouraged any kind of rapport. A few drinks and stories before dinner only worsened matters. After the four had eaten in silence and were waiting for the houseboy to remove the plates, Ellis apparently found the situation too oppressive, so he whipped out his revolver and shot the plates off the table.

Such bizarre behavior did not deter his superiors from giving him the most responsible assignments. From the Philippines he was ordered to the Naval War College. There, as a very junior captain between 1911 and 1913, he taught officers who became admirals and generals and later helped set the navy's course for victory in World War Two. On the staff with Ellis was Captain William S. Sims, one of the navy's most brilliant officers and one of Ellis's closest friends. Sims later became president of the War College. While at the college, Ellis wrote a series of papers on advanced base forces and the defense of several Pacific islands, including Guam, Peleliu, and Samoa. He also made numerous converts to his then-radical idea of offensive amphibious operations to seize islands as advanced bases for the navy in time of war. In a 1912 fitness report at the War College he requested that he be assigned "duty in making personal reconnaissances of ports in the Atlantic and Pacific likely to be occupied as advanced bases in time of war."

But the commandant had other plans for him in 1914. Assigned to the staff of the Advanced Base School at the Philadelphia Navy Yard, he made a reconnaissance of Culebra and Vieques islands near Puerto Rico for the 1914 advanced base exercise. Then, the secretary of the navy requested that he be assigned to a joint army and navy board scheduled to convene on Guam in March 1914 to prepare a defense plan for the island. On completion of the plan, he remained as military secretary and aide to Navy Captain William J. Maxwell, governor of Guam.

While on Guam in 1915, Ellis was confined to the hospital for several months, one of the first serious indications of his psychological and hyperactivity problems. His medical record reads, "March 6, 1915 . . . loss of self control and tending to hysteria. . . . Bad effects enhanced by short hours of sleep and long hours at desk work. Advise reduction in work and increase in recreation." A 28 June 1915 entry reads, "Very much depressed and extremely nervous."

During his Guam tour, Ellis had at least one confrontation with the governor and also one with a Japanese policeman on Saipan. The governor noted on his fitness report, "I considered Captain Ellis's manner and tone disrespectful and called him sharply to account for it." While visiting a native friend on Saipan, he expressed his resentment of the inquisitiveness of a Japanese policeman by knocking the man down a flight of stairs. Again, neither of these two incidents nor his frequent hospitalizations swayed his seniors' confidence in him.

On 2 January 1915, Colonel Lejeune was assigned as assistant commandant of the Marine Corps, World War One was six months under way, and the corps was busy with plans for expansion. Lejeune soon found that he needed a small staff to assist him. He immediately had three of the most promising junior officers in the Marine Corps transferred to his office. These were Pete Ellis, Thomas Holcomb, Jr., and Ralph S. Keyser. Holcomb later became the marines's first lieutenant general commandant, serving from 1936 through 1943.

The United States declared war on Germany on 6 April 1917. Three days later, Ellis was promoted to major. In June 1918, Brigadier General Lejeune and Major Ellis sailed together on board the USS Henderson for France. Lejeune, soon to be promoted to major general, was assigned command of the 2nd Army-Marine Division. Ellis, promoted to temporary lieutenant colonel, was assigned as adjutant of the 4th Marine Brigade, which along with the Army's 3rd Infantry Brigade comprised Lejeune's 2nd Division.

As part of the French Army, the 2nd Division, at Lejeune's request, was assigned the mission of assaulting Blanc Mont Ridge, a key German strong point on the Hindenburg Line, in early October 1918. Lejeune sent his aide for Ellis, and the aide reported back that the colonel was indisposed and that the indisposition could be expected to last several hours. Lejeune had the utmost confidence in Ellis – regardless of the indisposition – and wanted his advice on planning the assault. Later, Ellis prepared the plan for an assault which resulted in a penetration of the entire German defensive position forcing them to withdraw 30 kilometers, a Frenchman called it "the greatest single achievement of the 1918 campaign." General Henri Gouraud, whose plan Ellis recommended be discarded, rewarded Ellis with the Croix de Guerre and Palm and the Legion of Honor, grade of Chevalier. Ellis also was awarded the Navy Cross, not on the usual grounds of combat heroism but for excellence in his staff duties. The citation mentioned his imperviousness to fatigue and alertness under strain and sleeplessness, words which indicate that the nervousness and physical disorders diagnosed under headings such as neurasthenia and psychasthenia were becoming much more frequent and serious.

In 1919, Ellis's services were sought by both the navy and Marine Corps, but the routine of peacetime duty failed to supply mental stimulus to an officer of his caliber. From 1918 on, entries of hospitalization and sick leave in his record indicate a rapid nervous and physical decline. He took to drinking with increasing regularity. During 1919 and 1920, his friends noticed a very rapid decline in his physical appearance. In January 1920, navy doctors declared him unfit for active service and prescribed three months' sick leave.

In present times, Ellis might have been assigned to a rehabilitation program. But these were the passive days of the 1920s, so it was not surprising to find him being assigned, at his request, as the intelligence officer of the 2nd Marine Brigade in Santo Domingo. When the brigade commander was queried as to whether he "desired the services of Major Ellis" (he reverted to his permanent rank of major on 20 August 1919), the response was immediate, "Services desired and earnestly requested." When he reported in from sick leave on 17 April 1920, his orders to Santo Domingo were waiting for him. Tropical Santo Domingo was not exactly a health spa in the 1920s. It was the last place Pete Ellis should have gone to recuperate. A dry atmosphere would have been far better.

On 30 June 1920, Major General Lejeune was appointed commandant. Pete Ellis saw in this the opportunity for approval of the request he nude in his 1912 fitness report. On 20 August 1920, Ellis sent a letter to General Lejeune:

1. In order that the Marine corps may have the necessary information on which to base its plans for further operations in South America and the Pacific Ocean I have to request that I be ordered to those areas for the purpose of making the necessary reconnaissance.
2. In the performance of such duties I will undertake to adopt any personal measures (submit undated resignations, travel as civilian, etc.)…necessary to ensure that the United States shall not become embarrassed through my operations.

On 2 August 1920, Admiral Sims requested that Ellis be assigned to the staff of the Naval War College. Lejeune wrote to Sims, expressing regret that he could not comply with the request. Instead, Ellis reported to the commandant on 23 December 1920 and was assigned to the newly created operations and training division to work on his war plan. On 3 February 1921, he checked in at the Naval Hospital, Washington, D.C., where he stated that he had felt his latest breakdown coming on while he was in Santo Domingo. On 7 March, his problem was diagnosed as neurasthenia. On 17 March he began to subsist on the outside and report to the hospital every morning. His subsisting on the outside consisted of working night and day on his war plan in a dingy little office, Room 209, Headquarters, Marine Corps where a "No Admittance" sign was tacked to the door. The midwatch logs invariably showed the entry, "Lights burning in 209. Office occupied."[4]

On 9 April, Ellis requested a three-month leave to visit Belgium, France, Germany, and England. On 12 April, he was released from the hospital, allowing only a few days to tie up loose ends at headquarters before departing for Micronesia. The three months' leave was a cover for his mission to Micronesia. Before he could get away, he found himself back in the hospital on 18 April with the same old problem, neurasthenia. "Origin on duty

". . . nervous and tense, was emotionally unstable . . . coarse tremors of the hands and tongue," said the medical report. "Complained of insomnia, nausea and an irritative cough . . . prescribed hypnotics. . . . Developed what he describes as the 'shakes.'"

On 4 May, Ellis was discharged from the hospital to return to duty; on that same day, Lejeune, in a letter to the secretary of the navy, requested permission for Ellis to leave the United States while on leave to visit Belgium, France, Germany, and England. The next day, 5 May, the letter was returned approved by Franklin Roosevelt, acting secretary of the navy. If a written directive for his mission was ever given to Ellis, it has not survived.

Prior, to his departure, Ellis called at the commandant's office to say goodbye. During their farewell conversation, the commandant's secretary noticed Ellis hand Lejeune a sealed envelope which the general took without comment and slipped into his desk drawer. Ellis then departed. It was the last time they ever saw each other.

Looking at the mission in hindsight, the whole thing seems amateurish to a fault. There is no evidence of detailed planning. His cover as a trader was easily seen through by the German traders of Micronesia since he knew little or nothing about the business. The Navy Department apparently never bothered to tell the U.S. naval attaché in Tokyo about Ellis, although the attaché had primary intelligence responsibility for Micronesia. But with the laissez-faire atmosphere of the 1920s and the amateurish state of U.S. intelligence, permission for such a fishing expedition and the manner in which it was carried out were not so implausible as would be the case nowadays. To reconnoiter an area of such magnitude today might call for the combined resources of the civilian and military intelligence communities. But in May 1921, there was one lone, sick, and neurotic marine. Nevertheless, he was brilliant, courageous, and fired with a deep sense of duty. He was ready to embark on his mission with only the moral support of a pat on the back, a handshake, and wishes for good luck from the few senior officers who were privy to his mission. These included Generals Lejeune, Neville, Haines, and Logan Feland.

Ellis paid a last visit to his family in Pratt, Kansas. He told them he was going to travel for his health, but they would be unable to contact each other. If everything went well, they would hear from him in eight months. But if they did not hear from him, he wanted them to do nothing. There should be no inquiries through Senators Charles Curtis or Arthur Capper or through Congressman Homer Hoch, no publicity, no letters to the Marine Corps. Then he walked out the door of his boyhood home and vanished for almost a year. He was never seen in Europe. When he failed to return at the end of his ninety-day leave, an administrative officer at headquarters sent a brief memo to the adjutant-inspector, Brigadier General Henry Haines, "The leave granted Lieut. Col. Ellis has expired. How shall he be carried on the muster roll?" The memo came back with a note scrawled across the bottom, "Carry on leave," then, as if an afterthought, "until return" was added.

In late March 1922, Colonel Robert H. Dunlap, a close friend and confidant of Ellis on duty at Quantico, Virginia, received the following cablegram from Sydney, Australia:

> Impracticable here. Proceeding Japan. Everything all right cable Club Manila if not agreeable.
>
> Pete

He had just been released from a Sydney hospital where he had been treated for nephritis.

Years later, in 1948, the commandant of the Marine Corps asked General Douglas McArthur to search Japanese files for information on Ellis. Four messages were found, dated October 1921. They were exchanged between the consul general in Sydney, the foreign minister, and the minister of the navy. Using his cover as a trader for the Hughes Company, Ellis had requested a visa to visit the Marshall and Caroline Islands on business. The minister of the navy said the visa could be granted, but he wanted Ellis's itinerary in advance. Armed with his visa, Ellis tried to reach the Japanese mandated islands from Sydney, but no ships were available. His failure to get passage out of Australia forced him to seek transportation into the islands from Japan, which of course increased the risk.

He booked passage at Sydney on board the Tango Maru to Manila. Becoming sick en route, he was placed in a civilian hospital upon arrival at Manila. By chance, a Marine Corps officer recognized him and had him transferred to the naval hospital at Canacao, Cavite, where the admission entry in his medical record reads, "5-17-22. Complains of nervousness . . . very restless, twitching of muscles of face and arms...Diagnosis changed to nephritis acute."

On 19 June, Ellis sent the following secret message to Brigadier General Feland at Marine Corps Headquarters:

> It is essential to reach objective by northern route. I have gained complete authority and I do not think there will be any further difficulty. Delayed here while ill but all well now. I desire to continue and if necessary to take six months extension time. I possess necessary funds. Your reply is desired by radio to Navsta Cavite.
>
> Signed Ellis

Neither Ellis's serious illness nor his delay in getting into Micronesia swayed General Lejeune's confidence in him. The reply, signed by the assistant to the commandant, went out "priority" the same day Ellis's message was received:

> Extension granted for period of six months or as much of that time as may be necessary period.
>
> Signed W. C. Neville

Upon being released from the hospital, Ellis stayed at the Delmonico Hotel in the Intramuros (Walled City), Manila. Late in July 1922, he left Manila on board the SS *President Jackson* for Yokohama with a reservation through to San Francisco. The latter action was apparently an attempt to throw the Japanese off his trail. It was one of the last rational, albeit naive, acts of his life.

Early in August 1922, he landed at Yokohama and checked into the Grand Hotel. On 12 August, Commander Ulys R. Webb, Medical Corps, U.S. Navy, commanding officer at the Naval Hospital, Yokohama, received a telephone call from a very excited desk clerk at the Grand Hotel who said that an American guest was quite sick. He asked if a doctor could come quickly. Webb found a man in civilian clothing suffering from nephritis, and there was also evidence that he had been drinking heavily. Determining that immediate hospitalization was necessary, the doctor had the man sent to the Naval Hospital. Upon admission, the patient identified himself as Lieutenant Colonel Earl H. Ellis, U.S. Marine Corps, and said he was touring Japan while on leave. His medical record reads, "August 12, 1922 Diagnosis: #548 Nephritis acute…Probably from condition incident to service in the tropics. Patient also has probably been over indulging in alcoholics…23 August, to duty much improved, U. R. Webb, Comdr, MC, USN."

A week later, Ellis was admitted again, "9-1-22 #548 Nephritis acute. Readmitted, same symptom, same treatment. 9-14-22 Discharged to duty much improved, at his own request in order to continue his journey. U. R. Webb, Cmdr, MC, USN."

Captain Ellis M. Zacharias, in 1922 a lieutenant commander assigned to the naval attaché's office in Tokyo, wrote in his book Secret Missions (New York: G. P. Putnam's Sons, 1946):

> The attention of the naval attaché [Captain Lyman A. Cotten, USN] was directed to an American who had just arrived in Yokohama and who was seen frequently in rather shabby drinking places and geisha houses . . . As he [Ellis] told it during his lighter moments in Yokohama, he was selected by Washington to go to the mandated islands in the guise of an innocuous traveler "to find out what the hell was going on down there."…For several days we maintained our surveillance over the "agent" and watched him toboggan rapidly in Yokohama bars. Every one of his appearances there revealed more data on his proposed trip, not only to us but obviously to Japanese counterintelligence as well, and we realized that this "secret agent" had outlived his usefulness long before he could embark on his actual mission.

On 20 September, Webb had an ambulance pick up Ellis at the Grand Hotel and admitted him to the hospital. His medical report reads, "Poison, alcohol, acute. . . . Not duty. Due to his own misconduct…delirium tremens . . . so shaky cannot feed himself . . . throws everything in his room out of the window. Treated with whiskey, sedatives and food."

When Ellis sobered he found himself in a private room attended by Chief Pharmacist Lawrence Zembsch who acted more as jailer than nurse.

Cotten had never been informed of Ellis's mission. If Ellis had been under secret orders from the highest echelon of the government, Cotten would have been in serious trouble for terminating or otherwise disrupting the execution of those orders. Lieutenant Colonel Ellis was obviously in extremely poor physical condition and required immediate medical help which was not available in Japan. So he proposed to have Webb certify him as sick for further transfer to the United States for treatment.

Captain Zacharias said in *Secret Missions*, "Although originally motivated by security considerations, Cotten's concern about the Colonel's physical condition appeared fully justified after Dr. Webb's first examination . . . The Colonel was in no shape even for transportation back home, so we were advised to permit him to regain at least some of his strength in his, private ward before sending him on a strenuous journey by transport." Webb prepared the necessary report certifying Ellis as sick and requiring medical treatment m the United States. Upon receipt of Webb's report, General Lejeune revoked Ellis's leave and ordered him to report. But Pete Ellis never received those orders.

Webb gave Ellis his choice of going home by government transportation or buying his own ticket for a commercial liner. He decided instead to turn his back on the security of returning to the United States. On 4 October 1922, Ellis cabled his bank in San Francisco for $1,000. Two days later, he received it. On the night of 6/7 October, he slipped out of the hospital against Webb's specific orders not to leave and departed forever the official custody of the naval service.

Starting at the Grand Hotel in Yokohama where Ellis had been staying, Captain Gotten and his intelligence agents began to make discreet inquiries. They found he had paid his bill at the hotel and ordered an automobile to take some luggage to the Yokohama railway station. Gotten even went to the extent of enlisting the aid of the Japanese missing persons bureau and other local authorities in the search. Both U.S. and Japanese authorities searched Tokyo and Yokohama without success. Ellis probably departed from either Kobe or Moji, using the visa stamped in his passport at Sydney a year earlier as his "ticket" to the mandated islands.

Apparently, he first went to Jaluit in the Marshals where he stayed about two months. There he became acquainted with Arthur Herrman, a German trader. Herrman was in San Francisco on business on 23 May 1923. There he read about Ellis's death in a newspaper, then called on Major General George Barnett at Headquarters, Department of the Pacific. The following is from General Barnett's 25 May 1923 letter to the Major General Commandant. He reported Herrman said the following:

> (a) Stated that he saw Colonel Ellis in Kusaie, Eastern Caroline Islands, and that he also had a brother there who was acquainted with Colonel Ellis.

(b) That he left on the same steamer with Colonel Ellis, and went as far as Palew [Palau] with him in the Western Caroline Islands. This was about April 16, 1923.
(c) That Colonel Ellis at that time was in good health.
(d) That he (Herrman) had known Colonel Ellis for about two months, while at the Marshall Islands. While there Colonel Ellis had heard from the Japanese that there was to be war between the United States and Japan. A great many of the Japanese were drunk, and it was their intention of putting Colonel Ellis in jail.
(e) According to Mr. Herrman, Colonel Ellis was en route from Palew to New Guinea.
(f) That on the steamer between Kusaie and Palew, Colonel Ellis has [sic] eaten some canned eels and had drunk some beer, which made him (Ellis) very ill.
(g) That he (Herrman) saw Colonel Ellis at Jaliut [sic] and was later a patient at the hospital there.
(h) Herrman stated . . . that Colonel Ellis carried a considerable amount of money with him.
(i) . . . Mr. Herman stated that there was every evidence that the Japanese wanted no foreigners on the islands, and they were very anxious to get rid of Colonel Ellis.

This was the first smattering of information of Ellis's activities since he disappeared from the naval hospital at Yokohama on the night of 6/7 October 1922. Years later, others were to add bits and pieces to the story. In November 1923, Cornelius Vanderbilt III talked with a medical missionary, Miss Jesse Hoppin, when the Japanese allowed his yacht to lie to at Jaluit for repairs after a storm. She said she had known Ellis and had nursed him in her home when he was seriously ill at Kusaie. The Japanese, she recalled, had been furious with him when he entered certain forbidden areas. She had heard threats against his life and felt Ellis had sailed from the Carolinas just in time, though she was sure he was under surveillance wherever he went in the Pacific. She gave him a clean bill of health on his departure from Kusaie.

In 1926, Ellis's two sisters had a brief visit with Miss Hoppin between trains at Wichita when Miss Hoppin was returning to Kusaic after a leave to her home in Aubumdale, Massachusetts. Miss Hoppin added nothing new during this brief visit. She promised to write to Ellis's sisters, but she never did. In 1933, Miss Hoppin again returned to her home on leave. Now sixty-seven years old, she had spent most of her life in the Marshalls and had lost touch with the United States. Three days after her return home, a Marine Corps officer paid her a visit. Miss Hoppin was more reserved than she had been with Vanderbilt ten years earlier. She refused pointblank to discuss Ellis or his activities. The officer left convinced that the elderly missionary had been warned not to discuss the affairs of the islands to which she intended to return. In 1939, Miss Hoppin went to her home in the United States. The Japanese did not permit her to return to the Marshalls.

In March 1950, the commandant, hoping to learn more about Colonel Ellis's last days, sent Lieutenant Colonel Waite W. Worden to Koror to interview natives who knew Ellis. Colonel Worden's report revealed the following.

Upon arriving at Koror in April 1923, Ellis was met by the chief of native police, Jose Tellei, who checked all incoming passengers. Tellei told Colonel Worden that Ellis's papers showed him as a businessman. He said that neither the Japanese nor anyone else knew Ellis was a marine, but the commissioner of police, who was Japanese, directed that Ellis be followed at all times and further directed that the police wear civilian clothes. The Japanese police thought Ellis was a spy. Ellis stayed at Koror about three days, went to Ponape, then returned to Koror for six weeks. Tellei said everyone called him "Mr. Ellis," indicating that no one knew he was a Marine Corps officer.

When Ellis returned to Koror after his three-day visit to Ponape, he went to live with William Gibbon, a half-caste Englishman, and his native wife, Ngerdako. Gibbon was the only person at Koror who spoke English. After about a week, Ellis asked Gibbon to find him a house in the native area. He said he wanted privacy and didn't want to live in the Japanese community. Gibbon obtained the island chief's house for Ellis. The chief's house was owned by the community, but was unoccupied at the time because the chief then preferred to live in his own private house. Shortly after Ellis moved in, a twenty-five-year-old native woman, Metauie, came to live with him as a concubine. She lived with him until he died.

Metauie said Ellis drank constantly while at Koror. William Gibbon's widow Ngerdako confirmed this at the same time, saying that Ellis drank heavily, sake, beer, whiskey, anything he could get. Once he had no liquor and he came to Gibbon's house to demand something to drink. When Gibbon told him he had nothing to drink, Ellis, drunk at the time, tried to rip the walls apart with his hands, thinking Gibbon's supply of whiskey was hidden in the wall.

Although Ellis knew he was dying, he continued his daily search, Metauie said. He would leave the house every day saying he was going to take a walk. She didn't know what he was looking for.

Mrs. Gibbons said that he would walk around during the day, looking things over, and was constantly watched by the Japanese. Frequently the Japanese were discovered peeking into his window at night, and loitering on his premises. Ellis went out of the house on several occasions to beat up with his fists such Japanese as were peeking into his quarters.

Jose Tellei also stated that Ellis did a lot of walking around, looking things over, and was shadowed by the Japanese or native police at all times.

Near his end, Ellis must have realized his chances of making any sort of an intelligence find were quite remote. One can only guess at his despair and bitterness of spirit because his search had come to nothing. There was a cruel irony – *it was not their strength which the Japanese were trying to conceal. It was their weakness.* There were no Singapores, Gibraltars, or Verduns in the mandated islands before World War Two. The Japanese plan was to use these islands as an offensive springboard, not for defense. Much later, the Japanese skill in building improvised defenses, usually from local materials such as coconut logs and coral, was much in evidence. This became especially manifest in the toll of American lives it cost to take such positions. But these were somewhat hastily built after our Makin Island raid in 1942. For example, the elaborate cave system on Peleliu that cost one thousand marine lives was built between March and September 1944.

One morning Ellis went "crazy drunk," according to Ngerdako Gibbon, and by 1700 that day he was dead. She and her husband built a coffin for Ellis, and the next day they buried him in the native cemetery. Metauie, by 1950 a woman of about fifty-three, said she thought Ellis died from "too much sake." It is likely that Colonel Ellis died from the cumulative effects of drinking and his various diseases. There is also at least the possibility that he was poisoned by the Japanese, but the actual cause of death remains unknown.

The day before Ellis died, Captain Cotten was called by the Japanese Navy Ministry to receive news that Colonel Ellis had been located at Koror, but that the doctors there didn't expect him to live much longer. Captain Cotten asked the official at the Navy Ministry to send Colonel Ellis back as soon as possible. The Japanese official replied that details for his return would be arranged within 24 hours, and Colonel Ellis would be brought home at once.

The next morning, a call from the Navy Ministry informed the naval attaché that Colonel Ellis had died the night before. Captain Gotten saw in the act of picking up Ellis's remains at Koror a great opportunity to do some on-the-spot intelligence work. "I will send a representative to take charge of the ashes," he informed the Japanese, "This gentleman was an important personality in the United States, and we wish to bury him with the ceremony due his status."

Captain Cotten's request caught the Japanese spokesman off guard, because he was not prepared to handle such a request. After consulting with his superiors, he called Cotten back to say they interposed no objection to sending Chief Pharmacist Zembsch to Koror. After being carefully prepared for the trip in the attaché's office, Zembsch sailed from Yokohama on 4 June 1923 to bring back Ellis's remains.

In the 1950 interview, William Gibbon's widow stated that shortly after Ellis died, an American whose name she did not know arrived from Japan. Then she, her husband, and Jose Tellei dug up Ellis's body and cremated it in the open on a pile of rocks. The American placed Ellis's ashes in a small box he had brought with him. He then departed

Koror, saying he was going to the states via Japan. She said that he was in civilian clothes, of which he had many kinds, but he "looked like a soldier."

Metauie reported that when the American came, he went to the Koror government to inquire about Ellis. The Koror government called her, William Gibbon, and his wife to point out the burial place. Then the Japanese police, the American and a native working party disinterred the body in the presence of her, William Gibbon, Mrs. Gibbon, and Jose Tellei. Metauie stated further that the American had a small box. When the body was disinterred, it was cremated on some rocks in the open, after which the American placed the ashes in the small box. The American then waited for a Japanese ship, saying he would return to Japan and then go to America. The American was in civilian clothes. The Japanese police took all of Ellis's personal effects and turned them over to the Koror government. When the American picked up the ashes, she saw the box of effects in the government building and thought that the American took this box with him.

Jose Tellei stated that he was present at the time Ellis's body was disinterred, and he witnessed the cremation. He said that the American who picked up the ashes was a Mr. Lorenz (Lawrence Zembsch), whom he knew was a naval officer.

The Japanese kept the naval attaché advised of Zembsch's progress and of his arrival at Koror. But then the news abruptly ceased. On 13 August 1923, the Navy Ministry called the attaché to say that Zembsch would arrive by ship in Yokohama the next day. Dr. Webb, Lieutenant Commander Zacharias, and several members of the attaché staff went down to the pier to meet Zembsch.

After the ship was tied up, they waited a reasonable time for Zembsch to appear, then went aboard to locate him. They were greeted politely by the captain of the ship who personally conducted them to Zembsch's cabin. As they opened the door to the cabin, they saw Zembsch sitting on his bunk. He was unshaven, unkempt, and deranged in mind and physical appearance. Completely unmoved by Dr. Webb's appearance, he did not rise to greet him, but simply stared off into space. Clasped tightly in his arms was the white box used by the Japanese for the ashes of the cremated.

Despite the most attentive medical treatment, Zembsch remained in a catatonic stupor. Webb did not leave his bedside for four days, applying all known methods of mental therapy to get him back to a state of mental coherence. After showing some little improvement, he developed an acute case of amnesia which prevented him from remembering anything of the immediate past. Dr. Webb was convinced that he was heavily drugged. On 28 August, Webb finally got a statement from Zembsch that the Japanese had known Ellis for what he actually was.

Dr. Webb had scheduled another session with Zembsch on the afternoon of 1 September 1923. That morning Zembsch's wife had visited him at the hospital and was getting ready to leave right before noon. At 1142, a devastating earthquake struck the Yokohama area. The hospital was completely destroyed and both Zembsch and his wife perished in the ruins.

After U.S. authorities dug through the debris of the earthquake, the following was received by the American Consul General in Yokohama from the commander-in-chief, Asiatic Fleet:

> Ashes of LtCol Earl H. Ellis, born on 19 December 1880 died Palau, Caroline Islands 12 May 1923, were found in the ruins of receiving vault and identified by Lt. T. P. Riddle, ChC, USN, through a typewritten slip pasted to a strip of wood which had evidently been a part of the outer case of a small casket. Ashes being sent to the United States on instructions of the Department.

The remains were finally laid to rest on Pete Ellis's birthday, 19 December 1923, in his home town of Pratt, Kansas. Today the amphibious training building at the Marine Corps schools, Quantico, Virginia, is named Ellis Hall.

NOTES

[1] Operation Plan 712. A copy is on file with Head, Reference Section, History and Museums Division, Headquarters, U.S. Marine Corps, Washington, D.C. 20380. Ellis' plan has not been published. [Editor's note: HQMC has since published Ellis's study]

[2] The great majority of Marine Corps officers in the years following World War I saw the primary role of their service as a second army or as an expeditionary force. They figured that when the firebell rang, the senior Marines present at navy yards and other shore installations would scrounge up the Marines there and sail off to fight the war.

[3] "Neurasthenia" is a now-obsolete term describing a neurotic condition of debility, characterized by feelings of fatigue, worry, and inadequacy, by lack of zest and interest, by headaches and undue sensitivity to light and noise, and by functional disturbances of digestion and circulation. "Psychasthenia" is also an obsolete term used to describe a condition in which a person is unable to resolve doubts or uncertainties or to rest phobias, obsessions, or compulsions that he knows are irrational.

[4] HQMC was located in the Main Navy Building, 19th and Constitution Ave. in Washington

THE PROTOTYPE U.S. MARINE: EVOLUTION OF THE AMPHIBIOUS ASSAULT WARRIOR

Robert S. Burrell

> *Even though the Marine Corps' participation in amphibious assault principally occurred within a short four-year timeframe, the Pacific War seemingly perpetually defined U.S. Marines in terms of this mission. This has occurred to such a pervasive extent that both the Marine Corps and the public have erroneously superimposed "assault from the sea" onto the organization's distant past, as well as from World War II onward. It is obviously important to examine factors that contributed to the formation of this popular image.*

The Pacific War established the prototype United States Marine as an amphibious assault warrior who prosecuted fervent, and often sacrificial, frontal assault against formidable enemy fortifications yet emerged victorious. In his definitive history of the U.S. Marine Corps, Allan R. Millett defines the time when the Corps became an "Amphibious Assault Force" from 1900-1945.[1] Similarly, most studies focus on the Marines' agency in directing their own evolution during these five decades.[2] But, the "State Department" troops used in the "Banana Wars" of the 1920s and 30s bore scant resemblance in function or mentality to the archetypal amphibious assault warrior that emerged in the 1940s. Admittedly, prominent officers in the 1920s and 30s, including Earl Ellis, John Lejeune, and Holland Smith, developed innovative doctrines and techniques for ship-to-shore movement – to include the seizure of beachheads with the use of combined arms – but these visionaries did not foresee the ferocity of the battles that would occur inland subsequent to initial maneuvers.[3] The Marine Corps did not simply develop a Pacific warfighter in accordance with the visions of previous amphibious prophets of decades earlier but through four years of crucibles in combat.[4]

During four years of desperate and brutal warfare, the Corps increasingly relied upon the combat abilities of Marine riflemen as the most essential component in fighting Japanese. As historians Benis M. Frank and Henry I. Shaw have stated, the Marine regiment "experienced perhaps the most dramatic revolution" of all Marine Corps units in the war, and this was most evident at the lowest echelons of organization.[5] The Marine rifle squad of 1941 was comprised of nine men with eight Springfield rifles, one Browning Automatic Rifle (BAR), and one grenade launcher. By 1945, the firepower of the squad had tripled by expanding the unit to thirteen men who now wielded ten semiautomatic weapons (six M1 Garands and four M1 carbines), three automatic rifles (BAR), and nine grenade launchers (three M-8s and six M-7s). Additionally, the rifle squad was broken down into three maneuver units of four-man fireteams, giving the squad leader greater tactical flexibility to employ the increased combat power at his disposal. (The Marine Corps, in fact, originated this organization of the rifle squad, which the U.S. Army later adopted and both services continue to use over sixty years later.) The Marine Corps reorganized the Marine rifle squad to make it "more aggressive and efficient," yet, at the same time, it simultaneously increased the supporting arms available to this frontline unit.[6] For example, in 1942, the entire 1st Marine Division had only twenty-seven flamethrowers. By 1945, each of its nine infantry battalions independently wielded 24 flamethrowers a piece![7] These changes developed through reactionary responses to the particular enemy and topography faced in Pacific campaigns. Marines encountered a uniquely tenacious Japanese foe in the unique combat environment of the Pacific Islands, and this led to reequipping and reorganizing Marine infantry. This essay explores the effects that environmental conditions and Japanese agency had on the tactical learning process that generated not only specific capabilities but also a unique mentality and self image of an amphibious assault warrior – an archetype which has remained central to Marine Corps institutional identity despite subsequent changes in mission and capabilities.

Guadalcanal: Warfighting Transition

The hastily organized 1st Marine Division set out to seize the southern Solomon Islands in August of 1942. Specifically, this included the nearly simultaneous invasion of the islands of Gavutu, Tanambogo, Tulagi, and Guadalcanal. Marines caught the Japanese ill-prepared and undermanned on all four islands. Of the four objectives, the smaller islands of Tulagi, Gavutu and Tanambogo offered sufficient conditions to test the Marine Corps' amphibious assault doctrine as set forth in *Tentative Landing Operations Manual* (1938). In such cases, combined arms of naval guns and naval air supported the infantry's ship-to-shore maneuver with tanks and artillery assisting in the subsequent assault. But, amphibious doctrine did not prepare the Marines for clearing out the tenacious Japanese defenders who fought from fortified positions to the death, and, contrary to expectations, this is where the majority of fighting took place, rather than the shoreline.

Gavutu and Tanambogo, in close proximity to each other and connected by a short pier, offered little in the way of beachheads. However, only an estimated 1,000 enemy personnel had taken up positions there and 600 of those were laborers – leaving only 400 Japanese combat troops. Due to the element of surprise and shortage of manpower on these islands, the Japanese declined to defend many positions near the shoreline. Instead, the enemy retreated to a series of caves and dugouts (which they had also made effective use of during the preliminary bombardment). Excavating these dispersed defenders required the aggressive use of riflemen. As a result of these initial island battles, the Marines concluded that naval and aerial bombardment, as well as artillery support, offered little assistance in destroying what turned out to be a surprisingly tenacious underground foe. In contrast to doctrine, which emphasized combined arms assault, rifle squads worked independently using high explosives to destroy inland fortifications.[8]

The Prototype U.S. Marine

Marines on Guadalcanal in 1942 evacuate wounded by foot.

The unopposed landing on Guadalcanal, where the 1st Marine Division fought intermittently in the interior for another four months, failed to offer many lessons in amphibious assault. Still, as their most extensive campaign to date, it had a considerable impact on the Marine's conduct of war. As on the smaller islands, the lessons of Guadalcanal also focused on improving the intensity and resourcefulness of riflemen. During the invasion phase, the Marines were forced to rely upon the Navy's surface and air support. (The Navy reserved nearly all carrier positions for its own pilots – relegating most Marine pilots to land-based airfields, which were too far out of range to support nearly every Marine landings of the war.) When the Japanese fleet delivered to the U.S. Navy its second largest defeat in history at Savo Island, it decided to withdraw what remained of the Pacific Fleet – leaving the Marines stranded on Guadalcanal, where the Japanese subjected them to a series of ground attacks. The apparent unreliability of the U.S. Navy generated mistrust in supporting arms outside the Marine Corps' control - simultaneously increasing the Marines own preference for self-sufficiency and self-reliance.

As a result of the barely contested landing and subsequent rapid inland expansion on Guadalcanal, the 1st Marine Division concluded that the future assault forces should initially arrive light and without heavy equipment. As the campaign progressed, the wet and thick jungle environment restricted the use of vehicular support and reinforced emphasis on the Marine rifleman as the primary tool in combating the enemy. Similarly, Marines valued supporting arms proportionately with the degree to which they were man-portable.[9] This opinion eventually led to doubling the number of company's 60mm mortars while the number of heavier 81mm mortars in the battalions remained unchanged.[10] Topography and tactics of the enemy in and around Guadalcanal led the Corps to emphasize the proficiency of Marine riflemen – independent of bulky supporting arms.

Tarawa: Warfighting Trauma

General Holland M. Smith charged the 2d Marine Division with spearheading the assault on the Gilbert Islands in November 1943. The terrain of Betio Island on Tarawa Atoll posed a formidable obstacle for the division. A coral reef extended hundreds of yards outward from the island – creating a natural barrier to landing craft. Although the island contained a number of beachheads, over 2,000 Japanese and Korean workers had prepared hundreds of obstacles and fortified defenses, which 2,600 elite Japanese Navy troops effectively employed. More significantly, the Japanese Navy still posed a grave threat to the Pacific Fleet. Accordingly, the U.S. Navy decided that it needed to retain strategic surprise in order to get in and out of the Gilberts quickly, a choice that greatly hampered the assault force in a number of ways. The 2d Division initially planned to seize a nearby island to setup artillery pieces to provide accurate and timely indirect fire for the landing force, but the Navy's time constraints rendered this impossible. The Navy also limited preliminary naval and aerial bombardment to just three hours, ensuring that smoke and debris obscured the desired targets. This, in turn, reduced the effectiveness of naval supporting arms regardless of ammunition expenditure. The U.S. Navy's decision to attain strategic surprise left the majority of defenders unscathed. Again, the task of defeating the enemy fell almost solely upon the shoulders of the individual rifleman, who paid an enormous price of over 2,000 wounded and 1,000 dead to secure victory.

Fighting within the confined space of Betio's 291 acres over a short three days reinforced the Marine Corps' desire to make its infantry faster, correspondingly lighter, and more lethal. Although naval fires and air support did not perform remarkably well, they did increase combat power ashore without burdening the logistical footprint of riflemen. Since the Marines had not employed their own artillery and vehicles to their full effectiveness, General Julian Smith, Commanding General of the 2d Division, suggested after Tarawa that heavier equipment organic to the division was "excessive" and burdensome for atoll warfare. Instead, he wanted infantrymen as agile as possible during the first 48 hours, which included the elimination of the combat pack, mess kit, and lowering the amount of individual rations carried. While diminishing the need for entrenching tools, sandbags, and other defensive materials, General Smith stressed that the firepower of the rifle squad should considerably increase, including larger combat loads of hand grenades, demolition kits, and bangalore torpedoes. Until the war broke out, Marine engineers almost exclusively employed explosives, but now General Smith wanted all riflemen proficient in their use.[11] He also preferred increasing the number of flame throwers supporting the infantry.[12] Although combined arms remained important, after Tarawa, the capacity for Marine riflemen to overcome obstacles at the small unit level was the utmost priority.

A Marine rifle squad on Tarawa in 1943 moves inland from the beach

Marshall Islands: Warfighting Transformation

In January 1944, the Pacific Fleet invaded the Kwajalein Atoll of the Marshall Islands with the untested 4th Marine Division and the Army's veteran 7th Infantry Division, which had recently completed amphibious assaults in the Aleutian Islands. Despite the 7th Infantry Division's experience, the Commanding General of V Amphibious Corps, Holland M. Smith, ensured that the toughest objective fell to his Marine division. This reinforced the belief, valid or not, that Marines provided a superior amphibious force. And, this was an important distinction because the U.S. Army accomplished virtually all major amphibious landings in America's past and continued to provide the bulk of forces used for this purpose in the Pacific, including the major operations taken against Leyte, Luzon, and Okinawa. The assignment of objectives in the Central Pacific by naval officers implied that Marines were elite in comparison to soldiers, an image that Marine riflemen unreservedly embraced.

Marine infantry on Roi-Namur in the beginning of 1944 attack through fortified Japanese defenses.

The 4th Marine Division set out to seize the connected islets of Roi and Namur – so small that they could be measured in hundreds of yards. Enemy disposition and geography served the landing force in a number of major ways. Perhaps most notably, Kwajalein Atoll, due to a shortage of materials and misplaced priority of effort, contained perhaps the least prepared fortifications Marines would encounter in the Central Pacific. Furthermore, since the Japanese Navy had not contested the Gilbert landings, the U.S. Navy concluded that strategic surprise was not vital. This allowed the 4th Marine Division to emplace artillery, prior to the invasion, on four small islets situated near Roi-Namur. The circumstances made ideal conditions for the 4th Marine Division which, after a deliberately point-blank preparatory bombardment that lasted two full days, aggressively seized Roi-Namur from its nearly 4,000 defenders in a matter of 25 hours at the relatively small cost of several hundred casualties! In his after-action report, General Holland M. Smith concluded that "In the attack of coral atolls very few recommendations can be made to improve upon the basic techniques previously recommended and utilized in FLINTLOCK [Marshalls operation]."[13] The Marshalls Operation validated the idea of earlier Marine prophets that massive preparatory fires followed by rapid frontal assault of infantrymen constituted the ideal solution to seizing beachheads. Yet, contrary to prewar doctrine, General Smith stressed that the principle tactic in defeating the enemy inland consisted of rifle squads digging the defenders "out with hand grenades, flame throwers, and bayonets," a method of fighting at which Marines had only recently become quite proficient.[14] The Marshall's Campaign crystallized this concept of the amphibious assault warrior.

Marianas Islands: Warfighting Confirmation

The U.S. Navy's seizure of Saipan, Tinian, and Guam in the summer of 1944 was marked by different environmental conditions than those encountered in the previous two campaigns. These islands were considerably larger, giving the enemy a wider variety of defensive options. Yet, the Japanese remained fixated on the beachhead defense. By playing to the strength of the materially superior U.S. invasion forces, which had developed unparalleled expertise in establishing a beachhead by this time, the Japanese confirmed Marine Corps doctrine, tactical methods, and warrior identity. Of the three islands, perhaps Saipan offers the most revealing example. The island held considerable political ramifications for both nations, exemplified by the fact that Prime Minister Hideki Tojo resigned after its loss. As the principle objective of the Marianas campaign, Saipan received the greatest allotment of Japanese and American resources. The V Amphibious Corps planned to seize Saipan with the 2d and 4th Marine Divisions, leaving the Army's 27th Infantry Division in reserve – again testifying to the fact that soldiers were considered second-rate to Marines. The Corps Commander, Holland M. Smith, later confirmed this prevailing opinion during the battle when he fired the 27th Division's general for not being aggressive enough – a subject too complex and controversial to warrant further comment on in this short study.[15]

To contest the landings, the Japanese established main defensive lines about 500 meters from likely beachheads, supported by machineguns, mortars and artillery. Due to the number of landing areas available, the Japanese could not mass sufficient strength at any one point to repulse the invasion force. To ensure the Japanese could not redistribute their strength quickly, the U.S. Navy conducted a heavy two-day preliminary bombardment, primarily on locations to the south. After an amphibious feint near the northern shore, the Navy landed 8,000 Marines on the southwestern beaches in a period of twenty minutes! Since the enemy had organized no sizable reserve, they had relegated themselves to fighting a series of defensive engagements. Over the next three weeks, the Japanese counterattacked repeatedly from their retracting positions with support of indirect fire and tanks, but they could not match the numerically and materially superior invaders.[16]

Eventually, at the cost of 12,000 Marine and 4,000 Army casualties, Americans defeated 30,000 Japanese in a matter of twenty-five days.

A corpsman on Saipan in the summer of 1944 tends to Marine wounded.

The battles in the Marianas confirmed the amphibious assault warrior archetype developed in response to previous campaigns. Indeed, as historians Frank and Shaw have stated, "The refinement of existing tactics rather than the development of new ones marked the Saipan operation."[17] Indisputably, frontal assault was the Marines' normalized form of offense on Saipan. As such, frontline units developed "small unit leadership and small unit training" that could sustain massive casualties at levels over 50% and still maintain forward momentum. Due to emphasis on riflemen as the primary warfighting tool, each division parceled out supporting arms to infantry regiments who used them within their own sectors of advance as they saw fit. Rather than massing armor, tanks were also dispersed to regiments in an effort to further bolster the firepower of frontline infantrymen. Other than forming a straight line for the offense and defense, adjacent units made limited coordination in the seizure of objectives. Instead, units generally made forward progress within prescribed zones of action. Although the U.S. Army claimed that the Marines' conduct of war was suicidal and "contrary…to modern tactics," the technique of using neutralization fires followed by rapid and aggressive frontal assault worked well in seizing the shrinking defensive perimeter on Saipan. Despite the fact that some Japanese fortified positions were quite formidable, the overall distribution of forces was hastily organized. As the Japanese retreated into the interior the Marines kept them off-balance with rapid advances.[18] Correspondingly, the numerous Japanese counterattacks stood little chance of success against the materially superior combined arms and close combat ability employed by Marine riflemen.[19]

By late 1944, the geography and nature of warfare in Solomon, Gilbert, Marshall, and Marianas Islands had fashioned a prototypical Marine archetype that the Corps enthusiastically adopted. As the Marines expanded their ranks exponentially, it structured the training pipeline to produce more of these amphibious assault warriors. The Marine Corps had crossed a line from tactical ingenuity to institutional identity and, as will be demonstrated in the last campaigns, would find this ideal difficult to depart from.

Peleliu and Iwo Jima: Warfighting Rigidity

The islands of Peleliu and Iwo Jima are strikingly dissimilar in geography – all the more remarkable since the Japanese organized comparable defensive strategies in each case.[20] The enemy apparently took the lessons of Saipan seriously enough to make major revisions to their defensive doctrine. They decided to forego the beach defense in order to generate static and mutually supporting inland fortifications of extensive tunnels and pillboxes, supported with unprecedentedly heavy indirect fire. Also, the Japanese limited the use of counterattacks, which had not proven productive in the past. Although the Marines made some progress since the summer of 1944 in acquiring heavier tanks and artillery to combat fortifications ashore,[21] the U.S. Navy and Marine Corps expected and planned for contested beachhead assaults on these islands followed by Japanese counterattacks similar to those experienced on Saipan. Marine performance on Peleliu and Iwo Jima indicates that by 1944 the Marine Corps had fully embraced the archetype – a preferred warfighting style which it clung to regardless of its compatibility with the enemy disposition and terrain encountered in these later campaigns.

In September 1944, the Commanding General of the 1st Marine Division, William Rupertus, remained staunchly overconfident in the ability of his elite light infantry to destroy the well planned defenses on Peleliu. He remained so even after the short and poorly organized naval preparatory bombardment proved grossly inadequate in destroying the concrete bunkers and pillboxes of the well-prepared defenders. By leaving only one battalion of his entire division in reserve, Rupertus limited the tactical maneuver of his units to basic frontal assaults in their "respective zones of action." The enemy emplacements in the rocky cliffs of Umurbrogol Ridge – running down the length of the narrow island and surrounded by marshes – posed a significant natural and man-made barrier which greatly complicated the maneuver of the regiments and limited the use of tanks. As demonstrated by the data compiled in Table 1, the combat power of individual riflemen had significantly increased since 1942. More powerful individual weapons, larger combat loads of explosives, and heavier crew served weapons dispersed to support these riflemen all serve as indicators of the stress commanders placed on companies, platoons, and squads to perform the bulk of combat independently. Seizing each pillbox of the integrated Japanese defense scheme at a time with bazookas, flamethrowers, and demolitions, the veteran 1st Division incurred so many casualties in more than two months of fighting (Rupertus, in fact, had predicted the fight would last two or three days) that Rupertus reluctantly and tardily allowed the 81st Army Infantry Division to assist it in the mop up. The 1st Division alone incurred over 6,000 casualties in the destruction of 11,000 Japanese.[22]

Table 1: Comparison of Close Combat Weapons in Marine Infantry Regiments[23]

	1942 Guadalcanal	1944 & 1945 Peleliu & Iwo Jima
M1A1 .45 caliber Thompson submachine gun	507	-
.45 caliber automatic pistol	17	-
M1 .30 caliber semi-automatic carbine	943	1,794
M1 .30 caliber semi-automatic rifle	1,385	1,179
M1918M2 .30 caliber Browning Automatic Rifle	162	243
12-gauge shotgun	-	100
M2-2 flamethrower	-	81
60mm mortar	18	39

The seizure of Iwo Jima took place in February 1945 with the 3d, 4th, and 5th Marine Divisions. As exemplified at Peleliu, the Marine divisions tended to attack these carefully designed inland fortifications with a similar urgency as when storming heavily defended beachheads. Emphasis remained on the speed, aggression, and initiative of Marine riflemen. General Graves B. Erskine, Commanding General of 3d Marine Division, recognized maneuver as a superior tactic to frontal assault, but "the idea, found to be quite prevalent, that assault units must maintain an alignment and that physical contact between adjacent units is essential" proved difficult to dispel.[24] Historian Jon T. Hoffman pointed out that the predictable early morning bombardments followed by daybreak frontal assaults lacked imagination. In fact, the Marines attempted only a single night attack, and, due to virtually no training in such matters, it failed. Unfortunately, little in the Marines' arsenal of medium-sized tanks and artillery could destroy the mutually supporting fortifications on Iwo Jima – some of the strongest encountered in modern warfare, which the preliminary bombardment had again left virtually intact. While the 4th and 5th Divisions sustained 75% casualties in their infantry regiments, and the 3d division (which started out in reserve) sustained 60%, all three units maintained effective forward progress – a testament to Marines' emphasis on small unit leadership. However, the cost of 28,000 casualties to overcome 21,000 Japanese defenders in this month-long conflict remains tragically unparalleled in Marine Corps history.[25]

On Peleliu and Iwo Jima, extensive use of frontal assault employed over lengthy periods resulted in unprecedented casualties. Frontline units eventually passed a breaking point and their combat efficiency dramatically decreased. The system of sending Marine trainees to replace wounded (instead of designing a unit for unit swap) remains a controversial decision. Hasty integration of unskilled riflemen into squads and the resulting loss of unit cohesion and experience relegated Marines to the tactic most familiar to them – frontal assault – which, in turn, resulted in even greater losses and reinforced the vicious cycle of replacements all over again. In their frustrated attempts to overcome the staunchly entrenched enemy on Peleliu and Iwo Jima, Marines repeatedly requested increased naval gunnery support, but the U.S. Navy prioritized ammunition allocation in favor of the larger campaigns for Philippines and Okinawa. Ironically, when frontal assault tactics proved excessively costly on Peleliu and Iwo Jima, Marines routinely blamed the inadequacy of the Navy and Army Air Forces preparatory bombardments rather than questioning their own tactics. Essentially, Marines became frustrated when external supporting arms failed to soften up objectives sufficiently for the proven amphibious assault warrior methods to work properly.

A Marine rifle squad on Peleliu at the end of 1944 throws Molotov Cocktails at a Japanese position.

The Marine rifle squad, no matter how aggressive and lethal, encountered great difficulties in destroying the heavily fortified and well-planned static defenses on Iwo Jima. Supporting arms and armor internal to the divisions (especially artillery) were subsequently considered too light. The parceling out of tanks and artillery in nearly equal distribution down to battalion levels often robbed the regimental or division main effort of the desired mass and sustained fire to most effectively gain momentum. Concurrently, advancing nearly all frontline units forward simultaneously each morning along a broad front, instead of breaching the defenses and enveloping the enemy, proved costly (although the 3d Marine Division employed enveloping tactics to some extent on Iwo Jima).[26]

One could reasonably argue that employing frontal assault tactics, in which the Marines had established great proficiency, offered a better choice than developing a new style of offense at this late stage; however uncompromising employment of the amphibious assault warrior against the inland fortifications at Peleliu and Iwo Jima was probably not best suited for the terrain and defenses engaged. Ironically, once the rifle squad had evolved into the primary instrument for waging war, higher commanders could not easily retreat from that emphasis. By 1945, the Marine rifleman had developed into such a finely honed instrument of destruction that squad leaders, platoon commanders, and company commanders wielded the majority of combat power. Meanwhile, regiment and division officers relegated themselves to parceling out their own assets to assist frontline units simultaneously.

Conclusion

Initial encounters between Marines and their opponents in the southern Solomon Islands primarily consisted of amphibious landings followed by extensive inland fighting, yet still imparted a profound appreciation for Japanese tenacity. Additionally, the protracted combat within the dense vegetation on Guadalcanal limited the use of vehicular support and further maximized the use of aggressive foot-mobile infantry, who could work independent of heavy supporting arms when necessary. Later in the war, the topography of islands in the Central Pacific (Tarawa, Roi-Namur, and Saipan) combined with the Japanese doctrine of contesting the beachheads, offered model conditions for violently prosecuted amphibious assault from ship to shore. Yet, methods of using neutralization fires followed by infantry attacks failed to defeat the Japanese at the shoreline and usually resulted in vicious contests further inland over numerous but isolated defensive positions. These epic struggles for individual fortifications resulted in divisions and regiments distributing their available combat power to the smaller levels of organization at the forward edges of the battle space. Positioned at "the tip of the spear", the rifle squad evolved into the primary warfighting tool. This emphasis matured into a hallmark that Marines uniquely identified with and effectively employed. Charging forward into sheer death and destruction, the fighting spirit of the amphibious assault warrior seemingly matched the fatalistic fanaticism of his Japanese foe. The self-sacrifice, bravery, and tenacity necessary to prosecute such hazardous tactics gained the admiration of the

American public and concurrently gave the Marine Corps a cherished distinctiveness.[27] Once developed through the crucibles of combat, this prototypical style of warfare became so engrained into the fabric of the Marine Corps that it depended upon continued employment of the amphibious assault warrior ideal under the most adverse circumstances, even when it may have no longer presented the best solution to tackling the enemy disposition and topography encountered in drawn-out inland battles of Peleliu and Iwo Jima. Assuredly, World War II marked a watershed event in which the establishment of the amphibious assault warrior – deliberately designed to seize fortified Japanese islands – evolved into a cultural ethos and prototype U.S. Marine.

NOTES

Primary sources in this essay derive from numerous after action reports located on 35 reels of microfilm at Nimitz Library, U.S. Naval Academy, under the title *U.S.M.C. Operations Reports, 1941-1945*. Guadalcanal is located on reel 13, Tarawa on reel 4, Marshalls on reels 23, 32-33, Saipan on reel 9 and 34, Tinian on reel 10 and 14, Guam on reel 27, Peleliu on reel 5, Iwo Jima on reels 7, 19-22, 24 and Okinawa on reels 12, 25, 28, 29-32. For a Japanese description of the battles on Guadalcanal see *Japanese Monographs* 34, 35, 37, and 98, (Washington D.C.: Office of the Chief of Military History, Department of the Army), 1945-1960; for Tarawa see *Japanese Monographs* 48, 117, and 161; for Marshalls see *Japanese Monographs* 48 and 50; for Marianas see *Japanese Monographs* 49, 50, 90, 91, and 117; for Iwo Jima see *Japanese Monographs* 45, 48, 51, 94 and 96; and for Okinawa see *Japanese Monographs* 83, 96, and 135. One of the most complete locations of *Japanese Monographs* is located at the Military Historical Institute at Carlisle Barracks, Pennsylvania. Photos are provided courtesy of Special Collections and Archives Division of Nimitz Library.

[1] Allan R. Millet, *Semper Fidelis: The History of the United States Marine Corps*, (1980, New York: Free Press, 1991), vii-xviii.

[2] Perhaps Victor Krulak provided one of the most convincing accounts of the evolution of prewar amphibious doctrine and the Fleet Marine Force in the pre-war years, see Victor H. Krulak, *First to Fight: An Inside View of the U.S. Marine Corps* (1984, Annapolis, Maryland: Naval Institute Press, 1999), 71-87.

[3] For an excellent analysis of the inadequate readiness of the Navy and Marine Corps to conduct amphibious assault as late as July 1942, see William H. Bartsch, "Operation Dovetail: Bungled Guadalcanal Rehearsal," *Journal of Military History*, April 2002, 443-476.

[4] In his lectures at Command and Staff College and Amphibious Warfighting School, Jon T. Hoffman has previously discussed the idea that the Marines' conduct of amphibious warfare was not simply the product of foresight in the 1920s and 1930s. Also, in *Victory and Occupation*, Benis Frank and Henry Shaw have demonstrated the progression of infantry tactics. However, my argument differs by focusing on how the conduct of the enemy and the terrain encountered impacted that development.

[5] Benis M. Frank and Henry I. Shaw, Jr., *Victory and Occupation: History of U.S. Marine Corps Operations in World War II* (Washington D.C.: Headquarters, U.S. Marine Corps, 1968), 695. Also see L. M. Holmes, "Birth of a Fire Team," *Marine Corps Gazette*, November 1953, 17-23.

[6] Ibid., 701.

[7] Ibid., 702.

[8] First Marine Division (specific author unknown), "Division Commanders Final Report on the Guadalcanal Operation – Phase II," 108/323, no date, pages 1-16.

[9] Ibid. The foremost source on Guadalcanal is Richard B. Frank, *Guadalcanal: The Definitive Account of the Landmark Battle* (1990, New York: Penguin, 1992). To create an accurate picture of the Japanese side of the battle, Frank used translations of large portions of the 104 Volume Japanese study *Senshi Sosho* (War History). In 2003, Frank generously donated copies of those notes to Nimitz Library, U.S. Naval Academy. They are compiled in three volumes – the only English translations of the Guadalcanal portion of *Senshi Sosho* publicly available. Other authoritative secondary studies include: Allan R. Millet, *Semper Fidelis*, 363-387; and Jeter A. Isely and Philip A. Crowl, *U.S. Marines and Amphibious War: Its Theory, and Its Practice in the Pacific*, (Princeton, New Jersey: Princeton University Press, 1951), 72-152. No other secondary sources, however, measure up to the research of Frank on this topic. Also see Jon T. Hoffman, "The Legacy and Lessons of Operation Watchtower," *Marine Corps Gazette*, August 1992, 68-73.

[10] Frank and Shaw, *Victory and Occupation*, 851.

[11] Frank and Shaw, *Victory and Occupation*, 720.

[12] Julian C. Smith, Commander of the Second Marine Division, "Report on the Galvanic Operation," 23 December 1943, 1-5. D. M. Shoup, Commander Landing Team 2/2, "Report on the Galvanic Operation," 20 December 1943, 10. Dixon Goen., Commanding Officer, 2d Marine Regiment, "Report of Operation,

Galvanic," 18 December 1943, 12. The best secondary source on Tarawa is Joseph H. Alexander, *Utmost Savagery: The Three Days of Tarawa* (Annapolis, Maryland: Naval Institute Press, 1995). Other authoritative works include: Millet, *Semper Fidelis*, 393-399; Isely and Crowl, *U.S. Marines and Amphibious War*, 192-252; and Henry I. Shaw, Bernard C. Nalty, and Edwin T. Turnbladh, *Central Pacific Drive: History of the U.S. Marine Corps Operations in World War II* (Washington, D.C.: Headquarters, U.S. Marine Corps, 1966), 23-103. Also of interest see Jon T. Hoffman, "The Lessons and Legacy of Tarawa," *Marine Corps Gazette*, November 1993, 62-67; Joseph H. Alexander, "David Shoup: Rock of Tarawa," *Naval History*, June 1995, 19-25; and Robert S. Burrell, "Operation Galvanic: Remembering Tarawa Sixty Years Later," *Shipmate*, November 2003, 20-23.

[13] H. M. Smith, Headquarters V Amphibious Corps, "Operations Report of Flintlock Operation," 6 March 1944, 1-20. Quote is from page 11. An excellent secondary source is Bernard C. Nalty, *The United States Marines in the Marshalls Campaign* (Washington, D.C.: Headquarters, U.S. Marine Corps, 1962). Other authoritative works include: Millet, *Semper Fidelis*, 399-404; Isely and Crowl, *U.S. Marines and Amphibious War*, 253-309; and Shaw, Nalty, and Turnbladh, *Central Pacific Drive*, 177-220.

[14] Frank and Shaw, *Victory and Occupation*, 721.

[15] H. Schmidt, Commanding General Northern Troops and Landing Force, "Northern Troops and Landing Force Operations Report Phase I (Saipan)," 12 August 1944, 1-37. For more information on the relief of General Ralph Smith by General Holland M. Smith, see Edmund G. Love, "Smith Versus Smith," *Infantry Journal*, November, 1948; and Robert Sherrod, "The Saipan Controversy," *Infantry Journal*, January 1949. Also see Holland M. Smith and Percy Finch, *Coral and Brass* (New York: Charles Scribner's Sons, 1949); Shaw, Nalty, and Turnbladh, *Central Pacific Drive*, 312-319; and Harry A. Gailey, *Howlin' Mad vs. the Army: Conflict in Command, Saipan, 1944* (Navato, CA: Presidio Press), 1986. Perhaps the best account of "Smith versus Smith" is found in Isely and Crowl, *U.S. Marines and Amphibious War*, 342-347.

[16] H. Schmidt, Commanding General Northern Troops and Landing Force, "Northern Troops and Landing Force Operations Report Phase I (Saipan)," 12 August 1944, 1-37.

[17] Frank and Shaw, *Victory and Occupation*, 721.

[18] "Who Won the War?" *Infantry Journal* (January 1949), 2-3.

[19] H. Schmidt, Commanding General Northern Troops and Landing Force, "Northern Troops and Landing Force Operations Report Phase I (Saipan)," 12 August 1944, 28. A good description of the Marianas campaign can be found in Philip A. Crowl, *Campaign in the Marianas* (Washington: Office of the Chief of Military History, Department of the Army, 1960). Other authoritative sources include: Frank and Shaw, *Victory and Occupation*, 722-723; Millet, *Semper Fidelis*, 404-420; Isely and Crowl, *U.S. Marines and Amphibious War*, 310-391; and Shaw, Nalty, and Turnbladh, *Central Pacific Drive*, 231-568. Also see Leonard G. Lawton, "Tank-Infantry Team," *Marine Corps Gazette*, November 1945; and Jon T. Hoffman, "The Legacy and Lessons of the Marianas Campaign," *Marine Corps Gazette*, July 1994, 76-81.

[20] Due to the complexities of the extensive joint land campaign for Okinawa (during which the Marines remained subordinate to the Army for most of the battle) I have decided to focus on the battles of Peleliu and Iwo Jima for the latter stage of the war.

[21] By 1944 the Marine division had replaced its 76 light tanks with 46 medium tanks and doubled the number of 105mm howitzers from 12 to 24. Additionally, the Amphibious Corps retained the heaviest fire support and 155mm howitzers. Frank and Shaw, *Victory and Occupation*, 847-848.

[22] First Marine Division (specific author unknown), Special Action Report, "Phase II: Operational Phase," no date, 1-21; quote from page 3. Also see, Millet, *Semper Fidelis*, 421-425; and Frank and Shaw, *Victory and Occupation*, 723.

[23] Frank and Shaw, *Victory and Occupation*, 850-851. These numbers reflect the table of organization and do not necessarily reflect the exact numbers of weapons employed by the divisions in these campaigns.

[24] G. B. Erskine, Commanding General 3d Marine Division, "Action Report, Iwo Jima Operation," 30 April 1945, 35.

[25] H. Schmidt, Commanding General V Amphibious Corps, "Action Report Iwo Jima Operation," 3 June 1945, 1-3. H. Schmidt, Commanding General, V Amphibious Corps, "Special After Action Report, Iwo Jima Campaign," 13 May 1945, 1-10; E. A. Craig, Assistant Chief of Staff, G-3, "Special Action Report, Iwo Jima Campaign," 31 March 1945, 1-78; Isely and Crowl, *U.S. Marines and Amphibious War*, 392-579;

and Jon T. Hoffman, "The Legacy and Lessons of Iwo Jima," *Marine Corps Gazette*, February 1995, 72-77.

[26] Skillful secondary works include: George W. Garand and Truman R. Strobridge, *Western Pacific Operations: History of U.S. Marine Corps Operations in World War II* (Washington D.C.: Headquarters, U.S. Marine Corps, 1971); Millet, *Semper Fidelis*, 421-441; Isely and Crowl, *U.S. Marines and Amphibious War*, 392-579; Frank O. Hough, *The Assault on Peleliu* (Washington, D.C.: Headquarters, U.S. Marine Corps, 1950); William S. Bartley, *Iwo Jima: Amphibious Epic* (Washington, D.C.: Headquarters, U.S. Marine Corps, 1954); and Charles S. Nichols Jr. and Henry I. Shaw Jr., *Okinawa: Victory in the Pacific* (Washington, D.C.: Headquarters, U.S. Marine Corps, 1955). Also see Jon T. Hoffman, "The Legacy and Lessons of Peleliu," *Marine Corps Gazette*, September 1994, 68-72; and Jon T. Hoffman, "The Legacy and Lessons of Okinawa," *Marine Corps Gazette*, April 1995, 64-71. These latter essays prove very helpful.

[27] A mystique of the amphibious assault warrior archetype often bordered on the religious. For instance, after the terrible battle for Betio Island, General Julian Smith stated "I can never again see a United States marine without experiencing a feeling of reverence" This statement certainly stems from the nature of the sacrificial fighting to seize the island. "Arms, Character, Courage," *Time* (5 March 1945), 1.

THE TRUTH ABOUT PELELIU

Jon T. Hoffman

> *Through discussion of this controversial battle, Colonel Hoffman, Deputy Director of Marine Corps Historical Center, illuminates the character and leadership of the Corps' most famous warrior – Chesty Puller. His description of Puller, especially his actions at the battle of Peleliu, differs with many previous accounts, which characterized his tactics as bloody and one-dimensional. In addition, Hoffman's analysis provides greater insight into the conduct of the ferocious war in the Pacific and the tremendous leadership challenges required in its prosecution.*

During the afternoon of 23 September 1944, the hollow-eyed, scraggly, exhausted, numb survivors of the 1st Marines began to disengage from contact with the Japanese defenders on Peleliu, as the Army's 321st Infantry relieved them. Since the 15 September assault, the 1st Marines had lost 311 killed and 1,438 wounded out of a strength of 3,251. That casualty rate of 54% exceeded the eventual losses suffered by the 5th Marines (43%) and the 7th Marines (46%) in the same campaign.

Years later, some accounts of the battle mistakenly cited the casualties of the 1st Marines as the highest of any Marine regiment in the war. A few angry veterans and some authors called the regimental commander a "butcher" for his supposedly poor tactical leadership and callous disregard for the lives of his subordinates. Peleliu became a black mark on the otherwise enviable record of then-Colonel Lewis B. "Chesty" Puller. The contradiction seems stunning, yet history has been revised to lay more and more culpability for the debacle on the stocky shoulders of Puller. The truth about Peleliu does not leave him entirely blameless, but in fact, Chesty has gotten a bum rap.

The Battle

Marine Major General Roy S. Geiger's III Amphibious Corps drew the mission of seizing Peleliu to prevent its airfield from threatening General Douglas MacArthur's pending campaign in the Philippines. Geiger assigned the 1st Marine Division under Major General William H. Rupertus to assault the main objective, while the Army's 81st Infantry Division attacked nearby Angaur. Peleliu was six miles long and two miles across at its widest point (near the center of the island). The airstrip occupied the southern flatlands. In the north was a twisted series of coral ridges known as Umurbrogol Mountain.

The scheme of maneuver called for a landing on the southwestern shore. The 1st Marines, on the left flank, had by far the toughest mission. Once ashore, the regiment would have to wheel to the left while under the guns of the enemy in the high ground, attack north into a widening zone that would require immediate use of its reserve, then storm the Umurbrogol (which proved to be the heart of the Japanese defense). The plan called for the 5th Marines, in the center, to drive across the island and take the airfield and for the 7th Marines, on the right, to turn south and clean out the peninsula at that end of the island. The landing beaches of the 1st Marines presented a special problem: small bluffs flanking either end would allow the enemy to fire down the length of the shore.

Three days of naval preparatory fire inflicted little damage. On D-Day, Japanese artillery and mortars showered the Marines, while the enfilade fire of machine guns and antitank cannon swept over the sand. The division took heavy casualties and held only a tenuous perimeter the first night, but thereafter the issue was never in doubt. The cost, however, would not be determined until U.S. forces rooted out the last of the defenders.

On D+1 the 5th Marines reached the opposite shore. Over the next few days they occupied the lightly held eastern flatlands. The 7th Marines and two of its battalions completed the seizure of the southern promontory on D+3. Puller and his 1st Marines reached the Umurbrogol on D+2 and battered themselves against it for the next seven days. This particular area of the coral ridges turned out to be the enemy's main bastion and would be the very last ground conquered in the battle.

Elements of 2d Battalion, 7th Marines, the division's reserve, began to reinforce the 1st Marines on the night of D+2. Three days later, the remainder of the 7th Marines moved up and assumed responsibility for much of the Umurbrogol front. On the 23rd, against the wishes of Rupertus, Geiger ordered the 321st Infantry to join the fight on Peleliu and replace the depleted 1st Marines. Eventually the entire 81st Division came ashore and finished the campaign weeks after the last of the 1st Marine Division had returned to Pavuvu. Losses in the 1st Marine Division totaled 7,096 men, while the 81st Division's dead and wounded amounted to 3,089.

The Debate

The scale of casualties in the 1st Marine Division, but especially those in the 1st Marines, shocked everyone involved, because no one had anticipated the operation would be so difficult. (The following year, Iwo Jima and Okinawa would dwarf those numbers, with losses in 13 of the 15 Marine infantry regiments engaged exceeding those in the 1st Marines at Peleliu.) Puller was no exception. He himself had suffered through the battle with a severe infection in his thigh from a piece of shrapnel still lodged there from Guadalcanal. At a memorial service to dedicate the division cemetery on Peleliu in late September, the marks of his old wound and the recent battle were evident. He appeared thinner than usual, his face craggier, his eyes sunken and dark, his demeanor sullen. Major John S. Day, a division staff officer, observed that the colonel "looked like hell" and was limping badly. Years later, Puller called Peleliu "his toughest operation" of the war.

Major Day also had been struck by "how depressed [Puller] seemed at the casualties the 1st Marines had taken." In letters to friends and family written at the time, Chesty admitted "the fight was costly" and sympathized with those who had paid the high price: "May God rest the souls of our dead and make life less bitter for our maimed and crippled." But he said no more, giving his feelings for these men no greater space than he had accorded the loss of his own brother a few weeks earlier. He preferred instead to dwell with pride on what his outfit had done: "The performance of my officers and men was grand. They never failed to move forward when ordered to, and gained ground continually regardless of the enemy. If there is such a thing as glory in war, they have won it."

Condemnation of the decision to attack Peleliu and of Puller's part in the battle has increased over the years. While the former is probably justified, a thorough look at the records of the campaign shows that Chesty's performance does not rate the censure it has received. Most critiques are based on memories, often influenced by Puller mythology, that do not stand up against the facts.

Firepower

One of the most serious criticisms concerned Puller's use of firepower. Lieutenant Colonel Harold O. Deakin, the division plans officer, believed himself to be "charitable" in saying that the commanding officer of the 1st Marines "didn't have a total grasp of the use of naval gunfire, artillery, and supporting arms in general." Lieutenant Colonel F. G. Henderson, a member of the corps operations staff, agreed: "Puller refused to let you help him with fire support. He insisted that he was going to do it with Marine infantry, ram it in there." Major Gordon Gayle, a battalion commander in the 5th Marines, while not criticizing Puller, felt that his own regiment performed better and suffered lower casualties because it employed the lion's share of all the supporting fires requested during the campaign.

Later attacks against the Umurbrogol did benefit from much greater firepower, but the 1st Marines made as much use of supporting arms as the situation allowed. On D-Day, the Navy tallied 26 calls for naval gunfire. Observers in the 1st Marines initiated 15 of them, with one-third coming from the regimental headquarters. On D+1, it was 13 of 24, with 7 coming from Puller's command post. The share of recorded missions for the 1st Marines did not change appreciably until the end of its stay in the lines, when only one battalion was engaged. The war diaries and staff journals also show frequent use of air and artillery.

This activity may have been driven by the battalions and the regimental staff rather than Puller himself, but one item proves he was thinking about supporting arms. On D+1, the division received a message commending the ships for the naval gunfire provided that day. It began: "CO, 1st Marines very much pleased. . . ." An aversion to using firepower was not consistent with his prior record, either. In Nicaragua Puller had employed rifle grenades rather than an infantry assault "to save the men." On Guadalcanal he had called in fires repeatedly to support his infantrymen. In describing enemy casualties inflicted by his battalion, he had observed: "In the operations where supporting artillery, planes, and destroyer fire was furnished . . . the figures are much higher." Possibly, Puller was not the most skilled employer of supporting arms, but he was certainly aware of their value and used them when they were available.

It is true the 1st Marines was less creative in using firepower in this difficult situation. Later in the battle, other units came up with some unique ways to attack the Japanese defensive system. They used 155-mm guns for direct fire against caves in the face of ridges, hauled 75mm pack howitzers onto the heights to hit more inaccessible targets, and rigged long hoses to spray fuel where flamethrower-equipped tracked landing vehicles (LVTs) could not reach. While Puller and his subordinates were not as innovative as others, they also had little time to react. They first encountered the unexpectedly tough terrain and defenses of the ridge on D+2 and were relieved from the main Umurbrogol front barely 72 hours later. The ability of others to develop better ideas likely stemmed from their opportunity to understand the enemy's defenses before they confronted them.

The perception that Puller did not make full use of supporting arms also may have resulted from the fact that he had much less available than other regiments had when they fought in the ridges. At the start of the battle, the 1st and 5th Marines each had only a 75-mm howitzer battalion in direct support, whereas the 7th Marines had a 105-mm howitzer unit. The division had three battalions in general support, one each of 105-mm and 155-mm howitzers and 155-mm guns. The 155-mm howitzers were not in place until D+2, however, and then directed half their attention to the south in support of the 7th Marines until D+4. The 155-mm guns did not go into action for the division until D+4. Thus the 1st Marines did not have a full complement of artillery available until 19 September, at which point it was on the verge of being combat ineffective because of all the casualties. An Army observer thought the division's slow deployment of the heavy guns was inexcusable. In the meantime, Puller's regiment had requested additional artillery support. On D+1, for instance, the 1st Marines called in missions from the artillery battalion of the 5th Marines.

By the same token, the regiment conducted its entire fight with only Navy air support, whereas other units in the later stages of the battle would benefit from the presence of Marine aviators more skilled in attacking ground targets. The Marine fliers also made much greater use of napalm and 1,000-pound bombs, which had more effect than the ordnance generally used by the Navy. In addition, during the landing the 1st Marines' air liaison parties lost their jeep-mounted radios. These were not replaced until D+3 or later, which hampered the control of close-air support. The regiment also suffered from the limited availability of assets such as tanks and flamethrower LVTs, which were not concentrated against the ridges early in the battle. Moreover, other outfits would benefit from efforts to build roads into the Umurbrogol to give these weapons better access. Major General Julian Smith, a firsthand observer, recognized that Puller's men "had a terrifically hard job because the infantry had to fight its way forward without customary air and artillery support."

Before the battle was even joined, the 1st Marines had been victimized by the poor preparatory fires. The enfilading bunkers on the White beaches could have been knocked out if they had received attention. The 1st Marine Division had asked for fires "against areas which a study of the terrain and a knowledge of Japanese tactics would indicate were fortified," and Puller had identified the points as a major concern. But one battalion after-action report noted: "More NGF [naval gunfire] and some napom [sic] on the point just north of White One would have been a big help. This point was undamaged by preparatory fires." Thus, the 1st Marines suffered large initial losses that hampered it through the rest of the battle.

Tactics

Puller has been condemned more frequently for the tactics he employed. George McMillan, a Marine correspondent on Peleliu, summarized the "stereotype," saying Chesty "was a tragic caricature of Marine aggressiveness. Puller overdid it. In the minds of many Marine officers – I think the impression was widespread throughout the Corps – Puller crossed the line that separates courage and wasteful expenditure of lives." Captain Everett P. Pope (a company commander in the 1st Marines) knew Chesty was brave, but also thought that his commanding officer understood only one method of attack – "straight ahead." The young officer could never understand the orders to make repeated assaults against the Umurbrogol: "Why he wanted me and my men dead on top of that hill, I don't know. Don't know what purpose it would have served." Captain Nikolai Stevenson agreed there was no question of Puller's "bravery," but he "never cared about flanks, just straight ahead." He recalled Puller often answered the battalions' requests for assistance with: "Just keep pushing."

On one level, the operation required a speedy conquest of Peleliu, not only to provide support for the upcoming Philippines campaign, but also to allow the fleet to withdraw to safer waters. The former reason had evaporated by D-Day, but nothing indicates Geiger or Rupertus knew that until it was too late. The latter requirement had been driven home in the late-1943 Gilberts campaign.

While it might have been in Puller's nature to drive straight ahead in all situations (and that is open to debate), Marine Corps doctrine and Navy command decisions would have pushed him to that style of warfare at Peleliu in any case. General O. P. Smith (the assistant division commander) later gave an estimation of Chesty's tactical views that would have described most of the senior Marine commanders in World War II: "He believed in momentum; he believed in coming ashore and hitting and just keep on hitting and trying to keep up the momentum until he'd overrun the whole thing." General Lemuel C. Shepherd, one of the most respected Marine division commanders of the war, pressed the offensive on Okinawa with a similar outlook: "We will attack and attack vigorously, and we will continue to attack until the enemy is annihilated." Army General

George Patton, a premier practitioner of the amphibious art in the European theater, expressed the same philosophy: "We must attack . . . a commander, once ashore, must conquer or die." One need only look at Buna-Gona, Tarawa, Biak, Saipan, Guam, Iwo Jima, and Okinawa to realize both the Marine Corps and the Army often employed straight-ahead, attrition-style tactics against strong Japanese bastions.

On Peleliu, Puller faced a situation that gave him no opportunity to adopt elaborate schemes of maneuver. Within the Umurbrogol, the nature of the interlocking defenses meant that any assault deteriorated quickly into a frontal attack. There were attempts to get at the coral redoubt from the flanks, but in each case the Marines ran into supporting Japanese positions. There simply were no weak areas to exploit. As the commanding officer of 1st Battalion, 1st Marines, put it years later: "We did not discover the defenses until we were in the middle of them being fired at from three sides." The only real option for maneuver was that employed after the 1st Marines was relieved, a move along the lightly defended west coast. There is no indication that Chesty seriously considered that idea, but it was beyond his capability to execute it in any case. The vital beaches and rear areas had to be protected, and that required the 1st Marines to maintain an unbroken line throughout its zone. By the time the nature of the Umurbrogol defenses became apparent, the regiment already had exhausted its own reserve and that of the division, as well as a good portion of its front-line combat power. The forces available to Puller were too weak to exploit the coastal flank and guard all the uncovered portion of the ridges. It became possible only after the 5th and 7th Marines had completed their missions and the 321st Infantry had reinforced the division. Thus it was a decision for Rupertus, not Chesty, to make.

The only practical alternative Puller had was one advanced by Julian Smith, who felt that the division should have cleaned up the rest of the island and then attacked the Umurbrogol with all its resources, instead of letting a weakened regiment go it alone. Of course, that choice also was not Puller's to make, as Smith pointed out: "I wouldn't have assaulted as soon as the 1st Division did with Puller's regiment. . . . I would have put him on the defensive, and he would have been in fine shape." That undoubtedly was the best solution, but Rupertus was in a hurry to take Peleliu, and all his subordinates knew it. Years later Puller complained privately that the general gave him no options: "Orders were to attack dead ahead, and that was the only thing we could do, to take ground regardless of losses. . . . It was more or less of a massacre. There was no way to cut down losses and follow orders."

Other senior officers at Peleliu felt the same way. Colonel Harold D. "Bucky" Harris of the 5th Marines reported later that there was "plenty [of] pressure from above to speed up the attack." He felt "roughly used" when Rupertus pushed him too hard and believed that only Geiger's intervention had prevented his relief by the division commander. The operations officer of the 5th Marines agreed his outfit was "under the greatest of pressure from headquarters" and that Harris launched some attacks with "great reluctance." He remarked sarcastically: "You can imagine the fine impression we had at that time of division." The Army's senior observer was equally astonished by Rupertus's orchestration of the operation:

> There was not much effort on the part of the Division Commander to coordinate the action of the regiments or assist them by means at his disposal. . . . There were instances when it is believed that coordinated artillery fire and assistance from the 5th Marines would have aided the 1st Marines. . . . It was not until D+4 that the Division Commander visited any of the regimental command posts. . . . The regimental commanders appeared to know their jobs and had superior records as leaders in previous combat.

Lieutenant Colonel Arthur M. Parker, Jr., the executive officer of the 3d Armored Amphibian Battalion, placed the blame entirely on the general: "The cold fact is that Rupertus ordered Puller to assault impossible enemy positions at 0800 daily till the 1st [Marines] was decimated." Major Day agreed: "To blame Puller for the day-to-day attacks on the ridge line is really unfair. He was carrying out Rupertus' orders."

If Puller is to be faulted for heavy casualties in his regiment, it can only be in two areas. One was his failure to raise whatever concerns he might have had with his commander. Had he lodged a protest with Rupertus, he could have been relieved of command, which was not just theoretical in view of Harris's concern. Perhaps most important, Chesty would have been extremely reluctant to do anything that might call into question his own aggressiveness and courage. His bulldog character likely never allowed the thought of protesting orders to rise very close to the surface. As O. P. Smith observed: "As long as there was fighting going on, he wanted to be in it." None of Puller's fellow commanders bucked Rupertus, either.

One might also question the zeal with which Puller executed his orders after D+3, though the evidence is mixed regarding how much pressure he did apply to his subordinates. Major Raymond G. Davis, a battalion commander, did not detect any: "I never felt driven or forced, I felt supported." But some others believed they were compelled by Puller to go beyond the call of duty. One snippet of a radio conversation overheard by a reporter on 19 September lends support to that view; Chesty's "Go ahead and smash them" sounded like a call for an all-out assault, not a slow, probing attack. That, of course, may have been pure media hype, but the regiment did send companies into the attack again and again, long after they had lost their effectiveness. If Puller did not create or pass along the pressure, neither did he take action to damp it down. Like Confederate Lieutenant General Stonewall Jackson at the Civil War Battle of Chancellorsville, Chesty was a leader "whose resolution was invincible," who would push forward until the mission was accomplished or he and his men "had been annihilated." The 1st Marines had the reputation of being "the most aggressive of the regiments," and it lived up to that billing. While that aggressiveness probably increased casualties in the latter part of the battle, it was crucial to securing the vulnerable left flank of the division during the first two days of the operation, when a lack of determination in the face of enemy fire might have resulted in defeat.

The unknown factor in any evaluation of Puller on Peleliu is how much his inflamed leg affected his ability to command. It is conceivable that pain and fever may have had a significant impact on his judgment, while his lack of mobility prevented him from developing a true picture of what was happening. He certainly was aware of his high losses, but he may not have realized just how little he was achieving in return for those lives. It is significant that Geiger's action to relieve the 1st Marines appeared to be motivated as much by his assessment of Chesty's condition as it was by casualty figures.

If some Marines felt Puller was a butcher, many others respected and admired him. A rifleman in the 2d Battalion, 1st Marines, revered Chesty for his leadership from the front: "He was one of you. He would go to hell and back with you. He wouldn't ask you to do anything that he wasn't doing with you." Another Marine voiced almost exactly the same sentiment: "He was one of us! He led by example – not by sitting 500 yards behind the lines, issuing orders. . . He earned all his honors and accolades and perhaps some he never received." O. P. Smith praised Chesty's leadership: "I went over the ground he captured and I don't see how a human being had captured it, but he did. . . . There was no finesse about it, but there was gallantry and there was determination."

THE VITAL ROLE OF THE
U.S. MARINE CORPS RESERVE, 1893-1951

Chris Morton

> *Major Morton, former instructor of U.S. Marine Corps history at U.S. Naval Academy, explains the evolution of the Marine Corps reserve, a subject often overlooked in traditional studies. The development of the reserve force culminated with its ability to make ready the 1st Marine Division for Korea in 1950 – an event that clearly demonstrated the crucial role reserves now played in the Corps' emerging force-in-readiness mission.*

The contributions of the Reserve Component to the nation are often overlooked by historians and many military members alike. One need look no farther than our operations in Afghanistan (2001-3) and Iraq (2002-3) and the essential role the Reserve and played there to see that the nation depends heavily on this force. Several decades ago, this was also the case as America's military found itself involved as the chief United Nations force on the Korean Peninsula. Often neglected when studying the "Forgotten War" is the fact that, had it not been for the readiness and availability of the Marine Reservists, the most famous campaigns of the war would not have been possible.

The Naval Militia period

Despite America having learned from previous wars that there was a need for a reserve structure of citizen forces dedicated to service afloat, no national sentiment had developed for the organization and training of such forces until the late 1880s. This period witnessed the beginning of a movement to establish a naval militia "as a means for providing for the coast defense and meeting the increased demands of the regular naval establishment for men and vessels upon the outbreak of war."[1] The federal government recognized that

> the pressing need of such a reserve corps may be gathered from the established fact that if war was declared to-morrow the regular navy would be hard pressed to supply full complements of men to all its existing ships, while there would be absolutely none ready to man such coasting steamers as might be armed and pressed into service [for the purpose of coastal defense].[2]

Despite this recognition, the government took no action to establish such a force at the national level. Instead, the establishment of such organizations devolved upon the states.

In March 1888, the Massachusetts legislature passed the nation's first Naval Militia Act and established a naval reserve force (the Naval Militia) for the protection of the state's waters.[3] Several additional states would follow, with 15 having units by 1898 and 21 (plus the territory of Hawaii and the District of Columbia) by 1916. In almost every case, these Naval Militia units were part of the individual state's National Guard organization and were, therefore, similar in their relationship to the U. S. Navy as the National Guard was to the U. S. Army. Thus, these units were under the sole control of the state governor and not directly subject to the Navy Department or the President. Even so, the Navy Department began to see some potential utility to these units being properly trained, and, at the Navy's request, Congress appropriated funds to be distributed to those states with naval militia units for the support of these units (in proportion to the percentage of the whole "national" force) beginning in 1891.[4]

In many ways, the Naval Militia was more of a social club and a hobby of the social elite than it was a truly effective military organization. The members were often from prominent families and saw admission to the Naval Militia unit as an extension of their membership in the local yacht club. As such, Naval Militia battalions across the United States admitted members in a fashion similar to other social organizations of the period. The common procedure began with two members recommending an individual for membership. Such an individual then went before a committee on admissions, with a favorable report from the committee meaning that the candidate had been approved to join the unit.[5] Despite the largely cliquish composition of the units, membership was also seen as an opportunity to develop the martial skills of these young gentlemen. As a result, once admitted to the local unit, members were expected to attend weekly drills at the armory and the Battalion's cruise (usually two weeks) in the summer. Objectives of the drill periods were to train the men in close order drill, gunnery, signal flags, and the use of the broad sword, whereas the summer was spent on a naval vessel, when the federal government made one available, or in rowing drills and learning the art of sailing.

From the time of their formation in 1775, Marines served on naval vessels. This was also the case with the many of the state Naval Militia units. In most cases, the Marines of the state Naval Militias were an informal group; formed from within the Battalion's other divisions during cruise periods, but not held together as a unit when not at sea. The Marines began to assume a more permanent place within the Naval Militia organization when the 1st Marine Corps Reserve Company was formed as an adjunct top the New York Naval Militia in 1893.[6] Again, several other states (but not all) followed suit, among the more famous of their day were those of Massachusetts and Louisiana.

The Spanish American War provided the first true test of the Naval Militia organization. As the only reserve pool of trained sailors and Marines, the Naval Militia units provided the best means of rapid expansion of the naval services upon the outbreak of hostilities. As the Naval Militia units were responsible only to the governors of their various states, cooperation with those states was necessary. It took the deployment of a small (and, as it turned out, outdated) Spanish Fleet under the command of Admiral Pascual Cervera to gain that cooperation. Adm Cervera departed the Cape Verde Islands in April 1898, and this sent waves of panic up and down the Atlantic seaboard and into the Gulf Coast as people became convinced (with the help of the same American press that drew the US into the war) that the Spanish Fleet would arrive off their coast at any minute. As the fear of the Spanish fleet intensified, the governors responded to requests of the Navy Department by authorizing the members of their respective Naval Militia organizations to take a leave of absence from their units in order to enlist in the US Navy or Marine Corps.[7] Eventually, the Naval Militia provided 263 officers and 3,832 enlisted men to the Navy Department during the course of the war. The number of men who answered the call to the colors during this period was actually greater than the whole of the Naval Militia force in January 1898. As the tensions between Spain and the United States grew (and particularly after the sinking of the battleship USS *Maine*) the number of men willing to join these units increased. It is also interesting to note that the Naval Militia did a much better job providing men for service of the nation than did the National Guard (only about 50% of the original Guardsmen enlisted in the US Army).[8]

Naval Militia/Federal Reserve up to World War I

Following the successful conclusion of the Spanish-American War, the sailors and Marines who had joined the regular Navy or Marine Corps for the duration of the war were discharged and returned to the service of their various states. For almost two decades, the situation/relationship returned to *status quo antebellum*. However, the position of the Marines of the various state Naval Militias changed with the passage of the federal Naval Militia Act on February 16, 1914. This act placed the Naval Militias of the various states firmly under the control of the Navy Department.[9] Navy Department General Order Number 153 of July 10, 1915, created the Marine Corps Branch, Naval Militia and officially provided the role for the Marines

> to so organize, arm, uniform, equip, and train...that it may be eligible to be called forth by the President of the United States to serve the United States in the event of war, actual or threatened, with any foreign nation...or rebellion against the authority of the United States Government.[10]

General Order Number 153 also fixed the strength of a company within the Marine Corps Branch of the Naval Militia at three officers and forty-eight enlisted men, identical to regular Marine companies.

In addition to the Marine Corps Branch, Naval Militia, the United States Marine Corps Reserve was created by an act of Congress on August 29, 1916.[11] The Navy Department then used this act as the statutory authority for General Order Number 231 issued two days later to inform "all persons belonging to the Navy...[that]...a United States Marine Corps Reserve, to be a constituent part of the Marine Corps and in addition to the authorized strength thereof, is hereby established."[12] As American participation in World War I loomed, Congress passed the National Defense Act of June 3, 1916. From the perspective of the Naval Militia, the most significant provisions of this act were the ones that ended recruiting for the state militias effective April 1, 1917, and, more importantly, that the state naval militias would cease to exist once called to federal service.[13]

In anticipation of espionage and sabotage by German agents, several of the states activated their Naval Militia units (as well as National Guard) prior to the official outbreak of hostilities. When the United States declared war on April 7, 1917, the total strength of the federal Marine Corps Reserve authorized by Congress in 1916 was only thirty-six men. Fortunately, the U. S. Marine Corps could draw from the state Marine companies, which had a total strength of 1,046 officers and enlisted men. These units were mobilized for federal service when the US entered the war.[14] The addition of these trained men to the rolls of the active Marine Corps meant an almost immediate 10% increase in the size of the Corps.[15]

These men of the Marine Corps Branch, Naval Militia units were amalgamated into already established regular Marine units upon their arrival at naval stations, and the Marine Corps Branch, Naval Militia ceased to exist. This method of integrating the reserve forces into the active duty structure would remain the pattern for the first 50 years of the Marine Corps Reserve's existence. There are several possible explanations for this mobilization pattern and the basic competing interests are unit cohesion versus readiness. Due to the social club atmosphere of the Naval Militia units, the men often felt a great deal of unit pride. These men were very familiar with one another as they came from similar social backgrounds and lived and worked in the same area. Keeping this type of unit together as a fighting unit would certainly act as some level of a combat multiplier. On the other hand, one could easily make an argument (particularly in this pre-World War II period when affiliation was as much social as it was military) that it was impossible for the Reserve Marine drilling two hours per week to be as combat ready as the regular Marine training 5 days per week. With many of these already existing units not fully manned, it made sense to simply disperse these less well trained reservists to fill already existing vacancies rather than have complete units of less trained Marines. Additionally, there was a possible negative effect of leaving so many men from a single geographic area in the same unit. Should that unit go into combat, the losses sustained (all from that one area) could pose undue hardship on the home front. Eventually, beginning in the 1990s (Operation DESERT SHIELD/DESERT STORM), the Marine Corps opted for the unit cohesion combat multiplier as the overall training gap between regular and reserve has diminished, but individual mobilization would serve as the blueprint through Korea.

Due to this method of activation and the fact that the Corps considered all enlistments during World War I to be into the Marine Corps Reserve ("for the duration"), it is all but impossible to track the contributions made by any individual units of the Naval Militia. With the call to service for the war, the Corps took the opportunity to gain more control over the Reserve structure. Headquarters did not desire to continue with separate organizations at the state and federal levels. At its behest, Congress approved legislation in July 1918 that consolidated the Naval Militia, Marine Corps Branch and the Marine Corps Reserve and ended authorization to form units at the state level.[16]

The Post World War I Reserve

Following the conclusion of World War I, the Marine Corps Reserve program lapsed into obscurity. This was partly due to another provision of the National Defense Act of 1916 that troops called to federal service for the war "upon discharge...automatically became private citizens."[17] This meant that there was no manpower pool from which to form the post-war Marine Corps Reserve. However, the primary reason the reserve was not formed was a disinterest on the part of the federal government in funding a reserve structure. Despite the statutory authorization for a Marine Corps Reserve, no units were formed on the basis of the 1916 act due to Congress's failure to appropriate funds for their creation. Further action would have to be taken at the federal level for the Marine Corps Reserve to become a viable force.

Under the provisions of the 1916 Reserve Act, the Marine Corps maintained a reserve structure. However, in the immediate postwar period this structure was nothing more than a "registry of men with past service."[18] There was little public interest in matters of the military, particularly in maintaining a Reserve. As an "inevitable result, there was no allocation of funds. With little interest and no funds, there was little reserve."[19] The Major General Commandant of the Marine Corps[20], John A. Lejeune, continued to express interest in retaining a Reserve, reminding the Subcommittee of the House Committee on Appropriations for Naval Appropriation Bills on January 21, 1921, that "no appropriations have been made for a Marine Corps reserve. It is therefore a reserve in name only and will soon cease to exist."[21]

It took nearly four more years of lobbying before Congress would take action. On February 28, 1925, Congress approved *An Act To provide for the creation, organization, administration, and maintenance of a Naval Reserve and a Marine Corps Reserve*.[22] This act abolished the reserve structure created under the 1916 Reserve Act and recreated the Marine Corps Reserve. There were many changes over the 1916 law, the most significant being a provision for drill pay at the rate of one-thirtieth of the monthly base pay for the Marine's grade (on a basis similar to that of the National Guard and a practice that continues to this day). Another provision of the act authorized enlisted Marines to "be issued articles of uniform, bedding, and equipment" thereby limiting individual expenses associated with joining a reserve unit. Shortly after the passage of the 1925 law, the Marine Corps began to formulate an organizational structure and regulations governing the reserves. Chapter thirteen of the *Marine Corps Manual* published June 30, 1925, defined the mission of the reserve as "to provide a trained force of officers and men available to serve as reinforcements to the regular Marine Corps in time of war or national emergency."[23] This remained the mission of the reserve forces until 1940.

Major General Commandant Lejeune remarked on the progress of the reserve from its inception on July 1, 1925, in his annual report dated September 30th of that year:

> Under this new Reserve bill, the Corps has the opportunity to build up a real Reserve so that in the event of an emergency we shall be able to get the necessary officers and men to put the Marine Corps on an emergency footing. With this view, enrollment for the reserve commenced...Communications have been received from Reserve officers requesting authority to organize other companies, and headquarters has directed these officers to submit plans, and if they are satisfactory, the authority to organize other companies will be given.[24]

The original Fleet Marine Corps Reserve companies (referred to in Lejeune's annual report above) were formed in a similar fashion to the companies of the National Guard. There was no initiative taken on the part of Headquarters Marine Corps to direct unit location as the Reserve developed. Creation of the companies was purely an individual effort on the part of prominent citizens (and prior Marines). The primary determining factors for the creation of a unit were the ability to recruit a minimum of forty-five enlisted men into the unit as well as securing permission "to use the local National Guard or Naval Armory for storage of company property and for drill purposes."[25]

In the initial years of the Marine Corps Reserve, all recruiting was done by members of the units and was not controlled by the Marine Corps. The success of each individual unit was thus completely in the hands of the commanding officer. Marine Corps policy at the time recognized the importance played and personal investment made by the unit commanding officers in order to recruit and properly train the units. Therefore, there was no limit placed on the length of time that an individual could remain in command. As a result, it was not uncommon for unit Commanding Officers to remain in command for a decade or more. For example, Alfred A. Watters became commanding officer of the 310th Company in New Orleans on September 10, 1927, as a Second Lieutenant. He remained as the commanding officer until the unit mobilized for World War II in 1940 (Watters was a Lieutenant Colonel at this point).

Until the early 1900s, there was no permanent regimental or even company organization in the regular Marine Corps. All Marines were stationed aboard ships of the US Navy or at naval stations on guard duty. When necessary, expeditionary forces were formed from these scattered units. When the assigned mission was accomplished, these provisional organizations lapsed. By 1927, a company organization had been created consisting of two officers and sixty enlisted men and the companies were divided into three platoons. Therefore, when the newly created Fleet Marine Corps Reserve (FMCR) companies were established that same year, they had an identical structure. In 1929, the regular Marine Corps expanded their company strength to three officers and ninety-three enlisted men. As a result, the first of many reorganizations of the Marine Corps Reserve to mirror the structure of the regular Corps occurred by June of that year. This company organization would turn out to be short lived, but at its peak strength, the FMCR consisted of sixteen companies in sixteen different cities across the country.[26]

The Marine Corps expected the men attached to the FMCR companies to be able to augment the Corps in time of national emergency. This required some level of constant training to Marine Corps standards. Although there was no common training schedule established for units of the Marine Corps Reserve, a pattern had developed by the late 1920s that would continue as the standard through the Korean War period. The units held weekly drills of about two hours duration one night per week. The primary military objectives of drill periods were close order drill, classroom instruction, inspections, and gun drills.

One of the most significant drawbacks to this type of weekly training from a purely military standpoint is that field duty training was simply not feasible during the short period of time the Marines drilled during the week. Particularly problematic was that all of these units were located in major cities, meaning that suitable training areas were often some distance away. The end result was that all meaningful field training was accomplished during the two week summer training period (referred to as "summer camps" at the time – perhaps an indication of what level of training truly occurred).

In much a similar manner as the Naval Militia period, the Marine Corps Reserve of the 1920s and 1930s was as much a social group as it was a military organization. Again, the ranks were filled with men from prominent families (some were even practicing attorneys and physicians) who joined for the same patriotic and social reasons they joined other groups at the time. As a result, the units would also spend time socializing at the armory, either in an informal club setting (many of the armories at the time had at least one room set aside for this purpose) or at formal dinners or dances held by the unit.[27]

On October 31, 1929, the Marine Corps Reserve began a period of uncertainty when the federal government ceased drill pay.[28] The reserve appropriation was to be used only to support pay during annual training. In order to pay most expenses, such as maintenance of the gear and armory and transportation to summer training, many of the units resorted to collecting dues from the Marines. With no appropriation for drill pay, the requirement to attend weekly drills was suspended, but units could continue to drill without pay.[29] Despite such financial hardships, the Marine Corps Reserve persisted. This was due to a combination of factors. First was the fact that the men in the Reserve were, as mentioned previously, often members of the social elite. As a result, they were among the few who could afford to pay unit dues during the Great Depression. Also, those who remained affiliated with the Reserve at this time were among the most dedicated Marines of each unit. The end result was that

> in spite of having no pay, no clothing, and no armories or suitable places for training, many loyal and energetic individuals carried on and kept the reserve

alive. This gave the country a number of cadres for units when Congress, in 1935, again decided we needed the reserves.[30]

Were it not for the efforts of these few men during the early 1930s, the "Marine Corps reserve [would have] shriveled out of sight."[31]

Typical of individual sacrifice under the "New Reserve" was the 6th Marine Brigade (of the 19th Reserve Marine Regiment) of New York City. In a study published by the Commanding Officer of the unit in August 1932, he outlined the expenses of the unit above what the Marine Corps paid.[32] Dues were paid by the members of the unit at a rate of fifteen dollars annually for officers and three dollars annually for enlisted men. This fund was then used to cover expenses such as armory maintenance, camp expenses, transportation of the unit, and music for the band. In a three-month period before publication of the article, the unit spent almost four thousand dollars from private funds.

In spite of the fact that drill pay was no longer authorized, the reserve underwent another reorganization effective in late summer 1930. This reorganization resulted from experiments conducted by Headquarters, Marine Corps in early 1929 (before the suspension of drill pay) mostly in order to find ways to cut costs. Planners felt that "possibly the training of isolated companies was not for the best interests of the Reserve"[33] and that a regimental structure would reduce expenditures. The plan developed, termed the "New Reserve," called for the formation of reserve regiments composed of officers and men who would drill without pay, purchase most of their own uniform items, and also bear a large part of the reserve expense with private funds in order to save appropriated funds for training.[34] With this structure change, as well as the loss of funds, the Marine Corps Reserve reduced the overall number of units to thirteen battalions (in six regiments).[35] This "new" regimental/battalion organization was modeled on the structure of regular Marine battalions and was composed of a headquarters element, three rifle companies, and one machine gun company. The total authorized strength of these battalions were eleven officers and two hundred forty enlisted men.[36]

The year 1935 saw two significant events related to the Marine Corps Reserve. The first involved yet another structural reorganization. During the year, the regular Marine Corps restructured from infantry regiments into two Marine forces (one on each coast) whose mission was to be "sea soldiers" who could board naval vessels at a moments notice in order to be used to establish and secure advanced naval bases.[37] Under this plan, Headquarters Marine Corps began to question the viability of the reserve regimental structure, which had also proved too cumbersome for economical control. This structure was thus disbanded and reorganized as thirteen individual battalions (in thirteen cities) in order to "conform with regular Navy and Marine Corps policy of training smaller, more mobile units that could easily operate with the fleet."[38] As with all units of the ground reserve up to this point, every battalion was designated as an infantry battalion. These battalions was composed of a headquarters company and four rifle companies with a total authorized strength of twelve officers and two hundred fifty-eight enlisted men.[39] This organization would eventually expand to twenty-three infantry battalions by 1940 and would be the system in place when the Marine Corps Reserve was called to service for World War II.[40]

The second development of 1935 was the partial reinstitution of drill pay.[41] Congress appropriated funds for paying reserves for drill periods; however, the amount was insufficient to pay all members of the reserve for the statutorily authorized forty-eight drill periods. Over the course of the next three years, approximately seventy percent of the authorized complement of Marine reserves received pay for drill periods.[42] The remainder (largely the officers) continued to drill without compensation until the drill pay issue was finally resolved in the Naval Reserve Act of June 25, 1938, which increased the appropriation to a level allowing all reservists to return to full drill pay status.[43]

Mobilization of the Marine Corps Reserve for World War II began with President Franklin D. Roosevelt issuing Executive Order 8245 declaring a "Limited National Emergency."[44] Secretary of the Navy Frank Knox followed on October 5, 1940, with Dispatch 051751 placing "all organized reserve divisions...on short notice for call to active duty."[45] Major General Commandant Thomas Holcomb directed the twenty-three Marine Corps Reserve infantry battalions to report to their home stations for active duty no later than November 9th in Circular Letter 396 issued October 14th. The circular letter also declared that any Marine who "severs his connection with [the reserve] for any reason...[was] required by law to report to and register with [the] Local Board, Selective Service System."[46] This mobilization was the result of the rapid expansion of America's military as the nation prepared for its seemingly inevitable entrance into World War II. The Marine Corps was in the beginning of an expansion from 19,432 Marines (with no organized division size units in June 1939) to a post war size of 485,053 in six divisions (on V-J Day). As with the contribution of the Naval Militia units to the Spanish-American War and World War I, the Marine Corps Reserve of 1940 was able to provide trained men to fill the ranks of the active duty structure and allow for rapid expansion. When mobilized for service in 1940, the Organized Marine Corps Reserve numbered 239 officers and 6192 enlisted. This additional manpower represented an almost instantaneous 20% increase in the size of the Fleet Marine Force (28,345 in June 1940).[47]

Once the Reserve battalions arrived at their individual armories, they proceeded to their follow on duty station (San Diego, Quantico, or the Navy Yards at Philadelphia, Mare Island, Norfolk or Puget Sound) as soon as transportation became available. Upon arrival at these bases, the battalions were immediately "absorbed in units of the Fleet Marine Force" at the base.[48] This integration was the essence of the reserve mobilization for World War II. The reserves did not mobilize as units, per se, but as individual Marines to augment the regular units based upon the needs of those units for Marines with particular skills. Despite every Marine reservist being trained in the infantry specialty, not every vacancy in these pre-existing units required infantry skills. The end result was that some Marines integrated into infantry battalions while others were assigned to such units as armor, engineers, artillery, defense battalions, and motor transport.[49] This type of utilization of the Reserve for World War II demonstrated one of the fundamental weaknesses of the pre-World War II infantry only structure. Correcting these problems would be one of the focal points of Headquarters, Marine Corps when the Reserve was recreated following World War II. The integration of the Reserve battalions with already existing regular units effectively marked the hibernation of the Marine Corps Reserve until after the war.

The Korean War Era Marine Corps Reserve

Immediately following the conclusion of World War II, the Marine Corps began to plan for the reactivation of the reserve. This time, however (and unlike the initial period in the 1920s), Headquarters Marine Corps directed the organization from the beginning. One of the biggest hurdles that had to be overcome was the fact that one of the provisions the Marine Corps attached to the mobilization for World War II was that

> upon assuming active duty and proceeding to duty stations, all armories, storeroom space and office space formerly occupied by the battalions were vacated and all leases, occupancy permits and rent agreements were terminated.[50]

The reformation of the ground Organized Marine Corps Reserve (OMCR) began in December 1945, when recruiting officers across the country were directed to make "preliminary surveys of most major cities in an attempt to locate buildings that were available and would be satisfactory to house reserve units."[51] The lack of available armory facilities, even in areas with sufficient personnel willing to participate, necessitated further study on the part of Headquarters, Marine Corps. In order to locate facilities for the planned reserve units, boards of officers from Headquarters, Marine Corps were dispatched to the major cities beginning in February 1946. These Marines evaluated the cities on the basis of five primary criteria: 1) the male population of military age, 2) availability of suitable armory facilities, 3) geographic distribution of units in relation to planned mobilization points and field training areas, 4) availability of technically trained individuals to fill necessary billets, and 5) the presence of national guard or other service reserve units in the vicinity.[52] The board then recommended to the Commandant locations for the units to be activated and the first units were established by the end of that year. In fact, there were over 32,000 members of the Organized Marine Corps Reserve by the end of 1946.[53]

In addition to this direct involvement by Headquarters, Marine Corps on unit location, there was one significant policy change instituted following World War II concerned recruiting for reserve units. Reserve recruiters were created who were to act in similar fashion to the regular Marine Corps recruiters in order to staff the reserve units located in their area. As a result, the unit commanding officer was no longer solely responsible for recruiting for his unit, although he was expected to assist these recruiters in their efforts. This resulted in another policy change regarding the length of the commanding officer's tour. These tours were now to be rotated approximately every two years, as they were in the regular Marine Corps.[54]

The end result of these organizational changes directed by Washington was that the structure of the Marine Corps Reserve as it developed in the period following World War II bore little resemblance to the twenty-three infantry battalions of 1940. This post-war Marine Corps Reserve was designed to more closely mirror the composition of the Fleet Marine Force in order to better enable the reserves to augment the regular component with trained Marines. To this end, Headquarters, Marine Corps planned for the following units in the post-World War II ground Reserve: 16 infantry battalions, 2 tank battalions, 2 amphibian tractor battalions, 5 105mm howitzer battalions, 2 155mm howitzer battalions, 10 engineer companies, 4 signal companies, 2 heavy antiaircraft artillery groups, and 1 40mm battery.[55]

Until 1940, the standard was that the battalions and all of their subordinate companies were located in one geographic area. This meant that there were only a small number of areas capable of supporting large units. In order to maximize participation possibilities (and thus the strength of each individual unit), Headquarters realized that the overall unit organization of the inter-war period would need to be different as well. This resulted in the creation of more (and smaller) size units geographically dispersed throughout the nation. No longer would an entire battalion be located in a single city. The headquarters (and perhaps one or two of the companies) would be in one site and subordinate companies located in other areas (often as far as neighboring states). By the summer of 1950, the ground reserve consisted of 138 separate units in 126 cities in the United States and its possessions (one unit in Hawaii).[56]

Marines of the inter-war period continued the practice of weekly drills established in the 1920s. These drill periods were usually two hours in duration, and attendees were again authorized drill pay at the rate of $1/30^{th}$ monthly base pay for their rank for every drill completed.[57] Battalion objectives for the drill periods continued to be essentially the same as those of the pre-World War II reserves. Reservists were also, as with the pre-war period, required to attend active duty training for fifteen consecutive days for which they would receive full pay and allowances for the rank held and time served. All of this training focused on preparing the Marines for their mission "to provide a trained force of officers and enlisted men...for the integration into and assimilation by the Fleet Marine Forces of the regular Marine Corps in the event of mobilization or national emergency."[58]

In addition to the ground reserve, the Marine Corps recognized the need to expand their air reserve structure (which was virtually nonexistent prior to World War II). The Marine air reserve program had one great advantage over the ground reserves in getting underway following World War II, the Naval Air Stations constructed as training air bases during the war near major cities offered ideal training areas and facilities. With the Navy already in possession of the sixteen newly constructed airfields, the Marine Corps decided to form reserve aviation squadrons at each of these naval air stations.[59]

The Marine Corps established the fighter squadron as the base unit of the aviation reserve with a maximum authorized reserve strength at forty-five naval aviators, fifteen non-flying officers, and one hundred ninety enlisted men.[60] The primary mission of Marine air squadrons, both regular and reserve, was "training for close air support for ground forces making amphibious landings."[61] As such, the reserve aviators would be trained for fighter-bomber missions in the same vein as their regular brethren. This focus on close air support missions would prove critical in Korea, not only in support of Marines, but also in support of US Army ground operations (largely as a result of the Air Force's lack of emphasis on the close air support mission). The basic air weapon of Marine aviation in the inter-war period was the F4U Corsair and it became standard throughout the reserve with each squadron authorized eighteen.[62] By June of 1950, the Organized Marine Corps Reserve (aviation) consisted of 30 Marine Fighter Squadrons.

In contrast to the ground reserve, the air reserve did not drill once per week. These men would drill one entire weekend per month in order to allow more time for flight operations for the aviators and more time working on the aircraft for the crews.[63] An additional consideration leading to weekend drills proved to be the airfields themselves. The runways at some of the airfields were not equipped with lights, making nighttime operations impossible and further limiting the training value that could be obtained from weekly evening drill periods. Unlike the ground units who often had to travel to an annual training site, the squadrons were often capable of performing the necessary training locally. Therefore, it was fiscally prudent to remain in the local area even during the fifteen day summer training period.

In addition to the aforementioned organizational changes, the Marine Corps instituted several changes to the Reserve program as a whole in order to make it more attractive following World War II. Specifically, the Corps offered members of the Organized Reserve longevity pay which simply meant increased pay for every drill period and summer training period. Other pay related changes to the Reserve system included a retirement program being initiated and a more generous promotion system. Additionally, the focus of the Reserve in many specialties (aside from the infantry-only approach before 1940) resulted in Marines acquiring skills transferable to their civilian occupations. As if that were not enough, the Marine Corps Institute (long offering correspondence courses for earning high school and college credits) expanded its offerings to include a wide variety of technical courses. These changes, and the resulting size of the Reserve in June 1950, would ultimately serve the nation well on the Korean Peninsula.

The North Korean invasion of South Korea in the summer of 1950 caught America by surprise. The reliance of post-World War II foreign policy and military planners on the atomic bomb meant that our conventional military forces had been allowed to atrophy. The regular Marine Corps had been the subject of budget cuts at the hands of the President and Secretary of Defense that had virtually shattered their ability to rapidly respond to a strong premeditated act of aggression. The Marine Corps had two Divisions and two Wings (as mandated by the National Security Act if 1947) in name only. The peacetime table of organization for a Marine Division had been reduced to roughly half that of a wartime division and even these peacetime divisions were not fully manned.[64] It is in this context where the Marine Corps Reserve proved to be instrumental. By the time of the North Korean invasion, the reserve had steadily grown to a total of almost 130,000 (including all categories of Marine Reservists – about 40,000 in the Organized/Drilling Reserve). The Marine Corps had placed a much higher reliance on the Reserve structure to counterbalance the small size of the regular establishment and focused on a large, high quality force capable of rapid mobilization.

By early July, it was apparent that the forces in Korea at that point were insufficient to stem the tide of the North Korean onslaught. To provide additional firepower, the 1st Provisional Marine Brigade, consisting of 6,500 well trained Marines (and the only infantry regiment in the 1st Marine Division), was formed at Camp Pendleton, California, and deployed for the Korean Peninsula in mid-July 1950. These men were committed into the Pusan Perimeter to reinforce the U.S. Army and South Korean units already there.

As the situation in Korea deteriorated further, it became apparent that there was a need for a war-strength Marine division. General Douglas MacArthur (commanding officer of United Nations forces in Korea) had devised a plan for an amphibious envelopment of the North Korean army by landing at Inchon. In order to execute his plan, MacArthur asked the Joint Chiefs of Staff for the 1st Marine Division. However, as a combat unit, the 1st Marine Division had virtually ceased to exist with the deployment of the 1st Provisional Marine Brigade. Filling out the regimental combat teams of the war-strength 1st Marine Division required that the Marines of the 2nd Marine Division from Camp Lejeune, North Carolina be relocated to Camp Pendleton, but even that would not provide enough men. If the 1st Marine Division was to be built to wartime strength, the Reserves would be needed.

As a result of the immediate need to expand the size of the nation's conventional military forces, President Truman authorized the Defense Department to mobilize reservists for duty in Korea on July 19, 1950. The first twenty-two units of the Organized Marine Corps Reserve (ground) were ordered to active duty the following day. Over the course of the next fifteen days, the entire ground reserve received orders to active duty. By September 11th, a span of just 53 days, all units had reported for extended active duty.[65]

As with their call to duty for World War II, units were initially ordered to their training centers and then to follow on training at regular Marine Corps bases. As with the mobilization for World War II, the ground reserve units lost their identity the moment they transferred their members to units of the regular establishment and the individual units ceased to exist, making any attempt to discuss wartime activities at a unit level impossible. Immediately upon arrival at their follow on duty station, the Marines were "billeted, processed, and classified."[66] The urgency of the situation necessitated that those reservists best qualified, by virtue of previous training or military experience, for combat service with the 1st Marine Division be selected. Therefore, the Korean mobilization operated under the premise that reserve Marines fell into one of two categories — combat-ready or non-combat-ready.

Non-combat-ready Marines were those who did not meet the criteria mentioned above, as well as a subclass called the recruit class, which meant that the individual had either less than one year in the OMCR, had a poor drill attendance record, or had not yet completed recruit training. Many of these men remained at Camp Pendleton (except recruits, who were sent to San Diego) in order to receive sufficient training to then join units being rotated into the Korean theater. Others were sent to replace trained regular Marines in overseas security detachments and thus free those Marines for combat assignment.[67]

Combat-ready was defined as veterans of more than ninety days active service, or reservists for over two years with either attendance at one summer camp and seventy-two drills or two summer camps and thirty-six drills. Those individual Marine reservists determined to be combat-ready found themselves transferred into "already existing but severely undermanned" regular units and then sent to Korea.[68] Approximately 50% of the OMCR Marines (and all of the officers) were classified as combat ready and 2,891 were then immediately assigned to the 1st Marine Division.[69] It is in this augmentation of the 1st MarDiv where the Reserves made their first direct contribution to the war effort.

The impact made by the additional manpower from Marine Corps Reserve units was immeasurable. By September 15 (the date of the Inchon landing), "there were more Marines in the Far East than there had been in the total Fleet Marine Force two and a half months earlier, and 20 percent of these were reservists only six to eight weeks removed from their civilian pursuits."[70] These Marines of the 1st Marine Division would then lead the way on the campaign to recapture Seoul. Perhaps Major General Oliver P. Smith, the Commanding General of the 1st Marine Division, best expressed the value of the ground reserve when he said

> Without the reserves, the Inchon landing on September 15 would have been impossible....They needed no particular refresher course to renew the amphibious skills they had learned during World War II....Reserves were quickly integrated into the division and they all became Marines with as splendid a Marine spirit as the regulars.[71]

Units of the Organized Aviation Reserve also made a significant contribution to the Korean War. By 1950, the composition of the OMCR Aviation force was thirty Fighter (VMF) and twelve Ground Control Intercept Squadrons (MCGI) squadrons. The beginning of the Korean War found Marine aviation (both regular and reserve) in an enviable position relative to the ground forces. The Reserve squadrons were staffed at

94% of their authorized strength and approximately 95% of the officers had combat experience.[72]

Despite the high training level of the Reserve, the result of the regular aviation staffing was that demand for Marines of the Organized Aviation Reserve was relatively minimal and it never became necessary to activate this force completely. The first demand for Aviation Reservists came on July 23rd, with six reserve VMF and three MCGI squadrons receiving orders to active duty. In a similar fashion to the Ground Reserve, these initial squadrons were separated and augmented into units of the 1st Marine Aircraft Wing (MAW) to bring the regular units to effective combat strength.

The timely arrival of the reservists "more than doubled Marine aviation strength in the Far East, and the number of VMFs available for the Inchon-Seoul operation increased from 2½ to 6."[73] A significant percentage of these squadrons were composed of Organized Aviation reservists. In the 7-week period between activation and Inchon, "937 aviation reservists had moved from civilian life in the United States to combat operations in Korea."[74]

The contribution of the Aviation reserve has a deeper significance than pure activation numbers express. At the time of the Inchon landing, approximately 24% of the 1st MAW was composed of reservists called to the colors for the national emergency presented by Korea. Again, as with the OMCR Ground, without these men, the 1st MAW would not have been able to provide the vital close air support for the Inchon landing and follow on campaign to Seoul.

The Marine Corps Reserve grew in importance to the nation from the time of its inception until its ultimate battle test on the Korean Peninsula. It began as an extension of the state National Guard and grew to a force of tens of thousands members of the Organized Reserve force. It grew from, in many respects, a social club with little to no central control to a true military force with a prominent role in national defense under the auspices of Headquarters, Marine Corps. The Reserve played a role in every major conflict this nation faced from the Spanish American War to Korea and always provided a force that the nation could draw upon to augment its regular structure at times when rapid expansion became necessary. The ability to instantly expand the regular forces was an incredible combat multiplier in 1898, 1917, and 1940, but was absolutely essential to American success in 1950. This was the essence of the Reserve that had evolved by the Korean Conflict, an organization that would be ready when the nation was least prepared.

NOTES

Author's Note: To date, there are only three published histories focusing on the Marine Corps Reserve. The first of these was written in 1966 [Reserve Officers of Public Affairs Unit 4-1, *The Marine Corps Reserve: A History 1916-1966*, (Washington, D.C.: Division of the Reserve, Headquarters, United States Marine Corps, 1966)] on the fiftieth anniversary of the reserve and briefly covered the entire history of the reserve to the date published. The second was written by the Historical Branch of Headquarters Marine Corps in 1951 [Ernest Giusti, *Mobilization of the Marine Corps Reserve in the Korean Conflict*, Washington, DC: Headquarters, US Marine Corps, 1951] to detail the contributions made to the war effort by the Reserve. The most recent was completed in 1996 [Fourth Marine Division Battle Staff Historical Detachment, *History of the 4th Marine Division 1943-1996*, New Orleans: Fourth Marine Division, 1996)] as a history of the Fourth Marine Division.

[1] W. C. Whitney, (Secretary of the Navy) Annual Report for 1887; quoted in Harold Thomas Wieand, "The History of the Development of the United States Naval Reserve, 1889-1941" (Ph.D. diss., University of Pittsburgh, 1952), 12.

[2] "The Naval Militia," *Harper's Weekly* (New York), 06 June 1891; quoted in Works Projects Administration, *Historical Military Data on Louisiana Naval Brigade: From Feb 1st 1890 to Dec 31st 1895* (New Orleans: Jackson Barracks, 1940), 3.

[3] Kevin R. Hart, "Towards a Citizen Sailor: The History of the Naval Militia Movement, 1888-1898," *The American Neptune* 33 (October 1973): 258.

[4] U. S. Navy Department, *Laws and Regulations State and National, Relating to the Naval Militia* (Washington, D. C.: Government Printing Office, 1895), 49. The Navy Department also supplied many of the state Naval Militia organizations with older naval vessels to support their training.

[5] Harold Thomas Wieand, "The History of the Development of the United States Naval Reserve, 1889-1941" (Ph.D. diss., University of Pittsburgh, 1952), 37.

[6] Reserve Officers of Public Affairs Unit 4-1, *The Marine Corps Reserve: A History 1916-1966*, (Washington, D.C.: Division of the Reserve, Headquarters, United States Marine Corps, 1966), 3-4. The muster rolls of the various states do not all reflect Marine organizations. This may be an oversight, or some states may not have established "permanent" Marine units. This fact makes it incredibly difficult to determine the overall strength of this initial attempt at a "Marine Corps Reserve." The 1st Marine Company of the state of Louisiana perhaps experienced one of the more unique military activations during the 1905 Yellow Fever epidemic, when they were called to active service of the state to protect its citizens from "invading" forces from Mississippi. The Mississippians were in Louisiana in an effort to enforce a quarantine and prevent the spread of the epidemic, but the governor of Louisiana felt that the territorial integrity of his state had been violated and called on the Naval Militia to correct the situation. Fortunately, cooler heads prevailed and the standoff was resolved peacefully.

[7] Kevin R. Hart, "Towards a Citizen Sailor: The History of the Naval Militia Movement, 1888-1898," *The American Neptune* 33 (October 1973): 274-6. The understanding was that the men so granted a leave of absence would return to state service upon their discharge from active service.

[8] Ibid., 276. Author's Note – I can find no accurate/complete number of men from naval militia units who joined the Marine Corps during the Spanish American War.

[9] U. S. Navy Department, *Annual report of the Secretary of the Navy for the Fiscal Year 1918* (Washington, D.C.: Government Printing Office, 1918), 67.

[10] U. S. Navy Department, *Navy Department General Order No. 153 dated 10 July 1915*, released by Josephus Daniels, Secretary of the Navy, in *General Orders Navy Department Series of 1913* (Washington, D.C.: Government Printing Office, 1916), 1.

[11] *An Act Making appropriations for the naval service for the fiscal year ending June thirtieth, nineteen hundred and seventeen, and for other purposes*, Statutes at Large 39, sec. 417, 556-619 (1916).

[12] U. S. Navy Department, *Navy Department General Order No. 231 dated 31 August 1916*, released by W. S. Benson, Acting Secretary of the Navy, in *General Orders Navy Department Series of 1913* (Washington, D.C.: Government Printing Office, 1916), 27.

[13] "Two Centuries of Service: A Brief History of the Louisiana National Guard, 1948," TMs (photocopy), p. 10, Bruner Hall Military Library, Jackson Barracks, New Orleans.

[14] Louisiana, Adjutant General's Office, *General Orders No. 9 dated 06 April 1917*, Bruner Hall Military Library, Jackson Barracks, New Orleans.

[15] Major Edwin N. McClellan, *The United States Marine Corps in the World War* (Washington, D.C.: Government Printing Office, 1920), 12 and 76. There were 13,725 active Marines on April 6, 1917.

[16] Ibid., 76.

[17] Brigadier General Louis A. Toombs, *Annual Report of the Adjutant General of the State of Louisiana for the Fiscal Year Ending June 30, 1921* (Baton Rouge: Ramires-Jones Printing Company, 1921), Bruner Hall Military Library, Jackson Barracks, New Orleans, 2.

[18] Major Melvin L. Krulewitch, "The Marine Corps Reserve," *Marine Corps Gazette* 15 (November 1930): 43.

[19] First Lieutenant Lawrence C. Switzer, Jr., "The Reserves: Citizen Marines," *Marine Corps Gazette* 34 (November 1950): 103.

[20] From May 13, 1908, until January 20, 1942, the senior officer in the Marine Corps was titled the Major General Commandant. After 1942, the title Commandant of the Marine Corps (still in use today) was given to the senior officer. "Commandants of the Marine Corps," prepared February 1996. TD (photocopy). Marine Corps Historical Center Archives Reference Section - History and Museums Division, Washington, DC.

[21] Author Unknown, "The U.S. Marine Corps Reserve, 1955 (?)," TMs (photocopy), p. 13, Marine Corps Historical Center Archives, Washington, D.C.

[22] *An Act To provide for the creation, organization, administration, and maintenance of a Naval Reserve and a Marine Corps Reserve, Statutes at Large,* Vol. 43, Part I, 1080 (1925).

[23] United States Marine Corps, *Marine Corps Manual, 1926*, (Washington, DC: Government Printing Office, 1926), Located in Publications of the Federal Government, Navy Department, 1828-1947, Record Group 287, National Archives at College Park, MD.

[24] Reserve Officers of Public Affairs Unit 4-1, *The Marine Corps Reserve: A History 1916-1966*, (Washington, D.C.: Division of the Reserve, Headquarters, United States Marine Corps, 1966), 26.

[25] John C. Beaumont, Director, Division of Operations and Training to the Major General Commandant; 1855-25 over AO-119-tfh dated 18 October 1926, TD (photocopy), National Archives and Records Administration, Record Group 127, Washington, DC.

[26] Reserve Officers of Public Affairs Unit 4-1, 30. These companies were located in such cities as Boston, New York, Milwaukee, Philadelphia, New Orleans, St. Paul, MN, Portland, ME, Chicago, Seattle, Detroit, and Rochester, NY.

[27] Information regarding the typical drill periods of the reserves are drawn from Brigadier General N. Buckner Barkley, *SNAFU: Situation Normal, All f o u l e d up!* (New Orleans: by the author, 1981), 2; Commanding Officer, 1st Battalion, 22nd Reserve Marines to Major General Commandant, 01 October 1934, TD, File 1855-25/22 22nd Marines, U. S. Marine Corps General Correspondence Personnel Department 1933-1938, Records of the United States Marine Corps, Record Group 127, National Archives Building, Washington, DC; as well as interviews conducted by the author with Colonel Joseph Ingraham (12 September 1999), Major Bertram Verdigets (13 September 1999), Major Jack Kearney (19 October 1999), Master Gunnery Sergeant Bob Moore (08 September 1999), Jack Sands (22 September 1999), Sonny Edins (18 July 1999), and Walter Murray (10 July 1999).

[28] Reserve Officers of Public Affairs Unit 4-1, 36-7; "The 10th Infantry Battalion, USMCR," Document # AH-1265-hph dated 7 Feb 1950, Marine Corps Historical Center Archives Unit File Section - 10th Infantry Bn, Washington, DC, 3.

[29] "The 10th Infantry Battalion, USMCR," Document # AH-1265-hph dated 7 Feb 1950, Marine Corps Historical Center Archives Unit File Section - 10th Infantry Bn, Washington, DC, 3.

[30] Switzer, 104.

[31] "The New Marine Corps Reserve," *Marine Corps Gazette* 31 (March 1947): 12.

[32] Lieutenant Colonel J. J. Staley, "Membership in the Marine Corps Reserve What it Costs," *Marine Corps Gazette* 17 (August 1932): 37-38.

[33] Major Krulewitch, "The Marine Corps Reserve," 43.

[34] Brigadier General B. H. Fuller to Captain Alfred A. Watters, Commanding Officer, 310th Company, 04200 over 1855-25/428, 1855-25/22, AF-58-jah dated 4 August 1930. TD photocopy). National Archives and Records Administration. Record Group 127, Washington, DC; and Reserve Officers of Public Affairs Unit 4-1, 32-3.

[35] Reserve Officers of Public Affairs Unit 4-1, 44.

[36] Brigadier General N. Buckner Barkley, *SNAFU: Situation Normal, All f o u l e d up!* (New Orleans: by the author, 1981), 2; "Redesignated Marine Corps Group Will Appear in New Blue Uniforms During May," *Times-Picayune* (New Orleans), 07 April 1935, sec. 2, pg. 2; and "Marine Reserves Finish Two-week Training Session," *Times-Picayune* (New Orleans), 28 June 1931, 6.

[37] "Redesignated Marine Corps Group Will Appear in New Blue Uniforms During May," *Times-Picayune* (New Orleans), 07 April 1935, sec. 2, pg. 2

[38] Colonel William W. Stickney, "The Marine Reserves in Action," *Military Affairs* 17 (Spring 1953): 18.

[39] "Redesignated Marine Corps Group Will Appear in New Blue Uniforms During May," *Times-Picayune* (New Orleans), 07 April 1935, sec. 2, pg. 2; and "Marine Reserves of New Orleans Start Training," *Times-Picayune* (New Orleans), 15 June 1937, 7.

[40] Reserve Officers of Public Affairs Unit 4-1, 276-7. These units were also geographically dispersed throughout the nation – including the cities mentioned above as well as Washington, DC, Indianapolis, Galveston, TX, Seattle, San Francisco, Los Angeles, Toledo, Charlotte, NC, Portland, OR, and Roanoke, VA.

[41] "Redesignated Marine Corps Group Will Appear in New Blue Uniforms During May," sec. 2, pg. 2.

[42] "The 10th Infantry Battalion, USMCR," 3; and Author Unknown, "The U.S. Marine Corps Reserve, 1955 (?)," 30.

[43] Reserve Officers of Public Affairs Unit 4-1, 47-8.

[44] Reserve Officers of Public Affairs Unit 4-1, 59.

[45] Frank Knox, Secretary of the Navy Naval Dispatch 051751 dated 05 October 1940, TD (photocopy), Marine Corps Historical Center Archives Subject File Section - Reserves, Washington, DC.

[46] Major General Commandant T. Holcomb, Major General Commandant Circular Letter No. 396 to All officers, Regular and Reserve dated 14 October 1940, Marine Corps Historical Center Archives Subject File Section - Reserves, Washington, DC.

[47] Reserve Officers of Public Affairs Unit 4-1, 59; Allan Millett, *Semper Fidelis: The History of the United States Marine Corps*, (New York: The Free Press, 1991); and Henry Shaw, Jr., *Opening Moves: Marines Gear up for War* (Washington, DC: Marine Corps Historical Center, 1991). These numbers ("Organized") represent Marines in drilling units called to service. There was another category of Marine Reservists at this time (called Fleet Marine Corps Reserve and Volunteer Marine Corps Reserve) composed of men with reduced service obligations and no unit affiliation. With these men added, the Marine Reserve in 1939 numbered almost 15000 officers and enlisted, which was larger than the Fleet Marine Force at the time. Many Marines were individually called to service from these Reserve branches as well.

[48] Major General Commandant T. Holcomb to Commanding General Fleet Marine Force, Marine Corps Base, San Diego, California, 1855-40 over AO-283-njp dated 09 October 1940, TD (photocopy), National Archives and Records Administration, Record Group 127, Washington, DC.

[49] Colonel J. C. Craig, Jr. USMCR (ret), to Jack Sands 03 August 1995, transcript in the hand of Col. Craig, letter in the possession of Jack Sands, 900 City Park Avenue, New Orleans.

[50] Colonel Joseph C. Fegan, "M-Day for the Reserves," *Marine Corps Gazette* 24 (November 1940): 27-8.

[51] "Armory Difficulties for Reserve Units (Ground)," *Marine Corps Reserve Bulletin* (Washington, DC), September 1946, 1.

[52] "Marine Corps Reserve," *Marine Corps Reserve Bulletin* (Washington, DC), 01 May 1946, 2.

[53] Reserve Officers of Public Affairs Unit 4-1, 103.

[54] Ibid., 110.

[55] "Change in Composition of Organized Reserve (Ground)." *Marine Corps Reserve Bulletin* (Washington, DC), September 1946, 6.

[56] "Report of Mobilization U. S. Marine Corps Reserve Ground Units Based upon Actual Figures Furnished by Commanding Officers Prior to Departure for Initial Deployment Station" dated 13 Sep 1950, Marine Corps Historical Center Archives Subject File Section - Reserves, Washington, DC.

[57] "Marine Corps Reserve," *Marine Corps Reserve Bulletin* (Washington, DC), 01 May 1946, 4.

[58] TSgt Ronald Lyons, "The Marine Reserves – Ready," *Leatherneck* 33 (November 1950): 52.

[59] Al Idas and John Lambert, "History of Naval Air Station New Orleans," *Naval Air Station New Orleans Airshow '84 Program*, 28. The sixteen locations for Naval Air Stations built by 1942 are: Atlanta; Boston (Squantum), Mass.; Chicago (Glenview); Dallas (Grand Prairie); Detroit (Grosse Island), Mich.; Kansas City, Kan.; Long Beach, Calif.; Miami; Minneapolis, Minn.; Oakland, Calif.; New Orleans; New York City (Brooklyn); Philadelphia; Seattle; St. Louis (Robertson), Mo.; and Washington, DC (Anacostia). [Names in parenthesis are the official name of the air station if different from the city location, i.e. NAS Glenview instead of NAS Chicago.]

[60] Reserve Officers of Public Affairs Unit 4-1, 103.

[61] "Squadrons Assigned to Marine Air Detachments," *Marine Corps Reserve Bulletin* (Washington, DC), September 1946, 5.

[62] Captain Edwin Simmons, "The Reserves Fly High," *Marine Corps Gazette* 32 (September 1948): 11.

[63] Thomas Griffin, "Good Bayou," *New Orleans Item*, 24 April 1951, 9. This type of training would eventually become the standard across the Marine Corps Reserve and persists to this day.

[64] Ernest M. Giusti, *Mobilization of the Marine Corps Reserve in the Korean Conflict, 1950-1951*, (Washington, DC: Historical Branch, G-3 Division, Headquarters U. S. Marine Corps, 1951; reprint, 1967), 3-5. The peacetime division strength was 10,232 whereas the wartime table of organization prescribed a strength of 22,355. There were only 7,779 Marines in the 1st Marine Division and 8,973 in the 2nd MarDiv on 30 June 1950. Even if both the current MarDivs had been joined into a single unit, it still would have been 20% short of one war-strength division.

[65] Ibid., 10.

[66] Ibid., 11-12.

[67] Ibid., 12-14.

[68] F. C. Caldwell (Deputy Director for Marine Corps History) to Mr. Charles R. Gellner (Foreign Affairs Division Congressional Research Service), HDR-JCS-icm over 5750/17 dated 7 May 1973, Marine Corps Historical Center Archives Subject File Section - Reserves Correspondence 1950-1986, Washington, DC.

[69] Guisti, 13.

[70] Ibid., 1.

[71] Ibid., 16.

[72] Ibid., 32.

[73] Ibid., 15.

[74] Ibid., 14-15.

'ISSUE IN DOUBT': THE UNIFICATION CRISIS, 1945-1952

Robert S. Burrell

> *Following the destruction of the Japanese and German armies and navies in World War II, the U.S. Armed Forces turned inward to attack each other over the slimming national budget. In a series of bureaucratic battles in Washington D.C., the smallest of the services, the U.S. Marine Corps, faced off against its larger opponents in an epic struggle for survival. Ironically, the seven year confrontation eventually resulted in the strongest legislation to preserve the Corps functions in its history.*

In December of 1941 on a small central Pacific island named Wake – after two weeks of fighting the Japanese and battling an amphibious assault by superior forces – Major James Devereux radioed a stoic communiqué back to headquarters: "Issue in doubt." In the face of a rapidly advancing Japanese enemy that appeared unstoppable, Americans questioned the outcome of the entire Pacific War. Consequently, "issue in doubt" served as an analogous portrayal for America's numerous setbacks during the first six months of fighting the Japanese. Nearly two years later, one of Colonel David M. Shoup's battalion commanders evoked Devereux's phrase once again on D-Day at Tarawa: "Receiving heavy fire all along beach. Unable to land. Issue in doubt."[1] Essentially, the expression continued to serve as fitting description of an uncertain outcome in a difficult struggle.

Following the American victory in World War II, the Cold War brought about unprecedented changes in U.S. military policy – a revolution that jeopardized the future of the Marines. Chief proponents of abolishing the Corps were the Army and Army Air Force. In a rudimentary sense, the Army wanted more consolidated control over American ground operations while the Army Air Force wanted independent command of all air forces (to include Navy and Marine Corps aviation). The scheme of "unification" proposed reorganization of the Departments of Army and Navy and both respective Secretaries – replacing the entire existing system with three reorganized services (Army, Navy, Air) under a Secretary of the Armed Forces. In this skirmish dubbed "the unification crisis" (1943-1947), the U.S. Marine Corps came under systematic assaults that demanded its dismemberment, and the preponderance of this offensive did not finally end until 1952. Perhaps Deveraux's perceptive phrase "issue in doubt" best describes these seven years of bureaucratic tribulations.

The intense rivalry between the Army, Army Air Force, Navy, and Marines reached new heights during the Pacific War (1941-1945), and it was actually during this period that Chief of Staff of Army, General George Marshall, made the first serious proposal for merging the armed services together. Marshall submitted his idea to the Joint Chiefs of

Staff in November 1943. His suggestion resulted in the formation of the "Special Joint Chiefs of Staff Committee on Reorganization of National Defense" to discuss the question. The committee convened on the subject of unification but was incapable of any real action since Chief of Naval Operations, Admiral Ernest King, would never agree with Marshall's ideas. Since it was getting nowhere through the military bureaucracy, in 1944, the Army took its proposal to Congress for legislative action.

Proposed Organization of the Unified Armed Forces, 1944

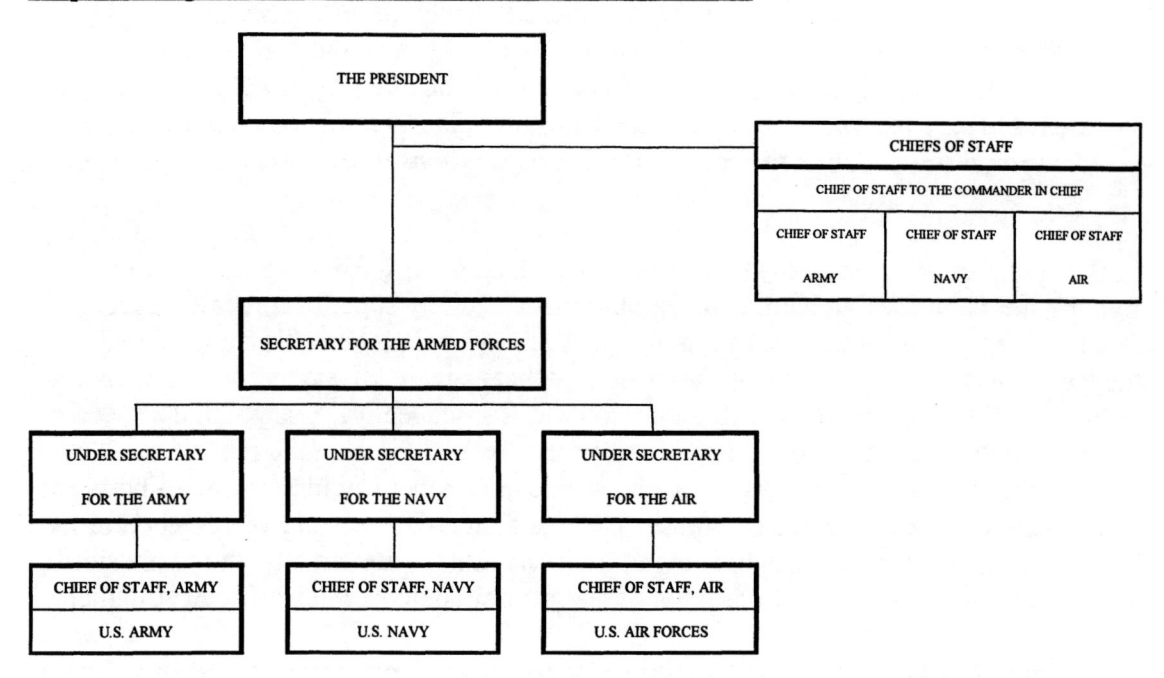

```
                    ┌─────────────────┐
                    │  THE PRESIDENT  │
                    └────────┬────────┘
                             │                    ┌──────────────────────────────────────────┐
                             │                    │            CHIEFS OF STAFF               │
                             │                    ├──────────────────────────────────────────┤
                             ├────────────────────┤  CHIEF OF STAFF TO THE COMMANDER IN CHIEF│
                             │                    ├──────────────┬──────────────┬────────────┤
                             │                    │CHIEF OF STAFF│CHIEF OF STAFF│CHIEF OF STAFF│
                             │                    │    ARMY      │    NAVY      │    AIR     │
                             │                    └──────────────┴──────────────┴────────────┘
                    ┌────────┴────────────────┐
                    │ SECRETARY FOR THE       │
                    │    ARMED FORCES         │
                    └────────┬────────────────┘
           ┌─────────────────┼─────────────────┐
   ┌───────┴──────┐  ┌───────┴──────┐  ┌───────┴──────┐
   │UNDER SECRETARY│  │UNDER SECRETARY│  │UNDER SECRETARY│
   │ FOR THE ARMY │  │ FOR THE NAVY │  │ FOR THE AIR  │
   └───────┬──────┘  └───────┬──────┘  └───────┬──────┘
   ┌───────┴──────┐  ┌───────┴──────┐  ┌───────┴──────┐
   │CHIEF OF STAFF,│  │CHIEF OF STAFF,│  │CHIEF OF STAFF,│
   │    ARMY       │  │    NAVY       │  │    AIR        │
   ├───────────────┤  ├───────────────┤  ├───────────────┤
   │   U.S. ARMY   │  │   U.S. NAVY   │  │U.S. AIR FORCES│
   └───────────────┘  └───────────────┘  └───────────────┘
```

In March 1944, Representative James W. Wadsworth introduced a resolution to the House of Representatives that would unify the armed forces.[2] The House created the "Select Committee on Post-war Military Policy" to investigate the matter. The committee became more commonly referred to as the "Woodrum Committee," after its chairman, Clifton A. Woodrum.[3]

Through the Woodrum Committee, Army General Joseph McNarney presented the War Department's plan for unification. The plan closely resembled Marshall's previous proposal of 1943. However, it provided only a basic blueprint for a merger, nothing more definitive. Despite the lack of detail, the key areas of contention with regard to the Marine Corps became clear rapidly. In fact, the plan failed to mention the Marine Corps altogether and when asked to clarify the matter, McNarney responded, "This is detail of organization which I don't believe I care to comment on at the moment."[4] With the War Department hiding its genuine intentions, the Marine Corps became gravely concerned with the Army and Army Air Force's surreptitious designs for postwar policy. Regardless, the Woodrum Committee finally concluded that issues of unification should be revisited after war's end and surmised that the time was not "opportune to consider detailed legislation which would undertake to write the pattern of any proposed consolidation, if indeed such consolidation is ultimately decided to be a wise course of action."[5]

In the summer of 1945, as Japan's end appeared imminent, unification supporters started building their case again. In July, the *St Louis Post-Dispatch* ran a provocative editorial about an Army-Navy merger that clearly stated the positions of the most influential participants.[6] The two most powerful American men to hold influence over future military policy, President Harry Truman and the man who would soon become his Chief of Staff and succeeding President of the United States, General Dwight Eisenhower, endorsed the merger proposal. The article argued that competition between the services throughout the war had caused numerous problems in wasted money, lost lives, and delays in planning. Specifically, the author pointed out that Marine General Holland M. Smith's firing of Army General Ralph Smith on Saipan in 1944 was indicative of the severe problems with service-based rivalry in the Pacific. Now that the war was winding down, supporters for closely integrating the Army, Navy and Air Forces appeared everywhere. At the moment, however, just how those designs would affect the Marine Corps remained less clearly defined.

Backdrop

As the United States faced off against the ideology and military threat of communism in 1945, it had difficult issues to solve concerning the size, organization, and mission of its military. The use of atomic bombs on Hiroshima and Nagasaki in August 1945 most strongly supported the importance of strategic air power and reduction of conventional forces, an idea that also appeared economically viable. Overwhelming air power through heavy bombers was a strategy that air enthusiasts applauded as long overdue. The fears of atomic attacks on the United States and a communist conspiracy to take over the world fueled increasing support for the development of atomic weaponry, as well as the strategic aircraft used for their delivery. Both of those developments aided the Army Air Force's longtime goal of an independent service. The new atomic era changed America's outlook on strategic delivery systems, but it concurrently endangered the Marine Corps' future.

Finding a viable mission had proved a tenuous struggle throughout the Corps' history. In the early 1900s, the advent of steel vessels in modern navies reduced the need for marines onboard ships. In the navies of most countries, marines were relegated to garrison duty on naval bases. As opposed to its counterparts, U.S. Marine Corps developed new missions for itself – first in the form of colonial infantry and later in the manner of amphibious assault. The extraordinary prudence of Marine leadership in preparing for the Pacific War in the 1920s and 1930s served as the greatest contribution to its later expansion. Incredibly, while retaining the impression of an all-volunteer force, Marines rapidly expanded from roughly 20,000 personnel in 1939 to almost 500,000 in 1945. To the institution's great credit, it served in some of the most difficult contests of World War II, firmly establishing an identity as amphibious assault experts. Even so, the Corps' functions and size were not clearly protected either by past precedent or congressional law. Despite the Marines' remarkable wartime achievements, the Army and Army Air Force questioned whether the United States would ever employ amphibious assault again.

Questions about the need for a Marine Corps did not simply derive from service rivalry but from reasonable doubts about the future necessity of costly amphibious assault. Battles against the new communist enemy in Asia, the Union of Socialist Soviet Republics, primarily required land and air forces. Even in a defensive situation, America had need of an army to protect the continental United States and an air force to counterattack with atomic warfare. But, simply stated, America no longer *needed* a Marine Corps. In the view of some, the Marine Corps had become a waste of funds. If a situation arose in which amphibious assault could be employed, the concentration of exposed naval forces required to prosecute such an endeavor made for a huge liability in an era of atomic warfare. Furthermore, many argued that the Army, which during the war had conducted larger and more numerous amphibious landings, in both the Pacific and the Atlantic, could fulfill the job if necessary.

More than anyone else, senior Marine officers understood the institution's precarious position within the U.S. military. Nevertheless, Marines would never consent to a course of action that diminished the prestigious organization to the role of the Navy's police force – guarding ships and bases. In essence, it refused relegation to the duties of other nation's marines. Therefore, Marine officers continued to argue the necessity of amphibious assault. All the same, Marines realized that the ability to seize island strongholds had much less relevance in the atomic era. Consequently, just as it had done during its colonial infantry and amphibious assault periods, the Corps began devising a new role and mission for itself – this time as America's force-in-readiness, basically fulfilling its slogan as "first to fight" by rapid sea deployment at a moment's notice. However, in 1945, the Marines' only bona fide option in the short term was to tenaciously argue that the nation needed an amphibious assault capability similar to that of World War II.

The unprecedented national debt incurred during the war logically resulted in a rapid shrinking of the military budget. President Harry Truman and the Congress cut large portions of military spending. The Navy faced reductions to its fleet, and the Marine Corps appeared one of the most superfluous institutions in the military. Due to the rivalries and jealousies between the services, Marine officers questioned whether they had many friends in the upper echelons of either the War or Navy Departments – for when it came down to disagreement over a diminishing pile of money, services interests turned cutthroat. As the Corps attempted to define its mission in the Cold War, few listened. Essentially, if the Marine Corps duplicated many aspects of the U.S. Army then it certainly remained a national luxury. To survive, it had to convince the American people (through Congress) to retain it in a form that resembled its current state or face the prospect of reductions that would relegate it to impotence. Considering the slim resources and intense service rivalries following World War II, it is not a stretch to say that the Marine Corps' struggle to play an active part in the postwar military appeared insurmountable.

Crisis

If anything, the squabble over shrinking resources in the post-war era created more open hostility between the services than during the conflict itself. The opposing camps settled in for a fight. Although President Franklin D. Roosevelt, a staunch Navy enthusiast, might not have approved of unification arguments, his successor and former Army officer, President Truman, fancied the idea. Unification supporters included the President and the senior leadership in the Army and Army Air Force. The main points of contention remained the transfer of Navy and Marine Corps air to a newly created Air Force and the restriction of the Marine Corps to a size no larger than a regiment. The Army wanted to ensure that the Marine Corps never resemble a regular ground army again.[7] Obviously, the Navy and Marine Corps continued to resist these ideas. At the very least, both naval services could agree on endorsing a strong peacetime naval force instead.

Truman's support of unification actually predated his presidency. While a Senator in August 1944, he wrote an extensive article in *Collier's* magazine endorsing the idea.[8] Once the Woodrum Committee disbanded in December 1945, the President introduced his proposal for combining the War and Navy Departments into a single Department of National Defense.[9] But, the Navy Department had not sat idly by as the War Department planned its postwar unification strategy. Instead, it began its own investigation for streamlining the armed services as early as May 1945.[10] Ferdinand Eberstadt, a military consultant, completed a study that advised increased coordination between the Army and Navy rather than a merger. The Secretary of the Navy submitted the proposal to the Senator David Walsh, Chairman on Naval Affairs, in October, two months before Truman came public with his.[11] Yet, remarkably, the twelve pages of conclusions and twenty-eight pages of discussion failed to mention the Marine Corps entirely. Headquarters Marine Corps could only be found in the proposal's organizational graph underneath the Chief of Naval Operations and alongside Aeronautics, Ordnance, Ships, Yards and Docks, Supplies and Accounts, Naval Personnel, Coast Guard, and Medicine and Surgery. Apparently, in their struggle for survival, the Marines would find few enthusiastic supporters in the Navy Department– the Corps would have to argue its specific place and function within the revised organization of the armed forces on its own.

In response to what he perceived as an institutional emergency, Commandant of the Marine Corps, A.A. Vandegrift, formed two groups to address the unification crisis under generals Gerald C. Thomas and Merritt A. Edson. Specifically, Thomas and Edson prepared position papers, monitored both the actions of the Executive branch and Congress, updated the press, and researched new missions for the Corps.[12] Perhaps one of the most influential groups in harnessing Congressional support for the Marine Corps was the clandestine "Chowder Society," made up of Marine officers working at Marine Corps Schools in Quantico, Virginia. The society was led by Colonels Merrill Twining and Victor Krulak. According to historian Alan R. Millett, the Chowder Society "developed into the Corps's political action arm, and its agents prowled the Pentagon and Congress arguing the Marine Corps case."[13]

The Marine Corps had its supporters in Congress, but the War Department held most of the bureaucratic power in the military. The struggle to gain support for or against unification quickly surfaced in the media and became a routine occurrence over the next few years. In December, John Cowles, chairmen of *Look* magazine, published a second article endorsing the merger of the Navy and War Departments.[14] He indicted that Chief of Staff of the Army, General George Marshall, and Chief of Naval Operations, Admiral Ernest King, duplicated war efforts and wasted as much time battling each other's departments as combating the enemy. Cowles wanted one service in the future, with no distinction between servicemen. That same month, Representative Henry D. Larcade submitted a pro-integration editorial from *Collier's* magazine to Congress.[15] The editorial stated that "lack of Army-Navy cooperation" was a major factor in the disaster at Pearl Harbor and in the ill-supported Marine invasion of Guadalcanal.[16]

Despite the War Department's rhetoric about the dangers of service rivalry, the real issue was not "unification" but what that term actually meant. The general plan called for the Army and newly created Air Force to absorb the Corp's existing duties, manpower, and equipment. Rather than mending fences with the Navy Department, the War Department's proposal had all the appearance of a consolidation of most of the military's resources under the Army and Army Air Force.

Marine officers began writing their Congressmen in opposition to Truman's idea, and more dissention from Congress quickly followed.[17] Representative Walter C. Ploeser wrote directly to the President and got to the heart of the issue: "A plan – the War Department Plan – which talks unification in one breath and then in the other advocates a separate air force must be subject to careful examination before it is taken at face value."[18] According to Ploeser, the Army simply wanted a monopoly under the guise of unification. The creation of a separate Air Force in the War Department actually worked against the idea of unification, and Ploeser pointed out that the Navy Department, with its many organizations, was a true example of a unified system.

Based on the history of the Pacific War, Representative Ploeser made a pitch for the Marine Corps that turned the President's proposal on its head: "Had the Marine Corps been larger it might have been possible for the Navy and Marine Corps, and their Coast Guard and Seebee [sic] units, to have wrested the victory in the Pacific without the necessity of transporting millions of men all the way from Europe to the Pacific. This brings up the consideration what should be the size of the Marine Corps under the system which I propose. My estimate would be 1,000,000 men and officers trained in all phases of amphibious warfare."[19] Such an expansion of Marines at a time of demobilization had no viable chance of gaining serious Congressional support. However, suggesting that the Marines Corps could replace the functions of the Army indicated exactly the redundancy that the Army found objectionable and threatening. All the same, a couple months later, Representative Donald L. O'Toole overtly made the argument to replace the Army with the Corps: as far as unification was concerned, the Marine Corps already worked well with the single department of the Navy – better to simply replace the Army by increasing the size of the Marine Corps: "Its men, noncommissioned officers, and officers have ever met the test of battle and emergency and have at all times in our history captured the imagination of the American people."[20]

As rhetoric between the Army and Marine Corps heated up, the Navy published its compromise plan in February – the one designed by Ferdinand Eberstadt for streamlining the Armed Services.[21] The Navy followed up with two articles opposing unification in *Seapower* magazine and another in *Naval Affairs* in March.[22] Staunch naval advocate, George Eliot, stated the Navy's fears effectively: "You [President Truman] are gambling the future of this country on the chance that your Secretary of the Armed Forces will always be impartial, uninfluenced, and evenly balanced, and that the Chief of Staff of the Armed Forces, his principal military advisor, will always, as he assumes office, forget all his ties with his own service, and at the same time acquire by some mysterious heavenly gift, a complete understanding of the needs and nature of the other two services."[23]

As the Navy openly voiced its opposition to the President's unification proposal, the Marine Corps sought to clarify its future role in the armed services. One of its most effective pitches came in the form of advertising the importance of amphibious assault to naval warfare. On the anniversary of the Iwo Jima landings, Vandegrift contended that the battle for Iwo Jima represented the climax of years of study and training for amphibious war. It demonstrated that "no beach, however strongly defended, can be held in the face of a well-organized and resolute assault from the sea. This is the fact of vital significance to any nation whose security depends upon maintaining supremacy on, over, and under the seas which lie between it and any possible aggressor. The ability to conduct effective and successful amphibious operations is a necessary and inevitable adjunct of sea-power."[24] Retaining the capability to seize an enemy beachhead remained the Corps' principle contention, but such reasoning did not prove persuasive to the White House, Congress, or War Department.

By April 1946, President Truman had had enough with the public debate of his proposal (although only opposition to unification actually disturbed him).[25] He announced that propaganda or lobbying by active duty officers would constitute insubordination, and he implied legal recourse for indiscretions. Truman's order dramatically shut the lid on public descent from naval officers. Nevertheless, if the Navy and Marine Corps could not speak out, their friends in the media continued to on their behalf. The *Utica Daily Press* in New York called the President's plan for the military "reckless" and further stated its alarm with the fact that that Truman "has told its naval critics to shut up."[26] One editorial poked fun at the Presidents' declaration by stating "And now – discipline. If the boss wants it, you had better go along. Even if you are an expert on the science of modern naval war you better defer to the judgment of an ex-artilleryman of World War I. Or else."[27] David Lawrence in the *United States News* put it this way: "Free speech is to prevail for all but the Navy. Mr. Truman has not rebuked the many Army and air officers who have recently been making speeches in favor of his plan to merger the armed services. But he seems irritated that those who have honest convictions in opposition should express them."[28] Lawrence stated that Truman's instruction delivered a blow to the Navy and "gallant Marines," who had fought their way across the Pacific seizing island bases for the Army Air Forces.[29]

In mid-May, Senator Edward Robertson presented an article to the Senate that the War Department must have found especially annoying. "Ex-Doughboy Pays Tribute to Marines" related American memory of Iwo Jima with the Corps' struggles in the unification crisis. The author, Henry McLemore (a former soldier turned Marine supporter), told Commandant of the Marine Corps, A.A. Vandegrift, to quit his worrying about unification. America loved its Marine Corps, and anyone in the War Department who questioned its utility should visit Iwo Jima and "imagine what it was like when the Marines went in."[30] These types of emotional appeals by the media appear to have been far more influential in garnering Congressional support than rational arguments about the need for amphibious assault. Accordingly, Headquarters Marine Corps increasingly mirrored such an approach over the next couple of years.

Climax

Despite the heated press, by the end of May, the War and Navy Departments attempted to compromise on many of the issues in Truman's plan. One major exception concerned the future of the Marine Corps. At least on paper, the War Department's view of the functions of the Marine Corps only slightly differed from the Navy's. Both agreed that Marines should serve in the seizure and defense of advanced naval bases as well as develop amphibious assault doctrine and equipment. However, the Army wanted to specifically direct that Marine operations should not involve "sustained land fighting."[31] The issue at stake for the Marine Corps predominantly derived from differing opinions about its size and disposition. Fundamentally, the Army did not believe the Corps should resemble another land army. Meanwhile, the Marine Corps consciously realized that it needed such redundancy in order to remain a viable fighting force in America's future.

In May 1946, making one of the most powerful speeches in his career (drafted chiefly by colonels Twining and Krulak),[32] Commandant of the Marine Corps, General A.A. Vandegrift addressed the Senate Naval Affairs Committee on the subject of unification. The General's exterior seemed to embody his nickname "Sunny Jim." Legendary Marine warrior, Smedley Butler, once described Vandegrift as "the damndest, fightin'est hillbilly not stillin' er fuedin'."[33] With his "cheery blue eyes and soft drawl of the spare Virginian," Vandegrift appeared before Congress, his uniform complete with seven rows of ribbons to include the Congressional Medal of Honor.[34] Vandegrift shamed the Congress into taking affirmative action on the Corps' behalf.

> In placing its case in your hands the Marine Corps remembers that it was this same Congress which, in 1798, called it into a long and useful service to the nation. The Marine Corps feels that the question of its continued existence is likewise a matter of determination by the Congress and not one to be resolved by departmental legerdemain or a quasi-legislative process enforced by the War Department General Staff. The Marine Corps, then, believes that it has earned this right – to have its future decided by the legislative body which created it – nothing more. Sentiment is not a valid consideration in determining questions of national security. We have pride in ourselves and our past but we do not rest our case on any presumed ground of gratitude owing us from the nation. The bended knee is not a tradition of our Corps. If the Marine as a fighting man has not made a case for himself after 170 years of service, he must go. But I think you will agree with me that he has earned the right to depart with dignity and honor, not by subjugation to the status of uselessness and servility planned for him by the War Department.[35]

The "bended knee" speech was a resounding success in swaying Congressional support.[36] After such a dramatic address, no assurances by Secretary of the Navy, James Forrestal, or by Secretary of War, Robert Patterson, about the "safety" of the Marine Corps could measure up to the fears expressed by Sunny Jim. The War Department would have to "tell it to the Marines."[37]

Undeterred, Army supporters continued to press forward. In June, the Congressional Joint Committee set up to investigate the Pearl Harbor disaster released its report declaring service rivalry as a principle cause of the American defeat. In an editorial in the *Washington Post* entitled "Merger Now" unification supporters used the Pearl Harbor findings to support their case. The editorial maintained that vested service interests were holding up commonsense legislation.[38] Similarly, the *Washington Star* made the case for consolidation of all air assets into the Air Force based on the latest report from the United States Strategic Bombing Survey. The author claimed that the revolutionary abilities of air power could "crush a country into complete submission without invasion."[39]

Continued opposition to unification failed to diminish the War Department's desire to curtail the Marines, and the explosive environment in Washington continued to boil over.[40] Probably the most provocative discourse came from Army Air Force General, Frank Armstrong, who spoke at a goodwill dinner for business in Norfolk, Virginia in December. He made the following comments to an audience consisting almost entirely of the naval community.

> You gentlemen had better understand that the Army Air Force is tired of being a subordinate outfit. It was a predominant force during the war, and it is going to be a predominant force during the peace…and we do not care whether you like it or

not. The Army Air Force is going to run the show. You, the Navy, are not going to have anything but a couple carriers which are ineffective anyway, and they will probably be sunk in the first battle. Now as for the Marines, you know what the Marines are, a small bitched-up army talking Navy lingo. We are going to put those Marines in the Regular Army and make efficient soldiers out of them.[41]

General Armstrong's speech simply added fuel to the fires of controversy, and Marine Corps supporters decided to take action. In January 1947, Representative James E. Van Zandt introduced House Concurrent Resolution 14 to "express the sense of Congress that the Navy and Marine Corps should be permitted to express views upon unification."[42] A number of Congressmen made similar pleas. By June, through the Secretary of the Navy, Representative Clare E. Hoffman had attained dozens of letters from admirals and Marine generals on the subject of unification and presented them to Congress.[43] All of them, to one degree or another, expressed sincere doubts on the direction and content of the unification bills. Essentially, Congress had made those opinions public knowledge despite the President's order to keep naval opposition quite.

General A. A. Vandegrift, in another remarkable speech given at the Navy Council Conference in February 1947, eloquently bid for active participation within the nation's security. He concluded his remarks with:

> I sincerely hope that we have your confidence that the Marine Corps is aware of its responsibilities and will persist in its efforts. Your confidence is in the last analysis the thing that will determine the question of success or failure of the armed forces of a nation...the weapon that conquered Iwo Jima was not produced in the vast arsenal of industry, but in the hearts of the American people who were represented there by the finest they could send to do battle with our mortal enemy. It is not too much to say that the future of the Marine Corps, of the Navy, or of the Nation itself rests finally not in our hands, but in your hearts."[44]

Representative George W. Sarbacher Jr. entered Vandegrift's comments into the Congressional Record with the preface, "I do hope that in future legislation we of Congress never allow the identity of this valiant organization to be lost or forgotten in the shuffle of unification."[45]

Following his discourse at the Navy Council Conference, Vandegrift spoke before the Senate Armed Services Committee. While conceding on the principle of increased integration, (in so far as it strengthened the cooperation between services and more closely restructured the civilian chain of command with the military one) he objected to the War Department's proposal on two matters that affected the Marine Corps.

> (1) "It affirms the existence of the Marine Corps without expressly stating the roles and missions which the Corps is expected to perform."
> (2) "It completely excludes the Marine Corps from participation in the joint bodies and agencies which the bill would establish."[46]

Vandegrift argued that only by intervening in the language of the bill could Congress guarantee retaining a Marine Corps in its current form: not doing so would result in fate determined by the President, the proposed Department of National Defense, or the Department of the Navy. Consequently, without specifying the roles and missions of the Marine Corps, Congress simply would not pass a unification bill. Essentially, Vandegrift's statements directly contributed to the War Department conceding on the first of his two points.[47] Concerning General Vandegrift's speech, Representative Mike Mansfield stated, "I shall personally question the value of such a merger if it contemplates subordinating the position of the corps. . . . I will do my very best to see that the marines, first to fight, are not the first to be liquidated."[48]

As Congressional support for the latest proposal on unification (House Bill 2319) slipped away, the press, in a feeding frenzy, increasingly pressed their case in support of the Marine Corps. In articles entitled "The Marines' Last Beachhead" and "General Vandegrift Should Be Heeded," authors described an ungrateful War Department attempting to dismember one of its most honorable members – the greatest enemy to the Corps was not the "Japs or Germans" but the U.S. Army, which had "envied since time immemorial the high estate of the Marine Corps in the eyes of the public, and a few Navy admirals are not above suspicion of jealousy."[49] Public sentiment for the Marine Corps irreparably damaged Congressional support for the unification proposal.

The Marine Corps had taken its case to the American people, represented by Congress, and the subsequent result would leave the Marine Corps in better shape than previously. House Bill 2319 was sent to Representative Clare Hoffman's committee, "Expenditures in the Executive Department." The Chowder Society asked the father of Iwo Jima veteran Lieutenant Colonel James Hittle, a good friend with Hoffman, to intervene on the Corps' behalf.[50] Vandegrift subsequently assigned Lieutenant Colonel Hittle to Representative Hoffman's staff for the purpose of working on what Hoffman would later describe as the "so-called" unification bill.[51]

Since President Truman had forbade military officers from speaking out on the merger issue, discussions taking place in the Hoffman Committee became a platform for voicing pro-Marine sentiment. Perhaps most damaging to the War Department, the committee made one classified report public – Joint Chiefs of Staff studies 1478. In those proposals General Eisenhower made the following stipulation:

> Land aspect of major amphibious operations in the future will be undertaken by the Army, and consequently the Marine Corps will not be appreciably expanded in time of war . . . the Navy will not develop a land army or a so-called amphibious Army, [and] . . . Marine Corps units to be limited in size to the equivalent of a regiment.[52]

Perhaps what most concerned Congressmen, especially those that supported the Marine Corps, derived from the manner in which War Department debated their actual plans for the Marines in secret boards while publicly presenting more ambiguous ideas. Spelling out the mission and roles of the Marine Corps increasing gained Congressional support since the wording in the War Department's unification proposal (H. R. 2319) simply could not be trusted. The direction of the Hoffman Committee eventually derailed H. R. 2319 so badly that unification proponents were forced to compromise in support of Hoffman's revised proposal, H. R. 4214, which gave the Corps legislative protection.[53]

Perhaps one of the Corps' opponents best described the revisions included in House Bill 4214 in a letter he sent to the Truman administration: "The mission of the Marine Corps is set forth in new language which has no basis of agreement among the services, limits the authority of the President over the Marine Corps, ignores the authority of the Chief of Naval Operations over the Marines, and ignores the position of the Navy in amphibious operations."[54] In other words, the Marines emerged in a stronger position in the Department of the Navy and in relation to the armed services than at any previous point in its history. All of which it had accomplished through Congressional support, despite only half-hearted assistance from the Navy and strenuous objections from the President and the War Department.

After much debate in committees and the floors of the Senate and House, by July, House Bill 4214 and its companion Senate Bill 758, adopted the basic language the Marine Corps requested. It allowed the Marine Corps to keep the aviation and combined arms required to carry out amphibious campaigns, the right to expand in times of war, and the broad task of performing "such duties as the President may direct."[55] House Bill 4214 eventually provided the basis for the National Security Act of 1947, which, among many modifications, finally gave the Air Force autonomy as a separate service.[56]

Signed by President Truman in July 1947, Section 206 (largely drafted by colonels Twining, Krulak and Hittle) put into Congressional law the duties and functions of the Marine Corps while, at the same time, restricted the President's authority to revise those definitions. Under the Department of the Navy, the Marine Corps was to provide "fleet marine forces of combined arms, together with supporting air components, for service with the fleet in the seizure or defense of advanced naval bases and for the conduct of such land operations as may be essential to the prosecution of a naval campaign."[57] However, although it legally spelled out the Marine Corps' functions, it notably did not give the Commandant of the Marine Corps a position on the Joint Chiefs of Staff, and it failed to define the Marines' size and budget – the struggle for the future of the Marine Corps was far from over.

Interval

Army proponents in Washington could not come to grips with the fact that the War Department had lost most of the substance in its bid for unification. Some fruitlessly hoped that Congress would reconsider. An editor for the *Washington Post* argued that the government had not gone far enough. Simply put, "unification has not unified the armed service," and, consequently, he decided to educate the "members of congress and most citizens" that assumed that it had.[58] Another author in the *Christian Science Monitor* complained about the "full failure of the unification of the armed services."[59] Yet indicative of how powerful the Marine Corps' public image had become, neither of the articles mentioned the organization at all, referring instead only to the Navy. Even though the Marines had arguably done the most to derail the War Department's proposals, few directly attacked it. Perhaps the Marine Corps had risen to such position of reverence that criticism of Marines proved counterproductive in garnering public support.

While the 1947 National Security Act defined the Marine Corps, if failed to protect its funding. As President Truman strove to downsize funds allocated to the military to one third of the national budget, the subsequent decrease in Marine Corps' resources nearly ruined the organization as a viable fighting force. By 1948, the Corps had been reduced from its wartime high of six divisions to two undersized ones. Commandant of the Marine Corps, Clifton Cates, became so concerned over the Corps' precarious position that he mandated training for all Marine Officers on the language in the National Security Act of 1947.[60]

The rivalry between the Army and Marine Corps continued unabated though 1948 and into 1949. In January, *Infantry Journal* presented an article "Who Won the War?" The editors voiced much displeasure over what they believed was the exaggerated credit given to Marine operations in the Pacific. They pointed out that soldiers liberated much more territory than Marines and sustained fewer casualties in the process. As a general rule, the "rush and die" procedures Marines used were "contrary…to modern tactics."[61] The editors of *Infantry Journal* concluded with, "There has too often been the implication that the Army has fought with less valor, or against inferior odds, but for the most part, the Marines have simply applied both energy and ingenuity to making the Corps and its record known."[62]

The anger that the Army expressed in the *Infantry Journal* was not hollow rhetoric. It had not given up its fight to rid itself of the institution that so successfully competed for its funding and missions. In January 1949, the War Department submitted a new proposal to the President. It planned to transfer the Marine Corps to the Army and all aviation, both Navy and Marine, to the Air Force.[63] Such a proposal really had little chance of getting past Marine supporters in Congress. Nevertheless, the President and his new Secretary of Defense could still affect financial aspects of the military, an outlet that would soon become the primary means of influencing the disposition of the services.

As the Navy and Air Force went toe-to-to over airpower during the famous "Revolt of the Admirals," the Army and Marine Corps squared off over ground resources. For one thing, Marines found training for their traditional role of amphibious operations difficult. Secretary of Defense, Louis A. Johnson, convinced the Chief of Naval Operations to assign nearly all amphibious shipping resources to train the Army. Curtailing the Corps' primary mission was not insulting enough, Johnson also forbid the celebration of the Marine Corps birthday. Marine air was in jeopardy as well. Giving a speech at the

Waldorf-Astoria Hotel in New York, Johnson stated that the paperwork for doing away with it were on his desk.[64] However, the most dangerous action that nearly emasculated the Corps was the President's cutbacks in funding. Under-funding led to large personnel shortages. By 1947, the two active Marine divisions consisted of only eleven battalion landing teams versus the eighteen required for full strength. Although the Marine Corps insisted it needed 114,200 Marines to fulfill its peacetime obligations, manpower fell to 83,609 men in 1948 and to 74,279 in 1950.[65] In the words of Victor Krulak, "we felt the dead hand of starvation everywhere."[66]

As the fights in Washington continued, Hollywood and the Marine Corps, in a major pitch to secure the Corps's future, teamed up to make *Sands of Iwo Jima* (1949) starring John Wayne. According to Wayne's son, Michael, the Commandant of the Marine Corps sent representatives to personally speak with his father. They pleaded with him to make the film on the basis that the Corps was fighting for its survival in Washington, and, if Americans saw the exploits of Marines in the Pacific, the public would want to keep the Marine Corps.[67] Purportedly, the Commandant's request served as one of Wayne's main incentives in agreeing to make the film. With help from the Marine Corps, the film went into production in the summer of 1949.[68]

The Marine Corps exhibited direct influence over the picture, which, despite its entertainment value, also doubled as both a recruiting and public relations piece. Technical advisors for the film included Medal of Honor winner Colonel D. M. Shoup, as well as Pacific veterans Lieutenant Colonel H. P. Crowe and Captain Harold G. Schrier. Even General Holland M. Smith was persuaded to come out of retirement and ensure the invasion scenes were conducted accurately. Actors underwent a type of "boot camp" training, to ensure they played the part of Marines correctly.[69] In order to create a realistic combat setting and offset the cost of the picture, the Marine Corps offered its base at Camp Pendleton, California, for filming. The reenactment of battles at Tarawa and Iwo Jima required a substantial amount of assistance from the Marines, who provided liberal numbers of weapons, jeeps, tracked vehicles, artillery, ships, and planes.[70] Of the sixteen thousand Marines stationed on Camp Pendleton, two thousand served in support of the movie, filling jobs that ranged from extras to technical advisors.[71] The Iwo Jima scene alone required 1,000 Marine extras, thirty tracked vehicles, destroyer escorts, LSTs (Landing Ship, Tanks), and two squadrons of Corsairs. According to the *New York Times*, the Marine Corps was "cooperating wholeheartedly in the venture."[72] As the most expensive film Republic Pictures had filmed to date (a budget estimated at over $1,000,000), the studio could certainly use all the help it could get. Producer Edmund Grainger stated that "without Marine cooperation, the picture would have cost at least $2,500,000."[73]

One of the top ten money-making films of 1950, *Sands of Iwo Jima* was nominated for four academy awards, including best story, best sound recording, best film editing and best actor. It also made John Wayne Hollywood's most popular star, graduating from his low budget westerns character to the role of American war hero. In the words of one film historian, from *Sands of Iwo Jima* onward, "John Wayne, rather than an actual military hero, served as the symbol of America's fighting men for a significant number of American moviegoers."[74] More importantly, *Sands of Iwo Jima* kept the image of Marines atop Mount Suribachi in the popular spotlight at a time when the Corps needed all the public assistance it could muster. One review commented that there was "so much savage realism in 'Sands of Iwo Jima,' so much that reflects the true glory of the Marine Corps' contribution to victory in the Pacific" that the film had "undeniable moments of greatness."[75] Arguably, despite significant attempts by the Army, Navy and Army Air Force to influence the writing of Pacific War history, *Sands of Iwo Jima* reinforced the perception in the popular media that the Marine Corps was the leading instrument in America's victory over Japan.

Later that year, when Representative Gordon L. McDonough wrote to Truman about his support for creating a permanent position for the Commandant of the Marine Corps on the Joint Chiefs of Staff, the President responded in August 1950:

> "I read with a lot of interest your letter in regard to the Marine Corps. For your information the Marine Corps is the Navy's police force and as long as I am President that is what it will remain. They have a propaganda machine that is almost equal to Stalin's. Nobody desires to belittle the efforts of the Marine Corps but when the Marine Corps goes into the army it works with and for the army and that is the way it should be."[76]

President Truman believed the Marine Corps both a redundancy and an anachronism and personally supported its transfer to the Army. However, hamstrung by the National Security Act, he continued to cut back its budget. Truman eventually planned to fund only six battalion landing teams in 1951. According to Victor Krulak, the President "intended to diminish progressively the fighting units of the Corps and, ultimately, to transfer what remained to the Army and Air Force."[77] Just five years after its unprecedented size in the Pacific War, U.S. Marine Corps diminished to a tattered skeleton of its former self, but that situation drastically changed with renewed conflict in the Pacific.

One of the greatest contributors to the survival of the Marine Corps was the North Korean Communist Army, which attacked and seized most of democratic South Korea in the summer of 1950.[78] In a miraculously speedy fashion that can probably not be overstated, the Marine Corps quickly called in reserves and deployed the 1st Marine Brigade to defend the rapidly shrinking allied perimeter around the port city of Pusan. Subsequently, under the direction of General MacArthur, the 1st Marine Division spearheaded the remarkable amphibious assault at Inchon in September, which almost immediately changed the war from a desperate defense of Pusan to total defeat of the North Korean Army. Perhaps one of the most brilliant strategic *ripostes* in military history, Inchon demonstrated the continued importance of both conventional forces and amphibious assault in the nuclear age.

The Marines served with great distinction in Korea for the next three years. Under the determined leadership of General "Chesty" Puller, the 1st Marine Division's fighting withdrawal from Chosin from November through December 1950, against several Chinese divisions in temperatures 30 degrees below zero, served as one of the Corps' most challenging military accomplishments. The combination of veteran Pacific War experience with a renewed urgency to prove the Marine Corps' usefulness resulted in incredible martial excellence and in terms of "sheer drama, valor and hardship matched the amphibious assaults of World War II."[79] Summing up Marines prowess in Korea, historians Merrill Bartlett and Jack Sweetman stated, "Even the Corps's critics had to admit that the Marine Corps's performance in Korea was far superior to that of the Eighth Army and X Corps."[80] The stellar deeds of Marines in the Korean War gave added vigor to their supporters in Washington and substantiated Marine Corps' claims as a fighting elite.

A great many journalistic reports from Korea praised the Marines while depictions of Army units sometimes presented negative criticism. Representatives Carl Vinson and Mike Mansfield as well as Senator Paul Douglas, used the glowing accounts of Marine exploits in Korea to sponsor new legislation to expand and clarify the organizations' responsibilities.[81] Proposals included a permanent position for the Commandant of the Marine Corps on the Joint Chiefs of Staff and a structure of no less than four Marine divisions and air wings. In contrast, Army generals and President Truman believed a Marine Corps conspiracy must have been slanting the truth about the performance of Marines as compared to soldiers in Korea. Consequently, Truman sent his former military aid, Army General Frank Lowe, to the theater in order to assess the situation. After touring the battlefield, Lowe's reports to the President, while condemning senior Army leadership in Korea, concurrently declared that "The First Marine Division is the most efficient and courageous combat unit I have ever seen or heard of."[82] In light of continued praise, new legislation to strengthen the Marine Corps gained increasing support.

Finale

As the Korean War dragged on to a stalemate, the President proved "unwilling to spend more political capital" in combating congressional legislation.[83] In June of 1952, President Truman signed into law the amendment to the National Security Act that gave the Commandant of the Marine Corps co-equality in the Joint Chiefs of Staff on any issue that concerned the U.S. Marine Corps. The revision included specific definitions on the size and functions of the Marine Corps that have since served as the organization's foundation. Specifically, it ensured the minimum force structure of the Corps would "include not less than three combat divisions and three air wings."[84] As well, it set legal parameters for Marines to assume the role of the subject matter experts on all matters of amphibious warfare, pronouncing that the Marine Corps "shall develop in coordination with the Army and Air Force, those phases of amphibious operations that pertain to tactics, technique, and equipment used by landing forces."[85] More importantly, the

Douglas-Mansfield Act (the common name for the 1952 revision) sanctioned the Marine Corps' new mission as force-in-readiness.[86]

Through its political maneuvering, combat excellence, and public relations programs, the Marine Corps, for seven years, thoroughly outflanked its opponents in the Army and Air Force. Victory in the unification crisis had a profound impact on the institutional advancement of the Marine Corps in relation to the other services. In fact, the bureaucratic battle with the War Department stimulated the most constructive legislation to determine the Marine Corps' scope and longevity since its inception in 1775. In sum, the revisions to the National Security Act finally ensured "a Marine Corps for the next 500 years," as stated by Secretary of the Navy James Forrestal to General Holland M. Smith, as he looked up at the first flag-raising on Iwo Jima in February 1945.

NOTES

[1] Michael Kernan, "...Heavy fire...unable to land...issue in doubt." *Smithsonian,* November 1993, 118; Rafael Steinberg and the editors of Time-Life Books, *Island Fighting* (Alexandria, Va.: Time-Life Books, 1978), 112.
[2] House Resolution 465, "Public Bills and Resolutions," Congressional Record, 9 March 1944, 2398.
[3] "Committee on Post-War Military Policy," Congressional Record, 24 March 1944, 3250.
[4] Demetrios Caraley, *The Politics of Military Unification: A Study of Conflict and the Policy Process* (New York: Columbia University Press, 1966), 28.
[5] House of Representatives Report No. 1356, "Postwar Military Policy," 10 December 1945. Also see "Reports of Committees on the Public Bills and Resolutions," Congressional Record, 15 June 1944 and 27 November 1944.
[6] "For Army-Navy Merger," *St. Louis Post-Dispatch,* 22 July 1945.
[7] Caraley, 66-69.
[8] Harry S. Truman, "Our Armed Forces Must Be United," *Collier's* 26 August 1944, 16, 63-64.
[9] Harry S. Truman, "Special Message to the Congress Recommending the Establishment of a Department of National Defense," 19 December 1945.
[10] James Forrestal, Secretary of the Navy, official correspondence to David Walsh, Chairman of the Committee on Naval Affairs, 27 May 1945, *Documentary History of the Truman Presidency, Volume 10.*
[11] James Forrestal, Secretary of the Navy, official correspondence to David Walsh, Chairman of the Committee on Naval Affairs, 18 October 1945, *Documentary History of the Truman Presidency, Volume 10.*
[12] Allen R. Millett, *Semper Fidelis: This History of the United States Marine Corps* (1980, New York: Free Press, 1991), 458,
[13] Millett, *Semper Fidelis,* 458.
[14] John Cowles, "We Must Unify Our Armed Forces," Appendix to the Congressional Record, 1945, A5464-5465.
[15] "Merger of the Army, Air Corps, and Navy," Appendix to the Congressional Record, 1945, A5594. Article with the same title transcribed from 22 December 1945 publication of *Colliers.*
[16] Ibid.
[17] "Unification of the Armed Forces," Appendix to the Congressional Record, 1946, A232.
[18] Walter C. Ploeser, Representative, to Harry S. Truman, President of the United States, official correspondence, 11 January 1946, Appendix to the Congressional Record, 1946, A113.
[19] Ibid.
[20] Donald L. O'Toole, remarks in the House of Representatives, 17 April 1946, "Unification of the Armed Services," Appendix to the Congressional Record, 1946, A2226.
[21] "The Merger Issue," *Naval Affairs*, February 1946, Appendix to the Congressional Record, 1946, A718.
[22] George Fielding Eliot, "Major Eliot Doubts Befits of Unification," *Seapower,* February 1946, 4, 30; Ralph A. Bard, "A Plan to Protect the Peace," *Seapower*, February 1946, 3; "One Department or Three Departments," *Naval Affairs*, March 1946, Appendix to the Congressional Record, 1946, A1142.
[23] Eliot, 3.
[24] A.A. Vandegrift, address on the anniversary of Iwo Jima, 19 February 1946, Vandegrift Papers, Marine Corps University Research Archives.
[25] "New Factor in Unification," *The Sun,* 12 April 1946?, Appendix to the Congressional Record, 1946, A2217.
[26] "Truman's Dangerous Policy," *Utica Daily Press*, 18 April 1946?, Appendix to the Congressional Record, 1946, A2283.
[27] "The Navy's Divergence," *Omaha World Herald*, 3 May 1946, Appendix to the Congressional Record, 1946, A2441.

28 David Lawrence, "Why Punish the Navy?" *United States News*, 19 April 1946.
29 Lawrence.
30 Henry McLemore, "Ex-Doughboy Pays Tribute to Marines," Appendix to the Congressional Record, 1946, A2678.
31 Robert P. Patterson, Secretary of War, and James Forrestal, Secretary of the Navy, to Harry S. Truman, President of the United States, official correspondence, 31 May 1946, Congressional Record, 25 June 1946, 7426.
32 Millett, *Semper Fidelis*, 459.
33 "Merger: Tell It to the Marines," *Newsweek*, 5 May 1947, 26.
34 Ibid.
35 A.A. Vandegrift, *Once a Marine: The Memoirs of General A. A. Vandegrift*, edited by Robert B. Asprey (New York: Norton, 1964), 317-318.
36 Millett, *Semper Fidelis*, 460.
37 "Merger: Tell It to the Marines," *Newsweek*, 5 May 1947, 26.
38 "Merger Now," *Washington Post*, 26 July 1946.
39 "The Air and the Future," *Washington Star*, 26 July 1946.
40 James Forrestal, memorandum to Clark M. Clifford, 7 September 1945, *Documentary History of the Truman Presidency, Volume 10*.
41 Caraley, 151n.
42 "Public Bills and Resolutions," Congressional Record, 14 January 1947, 330.
43 "The National Defense Establishment," Congressional Record, 30 June 1947, 7944.
44 "The United States Marine Corps and Its Part in National Security," Appendix to the Congressional Record, 1947, A1222
45 Ibid, A1220.
46 A. A. Vandegrift, statement to the Senate Armed Services Committee, 22 April 1947, *Documentary History of the Truman Presidency, Volume 10*.
47 T. A. Simms, letter to W. Stuart Symington, 23 April 1947, *Documentary History of the Truman Presidency, Volume 10*.
48 "The Marines' Last Beachhead?", Appendix to Congressional Record, 1947, A2229.
49 "The Marines' Last Beachhead?"; "General Vandegrift Should Be Headed," *News of Elmira N.Y.*, Appendix to Congressional Record, 1947, A2229. Quotes taken from the latter.
50 Millett, *Semper Fidelis*, 462-463,
51 Clare E. Hoffman, Representative, to A. A. Vandegrift, Commandant of the Marine Corps, official correspondence, 24 July 1947, Vandegrift Papers, Marine Corps University Research Archives.
52 Richard Tregaskis, "The Marine Corps Fights for Its Life," *The Saturday Evening Post*, 5 February 1949.
53 Millett, *Semper Fidelis*, 463.
54 Clark M. Clifford, presidential advisor, memorandum to President Harry Truman, 22 July 1947, *Documentary History of the Truman Presidency, Volume 10*.
55 "Unification of the Armed Services – Conference Report," Congressional Record, 24 July 1947, 9912.
56 Millett, *Semper Fidelis*, 463-464,
57 Gordon W. Keiser, *The U.S. Marine Corps and Defense Unification, 1944-47* (Baltimore, MD: Nautical & Aviation Publishing, 1996), 113.
58 Marshall Andrews, "Cry of Unification Still Far Cry From It," *Washington Post*, 3 May 1948?, Appendix to the Congressional Record, 1948, A2685.
59 Roscoe Drummond, "State of the Nation – Behind Armed Services Disunification," *Christian Science Monitor*, 13 May 1948?, Appendix to Congressional Record, 1948, A3028.
60 C. B. Cates to all Commanding Officers in the Marine Corps, "Support of the National Security Act," 3 March 1948, Cates Papers, Marine Corps University Archives.
61 "Who Won the War?" *Infantry Journal*, January 1949, 2-3.
62 Ibid.
63 W. Stuart Symington, memorandum with attached proposal to Clark M. Clifford, 14 January 1949, *Documentary History of the Truman Presidency, Volume 10*.

[64] Victor H. Krulak, *First to Fight: An Inside View of U.S. Marine Corps* (Annapolis MD: U.S. Naval Institute, 1984),120-123.
[65] Millett, *Semper Fidelis,* 465.
[66] Krulak, 123.
[67] Michael Wayne. See making of the film section of *Sands of Iwo Jima,* director Allan Dwan, starring John Wayne, DVD, Republic Entertainment, 2000. Other accounts state that John Wayne requested the part and needed no coaxing from the Marine Corps.
[68] William Milhon, "Sands of Iwo," *Leatherneck,* November 1949, 8-11.
[69] Lawrence H. Suid, *Guts and Glory: The Making of the American Military Image* (Lexington, Kentucky: University of Kentucky Press, 2002), 120.
[70] Ezra Goodman, "From the Halls of Montezuma to Hollywood," *New York Times,* 7 August 1949.
[71] Goodman; William Milhon, "Sands of Iwo," *Leatherneck,* November 1949, 8.
[72] Goodman.
[73] Goodman.
[74] Lawrence H. Suid, *Guts and Glory: The Making of the American Military Image* (Lexington, Kentucky: University Press of Kentucky, 2002), 135.
[75] T. M. P., "'Sands of Iwo Jima,' Starring John Wayne, At the Mayfair," *New York Times,* 31 December 1949.
[76] "From the Halls of Montezuma to the Shores of Korea – The Marines Can Win If We Give Them a Chance," Congressional Record, A6323. Truman apologized to Commandant of the Marine Corps, Clifton Cates, in regard to the language he used in responding to McDonough. Harry Truman, personal apology to Clifton Cates, 6 September 1950, Cates Papers, Marine Corps University Research Archives.
[77] Victor H. Krulak, *First to Fight,* 121.
[78] Millett, *Semper Fidelis,* 474.
[79] Millett, *Semper Fidelis,* 481.
[80] Merrill L. Bartlett and Jack Sweetman, *The U.S. Marine Corps: An Illustrated History* (Annapolis, MD: Naval Institute Press, 2001), 244.
[81] Millett, *Semper Fidelis,* 497.
[82] Millett, *Semper Fidelis,* 498.
[83] Millett, *Semper Fidelis,* 506.
[84] Committee on Armed Services, U.S. House of Representatives, *National Security Act of 1947* (Washington: U.S. Govt. Printing Officer, 1973), 16-17.
[85] *National Security Act of 1947*,16-17.
[86] Millett, *Semper Fidelis,* 518.

INCHON

Robert D. Heinl Jr.

Colonel Heinl details the decisions that initiated what some have described as the supreme amphibious operation ever conducted. Certainly, Inchon remains the most decisive turning point of war in the modern era and Marines constituted the primary ingredients to that success.

A hundred and eighteen years before the Communists invaded South Korea, Clausewitz wrote, "A swift and vigorous transition to attack – the flashing sword of vengeance – is the most brilliant point of the defensive."

The landing at Inchon in September 1950 is one of the most dramatic such transitions from defense to attack in the annals of war. It is also a story of strategic prescience and unflinching nerve on the part of a high commander and of professional expertise in the forces which were his instrument. Above all, Inchon is a triumph which could only have been achieved by American maritime power.

". . . Amphibious Operations Are a Thing of the Past."

One October afternoon in 1949, after paying compliments to colleagues of the naval services, the chairman of the Joint Chiefs of Staff (JCS) gave the House Armed Services Committee a forecast.

"I predict," said General of the Army Omar Nelson Bradley, "that large-scale amphibious operations will never occur again."

Within less than a year, the 1st Marine Division was fighting its way over the beaches and seawalls of Inchon, a Korean west coast port that few in Washington knew or cared about in 1949.

Our defense posture that year was less than brilliant.

Demobilization had gutted the armed forces. "America fought the war like a football game," said General Wedemeyer, "after which the winner leaves the field and celebrates." What remained was wracked by strategic controversy and interservice rivalry. The atom bomb, at the end of a conflict whose iron bombs had conspicuously failed to substantiate Douhet, Trenchard, and Mitchell, seemed to foreshadow an apocalypse in which future war – absolute and total –would be decided by aerial thunderbolts. In corollary, some said, sea power was through.

A sample of top thinking in the administration and Pentagon of those days can be found in a 1949 remark by Louis Johnson, then Secretary of Defense, to Admiral R. L. Conolly:

> Admiral, [said Johnson] the Navy is on its way out....There's no reason for having a Navy and Marine Corps. General Bradley tells me that amphibious operations are a thing of the past. We'll never have any more amphibious operations. That does away with the Marine Corps. And the Air Force can do anything the Navy can do nowadays, so that does away with the Navy.

Amphibious warfare, which General Bradley and many other senior officers decried, was a stepchild in the navy, too. The number of officers passed over while serving in amphibious billets was notorious. Op-343, amphibious warfare's front office in Chief of Naval Operations (CNO) was, headed only by a captain – in an organization containing 38 admirals and 335 other captains. Although the navy had 610 amphibious ships in commission in 1945, only 91 were left four years later. In 1948 the navy scrapped 510 landing craft and built one. The Fleet Marine Force – thirty-five thousand strong in 1948, Forrestal's last year – had already been slashed by Louis Johnson to twenty-three thousand. For 1950 the Defense Department was programming an FMF of six infantry battalions and eleven aviation squadrons. Naval aviation's first postwar carrier, *United States*, had just been abruptly canceled by the Defense Secretary, and the Marine Corps, back to the wall, was fighting to avoid being abolished outright or transferred to the army.

". . . The Worst Possible Place."

In the Far East, thanks largely to Douglas MacArthur, the United States appeared strong. To be sure, China had fallen. And Korea, like Germany, was divided into two parts, one Communist, one free. Yet there was not much concern over Korea nor had there been since 1947, when the JCS red-banded a memorandum which read:

> The Joint Chiefs of Staff consider that, from the standpoint of military security, the United States has little strategic interest in maintaining the present troops and bases in Korea.

Even as this paper was being shuffled about, the *In Min Gun*, or North Korean Peoples Army – a well-armed Communist force of fourteen divisions – was proceeding with careful preparations to conquer South Korea.

The opening scenario of the Korean War is a familiar one. On 25 June 1950 the North Koreans – as MacArthur later said – "struck like a cobra." The South Koreans reeled back, and so did American troops hastily committed from Japan. By mid-August the forces thrown together by the United Nations for the defense of South Korea were penned in a small perimeter around Pusan.

Besieging this perimeter, the main Communist armies were heavily concentrated far south, intent on pushing the defenders into the sea. Because of the presence of the Seventh Fleet, enemy supply lines ran by land down the length of Korea, with Seoul the focal point of their communications. The Communist spearhead was sharp and strong, but their flanks and rear were totally exposed.

On 4 July 1950 – no day for celebration in the Far East – when a weak infantry battalion was all we could field in Korea, General MacArthur had already decided how the Communists would be defeated. On that day he called a conference in Tokyo to consider a seaborne attack against the North Korean communications. What he had in mind was to land the 1st Cavalry Division at Inchon, seize Seoul, cut the enemy communications, and, as he was to repeat, "hammer and destroy the North Koreans." Anticipating his requirements, he had already radioed Washington for some amphibious engineer troops.

While MacArthur had no amphibious troops in July, he had an amphibious force. Early in 1950 – alone among the army's senior commanders in his faith in amphibious warfare – MacArthur had borrowed from the Pacific Fleet a tiny training force, one each of an AGC (amphibious force flagship), an APA (attack transport), an AKA (attack cargo ship), and an LST (Landing Ship, Tank) and a fleet tug. Besides the ships he got a 67-man Marine team from TTUPac (troop training unit), a TacRon (tactical air control squadron) and, most important, the staff of Amphibious Group 1. The PhibGroup commander, Rear Admiral James H. Doyle, had been Richmond Kelly Turner's's operations officer in the Pacific and was one of the few flag officers then in the navy with genuine enthusiasm for, and deep professional grasp of, landing operations. Doyle was conducting a training exercise in Tokyo Bay when the Communists attacked and of course became the Seventh Fleet's amphibious commander from that moment on.

Doyle and his people and the marines were only a nucleus, but their skills gave MacArthur what he urgently needed. Only because of Doyle could MacArthur start planning an amphibious assault while the roof was still falling in.

Events moved too fast to land the 1st Cavalry Division at Inchon. Every single soldier was needed to slow up the Communists in central Korea. Nevertheless, although he kept an open mind as to possible landings elsewhere (Kunsan, particularly), MacArthur visualized his objective as Inchon, and he never deviated from that concept during the weeks of retreat and disaster that lay ahead.

The reasons MacArthur kept Inchon in mind are evident. Inchon is the seaport of Seoul, Korea's ancient capital and first city. The excellent railroads left by the Japanese fan north and south from Seoul, as do the less excellent highways. The national telephone and telegraph nets radiate from Seoul. Kimpo, Korea's largest and best airport, lies between Inchon and Seoul. Inchon, in effect, is to Seoul what Piraeus was to Athens.

If, as a strategic objective, Inchon was all advantage, from the tactical viewpoint it was exactly the reverse. The amphibious bible of those days was USF-6 (naval amphibious doctrine), predecessor of NWP-22A. USF-6 set out seven criteria for a landing area:

(1) ability of naval forces to support the assault and follow-up operations
(2) shelter from unfavorable sea and weather
(3) compatibility of beaches and their approaches to size, draft, maneuverability, and beaching characteristics of assault ships and landing craft
(4) offshore hydrography
(5) extent of minable waters
(6) conditions which may affect enemy ability to defeat mine-clearance efforts
(7) facilities for unloading, and how these may be improved.

How did MacArthur's chosen objective measure up to the above criteria?

Inchon is a port of about the same size and general attractiveness of Jersey City. The tidal range at Inchon is 32 feet, a range only greatly exceeded in the Bay of Fundy. Tidal currents in the approach channels rarely drop below three knots and, in the main channel, reach 7 to 8 knots, close to the speed of an LCVP (Landing Craft Vehicle, Personnel). Inchon's approach, the Salee River (scene of marine operations in 1871) is a tortuous dead-end street with no room for turning or maneuver. Here, one sunken or disabled ship could block the channel from below and pen in anything above. Despite the currents, Inchon's waters are eminently minable and are commanded by heights and islands well suited for batteries that could shoot minesweepers out of the water.

Of beaches, in the common use of the word, Inchon has none. In the Joint Dictionary's definition of beach ("that portion of the shoreline designated for landing of a tactical formation"), Inchon in 1950 had certain stretches of moles, breakwaters, and sea-walls which Admiral Doyle's planners considered least objectionable. Beach exits were mainly the go-downs, railroad yards, and factory alleys of a congested Oriental city.

Underwater gradients approaching these "beaches" demanded a tidal height of 23 feet to get LCVP and LCM (Landing Craft, Mechanized) ashore, while 29 feet would be needed for LST. Tidal heights of this magnitude prevail at Inchon only once each month, for about 3 or 4 days.

Later on, General Almond, of whom we shall hear more, said Inchon was "the worst possible place where we could bring in an amphibious assault." But, because it was the worst possible place, it was also, in a sense, the best possible. There is an ancient Chinese apothegm that "the wise general is one able to turn disadvantage to his own advantage."

"I Wish I Had the 1st Marine Division."

Besides the physical obstacles to a landing at Inchon, there were two other obstacles which, if anything, might have seemed even more forbidding. One was to find the forces – landing forces and assault shipping – capable of executing such a near-impossible landing. The other was to convince an exalted body of doubters that an amphibious attack, even if practicable, was the correct counterblow to the invasion and that Inchon was the place. At this time, for example, a different strategy being urged on the JCS as well as any reporter who would listen, was that we should progressively bomb the communications and principal cities of North Korea and that, by the time this program reached the outskirts of Pyongyang, the Communists would sit down and negotiate.

Finding qualified amphibious troops presented difficulties because the only such we had were marines, and the last thing anybody in the Pentagon or White House of those days wanted to see was another exhibition of marine headline hunting, such as a victory. Besides, there weren't very many marines. Louis Johnson had seen to that.

From the outbreak of war, one officer in Washington had no illusions. In World War One he had commanded a platoon at Belleau Wood and a company in later actions. By the end of World War Two he had successively commanded (in combat) an infantry battalion, then a regiment, and finally a division. This officer – Clifton B. Cates – was commandant of the Marine Corps. To General Cates, the oddest thing about the outbreak of war in Korea was that nobody in the Defense Department, let alone Secretary of the Navy Matthews or Admiral Forrest Sherman, chief of naval operations, could find time to see the commandant of the Marine Corps. Some young planners on the Joint Staff were even suggesting that we could probably settle the Korean "emergency" without any marines at all. When General Cates finally did shoulder past the aides into Secretary Matthews's office on 30 June, the secretary remarked that the possibility of sending marines to Korea just hadn't come up in any conference he could recall. But this subject, nevertheless, had arisen. On 29 June, after vainly seeking an interview for four days, General Cates ran into Admiral Sherman in a Pentagon hall.

Cates: "Things look pretty grim over there. Why doesn't MacArthur ask for Marines?"
Sherman: (after a pause) "What do you have?"
Cates: "I can give you an RCT [Regimental Combat Team] and an air group from the West Coast."
Sherman: (another pause) "Leave it to me – I'll send a 'Blue Flag' to Joy." [Admiral C. T. Joy]

There was one more pause: as the situation worsened, Sherman waited two days – until after lunch on 1 July – before acting on Cate's offer.

The results of CNO's "Blue Flag," when at length sent to Admiral Joy in the Far East, were not long forthcoming. On 3 July, not to their unqualified satisfaction, the Joint

Chiefs of Staff – General Bradley, chairman; General J. Lawton Collins, army chief of staff; General Hoyt Vandenberg of the air force; and Admiral Sherman – had before them a dispatch from General MacArthur, asking for immediate movement of a marine regimental combat team with supporting aviation, to the Far East. Another message they had before them (at least those who read the New York *Herald-Tribune* that morning) was from David Lawrence, the highly informed Washington columnist:

> General MacArthur . . . has no trained amphibious forces. The United States Marines at San Diego are all packed up and ready to sail, and will be invaluable as reinforcements for MacArthur's troops. . . .Ships must be gotten out of "mothballs" immediately, though no such orders have been given, up to today at least. It takes weeks – not days – to transport men and supplies across the Pacific.

To underscore Lawrence's point the chiefs had an uninvited guest in "the tank." When, by chance, General Cates learned that MacArthur's request for marines was on the agenda, he announced he would attend, and he did.

Although, for a variety of reasons, the Joint Chiefs of Staff had small stomach for the decision, their session had but one outcome: after clearing with the White House (where President Truman himself had to approve), the marines were ordered to mount out. To the last, General Vandenberg tried to strip the force of its aviation but July 1950 was no time for interservice politics.

Orders for the marines to send a brigade to the Far East were not a complete surprise. While General Cates was still in the dark as to what Admiral Sherman might be doing on what the latter later called his "Cates to Sherman/to Joy/to MacArthur/to JCS" play, the commandant had, on his own responsibility, sent a war alert to the 1st Marine Division. By "just playing a hunch," as Cates put it, he had gained more than a day's lead time for organization of the 1st Provisional Marine Brigade and its aviation, MAG-33 (Marine Air Group).

Another officer who was taking time by the forelock was Lieutenant General L. C. Shepherd, Jr. Enroute to command Fleet Marine Force, Pacific (FMFPac) when the war exploded, General Shepherd cut short his fishing at Yellowstone, and reached Honolulu before breakfast on 2 July. Even before he could report in to Admiral Radford, the Pacific Fleet commander, his staff handed him the commandant's warning order and another (Sherman to Radford) alerting the commander-in-chief, Pacific (CinCPac) to prepare marine forces for Korean service.

Only taking time to call on Radford, an old friend, General Shepherd worked all day and into the night to organize the marine brigade for activation on 7 July. Brigadier General E. A. Craig, an officer of high reputation in World War Two, would be in command. When the brigade's orders were complete, General Shepherd, accompanied by his G-3 (operation's officer), Colonel V. H. Krulak, set out for Japan. Their mission was to make arrangements with General MacArthur for the marines' employment.

On 9 July Shepherd and Krulak arrived in Tokyo. Next morning the marines were escorted by MacArthur's chief of staff (Major General Edward M. Almond) into the supreme commander's office. After complimenting the Marine Corps with the graciousness of which he was past master, MacArthur said, "I wish I had the entire 1st Marine Division under my command again as I have a job for them to do."

Rising, MacArthur pointed the stem of his corncob pipe at Inchon and continued, would land them here and cut the North Korean armies off from their logistic support and cause their withdrawal and annihilation."

Shepherd reacted immediately: "Why don't you ask for the 1st Marine Division, General?"

"That's the kind of talk I like to hear," said MacArthur. "Do you think I can get it?"

Surely, the marine responded, MacArthur could get the division if he were to ask the JCS. In his own capacity, as the division's higher commander, General Shepherd went on, he could if ordered have the unit (at full peace strength less brigade units already committed) ready by 1 September. Could Shepherd take this up with General Cates asked MacArthur? No need, was the reply, he would assume responsibility. Good, said MacArthur, "You sit down and write me dispatch to the JCS."

Looking at the general's king-size desk and chair and imagining the general's glance over his shoulder, General Shepherd decided he could do a better job elsewhere. Excusing himself he went into the office of General Almond, a fellow alumnus of the Virginia Military Institute, and drafted MacArthur's message. When he took it in, Krulak recalled General MacArthur already seemed to be exuding "enthusiasm and resolute confidence."

The army reaction to MacArthur's proposal was conveyed in person since General Collins and his air force colleague Vandenberg were poised for a trip to Tokyo when the general's message arrived. Feeling he should remain in Washington, Admiral Sherman had asked Radford to go along from Pearl Harbor and represent him.

At Tokyo on 13 July, MacArthur confirmed that he intended to attack the enemy lines of communication on the west coast as soon as the *In Min Gun's* advance could be stopped. Inchon, he thought, was the best place, but he was also considering Haeju and Chinnampo. Then, and during staff talks next day, Collins was dubious as to the proposed amphibious counterthrust, especially when he learned the troop requirements. Still trying to divine whether the Russians would seize this convenient moment to march on the Rhine and points west, Collins told MacArthur: "General, you are going to have to win the war out here with the troops available to you in Japan and Korea."

MacArthur smiled and shook his head. "Joe," he said, "you are going to have to change your mind."

Later, MacArthur turned to Radford (the two theater commanders were side by side) and, testing General Shepherd's offer, asked what he thought the marines might be able to contribute. Radford had the right answer: "A brigade rapidly, and probably in the fall, the rest of a division."

Later, before leaving, speaking at least for himself rather than the chiefs, Collins did change his mind: privately, he told MacArthur, he thought a full marine division could be sent to the Far East. Thus encouraged, as soon as the visitors left, on 15 July, MacArthur sent his second request to the JCS for the 1st Marine Division and supporting aviation.

While these developments were in progress General Shepherd was on the West Coast. After briefing Radford ("I feel that there is a serious war in progress in Korea . . . for which Marines are trained and constituted," he said), Shepherd felt it imperative not only to see how the brigade was mounting out but, more important, to meet General Cates, there for the same purpose.

At Pendleton, General Shepherd disclosed MacArthur's plan. Cates, whose knowledge of the Korean situation and of the JCS deliberations was limited to what Admiral Sherman, a taciturn man, chose to disclose, was hesitant to commit a full division. An alluring offer was pending to assign marine forces to NATO. "Clifton, you cannot let me down on this," said Shepherd. "This is a hot war. We ought to be in it."

For a fighter like Cates, that clinched it. The two then conferred much of the afternoon and all evening on 12 July, and, when Cates took off for Washington, he knew what had to be done. At his immediate orders the staff at HQMC prepared plans for a war-strength division or, alternatively, to bring General Craig's brigade to war strength. The staff conclusions were quickly evident: to assemble a war-strength division from a corps numbering less than seventy thousand would require mobilization of the reserve. It would require transfer of practically all of FMFLant to the Pacific. It would require reactivation, organization, and mount-out – within days – of new regiments and new battalions made up of reservists, navy yard guards, and schools troops.

Nine days had elapsed since MacArthur's original request for a marine division, four days since his reiterated request, and still there was no reply. Learning that the brigade, however welcome, was nevertheless at peace strength, MacArthur on 19 July sent the chiefs still another message asking (1) that the brigade be brought to war strength, and (2) repeating for the third time that he needed a full marine division.

As General Cates knew by this time, approval of either, let alone both requests, would entail calling the reserve to the colors, and this information he quickly gave to the JCS when asked. With the *In Min Gun* in the very act of drubbing the 24th Infantry Division out of Taejon, the chiefs went to Blair House on 19 July and recommended mobilization of the marine reserve. Harry Truman nodded, signed the papers, and that afternoon warning orders alerted the ground reserve for active service.

While reservists packed seabags, a shabby tug of war was taking place to prevent mobilization of any of the Marine Corps's thirty reserve aviation squadrons.

Air Force Chief of Staff Hoyt Vandenberg had been unalterably opposed to sending any marine aviation to Korea ("from a sensitive feeling here at the Pentagon," wrote David Lawrence, "that the Marines should not have their own aviation."). Now, for reasons not recorded, Admiral Sherman – never a marine enthusiast – joined Vandenberg and on 20 July curtly vetoed the commandant's urgent request that aviation units be included in the call-up for Korea. While it was clear to Cates – and equally to MacArthur, who had so reassured Shepherd and Craig – that aviation had to be an integral part of the marine air-ground team, this view was evidently not accepted in Washington.

On 23 July, under increasingly sharp prods from the press (two days earlier, Lawrence had charged Generals Collins and Vandenberg with "having combined to squelch the opportunity of the United States Marine aviation units to fight in the Far East"), Sherman told Cates he could order up six fighting and ground squadrons. A week later, following what the commandant described as "a plain, forceful, and harsh" session on 31 July, between Carl Vinson, House Armed Services Committee chairman, and Admiral Sherman and Secretary Matthews, the admiral announced that two more aviation squadrons would be mobilized and that the Corps would be built up to two war-strength divisions and eighteen squadrons. Shortly before this disclosure, General Bradley sought out General Cates and asked if he "couldn't do something to stop Lawrence's critical articles," as (in the chairman's words) Cates "was the only one that could do it." "I thanked him for the compliment," Cates duly recalled.

Now that the marines were mobilizing, the Joint Chiefs at length – it was 20 July, ten days since the general's initial request – gave MacArthur a reply: yes, he could have a war-strength marine division, but no sooner than November. This date represented HQMC's view of an "orderly" buildup but was far from meeting the imperatives of war, as MacArthur quickly underscored in his fourth message:

> Most urgently request reconsideration of decision with reference to 1st Marine Division. It is an absolutely vital requisite to accomplish a decisive stroke and if not made available will necessitate a much more costly and longer effort both in blood and expense. It is essential that the Marine division arrive by 10 September 1950. . . . There can be no demand for its potential use elsewhere that can equal the urgency of the immediate battle mission contemplated for it.

Under cumulative impact of four dispatches, the chiefs at least gave him a prompt reply. Within forty-eight hours they countered that he must provide more information on his plans for the period before 10 September, and, by way of encouragement, said orders had been issued to bring the marine brigade, and of course its aviation, to war strength.

In his response next day, MacArthur did not identify Inchon as his objective (though it had been unwaveringly in his mind from the beginning) but he said this:

> Operation planned mid-September is amphibious landing of a two-division corps in rear of enemy lines for purpose of enveloping and destroying enemy forces in conjunction with attack from south by Eighth Army. I am firmly convinced early and strong effort behind his front will sever his main lines of communication and enable us to deliver a decisive and crushing blow. . . . The alternative is a frontal attack which can only result in a protracted and expensive campaign.

The general's *Reminiscences* recounts that this final message was greeted by "a silence of three weeks." This is not exactly true. On 25 July, the chiefs gave in. They ordered that the 1st Marine Division, commanded by Major General Oliver P. Smith, be brought to war strength (less one RCT) and mount out from San Diego between 10 and 15 August. Included in the JCS directive – another score for General Cates – was the phrase "with attached air" (actually only one-and-a-half more squadrons, but the precedent had been accepted). MacArthur's scheme now had its cutting edge.

". . . I Shall Crush Them!"

Never the most pliant of Washington's subordinates, General MacArthur had not yet fully disclosed his concept of an assault on Inchon. Troops were moving, ships were on the seas, and it was obvious the stakes were high, but the Joint Chiefs of Staff, military advisors to the president, did not yet know the name of the game.

"Frankly," General Collins later said, "we were somewhat in the dark."

Thus, on 20 August, General Collins, accompanied by Admiral Sherman, was sent to Tokyo, in Collins's words, "to find out exactly what the plans were." MacArthur, as he said in his *Reminiscences*, viewed the visit in a different light. "The actual purpose of their trip," he wrote, "was not so much to discuss as to dissuade."

Beside the JCS delegation, Admiral Radford and General Shepherd were both on their way to Tokyo, Admiral Doyle and staff were already there, aboard his flagship, Mount McKinley, and General O. P. Smith (en route by air from Camp Pendleton) would soon arrive. Alone among the key participants of the forthcoming operation, Vice Admiral A. D. Struble, soon to be designated as overall commander, was absent at sea, hammering the west coast of Korea.

There can be little doubt that General MacArthur looked on Admiral Sherman as the man he had to convince and therefore the key figure among the admirals and generals converging on Tokyo. The operation in MacArthur's mind was, above all, a naval operation, without the navy's ships and support, without the marines' amphibious troops, and without the professional knowhow of both navy and marines, the landing at Inchon – however brilliant a concept – could never become reality.

Moreover, General MacArthur already knew, there were serious reservations about the Inchon scheme, not only in his own staff but most certainly on the part of Admiral Doyle and his planners and generally among most senior navy and marine officers privy to the plan. In fact, the more the experts looked at Inchon, the more pessimistic they became.

For these reasons – and also because Sherman, at the height of his powers, was an officer of tenacious mind and purpose, professionally respected even by those who disliked him most – the admiral, short of MacArthur himself, was the dominant figure. And Sherman, in accordance with habit, was keeping his own counsel.

The panelled sixth-floor conference room m the Dai Ichi Building lay between the offices of Generals MacArthur and Almond. At 1730, 23 August, when the supreme commander entered the room, there were assembled Admiral Sherman and General Collins, representing the JCS, admirals Radford, Joy, and Doyle; generals Almond, Hickey, Ruffner, and Wright, all of MacArthur's staff; and a handful of key juniors. Curiously, neither marine general then in Tokyo (Shepherd and Smith) was invited, so the landing force interest was unrepresented save by a lieutenant colonel among Doyle's briefers.

A day or so before, concerned because MacArthur seemed oblivious of the enormous technical hazards posed by a landing at Inchon, Admiral Doyle had insisted to General Almond that MacArthur be briefed on exactly what the Inchon landing involved. Almond demurred, "The general is not interested in details." Doyle shot back: "He must be made aware of the details."

Now, following an introduction by General Wright, the operations officer, MacArthur puffed reflectively on his pipe for eighty minutes while nine officers of Amphibious Group I gave him nothing but details – details of intelligence, aerology, beaches, tides, currents, channels, communications, pontoonery, landing craft, boat waves, naval gunfire, and air strikes. After the last speaker uttered his last detail, Admiral Doyle rose and gave MacArthur the broad picture: "General, I have not been asked nor have I volunteered my opinion about this landing. If I were asked, however, the best I can say is that Inchon is not impossible." Then he sat down.

After a pause, MacArthur replied, "If we find that we can't make it, we will withdraw."

"No, General," said Doyle, "we don't know how to do that. Once we start ashore we'll keep going."

General Collins, who had "wanted to be darn sure just what these plans were," now knew and took the lead, "But not," he later said, "in any acrimonious way, as has sometimes been pictured." Why not Kunsan to the south? Or Posun-Myong, below Inchon? Sherman, said one account, was at first "lukewarm." However, when Doyle explained some of the dangers of the Inchon approaches, and mentioned the enemy shore batteries that could completely command the dead-end channel, Sherman sniffed, "I wouldn't hesitate to take a ship up there."

"Spoken like a Farragut!" exclaimed MacArthur.

History must regret that the conference room had no tape recorder. Thus we shall never know exactly what MacArthur said when the discussion had run its course. The several versions (including that in his *Reminiscences*) are at odds. But all who heard him that evening (dusk had fallen when he began to speak) agreed that his forty-five-minute reply, extemporaneous, without a note, was one of the compelling declarations of his career. Remembering that scene, Admiral Doyle said, "If MacArthur had gone on the stage, you never would have heard of John Barrymore."

The bulk of the enemy, MacArthur said, were committed against the Pusan perimeter. Frontal attack out of the perimeter would cost a hundred thousand casualties. The North Koreans were unprepared for an enveloping attack, least of all at such a place as Inchon. To land at Kunsan would be easier, to be sure, but the results would be "ineffective and indecisive." Nothing in war, he underscored, is more futile than short envelopments. With a deep cut across the Communists' lines of communications, they would soon be deprived of munitions and fighting power, and Inchon would become the anvil on which Eighth Army would smash the enemy from the south. "The amphibious landing is the most powerful tool we have. To employ it properly, we must strike hard and deep."

Adverting to what Wolfe's contemporaries in 1759 had disparaged as "a mad scheme," MacArthur likened the Inchon assault to Wolfe's surprise landing at the Anse du Foulon and his subsequent capture of Quebec As for the navy's objections, he recognize their validity. They were not, however, insuperable. Perhaps he had more confidence in the navy than the navy had in itself. "The navy has never let me down in the past, and it will not let me down this time," he said.

"I realize," he concluded, "that Inchon is a 5,000 to 1 gamble, but I am used to such odds . . ." Then his voice dropped so that the listeners strained to hear him: "We shall land at Inchon and I shall crush them!"

The effect was mesmeric. It might have been a minute before anyone spoke. Then Sherman said, "Thank you, a great voice in a great cause," and the meeting broke up. At dinner afterward, when all the navy and marine flag officers foregathered at Admiral Joy's Sherman said to General Shepherd that MacArthur had been "spellbinding."

"I wish," the admiral remarked next day, "I had that man's optimism."

Once the spell wore off, some listeners had second thoughts. After sleeping on the matter, the admirals and generals Shepherd and Smith met in Joy's office for what O. P. Smith described as "an indignation meeting." The consensus was that army planners were giving insufficient, if any, weight to the naval problems that loomed so large to the eyes of experience and that a more feasible landing area must be found. As General Shepherd noted, however, "Nothing of a concrete nature developed."

Lack of developments in any situation frustrated General Shepherd, and an opportunity to press for such developments at the highest level arose that morning. Almond asked that Shepherd come to the Dai Ichi Building. MacArthur wished to see him.

Before the appointment, General Shepherd (accompanied by Colonel Krulak) had forty-five minutes with Almond. The first matter raised by the marine was to urge that the brigade, which had been heavily engaged in the perimeter, be withdrawn from action since Inchon's D-day was but three weeks ahead. Almond replied shortly that the marines wouldn't be withdrawn until just before D-day as Eighth Army's General Walker couldn't spare them.

General Shepherd then voiced the reservations he felt about Inchon and, as he had previously during this visit to Tokyo, urged that Posun-Myong be substituted. Almond then disclosed that the real objective of the Inchon assault was to take Seoul, "that Inchon was decided upon and that was where it would be." He added that he didn't believe there were any troops in Inchon, and dismissed the amphibious landing as "a simple mechanical operation."

At this moment, perhaps fortunately, MacArthur entered the room and took General Shepherd and Colonel Krulak into his office. There, grasping the nettle, Shepherd again urged another objective. Instead of cutting off discussion, MacArthur launched into an analysis of the importance of capturing Seoul which, he said, "would quickly end the war."

"For a $5.00 ante," he concluded, "I have an opportunity to win $50,000, and I have decided that is what I'm going to do."

Landing at Washington's National Airport, Sherman and Collins flashed brief smiles for the photographers while public information officers assured reporters there was "nothing extraordinary" about the trip. Then, with more pensive mien, the two told Bradley and Vandenberg, there to meet them, of MacArthur's plans and his unswerving determination to go through with them. On 28 August – there seemed nothing else to do – the chiefs sent a message of tepid approval to Tokyo:

> We concur in preparations for executing a turning movement by amphibious forces on the west coast of Korea, either at Inchon in the event the enemy defenses there prove ineffective, or at a favorable beach south of Inchon if one can be located. We further concur in preparations, if desired by you, for an envelopment by amphibious forces in vicinity of Kunsan. We understand that alternative plans are being prepared to best exploit situation as it develops.

Thus, the Joint Chiefs of Staff reluctantly approved MacArthur's plan (Operation Chromite) to land at Inchon and cut the communications of the North Korean armies attacking the defensive perimeter around Pusan in southern Korea. MacArthur was determined to strike as soon as possible. For MacArthur, "as soon as possible" meant 15 September.

"One of MacArthur's greatest attributes," said Admiral A. D. Struble, soon to command the landings at Inchon, "was to get going *and to hit quick*."

High tide at Inchon on 15 September would put maximum high water over the harbor's mud flats, a tidal height of 31.2 feet. Twelve days later, on the 27th, there would be 27 feet (2 feet short of what the LSTs needed). Not until 11 October would there again be even 30 feet of water. September 15th was, therefore, the best date. This left just twenty-three days between arrival in Tokyo of Major General O. P. Smith (commanding general 1st Marine Division and thus landing force commander), and MacArthur's target date. It left no time whatever for rehearsals and barely enough for final mount-out, when the sea-borne elements of the division would reach Japan between 28 August and 3 September, some still in merchantmen, and – as in the case of Guadalcanal – would reembark and combat-load in assault shipping.

In this race against time and tide, back at the ranch at Camp Pendleton, things were humming.

When the 1st Marine Brigade shipped out for Pusan on 14 July, an aching void was all they left behind. Although the marine unit at Camp Pendleton m June 1950 was called a division, Defense Secretary Louis Johnson's surgery had effectively pared it barely to the strength of a brigade. Moreover, while the depleted headquarters of the nominal 1st Marine Division stayed behind when the brigade left, even this was in caretaker hands. By an ironic coincidence only days before Korea exploded, Major General G. B. Erskine, the division's steely commander and one of the corps's most distinguished World War Two tacticians, had been dispatched on secret orders to find out for the State Department what was happening to the French in Indo-China. Training and readiness were Erskine specialties and, although he had little to work with in 1948-49, what there was had been superbly prepared. Now, having fashioned a well-tempered weapon, it was Erskine's ill fortune not to wield it.

At war strength a marine division included 22,343 officers and men. The 3,386 people remaining when the 1st Brigade sailed in July represented fragments of the headquarters and service elements of a division, and little more.

". . . Few Cadres Left."

On 25 July 1950, the morning General O. P. Smith, the new division commander, broke his flag, there remained but twenty-one days before his division must mount out. During these three weeks the 2nd Division at Lejeune would be stripped to the merest cadre by transfer and redesignation of East Coast units. From some ten thousand reservists who began flooding in on 31 July, ninety-one officers and twenty-eight hundred enlisted men were to be selected and absorbed. From over a hundred posts and stations, navy yard marines to the number of one hundred thirty officers and thirty-five hundred enlisted were to join. In fact during one frantic four-day period, 1975 August, nine thousand officers and men reported for duty.

Amid this Niagara of people, the division staff had to plan movement to the Far East, receive war stocks of ammunition from depots as far away as New Jersey, and, not least, get units equipped. Fortunately there was Barstow to call on. Barstow reminded logisticians of a war surplus store. After World War Two, unlike others who left their gear where it stood, went home, and disbanded, the marines had cannily salvaged every weapon, every truck, every tank, every amtrac (amphibious tractor) within reach (and without much nicety as to original ownership). This trove eventually reached Barstow where, from 1946 on, items had been patiently overhauled, moth-balled, assigned serial numbers, and painted forest green when the olive drab or grey showed too conspicuously. "From this miser's lair at Barstow," recounted Andrew Geer in *The New Breed*,

> ...came the trucks, DUKWs, jeeps, trailers, and amphibian tractors that were to go once more to war. There were more veterans of Iwo Jima and Okinawa among the vehicles than among the men who would drive them.

The day after General Smith took over his new command, General Shepherd arrived from Honolulu for a visit. While at Pendleton, he telephoned General Cates, the commandant, in Washington. During this call, General Shepherd made two important Points: (1) that 1st Marine Aircraft Wing headquarters ought to go to Korea to assume command of air operations, and (2) that somehow the 1st Division *must* get its third infantry regiment, the 7th Marines.

Neither the White House, the secretary of defense, nor the JCS were not enthusiastic in mid-1950 about expansion of the Marine Corps. Thus, to obtain the 7th Marines, General Cates had first to convince the CNO, Admiral Sherman, and then fight it out with the JCS's Lieutenant General J. T. McNarney who (as Cates wrote) "personally checked every figure submitted and questioned many in detail." Fortunately, General MacArthur very much wanted a full marine division, and MacArthur's wishes could not lightly be flouted. Following a final confrontation with McNarney, Cates laconically jotted in his journal: "Can do. Few cadres left."

Few indeed. The 2nd Marine Division was so stripped that on 15 September 1950 – D-day at Inchon – it had but 3,928 officers and men on board. The 2nd Wing had bodily transferred MAG-15 to El Toro; this, with 1,230 pilots and ground crews from the reserve, completed the tactical air command that would support Operation Chromite. To denude the East Coast and the Atlantic of their marines was a risk, but so, to say the least, was the impending operation.

Operation Chromite

Accumulation of intelligence for Operation Chromite should have proved no problem. Inchon had been used by the army as a port for years after World War Two, but much elementary information was lacking. Japanese and American tide tables differed appreciably and nobody could say which was correct. Would Inchon's mud flats support infantry or vehicles at low water? How high were the seawalls at various stages of the tide? And so on.

By dint of furious search the planners found a transportation corps warrant officer who had operated boats all around Inchon Harbor, and this invaluable man promptly joined Admiral Doyle's staff. Aerial photos were needed, but Far East Air Forces had no suitable photo planes. The only aircraft capable of taking the very low-altitude pictures which would reveal the characteristics of the seawalls were two marine F4Us and a photo detachment aboard one of the carriers. Flying up to thirteen sorties a day with only two airplanes, this detachment, commanded by Major Donald Bush, completed its assignment in four days and turned over the results to a photo-interpretation team flown to Japan from Dayton, Ohio. And plans were afoot to verify all information by the surest means of all – personal reconnaissance.

There was one item of intelligence that no one knew. In August, Naval Mine Depot, Vladivostok, had sent training teams and several trainloads of mines to Chinnampo and Wonsan. Four thousand mines were being distributed from Chinnampo to Inchon, Kunsan, Haeju, and Mokpo. Undertaken quickly enough, minelaying could take Inchon out of play completely. What the odds on this might be, nobody could calculate, but it meant that the sooner MacArthur could collect his forces and strike, the more favorable those odds would be.

Aside from mining Inchon out of the game, the Communists could heavily reinforce the Inchon-Seoul area. They could intensify fortification sufficiently to unbalance MacArthur's strategic equations. Russian aviation or submarines could intervene. With or without Russian support, Chinese ground forces could join in (if they did, however, MacArthur predicted that the air force would "turn the Yalu into the bloodiest stream in all history.").

While intelligence estimates somewhat underestimated the strength of the Inchon-Seoul forces at five thousand to ten thousand, Inchon itself was not strongly held, thus indicating that the North Korean G-2s (intelligence staffs) tended to agree with General Almond's view of Inchon as "the worst possible place." The Inchon garrison comprised two battalions of infantry and two harbor-defense batteries of coast artillery, manning 76 mm and 106 mm guns. Engineers had plans for eventual fortification of Inchon, Russian land mines were already being laid, and, as mentioned, harbor-defense minefields were envisaged. (But there was one snag: although three hundred Russian pressure mines had reached Inchon on 29 August, they lacked cable harnesses. These the supply officer had on backorder.)

The tides dictated 15 September as D-day. That day, however, the tidal timing could hardly have been worse. Morning high tide came just forty-five minutes after sunrise. The next high tide would not crest until thirty-seven minutes after sunset. Morning tide would be many hours too soon for the underpowered, single-screw APAs and AKAs, in those days without modern navigational radar, to make a daylight approach up Flying Fish Channel to Inchon. On the other hand, thirty-seven minutes after sunset isn't ordinarily the best time for a landing, either.

The nub of this problem was how to land a marine division on two separate tides, one so early that normal assault shipping couldn't make it up the approach channels, the other so late that landings would have to be conducted by twilight and darkness. Paradoxically, a third problem helped solve the other two.

The island of Wolmi Do in Inchon harbor is the tactical key to the city. Wolmi Do's peak commands both harbor and town. No soldier in his right mind would consider landing at Inchon with having control of Wolmi Do.

General Smith's planners therefore concluded that Wolmi Do – which had to be secured initially – should be taken on the morning tide, and that the main landings at Inchon proper could then proceed in the evening. In this way, by solving the Wolmi Do problem separately, the main landings at Inchon could be simplified and streamlined.

But how could the Wolmi Do landing force – a battalion landing team (3/5) – get to its transport area in time for the morning flood just after sunrise? The usual shipping – APAs, AKAs, and LSTs – was out of the question. Admiral Doyle's chief of staff, Captain Norman Sears, proposed that the BLT be embarked in APDs and one LSD, all of which were adequately powered, maneuverable, and equipped with navigational gear suitable for the night approach. Then, to prove he had faith in his idea, Sears persuaded Admiral Doyle to let him command the Wolmi Do attack group.

After morning tide receded, the BLT on Wolmi Do would, although physically cut off, be on strong defensive ground and of course supported by the guns and aviation of the fleet.

In late afternoon, the remainder of the division would land over two widely separated beaches. Besides the obstacles of intelligence collection, of the tides, of the approach and of the capture of Wolmi Do, certain others remained before the Inchon plan could be firmed up.

One-third of the marine division – what today we call a marine expeditionary brigade, built around the 5th Marines and MAG-33 – was fighting in the Pusan perimeter. General Walker, commanding the Eighth Army, was, to say the least, unenthusiastic over losing his marines and had gone so far as to say he would not be responsible for the perimeter if the marines were withdrawn. General Almond – who knew little of landing operations – tried to persuade General Smith to go into Inchon without the 5th Marines. He even offered to provide a substitute army regiment (with no amphibious training, containing 40 percent recently drafted Korean civilian levies) and saw no reason why such a formation wouldn't do for an assault landing only two weeks ahead.

However, after a last-minute show-down with the naval commanders and Generals Smith and Shepherd, Almond and Walker yielded when General MacArthur ordered that the 5th Marines be released.

The plan for Operation Chromite contained the following missions:

- Seize the port of Inchon and capture a force beachhead line
- Advance rapidly and seize Kimpo airfield
- Cross the Han River
- Seize and occupy Seoul
- Occupy blocking positions north, northeast, and east of Seoul
- Using forces in the Inchon-Seoul area as an anvil, crush the Communists with a stroke from the south by Eighth Army.

To execute Chromite, General MacArthur, a unified commander, created a joint task force – Joint Task Force 7 (which was really a falseface for Seventh Fleet headquarters and its commander, Vice Admiral Struble). The troop component of JTF-7 ("expeditionary troops," it would have been entitled in the amphibious doctrine of the day) was to be a corps, since the assigned missions would require operations by two divisions.

The question of how to staff and organize the corps headquarters – and, most important, who would command it – went unsettled until mid-August. Early that month Admiral Sherman had suggested to MacArthur that General Shepherd be given the command. Such an assignment would have made sense not only because Shepherd, a lieutenant general (and thus of corps-command rank), was a veteran amphibious commander, but also because his headquarters (FMFPac) was organized for amphibious warfare, and, above all, was a going concern. General Wright, MacArthur's G-3, made these points in a memorandum of 7 August, urging that the marine headquarters be employed. General Hickey, MacArthur's deputy chief of staff, concurred emphatically and warned against "...the hasty throwing together of a provisional corps headquarters . . . at best only a half-baked affair." These recommendations stopped at the chief of staff's desk and rebounded with the obituary notation, "Return without action."

Three days later, when Wright again urged prompt formation of a corps headquarters, a provisional staff for this group was selected by General Almond, the chief of staff, from officers in MacArthur's headquarters. About that time, General Almond has related, he asked General MacArthur who was to command the corps, and was, he said, startled to hear the general reply, "It is you."

And so it happened that on 26 August, when Washington authorized activation of X Corps, an army organization, Major General Almond, who by dispensation remained as MacArthur's chief of staff, was named to command it.

But this corps headquarters for the first amphibious assault since World War Two had no amphibious qualifications. As Admiral Doyle later wrote, "The corps staff, with very few exceptions, had no amphibious training, experience, or basic understanding of amphibious operations." For this reason, X Corps could only enter the picture when the battle ceased to be amphibious. It was to embark in an MSTS transport without proper communications; its commander, Almond, would not even accompany Admiral Struble aboard the force flagship, Rochester.

To get around the amphibious impotence of X Corps, jointure of command did not take place until reaching the level of the attack force, under Admiral Doyle, and the landing force, under General Smith. Correspondingly, there was one further juncture of command below Doyle and Smith – that of Captain Sears's advance attack group with Lieutenant Colonel R. D. Taplett's 3rd Battalion, 5th Marines.

Considering the haste with which Struble had to organize it, the force was impressive: 71,339 officers and men in assault or follow-up landings, and two hundred thirty ships from seven navies, plus MSTS, and thirty Japanese LSTs, one commanded by a former battleship captain. Curiously, there was no air force participation in this joint task force. The inconvenient remoteness of shore bases from the objective area so curtailed air force time over target that air operations had to be left entirely to carriers positioned close by in the Yellow Sea.

The pre-D-day operations – settled only after heated debate – consisted of extensive diversionary strikes against Chinnampo, Ongjin, and Kunsan, and then two days of naval and air bombardment at Inchon, the latter especially planned, by exposing thin-skinned destroyers at short range, to tempt enemy shore batteries into opening fire. The principal points at issue were air force participation (strongly urged on MacArthur by Washington), and the duration of pre-D-day bombardment. Admiral Struble – whose experience had been in Europe and the Southwest Pacific – favored only one day of light bombardment, hoping for maximum surprise. Doyle and Smith, thinking in terms of the Central Pacific, wanted five days of everything that could shoot and fly. After considerable discussion, Admiral Struble decided on two days – a decision confirmed by events.

The landing plan called for seizure of Wolmi Do on the early morning tide, over Green Beach. Making the main effort in the late afternoon, the 5th Marines (Lieutenant Colonel R. L. Murray) would land in LCVPs over Red Beach and seize Observatory Hill, key terrain feature of Inchon town. Since the capacity of Red Beach was barely enough for one RLT, the 1st Marines (Colonel L. B. Puller) were to land in amtracs over Blue Beach. An added advantage of the Blue Beach landing was that it would put the 1st Regiment directly on the flank of any counterattack from Seoul and would also seal off Inchon from the South.

The limited duration of high water posed still another problem: the only time when LSTs could beach at Inchon would be amid early assault waves when front lines were but a block or so inland. Admiral Doyle nevertheless took the risk ("I had the utmost confidence in the Marines. In my book they could not fail," he later said) and accepted the major complication of bringing in eight rust-bucket LSTs (only one of whose skippers had previously beached or retracted) onto Red Beach at H + thirty minutes. Only if these ships – repossessed from the island trade, and aromatic with the fragrance of fishheads and urine – got in, to remain stranded overnight, could the landing force get the logistics needed to maintain it on the beach.

Fire-support would be provided by two heavy cruisers, two British light cruisers, eight destroyers, and four LSMR. Two marine F4U squadrons (VMF-214 and VMF-323, veterans of the fighting in the perimeter) would provide the bulk of the close air support, flying from CVEs. Navy ADs from the fast carriers would seal off the area and back up the marine squadrons. Although in the event this did not work out, planners hoped to get two light battalions of the 11th Marines into position on Wolmi Do to support the main landings.

As finally worked out and described here, the arrangements for Operation Chromite sound tidy and almost matter-of-fact. Could General Almond have been right after all when he called the landing assault "a simple mechanical operation?" ("It looked simple," General Smith later remarked, "because it was done by experts.")

To work up such a plan – or any plan – in such a time frame was a virtuoso performance. Again resembling Guadalcanal, the subordinate echelons (attack force/landing force) instead of responding to directives from higher headquarters, anticipated and almost completely dominated the plans on higher levels. General Smith issued his Inchon order on 27 August, whereas the X Corps order (theoretically the starting directive for the landing force) didn't come out until three days later and then only when advance drafts of the marines's order had been sent to X Corps to help them along. The final version of Admiral Doyle's numerous drafts was promulgated on 3 September; that of CJTF-7 (Commander Joint Task Force-7) appeared the same day (Admiral Struble wasn't even aware of the forthcoming operation until 22 August and could not get to Tokyo with his staff until the 25th).

General Smith's staff never had a chance to assemble in one place at the same time until after the landing. Part functioned as the marine brigade staff in the perimeter and had to conduct unrelated, hard-fought operations while moonlighting on plans for Inchon. Another echelon (on whom the main planning burden fell) flew with the division commander directly to Japan, while the remainder of the staff had to accompany the seaborne main body from the West Coast (and most of these officers had to stay in Kobe to run loading and embarkation).

In the journal he faithfully kept throughout two wars, General Smith ended his entry for 15 September 1950 with one sentence: *Operations have gone about as planned.* Since this article is concerned with the planning process for Operation Chromite, we can let Gen Smith's note tell the story.

Naturally, no battle really goes that smoothly (it was the elder Moltke who said, "No plan ever survives contact with the enemy") and Inchon was no exception. Generally, however, what Admiral Doyle and General Smith and their expert, highly professional staffs worked out, succeeded quite remarkably. D-day operations were completed on schedule with all objectives taken, at a cost of but 21 killed and 175 wounded. Twelve days later, after heavy fighting in and around Seoul, the Korean capital was reconquered, and – as MacArthur had predicted from beginning to end – the North Korean Peoples Army was destroyed. The *In Min Gun* had been hit so hard and so quickly, from the sea, that it was incapable of reaction or resistance until too late.

Cannae

Down at Green Beach, on Wolmi Do, today stands the only monument erected by Americans to the Inchon landings. Each year on 15 September (for the Koreans do not forget) delegations visit the impressive concrete cenotaph with its bronze plaque to lay wreaths in memory of those who recaptured Inchon and liberated Seoul. The wording of the memorial plaque is simple. It says that here the landing elements of the 7th U.S. Infantry Division landed at Inchon in September (no date given) 1950. Inexplicably, the 3rd Battalion, 5th Marines, whose leading elements landed at this spot three days before the infantry division, at 0633, 15 September 1950, is neither mentioned nor memorialized.

The revisionism implicit in this monument quite aptly bespeaks the larger camouflage of revisionism with which history has draped Operation Chromite. It is curious that so dazzling and decisive a victory should already be near forgotten or remembered only in a haze of inaccuracy.

There has developed, for example, a tendency to downgrade the Inchon-Seoul campaign as a kind of freak – an operation that shouldn't have succeeded but did. Was Chromite somehow unworthy because closely calculated long odds paid off? Taking MacArthur's hyperbole of 23 August that the odds against success were 5,000 to 1, writers who should know better have used this figure of speech as a serious basis for saying that Inchon was a mere gamble and next to foolhardy at that. How much wiser, instead of meaningless quantifications like 5,000 to 1, to view the operation with Admiral Doyle's informed conservatism as "not impossible." Speaking to somewhat the same point, O. P. Smith later said: "We had a break at Inchon, all right – we had the know-how."

Operation Chromite changed the entire course of the war. In immediate results alone, MacArthur's lightning campaign accomplished the following:

- It caused the disintegration of the North Korean perimeter about Pusan.
- By liberating Seoul and dislocating the Communist logistical system, it effected the destruction of the *In Min Gun*.
- It returned the United Nations to the 38th parallel and thus preserved the Republic of Korea.

Inchon must therefore by considered a masterpiece. Whether in virtuosity of execution, or – at the chill altitude of high command – as a Napoleonic example of nerve and acceptance of calculated risk, Inchon remains, in the words of David Rees, "a Twentieth-Century Cannae, ever to be studied."

More important than these military judgments, Inchon underscored in 1950 what America had nearly forgotten in the five years since its hour of greatest victory – what, indeed, it often forgets, save when it needs a victory – that America is a maritime power, that its weapon is the trident, and its strategy that of the oceans. Only through the sure and practiced exercise of sea power could this awkward war in a remote place have been turned upside down in a few days. As Thomas More Molyneux, author of one of the earliest complete works on amphibious warfare, wrote in 1759:

> A Military, Naval Littoral War, when wifely prepared and discreetly conducted, is a terrible Sort of War. Happy for that People who are Sovereigns enough of the Sea to put it into Execution! For it comes like Thunder and lightning to some unprepared Part of the World.

A FEATHER IN THEIR CAP? THE MARINES' COMBINED ACTION PROGRAM IN VIETNAM

Lawrence A. Yates

> *The Marine Corps has long touted the success of its Combined Action Platoons in Vietnam. Some prominent proponents of the program, such as retired Marine general Victor Krulak, have argued that a campaign to "win the hearts and minds" of the Vietnamese peasantry would have proven more successful in winning the war than the attrition strategy implemented by Army General Westmoreland. Dr. Yates, a historian from the Army's Combat Studies Institute, provides a more critical perspective on the Combined Action Program and argues that the effectiveness of this approach in Vietnam has not yet received enough critical examination.*

British counterinsurgency expert Sir Robert Thompson praised it as "the best idea I have seen in Vietnam"; U.S. Army Major General William DePuy dismissed it as "counterinsurgency of the deliberate, mild sort." The object of these conflicting assessments was the Combined Action Program (CAP) employed by the U.S. Marine Corps in Vietnam from 1965 to 1971. CAP united "a Marine rifle squad with a Vietnamese Popular Force platoon to provide village security and pacification in Vietnam."(1) The controversy the program generated from its inception persists today in the historiographical debate over the appropriate use of American military power against the Vietcong (VC) and North Vietnamese army (NVA). That debate is not going to be resolved any time soon. The purpose of this article is more modest: to outline the origins and evolution of CAP, to discuss some aspects of the CAP experience, and to conclude with a few observations relating CAP to the small wars tradition of the Marine Corps.

The Combined Action Program was the product of military necessity and strategic preference.(2) The primary mission of the marine combat forces that entered South Vietnam in the spring and summer of 1965 was to provide base security for the three enclaves they occupied in the I Corps Tactical Zone, comprising the country's five northern provinces. In the marine Tactical Areas of Responsibility (TAOR) at Phu Bai, Da Nang, and Chu Lai, U.S. military installations were vulnerable to attack from nearby hamlets and villages controlled, as was most of the rural population in I Corps, by the Vietcong. To secure the Phu Bai TAOR, marines and the local, part-time Vietnamese militia known as Poi Forces (PFs) formed a Joint Action Company.(3) In the fall of 1965, this improvised unit sent patrols into the area around the area and placed integrated platoons containing both marines and PFs in four villages north of Phu Bai in order to disrupt Vietcong activities and to obtain much needed intelligence. The success of this combined effort impressed Major General Lewis Walt, commander of the III Marine

Amphibious Force (III MAF). In November, Walt authorized similar operations in support of base security around Da Nang; in January 1966 he and his Vietnam counterpart extended the program of integrated operations by marines and PFs to all marine TAOR in I Corps.(4)

By this time, according to the *Pentagon Papers*, the Marine Corps "to a degree then unequalled among other American units was deeply engaged in pacification operations."(5) These endeavors undertaken in I Corps largely on III MAF's own initiative, quickly involved key marine officers in a stormy debate with the army-dominated U.S. Military Assistance Command Vietnam (MACV) over the appropriate strategy for winning the war. In articulating the marines' emphasis on pacification, Lieutenant General Victor Krulak, commanding general, Fleet Marine Force Pacific (FMFPac), contended that the "Vietnam conflict ultimately has to be decided among the people in the villages of South Vietnam," a point the Communists understood all too well, if MACV did not. In Krulak's opinion, MACV's war of attrition against North Vietnamese and Vietcong main forces was not only counterproductive, given the enormous pool of Communist manpower, but also largely irrelevant to the more important war being waged by the Vietcong political cadre and guerrillas for the support of the people. The people's loyalty, Krulak argued, was the "real prize" in the conflict; and to win the prize, Saigon and the United States had to put "the full weight of our top level effort into bringing all applicable resources…into the pacification process."

Krulak specifically recommended that the United States and South Vietnam neutralize VC political cadre in the villages and "comb the guerrillas out of the people's lives," thus denying the Vietcong food, sanctuary and intelligence. At the same time, to overcome the "provincialism" of the Vietnamese people and to help "win their allegiance and loyalty in an unbroken governmental chain stretching from the hamlet to Saigon," the United States had to "press" its ally to launch a major land reform program. The creation of a strong society also required reforms in health, education, agriculture, transportation, and communications – areas in which the U.S. military could play a direct role through the introduction of civic action programs. Americans were "far more efficient at civic action than the Vietnamese officialdom," Krulak judged, because they were "more aggressive, more resourceful, more compassionate and less venal." In I Corps the marines already had begun introducing a variety of civic action projects into coastal villages where most of the rural population lived. There was little hope, however, that these programs – much less more fundamental reforms – would succeed unless the people could be guaranteed protection from Communist reprisals. Emphasizing that "if the enemy cannot get to the people, he cannot win," Krulak concluded that "it is therefore the people whom we must protect as a matter of first business."(6)

All participants in the strategy debate of 1965 acknowledged this cardinal rule of counterinsurgency, but disagreed sharply over whose mission it was to provide village security. General William Westmoreland, the MACV commander, paid lip service to pacification, but in his commitment to waging a war of attrition against enemy main forces took the position that he "simply had not enough numbers to put a squad of Americans in every village and hamlet."(7) The marines for their part were conducting small-unit offensives to clear their expanding TAOR of VC cadre and guerrillas, but these operations were not designed to provide permanent security for the villages and hamlets.(8) Many Americans argued persuasively that it was up to the South Vietnamese to secure areas cleared by U.S. forces, but the Army of the Republic of Vietnam (ARVN) evinced little enthusiasm or aptitude for taking on the "village war."(9)

That left South Vietnamese Regional Forces (RFs) and PFs to perform the task. Of the two, the local volunteers known as PFs, who were organized into squads and platoons to defend the villages in which they lived, seemed ideally situated for the mission. The drawback was that, because they fell at the bottom of the South Vietnamese military hierarchy, PFs suffered the contempt and neglect of those above them. They consequently lacked leadership, motivation, discipline, training, and equipment. But home defense, the marines argued, gave the PFs a "powerful motivation potential."(10) The question was whether that potential could be realized. The experience with combined operations around Phi Bai and Da Nang in 1965 held out the promise that, under marine tutelage, the PFs could perform effectively. The mission of providing twenty-four-hour protection to villages and hamlets in I Corps thus fell to an expanded Combined Action Program. What had started as a limited experiment for the defense of U.S. military bases became the linchpin in 1966 in the marines' pacification strategy for winning the war.

On paper the CAP concept appeared simple and effective, marriage between marine tradition and the peculiar circumstances of Vietnam.(11) The critical unit in the program was the Combine Action Platoon,(12) formed by integrating a marine rifle squad of fourteen volunteers and a navy corpsman into a PF platoon of thirty-five men. Although district chiefs and their subordinate village chiefs retained control of PF units, the marine squad leader (a sergeant or in some cases a corporal) served as an adviser to the PF platoon leader and assumed de facto command of the platoon during combat operations. The remainder of the marine squad (three four-man fire teams, not including the navy corpsman and a marine grenadier attached to platoon headquarters) merged with the three rifle squads of a PF platoon. The marine fire team leaders served as squad leaders in the CAP platoon.

Once activated, a Combined Action Platoon lived in a compound built in or near a hamlet of the home village of the PFs. According to official accounts of the program, "Marine members of the CAP live in the same tents, eat the same food, and conduct the same patrols and ambushes as their Vietnamese counterparts." When not engaged in combat operations, the marines trained PFs in military fundamentals and counterguerrilla methods and offered advice on civic action projects proposed by village officials. The PFs, in return, furthered the marines' education in the language and customs of the people, provided knowledge of the terrain, and passed along vital intelligence. Marine leaders presumed that this interaction would encourage mutual trust and respect, both between the marines and PFs and between the marines and the villagers. As the inhabitants of a village grew accustomed to the marine presence and came to realize that the CAP platoon would not depart each day before sundown, they would gradually welcome the Americans into the community and provide information to help the platoon destroy the local Vietcong infrastructure and keep guerrilla bands at bay. Progress could then be made in improving living conditions in the village and in making the basic reforms that would shift the people's loyalty to the national government.

Once a village attained a respectable level of stability and the PFs acquired a high degree of military proficiency the marines could move on to a new community in need of protection. As the marines spread outward from minimally contested villages in their enclaves, they would, through an "oil spot" effect, create a security network that would gradually cover all of the highly populated coastal region in I Corps. The VC, isolated from the population, would become little more than a military nuisance, the insurgency would wither, and the marines could depart the country, "leaving behind a more substantial Vietnamese rural security structure."(13)

The CAP concept was ambitious. Whether or not the marines could implement it successfully depended in part on their ability to activate more Combined Action Platoons. The marines wanted III MAF to have 74 CAP platoons in the field by the end of 1966, but had to settle for 57 when confronted simultaneously with a Buddhist rebellion against the Saigon government, the reluctance of many district chiefs to assign PFs to the program, and large-unit operations that drained marine manpower. A variety of other disruptions, including the demilitarized zone (DMZ) campaign, the siege of Khe Sanh, and the 1968 Tet Offensive similarly delayed realization of the 1967 goal of 114 CAP platoons until 1969, the peak year for the program.

As the number of platoons increased, III MAF made administrative changes and reorganized command and control relationships. In 1967, for example, the program acquired Table of Organization and Equipment (TO&E) status, and Lieutenant General Robert Cushman, the new III MAF commander, placed CAP under the supervision of his deputy. Under this arrangement operational control of CAP marines was transferred from line units to Combined Action Companies (CACOs) and, at the next higher echelon, to newly created Combined Action Groups (CAGs). In January 1970 III MAF created the short-lived Combined Action Force (CAF) as a headquarters with command status for the four CAGs then in existence; CAF was deactivated that September as part of the troop withdrawal from Vietnam. As the marines added tiers in the CAP chain of command, the lines of coordination and control with the Vietnamese involved in the program invariably became more complex as well.(14)

Despite the magnitude of these changes and the added bureaucratic layers brought about by the expansion of CAP; the mission of the CAP platoon remained by and large unchanged. That mission had six parts: "destroy the Vietcong hamlet-village infrastructure; provide public security and help maintain law and order; protect the local governing structure; guard facilities and important lines of communications within the village and hamlet; organize local intelligence nets; and participate in civic action and psychological operations against the Vietcong." The marines in the platoon had additional missions: "conduct training in general military subjects and leadership for Popular Forces assigned to the platoon; motivate, instill pride, patriotism, and aggressiveness in the Popular Force soldier; conduct combined day and night patrols and ambushes; conduct combined operations with other allied forces; and ensure that information gathered was made available to nearby allied forces."(15)

Statistics were amassed by III MAF and FMFPac to prove that the Combined Action Program was an unqualified success. The basis for these statistics was a monthly reporting system initiated by General Walt in February 1966 that attempted to quantify "indicators" of pacification within a village. Although this system was replaced within a year by the more sophisticated Hamlet Evaluation System, both methods, according to FMFPac, confirmed the accomplishments of CAP.(16) CAP villages, for example, allegedly achieved high degrees of pacification much more rapidly than villages without CAP marines. FMFPac assessments of counterguerrilla operations further concluded that PFs belonging to CAP platoons enjoyed lower desertion rates and higher kill ratios and generated better intelligence than PFs working without marine supervision. In support of its figures and charts, FMFPac cited numerous examples of successful CAP field operations and constantly hammered home the point that "the clearest evidence of CAP effectiveness is the fact that the Vietcong have never been able to reestablish control over a village occupied by a CAP platoon."(17)

Critics then and later have regarded the mass of data and glowing reports of CAP activities as "Krulak's fables," mere propaganda in the continuing debate over strategy between the marines and MACV. The authors of the *Pentagon Papers* charged that "the Marine strategy was judged successful, at least by the Marines, long before it had even had a real test." Others questioned the methods used in compiling the statistics or asked whether it was even possible to quantify what in fact was a state of mind – a villager's sense of security or "a man's devotion to a cause." Also, the figures could be misleading. It was possible, a marine colonel claimed, for CAP marines to accumulate enough points on a survey to classify their village as "pacified," when in reality the Vietcong infrastructure, the most important of Walt's indicators, remained virtually undisturbed.(18)

It would be a mistake to dismiss FMFPac reports about CAP out of hand: many CAP platoons achieved significant successes in counterguerrilla operations and civic action. Still, the critics are correct in saying that the reports ignored or glossed over serious problems besetting the program, beginning with the recruitment and preparation of CAP marines. Initially, marines entering the program were to be combat-tested volunteers from line units – mature troops dedicated to helping the Vietnamese and free of xenophobia, racial prejudice, and other undesirable characteristics. To be sure, many such individuals volunteered, but others signed up to land what was perceived as a soft job, to escape the boredom of rear area duties, or to leave behind problems they encountered in their line units. Still other marines were "volunteered" by commanding officers who, reluctant to relinquish their best men to CAP, sent misfits and other "problem" leathernecks instead. The CAP screening process detected many of the unmotivated and undesirable candidates for the program, but others slipped through "perfunctory" interviews by saying what was expected of them – "pretending to Christian sufferance and forgiveness," as one of the less committed marines put it.(19)

Once screened, CAP marines were to receive at least two weeks of instruction in counterguerrilla skills and Vietnamese customs and language before joining their PF platoons. Judging from the testimony of a very small proportion of the marines who served in the program, it would appear, however, that a significant number of recruits either did not attend the course or found it wanting, especially with respect to language training, the program's "most glaring weakness."(20) For these marines CAP became an "earn while you learn" proposition in which the platoon itself provided the skills and knowledge they needed to survive and succeed.

It was not uncommon for a CAP platoon, once activated, to suffer supply and manpower shortages. Until the program attained TO&E status, it relied largely on marine or army line units for supplies. These units jealously guarded their materiel, making logistics an erratic and frustrating experience for CAP. To acquire equipment needed for operations, base protection, and civic action, CAP marines scrounged, begged, borrowed, bartered, and, not infrequently, resorted to "midnight requisitions."(21)

The same combination of initiative and ingenuity could not so readily correct the manpower deficit that plagued some CAP platoons. It was not uncommon for the PF contingent to be well below the thirty-five-man norm. A district or village chief, operating on his own agenda or punishing the marines for some slight, could withdraw PFs from the program without warning. Furthermore, PFs, as part-time militia, were not always present for duty. The marines themselves, particularly in the early days of the program and later during the withdrawal of American forces from Vietnam, frequently had to operate with rifle squads that were under strength and led by very young corporals. These conditions adversely affected the ability of CAP platoons to perform their missions and, more important, made it more difficult for them to defend against enemy attack.

Even under the best of conditions, a full-strength, forty-nine-man platoon could not by itself hope to defeat a large VC or NVA unit. While trying to keep the enemy at bay, CAP platoons would call in fire support from nearby bases and wait for reaction forces from line units or CACOs to arrive. Without outside support, compounds were often overrun. Indeed, so frequently were they overrun during the Tet Offensive that CAP platoons sought to reduce their vulnerability by operating thereafter as mobile units without a fixed base. The decision was controversial, since many marines regarded the compound as a symbol of CAP's twenty-four-hour presence and the "focal point for civic action." Proponents of the mobile concept countered that abandoning the "siege mentality" of the compound led to more frequent and meaningful contact with villagers, thus compensating for the decline in civic action projects.(22)

The vulnerability of CAP platoons exacerbated another sensitive issue: the relationship between CAP units and regular line units. According to the operating tenets of pacification strategy, the two forces were supposed to complement one another. CAP platoons would secure villages while marine or other friendly battalions maneuvered to clear the area of organized enemy forces. In the course of operations, line units would benefit from the intelligence and the knowledge of local conditions provided by the CAP platoons, while those platoons relied on line units for fire support and reaction forces should enemy troops in the vicinity of a CAP village attack.

What should have been a complementary relationship often degenerated into a fractious affair characterized by feelings ranging from ambivalence to outright hostility. Troops in line units constantly on the move resented what they perceived as the "easy" life of the stationary CAP marines who had "gone Asiatic"; moreover, battalion commanders fumed when they had to divert men and weapons to "bail out" a CAP platoon under fire, often under conditions only vaguely known to the troops mounting the relief mission. CAP marines countered by charging that line units ignored vital intelligence, provided only erratic support, and worst of all, failed to understand the nature of pacification. The mission of the battalion was to find and kill the enemy. The line marine regarded villages as combat zones, not pacification areas, and the people living in the villages as possible enemies, not potential friends. Generally insensitive to the needs of the inhabitants and often emotionally taut from the dangers and frustrations of field operations, line marines entering a CAP village posed a threat to the program. Whether inadvertently trampling on a garden or deliberately beating a VC suspect, the unwelcome intruders could wreck in minutes the progress CAP platoons had made over many mouths.(23)

Although CAP personnel often saw themselves as protecting villagers from friendly as well as Communist forces, the available evidence suggests that many of the CAP marines themselves had difficulty understanding the people and the society they were defending and, through pacification, trying to change. Virtually all marines entering the program brought with them the cultural baggage of Western society. CAP schools could impart – at least to those who attended them – a cursory overview of Vietnamese history politics, society, and culture, together with guidelines for what constituted proper behavior in the traditional society of the rural village. But in the time allotted, instructors could not begin to explain how customs varied from province to province or to analyze adequately the complex interactions in an agrarian society; the instructors could only hope that the marines in time would develop a higher level of toleration and understanding for a belief and value system quite different from their own. For eighteen-year-old marines, this was a tall order. Consequently, as one CAP veteran has observed, marines and PFs met "across a deep cultural gulf."(24)

That gulf often became deeper after marines joined a PF platoon. Sanitary conditions and the personal hygiene of the Vietnamese appalled many of the Americans who were assigned to CAP platoons. Moreover, the soap and toiletries ordered by the marines to alleviate the situation often ended up on the black market or in the possession of crooked officials. Corruption seemed endemic and in some locales contaminated the PFs who, as local henchmen of the district or province chiefs, ran "mafia-like" operations in which they used their paramilitary status to eliminate or intimidate the competition. Theft was another source of friction in some CAP villages, as PFs made off with rations, equipment, and personal items left unguarded by the marines. Recurring thefts generated ill feelings that occasionally led to incidents of threatened or actual violence. Less likely to cause violence but equally troubling to CAP marines were the rigid sexual mores of the Vietnamese villagers. Warned that "premarital sex is forbidden, but mutual masturbation by members of the same sex is not," marines were advised that it might be better to "acquiesce" in "what might seem to us homosexual advances" rather than "create an incident." One CAP marine probably spoke for all in observing that "one can expect an average group of young Marines to go only so far above and beyond the call of duty."(25)

Cultural differences reinforced marine complaints about the military dedication and prowess of the PFs. Rumor had it that PF platoons had been infiltrated by the Vietcong or at least had reached an understanding with the enemy about what was permissible in the conduct of military operations. Thus, many marines began their association with PFs by "trusting none of them." If the PFs subsequently failed to respond to training or did not carry their weight in the field, suspicion and distrust turned readily into dislike and contempt. By the time a marine finished his CAP tour, it was not uncommon for him to look upon the PFs "with a real sense of violence." This hostility was easily transferred to the villagers in general, with marines deliberately violating various taboos just "to get a rise out of the PFs" and those sullen Vietnamese who regarded the Americans not as saviors but as an occupation force. Surveys conducted in Vietnam in the late 1960s revealed racial prejudice ("Luke the Gook") and strong anti-Vietnamese feelings on the part of a significant number, albeit a minority of marines.(26)

This picture of mutual animosity can be overdrawn. There were, to be sure, CAP villages where the marines and PFs worked together well, each learning from the other; where marines were gradually, if not totally accepted into the community; and where the people assisted the CAP platoons in civic action and counterinsurgency campaigns. There were also marines who came to accept, if not fully comprehend, that PFs who resorted to theft did so out of economic hardship and familial responsibility; that corruption can be found in any society and in South Vietnam, if kept within limits, was regarded as acceptable and even as a mark of status; that family ties were key to a way of life based on a complex set of personal, impersonal, and mystical relationships; and that in the provincial world of the village, nationalism had little meaning except to a small, educated elite. "Outside Saigon and a few other places," one CAP marine recently noted, "there was no South Vietnam."(27) Caught in the middle of an ideological war in which neutrality could prompt severe retribution, villagers who otherwise might believe they had no stake in the conflict often ended up assisting the Vietcong out of a sense of self-preservation or because relatives, through persuasion or coercion, had joined the VC. Many CAP marines understood such arrangements and bore no grudge against the hapless victims of the war.

Nevertheless, the conflict, whatever its impact on village society, remained a fact of life, and it was the duty of CAP platoons to help sway the outcome. Both sides, through greatly divergent means, sought to transform traditional Vietnamese society into a modern nation-state. With a strong faith in the universal applicability of Western ideals and institutions and in the efficacy of reform and social engineering, CAP marines tried to convince villagers that an increasingly responsive government in Saigon offered the best blueprint for a more equitable, prosperous, and secure life. The effort was well intentioned, but good intentions could only effect so much: they could often atone for inadvertent breaches of village etiquette, but they could not transform overnight, or even in a few years, what history had taken centuries to set in place. Although progress in the village war *was* being made by 1971, the extent of that progress was, and still is, difficult to assess.

Amid this uncertainty, the last CAP platoon was deactivated in 1971, as Americans gradually withdrew from Vietnam. Supporters of the program have argued then and since that, had the CAP concept been applied throughout South Vietnam, the war's outcome might have been different. This seems an exaggerated claim, given the problems – both niggling and profound – that plagued the program. The question remains: What can be said about a program that engaged only a few thousand marines and left behind scant testimony as to its successes and failures? While some generalizations are possible, they do not always prove as illuminating as one might wish. There were good and bad, successful and unsuccessful CAP platoons. Accomplishments varied depending on such factors as time, place, and personnel, not to mention a host of other variables that were beyond the control of CAP marines. When engaged in counterguerrilla operations, CAP platoons often disrupted enemy activities, but few CAP units claimed to have eliminated the VC infrastructure from their respective villages. The effectiveness of PF training varied from one CAP platoon to another, allowing some CAP marines to relocate to new villages, but leaving others in place for the duration of the war. Moreover, despite the reforms and self-help programs that were introduced to improve the lives of the villagers, the persistence of traditional patterns of behavior caused many marines to demand in frustration, "Why do you do that? This is crazy!" The cultural gap, one CAP marine concluded, was simply "Unbridgeable."(28)

Marines who had conducted counterguerrilla operations, trained indigenous troops, and engaged in pacification programs in Latin America from 1915 to 1934 would have empathized with this sense of frustration. There, as in Vietnam, ethnocentrism came into conflict with alien cultures, as leathernecks tried to bring stability to Hispaniola and Nicaragua. The Chesty Pullers and Smedley Butlers of the small wars era fared reasonably well against the guerrilla bands arrayed against them, but they could not impose stability based on the type of representative democracy, free enterprise, egalitarianism, and military professionalism found in the United States. By the time the marines departed the area in the mid-1930s, they had come to recognize the limited effectiveness of American power and the limited applicability of American institutions in what would later be labeled Third World countries. The frustrations encountered in Haiti and Nicaragua dampened enthusiasm for pursuing the effort elsewhere.

This "lesson," however, did not find its way into the marines' professional journals, school curricula, or *Small Wars Manual*. The latter, for example, addressed the social and economic causes of revolution and explained how marines should interact with native populations, but it also perpetuated the notion that countries in the throes of revolutionary upheaval could be stabilized through the infusion of Western-style reforms.(29) Ethnocentrism toward the Third World remained undiluted when the United States entered Vietnam a quarter of a century later. As Edward Lansdale, one of the architects of that intervention, unabashedly avowed, "I took my American beliefs into these Asian struggles."(30) So, too, did most American policymakers and soldiers, however sophisticated their appreciation of the complex dynamics and nuances of Vietnamese society. In time hubris again yielded to disillusionment and frustration, much as it had at the end of the "banana wars" in Latin America. What the United States could not do in Haiti and the Dominican Republic – that is, restructure both countries according to an American blueprint – stood even less chance of succeeding in Vietnam. The United States had enjoyed complete control of an occupied country in Hispaniola. That was not the case in Vietnam, however. There Americans fought in an alien setting on behalf of a sovereign government that until the eleventh hour seemed unwilling or, perhaps more accurately, unable for fear of losing its hold on power to enact programs with enough grassroots appeal to win the allegiance of a large portion of the citizenry.

Just as the lessons of America's small wars in the first half of this century failed to prevent an encore performance in Vietnam, the "lesson" of Vietnam concerning the risks involved in trying to build nations for governments of countries fundamentally different from the United States is likely to be forgotten in the long term. A belief in the universal appeal and applicability of the American way of life is too deeply ingrained in the American character to expect otherwise. Despite what happened in Vietnam, Americans have not lost faith in the "middle way," that path of moderate and progressive reform through which the United States can lead the world to peace and harmony, while fending off the dangers of reaction on the Right and revolution on the Left.

It is in the context of ethnocentrism and cultural conflict that one must approach an assessment of the Combined Action Program. Many of the problems CAP encountered in Vietnam can be attributed to organizational growing pains. At the same time CAP was a small, but significant, part of a broader strategy that, despite its admirable intentions, was predicated on the existence of the "middle way" in Vietnam, that is, on the efficacy and relevance of American-style solutions. If the "middle way" existed at all, it contained so many obstacles that it could not be traversed easily or quickly. Given time, pacification might have worked; but time ran out. Alternative strategies appeared unattractive, so the Americans departed, the CAP platoons disbanded. Whether the Combined Action Program should be resurrected in another country under different circumstances is problematical. The possibility should not be dismissed out of hand. But before this innovative approach to local security is applied to another counterinsurgency effort, the CAP experience in Vietnam should be studied at length. For if the guiding strategy is infused with ethnocentrism and minimizes cultural differences, the prospects for the success of another Combined Action Program in the future would seem bleak.

NOTES

1. Thompson and Depuy quoted in Andrew Krepinevich, Jr., *The Army and Vietnam* (Baltimore, 1986), 174-75. The definition of CAP is taken from Bruce C. Allnutt, *Marine Combined Action Capabilities: The Vietnam Experience* (McLean, Va., 1969).
2. On the origins of the Combined Action Program, see Fleet Marine Force, Pacific (FMFPac), *The Marine combined Action Program Vietnam*, n.d. [but covers CAP from August 1965 through January 1967], in FMFPac documents, U.S. Marine Corps Historical Center, Washington, D.C.(hereafter cited as USMCHC); "Joint Action Company," in Third Battalion, Fourth Marines Command Chronology, September-October 1965, USMCHC; Jack Shulimson and Charles M. Johnson, *U.S. Marines in Vietnam: The Landing and the Buildup, 1965* (Washington, 1978), 133-38; Robert A. Klyman, "The Combined Action Program: An Alternative Not Taken" (Honors thesis, University of Michigan, 1986), 6-16; Michael E. Peterson, *The Combined Action Platoons: The US. Marines' Other War in Vietnam* (New York, 1989), 21-29; Allan R. Millett, *Semper Fidelis: The History of the United States Marine Corps* (New York, 1980), 560-66, 571-72.
3. In late 1965 the designation Joint Action Company was changed to Combined Action Company in accordance with military terminology that defines U.S. military operations with troops of another country as "combined" operations.
4. On expanding combined marine and PF operations throughout marine enclaves in I Corps, see Lewis W. Walt to Commanding General, I Corps, 5 January 1966; Lieutenant General Nguyen Chanh Thi to Commanding General, III MAF, 28 January 1966; Thi to various subordinates, 28 January 1966; Walt to Commanding Officer, I Corps Advisory Group, 4 February 1966; and Walt to Commanding General, Third Marine Division, 4 February 1966 – all attached to FMFPac, *Marine Combined Action Program Vietnam*. Note that in early 1966, the term "Combined Action Program" had not gained wide currency. As late as 1967 CAP and CAC (Combined Action Company) were often used interchangeably.
5. U.S. Congress, Senate Subcommittee on Public Buildings and Grounds, *The Pentagon Papers: The Defense Department History of United States Decision Making on Vietnam* (The Senator Gravel Edition), 4 vols. (Boston, 1975), 2:534.
6. Victor Krulak, "A Strategic Appraisal," December 1965, in Robert A. Klyman Papers, USMCHC. While my text relies on this paper to describe the marine approach to pacification, additional information can be found in Shulimson and Johnson, *Landing and Buildup*, 37-39, 46-48, 133-46; Neil Sheehan, *A Bright Shining Lie: John Paul Vann and America in Vietnam* (New York, 1988), 629-38; FMFPac, Operations of the III Marine Amphibious Force, USMCHC. Originally classified secret, the FMFPac volumes contain monthly reports, each of which includes a section on the pacification program. See also "III MAF Civic Action Summary," December 1965, Klyman Papers, USMCHC; Russel H. Stolfi, *U.S. Marine Corps Civic Action Efforts in Vietnam March 1965 – March 1966* (Washington, 1968); Shulimson and Johnson, *Landing and Buildup*, 37-39, 46-48, 133-46; Jack Shulimson, *US. Marines in Vietnam: An Expanding War, 1966* (Washington, 1981), 11-15, 229-58; Millett, *Semper Fidelis*, 566-71.
7. William C. Westmoreland, *A Soldier Reports* (Garden City, N.Y., 1976), 166. Similarly, Westmoreland argued, "Had I had at my disposal virtually unlimited manpower, I could have stationed troops permanently in every district or province and thus provided an alternative strategy. That would have enabled the troops to get to know the people intimately, facilitating the task of identifying the subversives and protecting the others against intimidation." Ibid., 147. The debate over strategy should not be seen in terms of the army versus the Marine Corps. Not all marine officers shared Krulak's views, while within the army a study commissioned by the chief of staff of the army challenged Westmoreland's attrition strategy. According to this study completed in March 1966, "Present US military actions against Communist regiments are inconsistent with that fundamental of counterinsurgency doctrine which establishes winning popular allegiance as the ultimate goal." Reference to this document, known as the PROVN study, together with a critique of Westmoreland's handling of the war can be found in Guenter Lewy, *America in Vietnam* (New York, 1978), 77-126. See also Millett, *Semper Fidelis*, 548-49; Reports, Commandant of the Marine Corps to Secretary, Joint Chiefs of Staff, "Status of the Development of Counter-guerrilla Forces," 1 February 1962 and 13 March 1962, Records of the U.S. Joint Chiefs of Staff, 1961, Record Group 218, 3360 Unconventional Warfare (10 February 1961) files, National Archives, Washington, D.C.

8. For marine small-unit counterguerrilla operations during the first two years of the war, see *U.S. Marine Corps Forces in Vietnam, March 1965 – September 1967: Historical Summary*, vol. 1, *Narrative*, USMCHC.

9. Millett, *Semper Fidelis*, 571; Lewy, *American in Vietnam*, 87-88, 97. In October 1966 Secretary of Defense Robert McNamara complained that ARVN had still not fully committed itself to the pacification program. *Pentagon Papers*, 4:350-51.

10. This description and assessment of the PFs is taken from FMFPac, *Marine Combined Action Program Vietnam*, 3-5.

11. Many marines regarded CAP as a direct descendant of programs the corps employed to train native constabularies in Haiti, the Dominican Republic, and Nicaragua during the 1920s and 1930s. Shulimson and Johnson note, however, that Combined Action Platoons were much more a "cooperative effort" than the "Marine-officered" units of the "banana war" era. *Landing and Buildup*, 134-35.

12. The Combined Action Program and the Combined Action Platoon share the same acronym, CAP. For the sake of clarity, I will use the acronym solely in reference to the former and refer to the latter as "CAP platoon(s)."

13. For a more detailed description of the organization and methods of the Combined Action Platoon, see FMFPac, Marine Combined Action Program Vietnam; Lt. Col. W. R. Corson, USMC, "Marine Combined Action Program in Vietnam," n.d. [1967], USMCHC.

14. Details regarding the expansion of CAP can be found in the FMFPac monthly reports and in the CAF and CAG command chronologies, as well as those of the line units that prior to October 1967 had operational control over CAP platoons. These documents are located at the Marine Corps Historical Center. For cogent summaries of CAP's growth, see Klyman, "Combined Action Program," 12-43, and Peterson, *Combined Action Platoons*, 31-83. See also, Shulimson, *Expanding War*, 239-43; Gary L. Telfer, Lane Rogers, and V. Keith Fleming, Jr., *U.S. Marines in Vietnam: Fighting the North Vietnamese, 1967* (Washington, 1984), 186-94; Charles R. Smith, *US. Marines in Vietnam: High Mobility and Standdown, 1969* (Washington, 1988), 288-94; Graham A. Cosmas and Terrence P. Murray, *US. Marines in Vietnam: Vietnamization and Redeployment, 1970-1971* (Washington, 1986), 139-61.

15. Smith, *High Mobility and Standdown*, 290-91. See also FMFPac, Operations of the III MAF, January 1967, 37.

16. Walt's system was based on five "progress indicators": destruction of enemy units; destruction of enemy infrastructure; government of Vietnam (GVN) establishment of security; GVN establishment of local government; degree of development of new life program. Each indicator received a value of twenty points and was broken down into related subdivisions. A score of sixty points indicated "firm GVN/U.S. influence," while a score of eighty points indicated pacification. The Hamlet Evaluation System was developed by the CIA to provide a uniform measure of progress throughout Vietnam. It "borrowed freely" from the marine system, but differed in several respects. According to FMFPac, however, the two systems reinforced one another and led to the same conclusions. Shulimson, *Expanding War*, 257-58. Allan Millett notes in his history of the Marine Corps that "a more sophisticated system of evaluating hamlet security showed that much of the Marine civic action program had produced no lasting GVN control." *Semper Fidelis*, 575.

17. FMFPac, Marine Combined Action Program Vietnam, 3, 7-17; FMFPac, Operations of the III MAF, monthly reports, 1966-1971.

18. *Pentagon Papers*, 2:535; Shulimson, *Expanding War*, 258; Klyman, "Combined Action Program," 3, 17-18, 77-78 n. 6. The marine colonel may have been exaggerating his point. According to Shulimson, each indicator "was dependent on the other, providing a balance to the total picture." In other words, a high score in four of the five indicators (needed to reach the eighty-point level) could not be achieved unless progress had been made in the area of the fifth indicator. Another complaint, however, has been that the determination of points for any given indicator was based as much on guesswork as solid analysis. Shulimson, *Expanding War*, 257; Klyman, "Combined Action Program," 77-78 n. 6.

19. Peterson, *Combined Action Platoons*, 32-34, 48. Peterson indicates that many volunteers came not from line units but from combat support and combat service support units. See also Klynian, "Combined Action Program," 19, 28, 37-39; David Sherman, "One Man's CAP," *Marine Corps Gazette* 73 (February 1989): 58; Edward E Palm, "Tiger Papa Three: A Memoir of the Combined Action Program," pt. 1, *Marine Corps*

Gazette 72 (January 1988): 369737; Edward Palm to Major Charles Driest, USMC, 5 January 1989, copy in author's possession; Harry A. Scarr, et al., *Marine Combined Action Capabilities: Training for Future Contingencies* (McLean, Va., 1971), C 9-10; James DuGuid interview, San Francisco, Calif., 14 October 1984; Col. Byron F. Brady interview, San Francisco, Calif., 12 October 1986; Eugene H. Ferguson interview, San Francisco, Calif., 13 October 1984; Igor Bobrowsky interview, San Francisco, Calif., 3 December 1982 – transcripts of each of the above interviews at USMCHC.

20. Klyman, "Combined Action Program," 23-25; Peterson, *Combined Action Platoons*, 24, 48; Sherman, "One Man's CAP," 58; DuGuid, Ferguson, Bobrowsky interviews. Palm recalled of his language training that "we went off to our respective villages armed with the Vietnamese equivalent of *La plume de ma tante* and other useless phrases." Another marine recalled that the Vietnamese dialect taught in the CAP school at Da Nang was of no use to him in his assigned village south of the base. Palm, "Tiger Papa Three," Pt. 1, 37-38; Scarr, et al., *Combined Action Capabilities*, C 34.

21. Peterson, *Combined Action Platoons*, 36, 47; William F. Lockridge interview San Francisco, Calif., 13 October 1984, copy at USMCHC; C.W. Miller taped telephone interview with Maj. Driest, 1988, notes from tape in author's possession.

22. Klyman, "Combined Action Program," 30-34, 45-46, 73 n. 14; Peterson, *Combined Action Platoons*, 56-62; "A Discussion of the Mobile CAP Concept," Enclosure 7 to "Fact Sheet on the Combined Action Force," 31 March 1970, FMFPac Records, USMCHC; Scar; et al., *Marine Combined Action Capabilities*, C 20; DuGoid, Brady, Ferguson, Bobrowsky interviews. A graphic account of a CAP compound being overrun is contained in F. West, Jr., *The Village* (New York, 1972), 1059727. DuGuid noted that he had yet to meet a CAP marine whose compound was not overrun.

23. Peterson, *Combined Action Platoons*, 35-38; Klyman, "Combined Action Program," 22; author's conversations with Jack Shulimson, Washington Navy Yard, 19 July 1989, and Brig. Gen. E. H. Simmons, USMC (Ret.), Washington Navy Yard, 20 July 1989; Brady, Miller, Ferguson, and Bobrowski) interviews.

24. Palm, "Tiger Papa Three," pt. 1, 35.

25. Peterson, *Combined Action Platoons*, 44-45, "97", 104; Palm, "Tiger Papa Three," pt. 1, 37; Edward F. Palm, "Tiger Papa Three: A Memoir of the Combined Action Program," pt. 2, *Marine Corps Gazette* 72 (February 1988): 69-70; Scarr, et al., *Marine Combined Action Capabilities*, C 4; Simmons, Brady, Miller, Ferguson interviews.

26. Peterson, *Combined Action Platoons*, 41-43, 88; Palm, "Tiger Papa Three," pt. 1, 40-41, Pt. 2, 67-68; Sherman, "One Man's CAP," 61; Simmons, Brady, Miller interviews.

27. Palm to Driest, 5 January 1989, copy in author's possession.

28. Lockridge interview; Palm, "Tiger Papa Three," Pt. 1, 35.

29. U.S. Marine Corps, *Small Wars Manual* (Washington, 1940). For an enlightening analysis of American ethnocentrism toward the Third World, see Howard J. Wiarda, "At the Root of the Problem: Conceptual Failures in U.S.-Central American Relations," *Central America: Anatomy of Conflict*, ed. Robert S. Leiken (New York, 1983), 261.

30. Stanley Karnow, *In Our Image: America's Empire in the Philippines* (New York, 1989), 348.

WHY THE ARMY AND MARINE CORPS SHOULD BE FRIENDS

Allan R. Millett

This final essay by Dr. Millett, a retired Marine Colonel and the foremost authority on Marine Corps history, appropriately expounds upon a recurring theme in this book – the traditional rivalry between the Army and Marine Corps. The author argues that both services need to reappraise their historical relationship from a broader viewpoint and recognize that they have much in common as a brotherhood in arms. And, ultimately, the nation's prosperity depends on the future success of both institutions.

Soldiers and Marines are cowmen and sheepherders. Remember the cowmen and the sheepherders of the Old West? They battled one another with unbridled contempt and ferocity over the grasslands of the open range, strewing the bodies of their animals and drovers everywhere. In the meantime, the banks, the farmers, the railroads, and the Plains winters put the independent cowmen and sheepherders out of business, even though everyone knew that Americans wanted both beef and wool. The US Army and US Marine Corps should learn that your enemies are not necessarily your enemies when you get into a turf fight.

To address the current issues of roles, missions, and budgets for a strategic future that offers little more than regional conventional wars and lesser interventions, the Army and Marine Corps should call a truce, and they should form an alliance that stresses the complementary capabilities of the two services and their partnership in joint operations. To do so will require a retrograde movement down memory lane and some new thinking about the relations of the two services during the course of the 20th century. The Chief of Staff and the Commandant already have formed an effective association, but they should have the full support of the officer corps of both services. We have met the enemy, and it is not us – or you.

Why Real Soldiers Do Not Like Jarheads

The officer corps of the US Army sometimes fears that the Army exists only to make the Marine Corps look better to the public and Congress. They believe, as Brigadier General Frank A. Armstrong, Jr., said in a speech in 1945, that the Marine Corps "is a small, bitched-up army talking Navy lingo. We are going to put those Marines in the regular Army and make efficient soldiers out of them." General Armstrong could be ignored – perhaps – but General of the Army Dwight D. Eisenhower thought the same thing. So did

General of the Army George C. Marshall, and he, too, thought the Marine Corps should just fade away.

Why did these distinguished officers regard the Marine Corps with fear and loathing? The tension between the Army and Marine Corps started in the War with Spain, flamed in the Boxer Rebellion and Philippine Insurrection, and exploded in World War I. While Major General William R. Shafter's Eighth Corps fought, sickened, grumbled, and died in the trenches at Santiago de Cuba, a small Marine battalion waged a neat little campaign at Guantanamo Bay – reported brilliantly by Stephen Crane – and got off the island in time for a victory parade in Washington, D.C. The soldiers came home to quarantine camps. The Marines who fought for the legation quarter in Peking in 1900 also got plenty of ink – and later a Charlton Heston movie. No one was gentle with the kind folks of Samar after the Balangiga Massacre (1901), but the punitive campaign cost General Jacob H. Smith, USA, his career, not Marine Colonel L. W. T. Waller. When the State Department announced it wanted a legation guard in Peking, it chose Marines. The Army received the less glamorous task of keeping the transportation routes open from Tientsin. In the Philippines the soldiers moved on to fight the Moros while the Marines paraded about the new naval stations at Subic Bay and Cavite.

In World War I the senior officers of the American Expeditionary Forces, including General John J. Pershing, opposed the formation of the 4th Brigade (Marines) of the 2d Division and resisted additional plans to form an all-Marine division in 1918. When the four most experienced divisions of the AEF went into serious action in May 1918, the American press found high drama in the 4th Brigade's battle for Belleau Wood and gave pallid coverage to the stiff fights by the Army at Cantigny, Vaux, Chateau-Thierry, Seicheprey, and the south bank of the Maine. For the rest of the war General Headquarters AEF tried to minimize the role of the Marine brigade, regarded as publicity-crazed. Relations did not improve in peacetime, despite the gallant efforts of Major General James G. Harbord, USA, who had commanded the Marine brigade at Belleau Wood. During the Hoover Administration the War Department sent out at least one proposal to sink the Marine Corps as an economy move. The move died in Congress, again proving that Marines had too much influence on the Hill.

If Army-Marine relations had taken on a burned odor by 1941, they became absolutely noxious in World War II. The War Department, including General Marshall, resented FDR's close ties to the Corps, cemented by his son James, a Marine reserve officer, and his personal friendship with Commandant Thomas Holcomb. The Army did not want to share its scarce materiel with the Marines in the mobilization period, but FDR ruled otherwise. It did like having Marine staffs running the two ad hoc joint amphibious corps on both coasts, formed in 1941. The Army resented the fact that the Marine Corps took only volunteers in 1941 and 1942 when it was coping with draftees. The press again seemed prejudiced toward Marines and insensitive to Army performance in the South Pacific, 1942-1943. Guadalcanal became famous, but who cared about New Guinea except the MacArthur idolaters? Everyone knew the 3d Marine Division assaulted

Bougainville and the 1st Marine Division took most of New Britain island, but what of the Army divisions that finished both conquests?

The focal point of Army-Marine hostility – for such it was – in the Pacific war became Lieutenant General Holland M. Smith, US Marine Corps, first commander of V Amphibious Corps and then Fleet Marine Force Pacific. A Marine partisan of terrible temper, Holland Smith treated almost everyone the same – including Marine officers – and that was not gently. He put himself at odds early with Lieutenant General Robert C. Richardson, Jr., USA, roughly his Army counterpart in the central Pacific theater. Holland Smith – so the Army thought – showed a wretched degree of incompetence and intolerance, which he inflicted upon Army units in operations in the Gilberts and Marshalls. He then relieved Major General Ralph C. Smith, USA, a very nice man and CG of the 27th Infantry Division, during the Saipan campaign. Always the cavalryman, Richardson rode to the rescue, but the relief stuck, and Smith vs. Smith boiled all the way to Washington for General Marshall, Commandant Holcomb, and Admiral Ernest J. King to adjudicate. The Army laid down the law: no more Army troops would serve under Holland M. Smith. The corollary became: no Marine general should or could command a corps or field army.

In the locust years of 1945-1950 the Army argued that (1) no future major war would require amphibious landings or that the nuclear threat made such ventures suicidal, a glowing Gallipoli; and (2) the Army could make any necessary amphibious landings since it had done so many times not only in the Pacific, but in the European theater as well. Although the Marines had made some minor doctrinal and equipment contributions, they no longer monopolized expertise in the amphibious specialty. Whatever Marines thought they could do, good old infantrymen, combat engineers, and assault amphibious transportation battalions could do as well or better. General of the Army Omar N. Bradley, Chief of Staff and then Chairman, JCS, went on the record: the United States did not need even one division prepared for amphibious assaults. But once again the Marines struck back through Congress and arranged for their preferred roles and missions to be written into the National Security Act of 1947, an act of rank treason toward poor old Captain Harry S. Truman, the Commander in Chief. The President was right when he said the Marines and Russians had similar propaganda machines.

When hard-pressed by circumstances beyond its control to fight in Korea and Vietnam, the US Army found the Marines to be reluctant allies and uncharitable comrades. The Marines, as always, got too much unearned publicity. They saved the Pusan perimeter, seized Inchon, recaptured Seoul, and fought their way out of the Chosin reservoir area. The 1st Marine Division then became a focal point of criticism of 8th Army's conduct of the campaign of 1951. In Vietnam the Marines got to fight their war in the I Corps area and made too much of their hard service along the DMZ. In both wars the Marines did not want to share their tactical aviation for close air support, and their conduct of helicopter operations showed more hubris than skill. Marine generals like Victor H. Krulak made life miserable for General William C. Westmoreland because of their obsession with pacification and working with the Vietnamese military and paramilitary forces.

In both wars the Marines always seemed to require more logistical support from the Army: transportation, engineering equipment and supplies, communications equipment, and ordnance. They always went into battle without enough artillery and tanks. They took what appeared to be excessive casualties because of their aggressiveness and poor use of supporting anus. They seemed to measure success by their own dead, not the enemy's. A little Army joke took root in Vietnam: Why are Marines like bananas? Answer: they grow green, turn yellow, and die in bunches. Marine Corps field staffs plan with all the care and foresight of teenagers, and they expect instant miracles from a tactical approach that resembles a rugby scrum. Marine battalions go into battle with too many flags (where's the next Suribachi?), cameras, and bodybags. In the operations large and small that followed in the 1980s and 1990s, soldiers thought they saw the same behavior in Lebanon, Grenada, Panama, and the Gulf War. Army officers knew that Marines studied maneuver warfare, talked the nuances of AirLand Battle, and even started to act like professionals in the fields of logistics and intelligence, but might it only be the Marine version of Russian deception operations?

Army officers – and I base my impression on 25 years of teaching them – often believe that the Marine Corps conducts a shameless guerrilla war upon the Army in Congress and extracts every additional budget increment from funds that should rightfully go to the Army. They resent the fact that the Douglas-Mansfield Act of 1952 mandates a Fleet Marine Force of three divisions and three aircraft wings. They wait each recurring cycle of defense reorganization as an opportunity to check Marine access to influential civilians in the executive branch and Congress. They do not like the current practice of rotating the job of Commander-in-Chief Central Command between the Army and the Marine Corps. (How can a Marine command a field army if he is not an honor graduate of the Army Command and General Staff College?) The generations of Army officers pass with the years, but the rap on the Marine Corps lives on. Why do the myths persist? In part, they exist because they are true. But whatever the unhappiness of the past, the Jarheads' sins are exaggerated and invariably overlook the fact that the Marine Corps has a good case against the US Army.

Why Real Marines Do Not Like Doggies

All real Marines know that the US Army would rather plan than fight and that when it comes to slaughter, it stays away from water. The Army has never seen an amphibious operation it likes – or at least can conduct with any degree of skill and ardor. Yet the Army is perfectly willing to throw its soldiers out of perfectly good airplanes or ferry them into hot LZs in mini-helicopters that cannot carry enough troops to give the grunts on the ground a fighting chance. The Army officer corps talks as if it reveres Patton and the panzer generals, but the soul of the Army is artillery-red and thrills only as the barrels of massed howitzers begin to glow. The perfect campaign is one that can be fought with a few FIST teams and battalions of mobile artillery. Marines think the Army really would like to fight a Verdun without the infantry.

Marines believe that the Army is paranoid and disingenuous in its criticism of Marine operations. Since late in the 19th century Marine officers have attended Army branch, intermediate, and senior schools, and they often learn their trade from Army manuals, from Army instructors, using Army-developed weapons and equipment. The only distinctive operational difference is the amphibious mission, which the Army never wanted and said so in writing as early as 1927 in a joint action manual adopted by the Army and Navy. The Army knows how to criticize amphibious assaults whenever the Marines plan and execute them, but not its own landings. The Army has been fortunate that it had a few fine soldiers who could save such bungled operations as the landings at Salerno, Anzio, and Omaha Beach. The Army lost more dead at Omaha Beach in one day than the Marines lost on Tarawa in three.

Marines are suspicious that Army generals, under whom they have often served, are much too careless with Marines' lives. This suspicion started in World War I when General Harbord forgot about artillery and reconnaissance at Belleau Wood. The battle of Soissons and the Meuse-Argonne campaign simply reinforced this impression. (Just whose idea was it to attack across the Meuse on the morning of Armistice Day?) It continued in World War II. If Douglas MacArthur loved the 1st Marine Division, it did not reciprocate his admiration then or in Korea, and Marines pitied the soldiers who fought and died for the greater glory of the American Caesar. Holland Smith had no monopoly of disdain for the 27th Infantry Division, but Marines remember all the other Army divisions with whom they worked well: the Americal and 25th Infantry Divisions on Guadalcanal, the 37th Infantry Division on Bougainville, the 77th Infantry Division on Guam, the 81st Infantry Division on Peleliu, the whole XXIV Corps on Okinawa (except, again, the 27th Infantry Division). The aviation squadrons of the 1st Marine Aircraft Wing relished the opportunity to provide close air support for the US 6th and 8th Armies in the Philippines. The biggest residual unhappiness left from World War II, in fact, has nothing to do with Smith vs. Smith, but the refusal of Lieutenant General Simon Bolivar Buckner, Jr., USA, to envelop the Naha-Shuri Castle-Yonabaru line on Okinawa. With the veteran 2d Marine Division available and willing to conduct an amphibious envelopment of the Japanese 32d Army, Buckner decided instead to plunge ahead in great AEF fashion and sent thousands of Marines and soldiers to their deaths, including his own.

If Major General Edward M. Almond had a difficult time in Korea as the X Corps commander, he had Buckner in part to blame for his tense relations with the 1st Marine Division. The fact that he was MacArthur's corps commander of choice did not help either. But the real difficulty was that MacArthur and the rest of the Army would not accept Lieutenant General Lemuel C. Shepherd, Jr., USMC, a star performer in the field since Belleau Wood, as the X Corps commander. Many Marine officers knew that Holland M. Smith was not a great corps commander and that he depended upon Brigadier

General Graves B. "Bobby" Erskine to make things work. But what about the splendid World War II performance of Lieutenant General Roy S. Geiger, Jr., USMC, who proved in four campaigns that he could command anything that flew, walked, and shot, regardless of uniform? Lem Shepherd and Roy Geiger were certainly better than many of their Army counterparts in both wars.

In Vietnam and the Gulf War, Marine officers believed they saw the same callous Army generalship at work again and the same unfair criticism of Marine operations. "Search and destroy" and "body count" were created at MACV [US Army Military Assistance Command], not at the headquarters of the III Marine Amphibious Force. Holding Khe Sanh was not a Marine idea, but a requirement from General Westmoreland. The bloody operations along the DMZ in 1967 and 1968 came with Operation Dye Marker, the creation of the McNamara Line, a concept from a former Air Force officer who confused the PAVN [Peoples Army of Vietnam] with Algerian guerrillas. And whose brilliant idea was it to introduce the M-16 in the middle of a shooting war so the troops could get battlefield on-the-job training on rifle cleaning and disassembly? And if the 1st Marine Aircraft Wing did not fly enough close air support missions for anyone in South Vietnam, please check with the wizards of 7th Air Force and Washington who thought that air interdiction wins wars. As for the Gulf War, the I Marine Expeditionary Force accepted the grim task of fixing the Iraqi army in Kuwait while the 3d US Army (Patton lives!) drove to glory, only to be criticized by CINCCENTCOM because it did too good a job. (Don't let the Mother of All Briefings fool you about feelings!) Accounts of the war written by Army officers who should know better hardly admit that I MEF was in-theater, had tanks and heavy guns, and supported itself.

Marines believe that the Army refuses to acknowledge that it owes anything to Marine innovation. Although Army officers will concede that individual Marine officers with whom they've served can be quite clever and bold, they cannot accept the fact that the US Army has borrowed concepts from the Marine Corps, just as the Marine Corps has borrowed concepts (and much more) from the Army. For example, the Marine Corps first broke the infantry squad into fire teams in World War II. It championed the amphibian tractor, which worked well in European river crossings, if not landings. The Marine Corps developed doctrine for effective close air support; the problem for the Army is getting the Air Force to accept the doctrine. The Marine Corps made the first institutional commitment to make the helicopter an instrument of tactical mobility. The first tests of this experiment came in Korea in 1951 by Marines. It is now pioneering in tilt-rotor development with the V-22A "Osprey." The Army even moved toward Marine concepts of recruit training and made its trainers wear the old "Smokey the Bear" campaign hat. It is not the Marine Corps' fault that the Army cannot apply the gentle personal touch known to the graduates of Parris Island.

The Army continues to grouse about Marine Corps political influence in Washington, but it badly exaggerates Marine clout. For example, Presidents and cabinet officers since FDR have been more pro-Army than anything else. The real problem is that they tend to be anti-military. The Army complains because George Shultz, Jim Baker, Don Regan, John Warner, John Chaffee, John Glenn, Bud McFarlane, Paul Douglas, Mike Mansfield, George Smathers, and many others are former Marines. What is one to make of the fact that former Army officers and enlisted men who held high places include Harry S. Truman, Louis Johnson, George C. Marshall, Dwight D. Eisenhower, Maxwell D. Taylor, Alexander Haig, Ronald Reagan, Caspar Weinberger, Henry Kissinger, James Wadsworth, Sonny Montgomery, Robert Dole, and many other distinguished members of Congress? The answer is quite simple: these men retain some service fondness, but their job descriptions do not allow them to advocate service positions. Was Les Aspin a special friend of the Army, Ron Dellums a great champion of the Marine Corps? Marines believe the key to effective lobbying is with members of Congress who have no military experience (or bias) at all, regardless of party affiliation.

Marines resent the fact that the Army is jealous of Marine aviation. The Marine Corps has paid a high price to preserve a fully capable fixed wing and helicopter force of around 1000 aircraft. This price is not paid just in dollars, but in personnel training and assignments, constant tension with the Navy's aviation leadership, constant conflict with Marine traditionalists who do not like fat aviation technicians and pilots who don't want to shoot rifles, and in dealing with an Air Force which will hardly concede any expertise to naval aviation, yet wants to control it in every operation, large or small. As long ago as the 1920s Marine planners saw that tactical aviation and ground forces could be integrated in combat to enhance each other's capabilities. Marines wonder why the Corps should be punished for discovering what is now a truism of modern warfare. The Marine Corps managed to hold on to its aviation force in the reorganization battles of the early Cold War, and it knows that the Army wishes it had, too.

In truth, there is much about the modern Army that Marines do not understand. One is the stress of mobilization and expansion. It is one thing to create six divisions for the Fleet Marine Force from two small brigades; it is quite another to field 89 divisions on an active-duty division base of 11 divisions. In 1941 the Army had about 130,000 officers with any peacetime training to lead a wartime Army (including the USAAF) of more than 11 million. The Marine Corps has a Select Reserve smaller than the active-duty force; the Army's is larger. The Marine Corps does not and never will deal with a reserve component with the political influence of the Army National Guard. The number of Marine Reserve generals cannot even make up a squad, and the most influential of them in Congress is a staff director, not a Congressman. Marines do not fully appreciate how much of the Army is dedicated to administrative and logistical functions, some of which helps the Marine Corps – or used to. They also do not fully understand the feudal relationships between Army senior generals. In the Marine Corps the Commandant is the Pope, but in the Army the Chief of Staff is the king only by the grace of the nobles. Marines do not understand the Army fixation with planning and documentation. They do not appreciate that the Army's 19th-century icon is Helmuth von Moltke the Elder, while the favorite Marine general of the era is Stonewall Jackson. Marines seize the hour, and soldiers seize the week. The heart of the matter is that one service has always been seven to ten times larger than the other.

Marines actually know a great deal about the Army from joint service, schooling, and reading. They wish the Army knew more about the Marine Corps because almost every day they see Army officers saying things that clearly show that they haven't a clue about how the Fleet Marine Force is organized and does business. Instead they believe all the Army has to offer is tired Marine Corps jokes.

Why the Marine Corps and the Army Should Be Friends

Like the cattlemen and the sheepherders, the Army and the Marine corps have much more in common – win or lose – than they are ready to admit. The good health of both services depends upon a case for their mutual existence that cannot be made in Washington and at the headquarters of the unified and specified commands until the Army and the Marine Corps band together at every level. Our shared problem at the end of the Cold War is much like that at the end of World War II. We are faced with a perceived strategic environment in which major war is unthinkable and conventional military forces in large numbers are too costly. Even though nuclear weapons are no longer the lethal currency of the hour, we are again being told that men with rifles on the ground, supported by tactical aviation and supporting arms, are as irrelevant as the knights of old. Advanced electronics, airframes and seaframes, and precision-guided munitions will do the job. The United Nations can provide the global police force.

Perhaps, but we have heard this siren's song through the ages, and it never quite works that way. The Army and the Marine Corps share a common insight about the nature of war, and since it tends to be the minority opinion, it needs constant and articulate expression. War is the collective expression of the will of people to fight for something they hold dear and for which they are willing to die. Who holds those values, what those values are, and just how much those values will call forth in sacrifice may vary with time, place, and people. Clearly, the Iraqis are not the Somalis or the Serbians. Destroying places and people either with nuclear weapons or precision-guided munitions means nothing unless it destroys the enemy's will to wage war.

Most 20th-century American political leaders know nothing about the relationship of violence and politics, unless they have been big city mayors or represent a minority urban constituency. Some governors, but not many, might qualify. The average American politician, if faced with an inescapable decision on war and peace, would rather throw dollars than lives at the problem. It was no accident that the United States spent the most money and lost the fewest lives in World War II. Yet there are plenty of crises in which military force is the unavoidable option and in which we must be prepared to lose lives and to do so over an extended period of time. That was not the case in the Gulf War, but it was certainly the case in Korea, Vietnam, Central America, Afghanistan, and the Horn of Africa. The number of lives lost may not be large in absolute terms, but they may be proportionately large when compared with the number of people deployed. Such is a characteristic of counterinsurgency and peacekeeping operations. Who is ready to teach this lesson to American politicians if not the Army and the Marine Corps?

Another lesson that our political leadership needs to hear is that the American public needs constant reassurance and nurturing when it comes to matters military. The Army and the Marine Corps cannot dodge this problem in recruiting or any other phase of public relations by claiming that they are really only a place where young men and women learn technical skills without hazard, a sort of global technical institute in which the students only happen to wear uniforms. The Air Force and the Navy, at least in recent memory, expose only career-committed officers who fly to the threat of death on a routine basis. Even if every service death is tragic, it is somehow less traumatic if the deceased is a 30-year old captain, not a 20-year old PFC. If this observation seems callous, walk around Arlington National Cemetery and test your reaction. Army and Marine officers know what it is like to write many letters, not one or two, or to reconstitute a platoon that has disappeared in a firefight, not just rearrange a squadron flight schedule. American politicians have a way of forgetting about what war costs, and Army and Marine Corps senior officers are the best prepared to remind them. During the Missile Crisis of 1962 the Kennedy brothers had almost ordered an invasion of Cuba when Marine Commandant David M. Shoup conducted a little tutorial on Tarawa and the comparative vastness of the proposed objective area.

Together we face a political elite who act on the apparent belief that force is either anachronistic or, if necessary, can be applied cheaply and painlessly. We can only hope that the critical educational process now underway, directed by the veterans of World War II and Korea, will have some influence on the politicians whose intellectual and emotional roots remain fixed in the illusions of the 1970s. Our problem is that we share the national defense arena with two other services, the Air Force and the Navy, who are predisposed institutionally to represent a different vision of warfare. I think that as long as the Soviet Union was the principal threat, the Air Force and the Navy held the strategic high ground. We did not want to occupy Russia; we did not really want to reform Soviet society or dismember the Soviet empire. What we required was the deterrence or destruction of Soviet nuclear forces and those conventional forces poised to overrun western Europe. Unless the Air Force and the Navy assured that nuclear deterrence would hold, we could not hope to wage and win a conventional war in Europe. The Navy and the Air Force are now attempting to reposition their forte in strategic deterrence to a neo-romantic view that airpower and seapower can have equal effect on regional conflict.

For the Navy this strategic faith goes all the way back to the Mahanian era of the late 19th century, if not before. Much of the Navy's statement about the wonders of projecting military power inland from the sea sound like the musings of Rear Admiral Robert Shufeld in the 1880s. For the Air Force the time window is less dramatic, but no less decisive. In a 1943 version of the Army's manual of operational doctrine, the Army Air Forces asserted that airpower and land power were now co-equal, but this argument included some hopeful notions about the effect of strategic bombardment. For the first time during the Korean War – and echoed thereafter through the Gulf War – the Air Force has argued that tactical aviation could win wars with ground forces playing a subordinate role. Guilio Douhet lives, but he has returned without his strategic clothing. The inspired application of airpower in the Gulf War offers an interesting lesson: the destruction looked worse than it was when one balanced the actual reduction of Iraqi capability against the vivid images of exploding structures and mangled civilian bodies. Filtered through television, airpower has become a force for peace through premature negotiation.

At the moment American defense analysts have brought scenario-generation to a level of imagination we once reserved for Robert Heinlein and Stephen Spielberg. Such exercises have some value, but we must remember – and remind others – that the essential nature of war is its unpredictability. We are likely to fight next someone we do not now identify as a great threat. The only enemy we identified correctly in this entire century was Japan. However, one common thread runs through all our wars and lesser engagements in this century. None of them involved only air and naval forces, and none of them were decided by air and naval forces alone. If you are ready to show the flag, you had better be ready to show something else, too, since the street gangs of the globe are not easily impressed by air and naval parades. The Army and the Marine Corps learned these truths long ago; they must preserve the wisdom that only the dead have seen the end of war.

BIOGRAPHICAL DIGEST

COLONEL and BREVET BRIGADIER GENERAL ARCHIBALD HENDERSON:

Serving as Commandant of the Marine Corps for an incredible 39 years, heritage has dubbed Archibald Henderson the "grand old man of the Marine Corps."

Archibald Henderson was born in Colchester, Virginia, on 21 January 1783. He was appointed a second lieutenant in the Marine Corps on 4 June 1806. During the War of 1812, as a captain, he served as commander of the Marine guard on board the frigate *Constitution* and for his gallant service with that famed vessel received the brevet rank of major.

In 1820 at the age of 37, he was appointed the fifth Commandant of the Marine Corps, a responsibility he held until his death almost 39 years later. During his tenure of office, Henderson saw the Corps through a host of small campaigns and seaborne operations and personally led a Marine regiment in the early campaigns of the Seminole War.

He commanded the Corps during the Mexican War, and by the time of his death on the eve of the Civil War, had insured the continued role of his beloved Marine Corps as a strong armed force in the American military structure. Henderson passed away quietly during a nap on the afternoon of 6 January 1859.

COLONEL CHARLES G. McCAWLEY:

Charles G. McCawley, born in Philadelphia on 29 January 1827, was the son of Captain James McCawley, USMC, who died in 1839. He was commissioned a second lieutenant in 1847, in time for the assault of Chapultepec. For gallantry in that attack, he was brevetted a first lieutenant.

During the Civil War he was present at the capture of Port Royal, South Carolina, and in other landings along the Atlantic coast. He was brevetted again, this time to major, for gallant conduct in the unsuccessful assault of Fort Sumter in 1863.

A methodical man, his tenure as Commandant was distinguished by improved administrative practices, higher enlistment standards, better training, getting a quota of Marine officers from the Naval Academy, better officer selection and instruction, enforcement of uniform regulations, standard tables of organization, and regularization of staff and command procedures. It was under Colonel Commandant McCawley that both the typewriter and the telephone were introduced into the Corps. While McCawley was Commandant, John Philip Sousa served as leader of the Marine Band.

In ill health at the time of his retirement, he returned to his home in Rosemont, Pennsylvania. He died there in October 1891 at the age of 64.

MAJOR GENERAL GEORGE BARNETT

Major General George Barnett, 12th Commandant of the Marine Corps. He entered the Marines from the U.S. Naval Academy in 1883. After serving onboard the USS *Pinta* and USS *Iroquois,* he was promoted to first lieutenant 1890.

In 1896, he served onboard the USS *Vermont* as well as on the USS *San Francisco* and USS *New Orleans* in 1897. It was on the *New Orleans* that he participated in the Spanish-American War in several bombardments of the forts at Santiago, Cuba. As a Captain, he served on the USS *Chicago* in 1898. As a Major in 1901, he commanded a battalion of Marines on the USS *Panther* and protected American interests in Panama.

In 1902, Major Barnett commanded another battalion of Marines headed for the Philippines but was transferred to duty with the Asiatic Fleet until 1904, at which time he rejoined the First Brigade Marines in the Philippines. In 1905, Lieutenant Colonel Barnett commanded an expeditionary battalion onboard the USS *Minneapolis* which participated in the Cuban Army of Pacification. He served in Cuba until 1906.

From 1910-1913, Colonel Barnett, commanded the First Regiment of Marines in Cuba. In 1914, he was appointed Major General Commandant of the Marine Corps and again promoted to brigadier general in 1916. During his tenure, he oversaw the deployment of Marines to Vera Cruz, Mexico, in 1914, as well as extended interventions in Haiti and Santa Domingo. However, Barnett's most important contribution was ensuring Marine participation in France during World War I, during which the Marine Corps expanded to more than three thousand officers and approximately 75,500 enlisted men. Major General Barnett was relieved as Commandant of the Marine Corps in 1920. He retired in 1923 and died in 1930.

LIEUTENANT COLONEL EARL H. ELLIS:

Lieutenant Colonel Earl Hancock "Pete" Ellis was a brilliant planner and a principal staff officer to General John A. Lejeune in World War I, who forecast the amphibious struggle for the Pacific more than 20 years prior to World War II. Believing war with Japan was inevitable, Ellis traveled among the Japanese in the forbidden Carolinas and died there under mysterious circumstances on 12 May 1923.

Colonel Ellis was born on 19 December 1880 at Iuka, Kansas, and began his career in the United States Marine Corps in 1900 as a private. On 6 December 1901, he became a second lieutenant.

In 1917, Major Ellis left Quantico for France where he served in many capacities, including the staff of General John A. Lejeune. He participated in the St. Mihiel Offensive and in the Meuse-Argonne Offensive. He was awarded the decoration of Chevalier of the Legion of Honor by the President of the French Republic, and the U.S. Army Citation Certificate by the Commanding General of the American Expeditionary Forces.

Colonel Ellis died at the age of 43 at Parao (Palau), Carolina Islands on 12 May 1923, and his remains were returned to the United States for burial.

MAJOR GENERAL SMEDLEY D. BUTLER

Major General Smedley D. Butler, later known to thousands of Marines as "Ol' Gimlet Eye," was one of the most colorful officers in the Marine Corps history. He also earned the rare distinction of winning two Medals of Honor.

Congress appointed Butler a second lieutenant in 1898. In 1900, he served with distinction in China. During the Boxer Rebellion, he was wounded at the Battle of Tientsin and earned a brevet promotion to Captain. From 1901 through 1909, Butler served at various posts in the continental United States and on a number of Navy ships. In 1909, he commanded the 3d Battalion, 1st Marine Regiment on the Isthmus of Panama. Later, in 1912, he commanded an expeditionary battalion organized for service in Nicaragua, where he participated in the bombardment, assault and capture of Coyotepe.

Major Butler earned his first Medal of Honor following action at Vera Cruz, Mexico in 1914, where he commanded the Marines who landed and occupied the city. The following year, he was awarded the second Medal of Honor for bravery and forceful leadership as Commanding Officer of detachments of Marines and seamen of the USS *Connecticut* in repulsing Caco resistance on Fort Riviere, Haiti.

During World War I, he commanded the 13th Regiment of Marines in France. When he returned to the United States in 1919, he became Commanding General of the Marine Barracks, Quantico, Virginia, and served in this capacity until 1924. In 1926, he assumed command of the Marine Corps Base at San Diego, California. In 1927, he returned to China for duty with the 3d Marine Brigade. He retired from active duty in 1931 and died at the Naval Hospital, Philadelphia on 21 June 1940.

LIEUTENANT GENERAL JOHN A. LEJEUNE:

Lieutenant General John A. Lejeune, often referred to as "the greatest of all Leathernecks," during his more than 40 years service with the Marine Corps, led the famed Second Division (Army) in World War I, and was Major General Commandant of the Marine Corps from June 1920 to March 1929.

Lejeune graduated from Louisiana State University in 1884 and from the U.S. Naval Academy in 1888. He was commissioned a second lieutenant in the Marine Corps on 1 July 1890. During the 1890s and early 1900s Lejeune, as both a Lieutenant and Captain, served on a great number of U.S. Navy ships and at various naval stations. In 1903 and 1904, Major Lejeune was dispatched to Panama with a battalion of Marines. He then redeployed to Panama in 1906. In 1907, he commanded the Marine Barracks at Cavite Navy Yard, Philippines. He later commanded the First Brigade of Marines in the Philippines from 1908-1909. In 1912, Lieutenant Colonel Lejeune deployed to Cuba with the Second Provisional Brigade Marines. In 1913, he commanded the Second Advanced Base Regiment which secured Vera Cruz, Mexico in 1914.

In June 1918, General Lejeune arrived in France. He was originally assigned to command a brigade of the 32nd Division. He later commanded the Fourth Brigade of Marines of the Second Division. In late 1918, General Lejeune assumed command of the Second Army Infantry Division and remained in that capacity until 1919. He was the first Marine officer to hold an Army divisional command. In 1919, he was appointed Commanding General, Marine Barracks, Quantico, Virginia. He then was appointed Major General Commandant of the Marine Corps in 1920. General Lejeune was relieved as Commandant in March 1929.

MAJOR GENERAL MERRITT AUSTIN EDSON:

Major General Merritt Austin Edson was known as "Red Mike" by most Marines. His nickname, originating from his red beard worn in Nicaragua days, was also his code name during this time period.

General Edson joined the Marine Corps Reserve on 26 June 1917. Thus began a career which was to be characterized by its diversity and distinguished even by the high standards of the Marine Corps. Fighting ashore in Nicaragua from February 1928 to 1929, he fought twelve separate engagements with the Sandino-led bandits and denied them the use of the Poteca and Coco River valleys.

Before WWII he commanded the first Marine "Raider Battalion" (an elite parachute battalion) and during the war he fought at the battles of Guadalcanal, Tarawa, Saipan and Tinian. General Edson is best known for his exemplary performance in these Pacific campaigns.

In addition to the Medal of Honor, General Edson was awarded two Navy Crosses, a Silver Star and two Legions of Merit, his numerous other decorations included the Presidential Unit Citation with two bronze stars. He retired from active duty on 1 August 1947 and died on 14 August 1955

GENERAL DAVID M. SHOUP

General David Monroe Shoup was a World War II Medal of Honor recipient and 22nd Commandant of the Marine Corps. He is probably best remembered for his phenomenal leadership at the battle for Tarawa, where he stepped up from a career consisting mostly of staff positions to become the commander of the landing force on Betio Island.

Shoup was commissioned a Marine second lieutenant in 1926. He served expeditionary duty with the 6th Marines in Tientsin, China in 1927. In 1929, Shoup was assigned to the Marine detachment aboard the USS *Maryland*. In 1934, First Lieutenant Shoup was again ordered to China, serving briefly with the 4th Marines in Shanghai and, subsequently, at the American Legation in Peiping.

He served as an observer of the 1st Marine Division on Guadalcanal in 1942 and the 43d Army Division on New Georgia in 1943, earning a Purple Heart in the latter operation. In 1943, Colonel Shoup was placed in command of the 2d Marines, the spearhead of the assault on Tarawa. During this action he earned the Medal of Honor as well as a second Purple Heart, while commanding all ashore ground troops. In 1943, he became Chief of Staff of the 2d Marine Division, and served in this capacity during the battles for Saipan and Tinian in 1944.

In 1957, he became Commanding General of the 1st Marine Division and of the 3d Marine Division in 1958. In 1959, President Dwight D. Eisenhower nominated Lieutenant General Shoup to be the 22d Commandant of the Marine Corps. Upon assuming his post as Commandant of the Marine Corps on January 1, 1960, he was promoted to four-star rank. His time in office saw the beginning of limited operations in Vietnam. He died on January 13, 1983.

LIEUTENANT GENERAL LEWIS B. PULLER:

Lieutenant General Lewis Burwell Puller, colorful veteran of the Korean fighting, four World War II campaigns and expeditionary service in China, Nicaragua and Haiti, and arguably the highest decorated Marine of all time, was the only Leatherneck ever to win the Navy Cross five times for heroism and gallantry in action. He often is referred to by his nickname "Chesty" – bequeathed on him by his peers for his muscular physique and barrel chest.

A Marine officer and enlisted man for 37 years, General Puller served at sea or overseas for all but ten of those years, including a hitch as commander of the "Horse Marines" in China. Excluding medals from foreign governments, he won a total of 14 personal decorations in combat, plus a long list of campaign medals, unit citation ribbons, and other awards. In addition to his Navy Crosses (the next-highest decoration to the Medal of Honor for Naval personnel), he holds its Army equivalent, the Distinguished Service Cross.

Promoted to his final rank and placed on the temporary disability retired list 1 November 1955, he died on 11 October 1971.

GENERAL ALEXANDER A. VANDEGRIFT:

General Alexander Archer Vandegrift, who earned the Medal of Honor in World War II, and served as the eighteenth Commandant of the Marine Corps, from January 1, 1944 to January 1, 1948.

The General commanded the 1st Marine Division in the battle for Guadalcanal, and the I Marine Amphibious Corps in the landing at Empress Augusta Bay, Bougainville, during World War II.

For outstanding service as Commanding General of the 1st Marine Division during the attack on Guadalcanal, Tulagi, and Gavutu in the Solomon Islands on August 7, 1942, he was awarded the Navy Cross, and for the subsequent occupation and defense from August 7, to December 9, 1942, was awarded the Medal of Honor.

On January 1, 1944, as a lieutenant general, he was sworn in as the eighteenth Commandant of the Marine Corps. On April 4, 1945, he was appointed general, with date of rank from March 21, 1945, the first Marine officer on active duty to attain four-star rank.

He left active service on December 31, 1947, and was placed on the retired list, April 1, 1949. He died November 20, 1969

GENERAL CLIFTON B. CATES:

Clifton B. Cates commissioned a second lieutenant of Marines in 1917 after attending the Missouri Military Academy and University of Tennessee Law School.

Six months later, he sailed with the 6th Marines to France. He served in five campaigns, during which he was once gassed and twice wounded. He was awarded the Navy Cross for extraordinary heroism in action at Bouresches on 6 June 1918. Following the war, he was a White House aide and aide-de-camp to Commandants Barnett and Lejeune.

In May 1942, Colonel Cates was given command of the 1st Marines, which he led in the Guadalcanal campaign. Later in the war, after commanding Marine Corps Schools at Quantico, he commanded the 4th Marine Division at Tinian and Iwo Jima.

On 1 January 1948, General Cates was promoted to general and became Commandant, where he served through the Korean War. Carrying out his predecessor's objective of obtaining a well-defined statutory position for the Marine Corps, General Cates contributed to the passage of Public Law 416, which set the Corps' active strength at three divisions and three aircraft wings. He retired in 1954, and died in 1970.

LIEUTENANT GENERAL VICTOR H. KRULAK:

Lieutenant General Victor H. Krulak performed duty in some of the most pivotal periods of Marine Corps history. Remarkably, he was intimately involved with central decisions affecting the Corps' direction for over thirty years –perpetually in the thick of the action, both in peacetime and war.

Victor Harold Krulak was commissioned a Marine second lieutenant upon graduation from the U.S. Naval Academy, 31 May 1934, beginning a thirty-four year career that encompassed three phases of Marine history – Colonial Infantry, Amphibious Assault, and Force in Readiness.

Lieutenant Krulak served in China in 1936, gaining the unique distinction as a "horse Marine." As a Captain in the early 1940s, he served on the staff of General Holland M. Smith, then Commanding General of Amphibious Corps, Atlantic Fleet. In this capacity, Captain Krulak worked closely with the development of amphibious assault. In 1943, Major Krulak commanded 2d Parachute Battalion in the World War II. Later, Lieutenant Colonel Krulak served in numerous Pacific Campaigns, including the Northern Solomons, where he earned the Navy Cross for extraordinary heroism and the Purple Heart for wounds received in combat.

In both the Korean and Vietnam Wars, Lieutenant General Krulak served in key capacities, the foremost being that of Commanding General, Fleet Marine Force, Pacific, which he led from 1964 until his retirement in 1968.

SUGGESTED READINGS AND FILM

The essays selected in *Crucibles*, while some of the best available articles on the Marine Corps' institutional history, are certainly not definitive in nature but rather starting points for thought and discussion. A more thorough examination of the subject requires further reading. Additionally, perhaps the best way to observe the evolution of the Corps' public image can be done by way of film rather than text. In this regard, I have included a list of essays, books, and movies which compliment the topics discussed in *Crucibles*.

ESSAYS

Condon, John P. "U.S. Marine Corps Aviation." Edited by John M. Elliott. Washington D.C.: Deputy Chief of Naval Operations, 1987.

Love, Edmund G. "Smith Versus Smith." *Infantry Journal*. November, 1948.

Melshen, Paul. "He Served on Samar." *U. S. Naval Institute Proceedings*. November, 1979.

Millett, Allan R. "The U.S. Marine Corps: Adaptation in the Post-Vietnam Era." *Armed Forces and Society*. Spring 1983. 363-392.

Sherrod, Robert. "The Saipan Controversy." *Infantry Journal*. January, 1949.

Shulimson, Jack. "Military Professionalism: The Case of the U.S. Marine Officer Corps, 1880-1889." *Journal of Military History*. April 1996. 231-242.

BOOKS

Bartlett, Merrill L. *Lejeune: A Marine's Life, 1867-1942*. Annapolis, Maryland: Naval Institute Press, 1996.

Bartlett, Merrill L. and Jack Sweetman. *The U.S. Marine Corps: An Illustrated History*. Annapolis, Maryland: Naval Institute Press, 2001.

Caputo, Philip. *A Rumor of War*. 1977, New York: Ballatine Books, 1978.

Cameron, Craig. *American Samurai: Myth, Imagination, and the Conduct of Battle in the First Marine Division, 1941-1951*. New York: Cambridge University Press, 1994.

Krulak, Victor H. *First to Fight: An Inside View of the U.S. Marine Corps*. 1984, Naval Institute Press, 1999.

Millett, Allan R. *Semper Fidelis: The History of the United States Marine Corps*. 1980, New York: Free Press, 1991.

Ricks, Thomas E. *Making the Corps*. New York: Scribner, 1997.

Schmidt, Hans. *Maverick Marine: General Smedley D. Butler and the Contradictions of American Military History*. Lexington, Kentucky: University of Kentucky Press, 1987.

Sledge, E.B. *With the Old Breed at Peleliu and Okinawa*. 1981, Annapolis, Maryland: Naval Institute Press, 1996.

MOVIES

55 Days at Peking. Directed by Andrew Marton and Nicholas Ray. Starring Charlton Heston and Ava Gardner. 1963, Best Film and Video, 1991. (150 minutes)

A Few Good Men. Directed by Rob Reiner. Starring Tom Cruise, Jack Nicholson, and Demi Moore. Columbia Pictures, 1992. (138 minutes)

Battlecry. Directed by Raoul Walsh. Starring Van Heflin and Aldo Ray. 1955, Warner Studios, 2001. (169 minutes)

The D.I. Directed by and starring Jack Webb. 1957, Warner Studios, 1995. (106 minutes)

Flying Leathernecks. Directed by Nicholas Ray. Starring John Wayne and Robert Ryan. 1951, Turner Home Entertainment, 1992. (102 minutes)

Full Metal Jacket. Directed by Stanley Kubrick. Starring Mathew Modine and Vincent D'Onofrio. 1987, Warner Studios, 2001. (116 minutes)

The Great Santini. Directed by Lewis John Carlino. Starring Robert Duvall and Blythe Danner. 1980, Warner Studios, 2004. (118 minutes)

Guadalcanal Diary. Directed by Lewis Seiler. Starring Preston Foster and Lloyd Nolan. 1943, Twentieth Century Fox, 2002. (93 minutes)

Halls of Montezuma. Directed by Lewis Milestone. Starring Richard Widmark, Robert Wagner, and Jack Webb. 1950, Twentieth Century Fox, 2002. (113 minutes)

Heartbreak Ridge. Directed by and starring Clint Eastwood. 1986, Warner Studios, 2000. (130 minutes)

Retreat, Hell! Directed by Joseph H. Lewis. Starring Frank Lovejoy and Richard Carlson. 1952, Republic Studios, 1989. (95 minutes)

Rules of Engagement. Directed by William Friedkin. Starring Tommy Lee Jones and Samuel L. Jackson. 2000, Paramount Studio, 2001. (128 minutes)

Sands of Iwo Jima. Directed by Allan Dwan. Starring John Wayne and John Agar. 1949, Republic Studios, 2003. (109 minutes)

Wake Island. Directed by John Farrow. Starring Brian Donlevy and Robert Preston. 1942, Universal Studios, 2001. (88 minutes)

What Price Glory? Directed by John Ford. Starring James Cagney and Corinne Calvet. 1952, Twentieth Century Fox, 1991. (120 minutes)

Windtalkers. Directed by John Woo. Starring Nicholas Cage and Adam Beach. MGA/UA Video, 2002. (153 minutes)

COMMANDANTS OF THE MARINE CORPS

1775 - 1783	Major Samuel Nicholas
1798 - 1804	Lieutenant Colonel William Burrows
1804 - 1818	Lieutenant Colonel Franklin Wharton
1819 - 1820	Lieutenant Colonel Anthony Gale
1820 - 1859	Colonel Archibald Henderson
1859 - 1864	Colonel John Harris
1864 - 1876	Brigadier General Jacob Zeilin
1876 - 1891	Colonel Charles McCawley
1891 - 1903	Major General Charles Heywood
1903 - 1910	Major General George Elliot
1911 - 1914	Major General William Biddle
1914 - 1920	Major General George Barnett
1920 - 1929	Major General John Lejeune
1929 - 1930	Major General Wendell Neville
1930 - 1934	Major General Ben Fuller
1934 - 1936	Major General John Russell
1936 - 1943	Lieutenant General Thomas Holcomb
1944 - 1947	General Alexander Vandegrift
1948 - 1952	General Clifton Cates
1952 - 1955	General Lemuel Shepherd Jr.
1956 - 1959	General Randolph Pate
1960 - 1963	General David Shoup
1964 - 1967	General Wallace Greene Jr.
1968 - 1971	General Leonard Chapman Jr.
1972 - 1975	General Robert Cushman Jr.
1975 - 1979	General Louis Wilson
1979 - 1983	General Robert Barrow
1983 - 1987	General Paul Kelly
1987 - 1991	General Alfred M. Gray
1991 - 1995	General Carl E. Mundy Jr.
1995 - 1999	General Chuck Krulak
1999 - 2003	General James L. Jones
2003 -	General Michael W. Hagee

LtCol Franklin Wharton
1804-1818

MGen Charles Heywood
1891-1903

Gen Wallace Greene Jr.
1964-1967

Gen Alfred M. Gray Jr.
1987-1991

BGen Jacob Zeilin
1864-1876

MGen Ben Fuller
1930-1934

Gen Leonard Chapman Jr.
1968-1971

Gen Chuck Krulak
1994-1999

MARINE CORPS BATTLE HISTORY

1775-1783	Revolutionary War	1941-1945	World War II
1798-1801	Quasi War		*Pearl Harbor*
			Wake Island
1801-1805	Barbary Wars		*Bataan & Corregidor*
1812-1815	War of 1812		*Midway*
	Bladensburg		*Guadalcanal*
	New Orleans		*New Georgia*
			Bougainville
1835-1842	Florida Indian Wars		*Tarawa*
1846-1848	Mexican-American War		*New Britain*
			Marshall Islands
	Chapultepec		*Marianas Islands*
1861-1865	American Civil War		*Peleliu*
			Iwo Jima
1898	Spanish-American War		*Okinawa*
1898-1902	Philippine War	1950-1953	Korea
1900	Boxer Rebellion		*Inchon*
			Chosin
1909-1912	Nicaragua	1958	Lebanon
1914	Vera Cruz	1962-1975	Vietnam
1915-1934	Haiti		*Khe Sanh*
			Hue
1916-1924	Santo Domingo		
1917-1918	World War I	1965	Dominican Republic
	Belleau Wood	1981-1984	Lebanon
	Soisson	1983	Grenada
	St. Mihiel	1987-1991	Persian Gulf
	Blanc Mont		
	Meuse-Argonne	1988-1990	Panama
1926-1933	Nicaragua	1992-1994	Somalia
		2001-2002	Afganistan
		2003-2004	Persian Gulf

BIBLIOGRAPHY

The cover photo of two Marines attacking a Japanese pillbox on Iwo Jima in 1945 with flamethrowers as well as the picture of the flag raising on Mount Suribachi before the Table of Contents are provided courtesy of the Marine Corps University Research Archives. The photo on the title page of Marines storming the beaches of Iwo Jima is provided courtesy of Special Archives, Nimitz Library, U.S. Naval Academy. Photos and most of the textual information, often verbatim, in the biographical section are provided courtesy of the United States Marine Corps History and Museums Division.

Original works included in this book are printed by consent of the respective authors. Other essays are reprinted from previously published sources. Their inclusion is done only with the permission (either directly or through a copyright agency) of the following publications.

Alexander, Joseph. "Sea Soldiers Ashore: U.S. Marines in World War I." *Marine Corps Gazette*. November 1983. 61-67. Reprinted courtesy of the *Marine Corps Gazette*. Copyright retained by the *Marine Corps Gazette*.

Brooks, David C. "U.S. Marines and Miskito Indians: The Rio Coco Patrol of 1928." *Marine Corps Gazette*. November 1996. 64-71. Reprinted courtesy of the *Marine Corps Gazette*. Copyright retained by the *Marine Corps Gazette*.

Burrell, Robert S. "'Issue in Doubt': The Unification Crisis, 1945-1952." Printed by permission.

Burrell, Robert S. "The Prototype U.S. Marine: Evolution of the Amphibious Assault Warrior, 1941-1945." Printed by permission.

Cosmas, Graham A. "*Cacos* and *Caudillos*: Marines and Counterinsurgency in Hispaniola." *New Interpretations in Naval History: Selected Papers from the Ninth Naval History Symposium*. Edited by William R. Roberts and Jack Sweetman. U.S. Naval Institute Press, 1991. 293-308. Reprinted by permission.

Cosmas, Graham A. and Jack Shulimson. "The Culebra Maneuver and the Formation of the U.S. Marine Corps Advance Base Force, 1913-14." *Assault from the Sea*. Edited by Merrill L. Bartlett. Naval Institute Press, 1983. 121-132. Reprinted by permission.

Dawson, Joseph G. "With Fidelity and Effectiveness: Archibald Henderson's Lasting Legacy to the U.S. Marine Corps." *Journal of Military History*. October, 1998. 727-753. Reproduced with the permission of *Journal of Military History*. Permission conveyed through Copyright Clearance Center, Inc.

Heinl, Robert D. Jr. "The Cat With More Than Nine Lives." *U.S. Naval Institute Proceedings*. June 1954. 659-671. Reprinted from *Proceedings* with permission; Copyright © (1954) U.S. Naval Institute/ <http://www.navalinstitute.org/> www.navalinstitute.org.

Heinl, Robert D. Jr. "Inchon." *Marine Corps Gazette*. September (part I) and November (part II) 1967. 21-28 and 45-50 respectively. Reprinted courtesy of the *Marine Corps Gazette*. Copyright retained by the *Marine Corps Gazette*.

Hoffman, Jon T. "The Truth About Peleliu." *U.S. Naval Institute Proceedings*. November, 2002. 50-54. Reprinted from *Proceedings* with permission; Copyright © (2002) U.S. Naval Institute/ <http://www.navalinstitute.org/> www.navalinstitute.org.

Jennings, Kenneth A. "Sandino Against the Marines: The Development of Air Power for Conducting Counterinsurgency Operations in Central America." *Air University Review*. May 1986, 85-95. Reprinted by permission.

Linn, Brian McAllister. "We Will Go Heavily Armed: The Marines Small War on Samar." *New Interpretations in Naval History: Selected Papers from the Ninth Naval History Symposium*. Edited by William R. Roberts and Jack Sweetman. U.S. Naval Institute Press, 1991. 273-292. Reprinted by permission.

Marshall, Heather P. "The China Marines and the Crucible of the Warrior Mythos, 1900-1941," Printed by permission.

Millett, Allan R. "Why the Army and Marine Corps Should Be Friends." *Parameters*. Winter 1994. 85-97. Reprinted by permission.

Morton, Chris. "The Vital Role of the U.S. Marine Corps Reserve, 1893-1951." Printed by permission.

Reber, John J. "Pete Ellis: Amphibious Warfare Prophet." *U.S. Naval Institute Proceedings*. November 1977. 53-64. Reprinted from *Proceedings* with permission; Copyright © (1977) U.S. Naval Institute/ <http://www.navalinstitute.org/> www.navalinstitute.org.

Showalter, Dennis E. "Evolution of the Marine Corps as a Military Elite." *Marine Corps Gazette*. November 1979. 44-51, 54-58. Reprinted courtesy of the *Marine Corps Gazette*. Copyright retained by the *Marine Corps Gazette*.

Shulimson, Jack and Graham A. Cosmas. "Teddy Roosevelt and the Corps' Seagoing Mission." *Marine Corps Gazette*. November 1981. 54-61. Reprinted courtesy of the *Marine Corps Gazette*. Copyright retained by the *Marine Corps Gazette*.

Yates, Lawrence A. "A Feather in Their Cap? The Marines' Combined Action Program in Vietnam." *New Interpretations in Naval History: Selected Papers from the Ninth Naval History Symposium*. Edited by William R. Roberts and Jack Sweetman. U.S. Naval Institute Press, 1991. 309-326. Reprinted by permission.

INDEX

A

advance base force, 110-116, 120-121, 125-126, 131, 135
Advanced Base Operations in Micronesia, 176
Aguinaldo, Emilio, 68
Almond, Edward M., 295

B

Badger, Charles J., 116
Bainbridge, William, 50
Baker, Newton, 127
Banana Wars, 126, 147
Bancroft, George, 54
Barnett, George, 117-121, 126-132, 184
Bell, J. Franklin, 101
Belleau Wood, 9, 11, 16, 35, 129, 131-132, 259, 292, 295
Biddle, William P., 112-115, 117
Borah, William E., 105
Bougainville, 11, 292, 295
Boxer Rebellion, 56, 67, 71, 83, 85, 87, 89, 92, 292
Bradley, Omar, 255, 293
Buckner, Simon B., 295
Buna-Gona, 212
Butler, Smedley, 35, 83, 85, 87, 91, 92, 93
Butler, Thomas H., 83, 103, 106

C

Calhoun, John C., 46
Camp Lejeune, 227
Camp Pendleton, 227-228, 248, 264, 268
Capper, Arthur, 181
Cates, Clifton B., 247, 259-264, 269
Central Pacific Campaign, 2, 13, 195, 197-198, 274
Cervera, Pascual, 216
Chapultepec, Mexican Military Academy, 55, 56
Charlemagne, Massena Peralte, 136-137, 140-141
Chosin Reservoir, 250, 293
Clausewitz, Carl von, 255
Cole, Eli K., 100
Coontz, Robert E., 175
Craig, E. A., 260, 262
Crowninshield, Benjamin, 45, 46
Cuba, 71, 110, 112, 121, 130, 299
Culebra Island, 34, 109, 111, 115-121, 126, 178

Culebra maneuver. *See* Culebra Island
Curtis, Charles, 181
Cushman, Robert, 280

D

Daly, Dan, 11, 85
Daniels, Josephus, 113, 127
Dartiguenave, Sudre, 136
Day, John H. A., 75
Denny, Frank L., 32, 101-102, 106
DePuy, William, 277
Dewey, George, 7, 112
Dobbin, James, 56
Dole, Robert, 297
Dominican Republic, 10, 16, 112, 121, 130, 135-141, 143-144, 286
Douglas-Mansfield Bill, 38, 251, 294
Doyle, James H., 257-258, 264-266, 270-271, 273-276
Duncan, Donald, 11
DuPont, Samuel, 25

E

Eberstadt, Ferdinand, 239, 241
Edson, Merritt A., 147-157, 167, 239
Eisenhower, Dwight, 13, 237, 245, 291, 297
Elliot, George F., 26, 97
Ellis, Earl H., 116, 121, 132, 144, 175-184, 189, 191
Eniwetok, 177
Erskine, Graves B., 268, 295
Evans, Robley D., 27, 28
Executive Order 969, 31

F

Farragut, David G., 25, 266
Fifth Marine Division (5th Marine Division), 200
First Marine Aircraft Wing (1st Marine Aircraft Wing), 295, 296
First Marine Division (1st Marine Division), 5, 11, 192-193, 199, 207, 208, 211-212, 215, 227-228, 249-250, 255, 259, 260-264, 268-269, 292-293, 295
flag raisings on Mount Suribachi, 294, 251
Fort Fisher, 6, 27
Foss, George E., 105

Fourth Marine Division (4th Marine Division), 195, 196-197, 200
Fullam, William F., 26, 28-32, 34, 98-100, 103-105, 111, 113-114

G

Gale, Anthony, 46
Gallipoli, 9-10, 132, 177, 293
Geiger, Roy S., 207-208, 211-212, 214, 295
Gibbons, Floyd, 129, 131
Gilbert Islands, 194, 196
Grenada, 294
Guadalcanal, 11, 16, 36, 147, 192-193, 208-209, 240, 268, 274, 292, 295
Guam, 9, 13, 178-179, 197, 212, 295

H

Haiti, 10, 121, 130, 135, 136-144, 286
Hale, Eugene, 104
Harbord, James G., 35, 129-130, 292, 295
Harllee, William C., 85, 141-142
Hatcheelustee Creek, Battle of, 52
Hawaii, 10, 216, 225
Hayes, Thomas, 83
Henderson, Archibald, 22-25, 43-44, 60
Herbert, Hilary A., 27
Heywood, Charles, 110
Hiroshima, 237
Hittle, James D., 245-246
Hoch, Homer, 181
Hoffman Committee, 245-246
Hoffman, Clare E., 244
Holcomb, Thomas, 179, 223, 292-293
Holmes, Isaac E., 54
Hoover, Herbert, 34-35, 170
House Armed Services Committee, 38, 244-255, 263
House Bill 4214, 246
House Committee on Naval Affairs, 22-23, 130
Huerta, Victoriano, 113, 116, 125
Hull, Isaac, 50

I

Inchon, 293
Iwo Jima, 11, 13, 15, 199-200, 202, 208, 212, 241-245, 248, 251, 269

J

Jackson, Andrew, 22-24, 39, 47, 50
Jackson, Stonewall, 213, 297
Johnson, Hiram, 170
Johnson, Louis, 37-38, 256, 259, 268, 297
Jones, Thomas Catesby, 50

K

Kennedy, John P., 57
Khe Sanh, 15, 280, 296
King, Ernest J., 293
Kissinger, Henry, 297
Knox, Frank, 223
Korean War, 221, 224, 228, 250, 256, 293, 295-296, 298, 299
Krulak, Victor, 15, 240, 242, 246, 248-249, 261, 267, 278, 281, 293
Kwajalein Atoll, 196

L

LaFollette, Robert M., 105
LaGuardia, Fiorello H., 35
Larcade, Henry D., 240
Lebanon, 294
Lee, Harry, 137, 142
Lejeune, John A., 2, 33, 85, 91, 97, 116-121, 125-127, 129-132, 164-169, 175-182, 184, 191, 219-220, 269
Lodge, Henry Cabot, 104
Long, Charles G., 100, 117
Lowe, Frank, 250
Luce, Stephen B., 29, 105, 106
Ludendorff, Erich, 130, 132

M

Maas, Melvin J., 35
MacArthur, Douglas, 15, 34-35, 176, 207, 227, 249, 256-276, 292, 295
Mackenzie, Alexander S., 50
Madero, Francisco, 113
Mahoney, James, 100
Mameluke sword, 49
Manderson, Charles F., 26
Mansfield, Michael, 245, 250, 296
Marianas Islands, 197-198
Marine Advance Base School, 110
Marine Band, 49, 60
Marshall Islands, 176-177, 185, 196-197
Marshall, George C., 235, 240, 291-293, 297
McCawley, Charles G., 25, 86, 102, 106
McDonough, Gordon L., 249
McLemore, Henry, 242
Metcalf, Victor H., 30, 99
Mexican-American War, 54
Mexico City, 6, 55-56, 60
Meyer, George von L., 112
Miskito Indians, 149-157
Mount Suribachi, 249

Index

N

National Security Act of 1947, 14, 37, 227, 246-251, 293
Naval Militia, 215-218, 221, 223
Naval War College, 15, 178, 180
Navy Bureau of Navigation, 29-32, 99-100
Navy Bureau of Ordnance, 110, 112, 114-115
Neville, Wendell C., 32, 117, 121, 181-182
Newberry, Truman H., 30
Nicaragua, 10, 112, 144, 147-153, 156, 161-164, 167-171, 209, 285
North American Treaty Organization, 16, 132, 262

O

Okinawa, 11, 13, 208, 211, 269, 295
Organized Marine Corps Reserve, 223-224, 226-229

P

Panama, 294
Patterson, Robert, 243
Patton, George, 212
Pearl Harbor, 10, 31, 114, 240, 243, 261
Peleliu, 13, 178, 187, 199-200, 202, 207-209, 211-212, 214, 295
Persain Gulf War, 299
Pershing, John J., 9, 127-131, 133, 292
Persian Gulf War, 296, 298
Philippine War, 1, 56, 68, 76-77, 292
Philippines, 9, 67, 70-77, 97, 101-111, 114, 175-178, 207, 211
Ploeser, Walter C., 240
Polk, James K., 55
Porter, David D., 25, 26, 72, 74, 76
Puller, Lewis B., 15, 85, 207-214, 250, 274
Pusan Perimeter, 16, 227, 249, 256-266, 268, 272, 276, 293

Q

Quick, John, 85

R

Reagan, Ronald, 297
Rice, Alexander, 25
Richardson, Robert C., 293
Robertson, Edward, 242
Robison, Samual S., 143
Rodgers, John, 50
Roosevelt, Franklin D., 115, 181, 223, 239
Roosevelt, Theodore, 29, 31, 33, 68, 97, 111
Rowell, Ross, 163-164, 167, 171
Royall, Kenneth C., 38
Rupertus, William H., 199, 207-208, 211-213

S

Sacasa, Juan, 168
Saipan, 12, 13, 15, 179, 197, 199, 202, 212, 237, 293
Saltonstall, Leverett, 38
Samar Island, Philippines, 67-78, 292
Sandino, Augusto, 1, 148, 150-156, 161-171
Sarbacher, George W. Jr., 244
Schilt, Christian, 166, 167
Scott, Winfield, 55, 56
Second Marine Division (2d Marine Division), 132, 194, 197, 295
Seminole Indian War, 24, 51-53
Senate Bill 758, 246
Senate Naval Affairs Committee, 25, 27, 30-36, 55, 102-105, 242
Shepherd, Lemuel C., 211, 260-269, 272, 295
Sherman, Forrest, 259
Sherman, John, 26
Shoup, David M., 91, 235, 248, 299
Sims, William S., 32, 98-99, 103-104, 119, 132, 178, 180
Small Wars Manual, 78, 286
Smith versus Smith controversy, 12, 197, 237, 293, 295
Smith, Holland M., 12, 129, 191, 194-195, 197, 237, 248, 251, 293, 295
Smith, Jacob H., 68, 71-72, 292
Smith, Julian, 210, 212
Smith, Oliver P., 228, 264
Smith, Ralph, 12, 237, 293
Soissons, Battle of, 129
Solomon Islands, 12
Spanish-American War, 9, 84, 97, 110, 216, 217, 223, 229
Stevenson, Adlai E., 26
Stewart, Charles, 45, 50
Stimson, Henry Envoy, 148

T

Taft, William Howard, 105-106, 112
Tarawa, 11, 194, 202, 212, 235, 248
Third Marine Division (3d Marine Division), 200, 202
Thomas, Gerald C., 239
Thompson, Smith, 46
Tinian, 197
Toucey, Isaac, 60
Truman, Harry S., 30, 227, 237-242, 245-260, 263, 293, 297
Turner, Richmond, 257
Twining, Nathan C., 114, 240, 242, 246

U

U.S. Military Academy, 4, 48, 56, 58
U.S. Naval Academy, 2, 100, 130
Umurbrogol Mountain, Peleliu, 199, 207-212

V

Van Zandt, James E., 244
Vandegrift, Alexander A., 36-37, 239, 241-242, 244-245
Vandenberg, Hoyt, 260-261, 263, 267
Veracruz, Mexico, 7, 54-55, 120-121, 125, 127
Vietcong, 277-281, 284-285
Vietnam War, 3, 14-15, 156-157, 277-286, 293, 296, 298
Vinson, Carl, 35-38, 250, 263

W

Wadsworth, James W., 236, 297
Waller, Littleton Waller Tazwell, 32, 67, 68, 71-78, 84, 87-88, 177, 292
Walsh, David, 239
Walt, Lewis, 277
War Department, 21, 33, 35-36, 103, 128, 130, 236, 239-247, 251
Washington riots of 1857, 58
Wayne, John, 3, 14, 248
Webb, James, 14
Weeks, John W., 104
Weinberger, Caspar, 297
Wells, Clark W., 136
Westmoreland, William, 15, 278, 293, 296
Wharton, Franklin, 45
Wood, Leonard, 31, 101
Woodrum Committee, 236, 239
Woodrum, Clifton A., 236
World War I, 7, 9, 11, 14, 34, 56, 121, 125-126, 132-135, 140, 156, 169, 177, 189, 217-219, 242
World War II, 2, 3, 5, 6, 11, 14, 36, 126, 129, 169, 171, 195, 202, 211, 218, 220-228, 235, 237-239, 250, 295, 296, 298-299

Z

Zelaya, Jose Santos, 150